Religion
at the Corner
of Bliss
and Nirvana

Religion
at the Corner
of Bliss
and Nirvana

Politics, Identity, and Faith
in New Migrant Communities

EDITED BY LOIS ANN LORENTZEN,

JOAQUIN JAY GONZALEZ III,

KEVIN M. CHUN, AND HIEN DUC DO

DUKE UNIVERSITY PRESS

Durham and London 2009

ISBN 978-0-8223-4528-2 (cloth : alk. paper)
ISBN 978-0-8223-4547-3 (pbk. : alk. paper)

Contents

Preface

Advancing Theory and Method

LOIS ANN LORENTZEN, KEVIN M. CHUN,
JOAQUIN JAY GONZALEZ III, AND HIEN DUC DO

Nestled in the bucolic hills of northern California lies a Buddhist religious center founded by a Chinese venerable master who was born in Manchuria at the beginning of the twentieth century. According to the center's official website, the organization was established as an ideal "way-place for the propagation of the Proper Dharma."[1] Further, the grounds of the compound cover 488 acres, or "about twenty-five times the size of the grounds of the White House." Originally built in the 1930s as a state hospital compound, all of its buildings and streets have been renamed and refashioned into "a wellspring from which Buddhism flows into the world" and a "place to which Buddhism throughout the world returns." When exploring this vast complex, one encounters buildings with names such as Joyous Giving House, Five Contemplations Dining Hall, Rebirth Hall, and the Jeweled Hall of Ten Thousand Buddhas, which, in its former life, served as an indoor gymnasium. Wild peacocks roam the grounds under street signs demarcating "Boddhi Way" and "Mindfulness Way," which serve as ever-present reminders of the Buddha dharma and the holy decree for this site. This rich religious and cultural landscape provided the inspiration for our book title because it embodied themes that we witnessed among the immigrant communities discussed herein. First, there is a theme of direction and guidance—all of the immigrant communities in this book turned to their faiths for direction and guidance in times of transition, dislocation, and relocation. For the Buddhist congregants at the northern California religious site, the street signs that metaphorically pointed the way to the proper dharma and spiritual transformation symbolized this guidance. For the immigrants in our study, faith traditions, teachings, institutions, and devotional practices pointed to a spiritual "center" that anchored their daily lives.

Another theme revolves around adaptation and synthesis. The religious lives of the immigrants in our study extended well beyond replicating "home" in a new land. Rather, their religious activities and identity formations represented a dynamic process of adaptation to new physical and cultural environments and an ongoing synthesis of cultural elements from their countries of origin, the United States, and elsewhere. For instance, the Buddhist religious site in the example above might at first glance appear to be a transplantation of Chinese Buddhism and culture to an American location. However, a more complex picture of this site emerges upon closer inspection: the transnational activities of its monks and congregants (many of whom move through its Asian and North American organizational network) and its ongoing dialogue with its surrounding northern California community have contributed to an altogether unique religious and cultural identity. The Buddha dharma street signs manifest this unique, hybrid identity—they are inscribed in English, reference ancient Buddhist tenets, and are most likely not found anywhere else in the world. In essence, the distinct characteristics of these signs capture the vibrancy and heterogeneity of the immigrant religious communities in this book. For some, the signs also symbolize their hopes and beliefs in a new, idealized religious space in America, thus reflecting historical immigrant narratives of renewal, reinvention, and regeneration.

This book reflects the findings of a four-year study conducted by researchers from the Religion and Immigration Project (TRIP) at the University of San Francisco to analyze the role of religion in the civic and political processes of new migrants.[2] When we started our fieldwork in 2001, few studies existed that explored the multiple and complex ways that religion provides both sites of resistance to assimilation as well as resources that facilitate civic incorporation in the United States. Fortunately, the literature on religion and recent immigrants to the United States is growing, and we have benefited from a number of excellent studies (Carnes and Yang 2004; Ebaugh and Chafetz 2000, 2002; Foley and Hoge 2007; Haddad, Smith, and Esposito, 2003; Hondagneu-Sotelo 2007; Jeung 2004; Kniss and Numrich 2007; Leonard, Stepick, Vásquez, and Holdaway 2005; Levitt 2007, 2001; Vásquez and Marquardt 2003; Warner and Wittner 1998). What the literature has in common is a desire to problematize traditional portrayals of ethnic communities as monolithic and static and to demonstrate how groups and individuals negotiate multiple religious, cultural, and national identities along a vast array of value, attitudinal, and behavioral domains. We hope to contribute to this body of literature a set of theoretical frameworks that are new or understudied in religion and migration literature, including theories that address sexual migration and acculturation. We also aim to provide ethnographic case studies that revisit, challenge, and reinterpret existing theories related to social capital, civic incorporation, and transnational migration.

RESEARCH DESIGN AND METHODS

Community-based ethnographic research shapes this volume. Data from our four-year study include ethnographic field notes from each study site; semi-structured family interviews for five immigrant families at each study site; and interviews with individuals. The first data collection phase involved ethnographic field observations at each site. Participant observation was our primary investigative technique because it afforded rich opportunities to study the daily interactions and rituals of congregants in their own time and space. Our ethnographic field notes consisted of detailed observations made by our research staff during weekly visits to each site. The consequent extensive ethnographic database allowed us to examine the actual processes we were studying. The notes included comprehensive descriptions of all aspects of religious and spiritual life (religious and social activities, rituals, texts, religious objects, etc.), as well as interpersonal relations and exchanges between individuals and groups that could be associated with themes explored at a particular site (civic and political incorporation, sexual migration, acculturation, transnationalism, social capital, etc.). The comprehensive field notes generated "thick descriptions" (LeCompte and Schensul 1999; Geertz 1973) — that is, detailed narratives of events, behaviors, conversations, interpretations, and explanations that illuminate how meaning and identity are constructed in the religious and civic lives of new immigrants. Our guiding research agenda was to explore the role of religion as a primary variable in the civic and social incorporation of recent migrants.[3]

Our family interview data consisted of audiotaped responses to semistructured interview items. All members of a designated family who were at least seven years of age were recruited for these interviews. The semistructured format of the interviews allowed each family member to elaborate on their unique immigration experiences. This included extended discussions on how their religious and spiritual lives help them cope with displacement and relocation. We also conducted semistructured interviews with numerous individuals who were not part of religious sites or families and individuals who frequented nontraditional religious sites, such as day laborers, gang members, transgendered sex workers, and other study participants. Interviews were conducted by multilingual researchers who were fluent both in English and in the respective languages and dialects of the five ethnic groups under investigation. Most of the research interviewers belonged to the five ethnic communities and were screened for cultural competence in interpersonal and communication skills. In addition, research interviewers attended three two-hour training sessions in interviewing techniques.

Although we began with a congregational model, we soon discovered that our sites "leaked" well beyond established religious sites and congregations. In some cases, we did indeed remain with congregations or religiously based social service sites, although we emphasized multilevel strata including families and individuals. In many cases, however, we followed our subjects outside the walls of traditional religious sites or congregations to places such as tattoo removal clinics, brothels, single-room occupancy hotels, and the streets of San Francisco, El Salvador, Vietnam, Taiwan, China, and Mexico. We began our study of a tattoo removal program for example, in a religiously based social service agency. We soon realized that we needed to follow gang members to the streets, to hospitals where tattoos were removed, to juvenile detention centers, to homes, and eventually to prisons in El Salvador. On the streets of San Francisco we encountered migrant transgendered sex workers and followed them to single-room occupancy hotel rooms, social service sites, and eventually to altars and shrines devoted to Santisima Muerte throughout Mexico. Had we stayed within the walls of a religious site or remained bound to a congregational model, we would have missed the strong and vibrant religiosity expressed by this highly marginalized group of migrants.

Hermeneutic phenomenology guided the analyses of our ethnographic data. This entailed analyzing and interpreting how people are situated in their worlds, constituted by their worlds, engaged in daily activity, and moved by their concerns in their everyday lives (Chesla 1995). This analytic approach offered multiple angles from which to examine the everyday lives of new immigrants. Conceptual connections between field-note text, codes, and multimedia data (e.g., photos, videotaped images, and audiotaped narratives) were examined. This process enabled us to develop conceptual networks of knowledge that contributed to emergent theory. Analyses of interview data similarly involved interpretive phenomenology to examine narratives related to each questionnaire domain. This involved reviewing entire interview narratives for each ethnic group to track holistic themes and then formulating detailed interpretations of each interview and marking text that addressed each of the identified themes. The combination of comprehensive descriptive data from ethnographic observations with individual narratives provided rich, in-depth understandings of the heterogeneous, complicated, incorporation processes for a broad range of immigrant groups.

Study Sample and Sites

Our ethnographic observations during the study's first year canvassed broad cross-sections of people at our study sites. To this end, we made a conscious effort to observe and record the diverse range of voices comprising the ethnic and religious groups under investigation. Study participants included first- and second-generation immigrant adults and youth of Chinese, Filipino, Vietnamese, Mexican, and Salvadoran descent. Although there is a tremendous range of ages in our ethnographic and family interview samples (from elementary-school-age children to adults ninety years of age), the majority of our adult participants are first-generation immigrants of low socioeconomic status who have relatively little formal education and who have either minimal or no skills in speaking and writing English. The majority of our youth sample, however, was enrolled in the public education system and possessed bilingual skills.[4]

Study sites were selected according to their sociopolitical and historical significance to each of the five ethnic minority groups; their high level of migrant membership, participation, and leadership; their emphasis on religious and social services for new immigrants; and their central location in neighborhoods with a high proportion of the specified ethnic populations. Prospective sites were evaluated on these four main criteria through exploratory field observations and individual interviews with religious and civic leaders and community members. Archival research of community records, historical documents and books, and printed media also aided our evaluation and selection process. Eleven sites constituted the final selection for our investigation.

Chinese Immigrant Sites:
1. A Chinese orthodox Mahayana Buddhist temple and monastery in San Francisco Chinatown that serves approximately 300 congregants per year.
2. A Chinese American Presbyterian Mission in San Francisco Chinatown that serves over 1,000 adults and youths per year.

Filipino Immigrant Sites:
1. A Roman Catholic church in the South of Market district of San Francisco with approximately 1,000 parishioners.
2. An indigenous Filipino Christian church in Daly City, California, with approximately 1,500 members.

Vietnamese Immigrant Sites:
1. A Roman Catholic church in downtown San Jose, California, with approximately 2,500 parishioners.
2. A Vietnamese Theravedic Buddhist temple in San Jose, California, that serves approximately 2,000 congregants.

Mexican Immigrant Site:
1. A Presbyterian church in the Mission District of San Francisco with approximately 150 congregants.

Joint Mexican and Salvadoran Immigrant Sites:
1. A charismatic Roman Catholic church in the Mission District of San Francisco with approximately 300 parishioners.
2. A Pentecostal church in the Mission District of San Francisco with approximately 300 congregants.
3. A Roman Catholic social service agency that serves approximately 14,000 immigrants per year.

It is important to note that these sites were the starting points for our study. The research quickly expanded into the numerous nontraditional sites mentioned above and discussed throughout the volume. The Filipino team, for example, not only observed rites and rituals at convents, seminaries, schools, monasteries, temples, grottoes, and churches but also participated in Bible studies, prayers, meditations, outreach events, picnics, masses, baptism, weddings, confirmations, house blessings, and funerals. They ate *almusal* (breakfasts), *tanghalian* (lunches), *hapunan* (dinner), and *merienda* (snacks) with their research subjects. The Mexican and Salvadoran teams found themselves in skid row hotels, prisons, detention centers, brothels, street corners, prayer meetings, indigenous baptism rituals, homes, and marches. Members of the Vietnamese team attended Catholic masses and Buddhist services as well as technical skills courses, language classes, social activities, and festivals. The Chinese team regularly visited children's after-school programs, festivals, and family events, and took long bus rides to remote Buddhist centers.

The Transnational Social Field

A paradigm of transnational migration guided our study of new immigrant communities. We assumed that our geographic site would not be limited to the San Francisco Bay Area; transnational lives and bilocalism more accurately describe the new immigrant communities of San Francisco. These immigrants, especially Salvadorans, Filipinos, and Mexicans, maintain active social inter-

action and community involvement across borders. Travel between sending and receiving countries is common and frequent—often taking place at least once in a given calendar year. For some, dual citizenship, including voting in elections in both countries, is possible. As Nina Glick Schiller writes, "Persons in the sending and receiving societies become participants in a single social unit" (1999, 99). Thus, comparative research in which both sending and receiving societies are explored is critical to properly understand the realities of the new immigrants. Researchers with gang members for example, quickly concluded with Elana Zilberg that "the complex flows and the multiple geopolitical scales of analysis at work in the urban barrio make it impossible to engage with the cultural politics of one side of this social field (Los Angeles) without simultaneously accounting for those at play on the other side (San Salvador)"; thus San Francisco and San Salvador became a single social unit" (2004, 769).

Religious groups also reflect this transnational dynamism. Our research field thus encompassed the San Francisco Bay Area as well as numerous "other sides" and sites. The Filipino research team conducted extensive fieldwork in the Philippines, in the cities and provinces of Manila, Quezon City, Laguna, Cavite, Cebu, Tagaytay, and Bohol. They also worked with colleagues at De La Salle University (Manila and Canlubang) and at the University of the Philippines (Quezon City and Los Baños). Jonathan Lee's primary research site was in

Taiwan and secondarily in San Francisco. Other members of the Chinese team traveled to Hong Kong and Taipei to gather more information about the transnational activities and social fields identified by subjects based in San Francisco. Researchers from the Mexican and Salvadoran teams collaborated with researchers in Mexico and El Salvador and conducted extensive fieldwork in those respective countries. Patricia Fortuny Loret de Mola conducted fieldwork with Maya in the Yucatán Peninsula and then followed them to San Francisco for further fieldwork. The Vietnamese team's study took them to Ho Chi Minh City, Vietnam, as well as to a smaller city forty-five kilometers to the south; researchers traced the close transnational ties between a Catholic church in Vietnam that is "partnered" with a San Jose, California, church, and the transnational religious field inhabited by linked Buddhist temples in Vietnam and northern California.

The point is that we ended up conducting our research in much the same way that our subjects lived their lives—coming and going, reinforcing and complementing transnational connections. Once we identified instances of transnational activities and ties, we explored their nature and extent and outlined the spatial or geographical demarcations of the transnational social field in which they occurred. We examined the significance of transnational activities to the character and settings of our study sites. Fieldwork and collaboration with researchers in countries of origin focused on what was actually exchanged in the identified transnational social fields, how these exchanges occurred, and how they directly or indirectly shaped the character and activities of our study sites in the United States.

Embodying the Transnational Social Field

In many ways our research team embodied the transnational social field we were studying. The entire Chinese research team had personal and family ties to the social fields they were investigating. Selina Lui, our Cantonese-speaking research team member, was born and raised in Hong Kong and later relocated to the United States for her graduate education in counseling psychology. She had extensive family and social networks in Hong Kong and the United States, which included active membership in a transnational Chinese Baptist community. Maureen Lin, our Mandarin- and Taiwanese-speaking research assistant, was born and raised in Taichung, Taiwan, moved to Canada during her high school and college years, and eventually relocated to San Francisco for her graduate education in counseling psychology. Kevin Chun, a fourth-generation Chinese American, has family roots in the San Francisco Chinatown community that span over a century. His first-generation family ancestors have historical ties to Guangdong province in China and to Hawaii when it was a U.S. territory.

The Filipino research team consisted of Joaquin Jay Gonzalez III and the research assistants Andrea Garcia Maison, Dennis Marzan, and Claudine del Rosario—all Filipino Americans and keen bilingual and bicultural observers. The second-generation immigrants Andrea and Claudine were born and raised in the East Coast of the United States. Dennis and Jay were born in the Philippines and are first-generation immigrants to California. Dennis immigrated at the age of twelve and Jay when he was twenty-four years of age. Jay also lived in Singapore for five years. Jay and Dennis live the transnational lives of their subjects, with family, friends, and social networks in both the United States and the Philippines.

The Vietnamese team members were all born in Vietnam and are refugees, although they took different routes coming to the United States. Hien Duc Do, sociologist and team leader, arrived as a teenager at the end of the Vietnam War in 1975. The research assistant Tommy Luu came to the United States as a young child, whereas Minh Tuan Nguyen arrived later as an unaccompanied young adult, leaving family behind. Now Vietnamese Americans, all members of the team are bilingual, bicultural, and active community members.

The Mexican and Salvadoran teams boasted a first-generation Salvadoran migrant, Rosalina Mira, in addition to Liliana Harris, who migrated from Mexico only months before the study began; Luis Enrique Bazan, a recent migrant from Peru where he had worked with street children; Susanna Zayarsky, a Russian migrant who has worked as a journalist in Argentina; Patricia Fortuny Loret de Mola, a Mexican anthropologist based in Yucatán; and Lois Lorentzen, a native-born Euro-American. The majority of the team led both personal and professional transnational lives throughout the course of the project.

The unique family origins, cultural socialization experiences, and life experiences of our researchers enriched their perspectives on acculturation, cultural and ethnic identity formation, and social stratification issues for new transnational migrants. Moreover, their diverse religious traditions, interdisciplinary perspectives, and ethnic backgrounds afforded them unique insights into the many facets of religious life for migrants in the San Francisco Bay Area.

COMMUNITY DISSEMINATION

Our team was dedicated to activism and community advocacy, as well as to academic research. Our research enabled us to inform public policy and promote social justice by giving voice to migrant concerns. We were fortunate in that our funders and the University of San Francisco encouraged us to sponsor community-based workshops and to disseminate our findings beyond the academy.

The Chinese team provided funding and support for Family Day at the Presbyterian Mission, an event that brought together over two hundred new immigrants for educational and informational sessions on health, parenting, and education. The team also supported Respecting Elders Day at the Buddhist Temple, an event that gathered over one hundred new immigrant seniors and their family members for an annual celebration to honor their achievements and lives. Members of the Chinese team routinely acted as translators for congregants, provided instrumental support by assisting with academic tutoring and completion of daily tasks or chores. These examples of community involvement are consistent with a participatory-action research approach, and are also culturally appropriate given Chinese cultural norms of reciprocity and collectivism, and the need for more staffing at nonprofit community sites with limited resources. The team also published in *Sing Tao Daily News* (the largest Chinese language daily in North America and Asia), provided radio interviews, and broadcast news (in Cantonese) of social services and activities offered to migrants by local Chinese religious groups over KUSF, the University of San Francisco's radio station.

The Vietnamese team shared research findings with the Vietnamese community in San Jose, California, and provided radio and newspaper interviews. The team also collaborated with the actors Van Pham Mai and Hung Nguyen and the director Victoria Rue of the Vietnamese theater company, San Khau Viet, to conduct theater workshops at two project sites: a Vietnamese Buddhist temple and a Vietnamese Catholic church. The community theater group produced a play based on project research and findings.

The Mexican and Salvadoran team cosponsored numerous events including Immigrant Pride Day 2002, the Migrant Face of God Conference (with a local interreligious immigrant rights organization), and the Celebration of Day Laborers. Team members regularly wrote for the popular press in both Spanish and English, and they were interviewed by local and national radio and television. The team was most proud of helping cofound the theater troupe El Teatro Jornalero. We invited the theater director Roberto Gutiérrez-Varea and the cultural worker Francisco Herrera to conduct workshops with day laborers. The day laborer actors quickly decided that they wanted to stage original theater productions based on their life experiences. El Teatro Jornalero now regularly performs to standing-room only crowds in San Francisco; their productions are frequently covered by Univision and Telemundo (national Spanish language television networks).

The Filipino team participated in Immigration 101a and Immigration 101b, workshops on legal rights and employment opportunities for newly arrived Filipino immigrants. They also sponsored Filipino Immigrants and their Churches: Helping Shape the New San Francisco Community, the first ever gathering of local Filipino American religious leaders to discuss the role of churches in the lives of new migrants. Team members published in the popular press both in the United States and in the Philippines (in English and Tagalog). Team leader Joaquin Gonzalez III was appointed to the Immigrant Rights Commission of the City of San Francisco and was recognized with a Special Congressional Citation from then House minority leader Nancy Pelosi for his "outstanding and invaluable work to the community."

THEORETICAL FRAMEWORKS

This volume draws from the multiple academic disciplines represented by our research team, including psychology, sociology, political science, art history, communication studies, anthropology, and religious studies. Theories that influenced our research come from acculturation studies in psychology, gender and sexuality studies, ethnic studies, migration studies, and sociology of religion; we also utilized theoretical frameworks related to transnationalism and globalization, border studies, class and structural analysis, and political and social capital.

We hope to bring new theoretical and conceptual frameworks to understand the role of religion in new migrant communities. Literature in migration studies, including that on religion, rarely references widely used models in the psychological literature on acculturation. We wanted to bring together literatures that are virtually never in dialogue, even when they address the same subject, such as migrants and acculturation processes. Sociologists of religion may not be convinced by acculturation theory, but we contend that at a minimum they should be exposed to this set of psychological approaches. Conversely, acculturation theorists in psychology could benefit from familiarity with the wide array of sociological, economic, and political literature related to migration. Similarly, the literature on religion and migration rarely, if ever, addresses the phenomenon of sexual migration, one of the foci of this volume. Theorists of migration studies, queer studies, and human rights could profit from dialogue with each other; as Howe writes in this volume, sexual migrants and the legal status of lesbian, gay, bisexual, and transgender (LGBT) migrants pose particular challenges to concepts of human rights and citizenship.

We decided to organize this book thematically rather than by ethnicity in order to break standard ways of examining communities as entities with minimal connections to each other. All too rarely do scholars in Asian American studies and Latin American or Latina and Latino studies, for example, compare and contrast data across disciplines. One of the great joys of our research process was the monthly daylong team meeting in which we shared reflections across academic disciplines and ethnic communities; we used case studies from our diverse groups to interrogate theories related to gender and sexualities, acculturation, political and social economy, and transnationalism. The following theoretical debates shaped our discussions and the eventual writing of this volume.

Gender and Sexualities

Research on gender and sexuality remains marginalized within migration studies. The household and family are the most studied (although still understudied) aspects of migration that acknowledge the importance of networks, as opposed to individual actors, in migration processes. Generally this research, while acknowledging family ties, does not explicitly analyze gender relations and sexual identities, although gendered divisions of labor have been well studied by migration scholars. Our essays build upon recent work on "sexual migration," a new theoretical intervention in the social sciences concerned with the motivations and processes associated with crossing transnational boundaries based partially or wholly on one's gender and/or sexuality (Cantú 1999; Parker 1997). Gender and sexual orientation may be key variables in the decision to migrate. Although feminist scholars have increasingly brought gender into migration studies during the last two decades, most immigration studies still treat gender relations and sexual identities as peripheral.

Research on the particular citizenship demands faced by lesbian and gay couples hoping to establish their legal legitimacy as same-sex couples in the United States is virtually nonexistent. We appreciate the new work that directly addresses the work of faith-based organization in promoting migrant rights, at times placing religious groups in direct opposition to the state (Hondagneu-Sotelo 2007). To our knowledge, however, the crucial role that religious organizations may play in helping LGBT migrants negotiate complex legal and social aspects of migration to the United States is invisible in the burgeoning literature on religion and immigration. The complex challenges faced by queer migrants are also largely unknown within the LGBT community (Donayre 2002;

Ranck 2002). Cymene Howe suggests, in this volume, that the legal mechanisms and community-based interventions that aid lesbian and gay migration
are a fundamental element of sexual migratory practices. Howe addresses the
role that religious communities might play, conceptually and pragmatically, in
LGBT migration. Utilizing human rights epistemologies and the philosophical
framework of a particular religious organization, Howe poses a series of questions that emerge surrounding the theory and practice of LGBT and same-sex
couple migration. Special challenges to notions of citizenship are posed by
LGBT migrants; by virtue of both their legal status and their sexuality, they face
difficulties in claiming full citizenship. Howe claims that religious communities, although not known for being champions of LGBT rights, may have the
networks, tools, and philosophical resources best suited to address the legal and
epistemological liminality of LGBT migrants, thus challenging human rights at
the level of both theory and practice.

The role of religion in constructing and transforming gender identities
and relations remains relatively unexplored. Feminist and social movement
theorists are often quick to discount positive reports of their religious life by
Pentecostal women, for example. Robin Leidner writes that "feminist ideology
defines the constituency of the contemporary women's movement extremely
broadly—all women should benefit from the struggle, all could contribute to
it, none should feel excluded. The reality has been somewhat disappointing"
(2001, 47). The migrant Pentecostal women featured in Lorentzen's essay in this
volume reported positively of their experience in the church; they claim that
they enjoy public roles and that their male partners increased participation in
the home. Lorentzen challenges social movement and feminist theory by exploring the paradoxical characteristics of Pentecostalism in a migrant church;
it is both oppositional to the status quo and upholder of it. Questions of identity are also central in this migrant Pentecostal church; religious, theological,
migrant, and gender identities are continually renegotiated and shifting. Transnational migration networks may also emerge based on gender/sexual identity
as is evident in the case of transgendered sex workers who travel between San
Francisco and Guadalajara, Mexico (see Howe, Zaraysky, and Lorentzen in this
volume). The politics of citizenship, legitimacy, social acceptance, and identity
construction are especially challenging for outwardly LGBT migrants; those
who engage in sex work face even greater challenges and increased marginalization. We argue that the devotional practices offered to La Santisima Muerte
offer transgender sex workers both a sense of shared community as well as an
affirmation of identity.

We hope that these essays encourage other scholars to push the edges of theoretical debates within migration studies concerning sexual migration, gender identity construction, gender and religion, and transnationalism and gender.

Acculturation

Acculturation theory remains the predominant theory in psychology that specifically addresses psychosocial adjustment and adaptation experiences among new immigrants and refugees. Although the Chinese team members' research training has mostly focused on the scientific method and statistical analyses, they decided to broaden their investigative lens by using ethnographic methods that more fully capture the multidimensional and dynamic properties of acculturation. This represented a paradigm shift from traditional acculturation studies that typically rely on individual self-report measures with limited data points.

Current debates in acculturation research are mostly concerned with understanding the nature and specific characteristics of acculturation. Specifically, researchers have called for more innovative assessment methods that can more effectively assess the fluctuating and multifaceted nature of this construct (e.g., Bornstein and Cote 2006; Chun, Balls Organista, and Marin 2003). Along similar lines, researchers believe that greater attention should be given to contextual or environmental factors that potentially influence acculturation. In some respects this has moved the field a little closer toward sociological research on immigration, which has paid more attention to the social, historical, and political dynamics underlying resettlement.

Chun references current theoretical models of acculturation in his essay on religious organizations in San Francisco Chinatown. Acculturation is basically defined as a multidimensional and dynamic process of cultural acquisition and maintenance when distinct cultures come into sustained contact. Acculturation is multidimensional because cultural acquisition and maintenance can occur along different dimensions of psychological functioning. For instance, a new immigrant may exhibit shifts in behaviors, beliefs, attitudes, and values as a result of immersion in a new cultural environment. Acculturation is dynamic because the rate and nature of cultural acquisition and maintenance are constantly in flux depending on social conditions and environmental factors. The construct of acculturation is receiving greater attention in the social science literature, especially in the field of psychology where it has been linked with experiences of stress and the resultant difficulties in psychological adjustment. In his essay, Chun attempts to expand the scholarly discourse on acculturation theory along several fronts. First, his essay attempts to bridge the conspicuous gap between the psychological literature on acculturation and the current literature on religion and immigration. He primarily achieves this by exploring how two religious organizations in San Francisco's Chinatown—a Presbyterian mission and a Buddhist temple—serve as important sites of acculturation. Second, he attempts to broaden the discussion of acculturation theory by examining how contextual factors, including the institutional cultures and histories of religious organizations, shape individual experiences of acculturation among its members. Third, Chun spotlights youth acculturation experiences that have received relatively little attention in the psychological literature. Fourth, he explores whether religious practices and values are maintained or are transformed during acculturation. Surprisingly, there is a paucity of psychological research on acculturation and religion despite the fact that religious faith and organizations figure prominently in the lives of many Chinese immigrants. Finally, his essay is based on ethnographic methods that offer new opportunities to observe and analyze the complex characteristics of acculturation.

Hien Duc Do and Mimi Khúc illustrate the multiple roles that a Vietnamese American Buddhist temple occupies in the United States, including as a site of resistance, a place of worship, a center for cultural and religious preservation, a transnational tie between the United States and Vietnam, and a link between the global and the local. Do and Khúc begin their essay by presenting a historical overview of acculturation models in the field of sociology. In this presentation, they emphasize how these acculturation models offer an important macro-level or societal perspective of immigration. Do and Khúc then provide an in-depth discussion of the history, structure, and activities of a Buddhist temple in San Jose, California. These authors pay close attention to how these facets of the temple embody different manifestations of acculturation, adaptation, and innovation in response to the distinct needs of their Vietnamese American congregants and their new American cultural setting. This essay shares a major theme that also runs throughout Chun's essay—religious sites offer novel and rich opportunities to investigate the complex and multilayered process of immigrant adjustment and adaptation.

Transnationalism

New immigrants often maintain active social interaction and community involvement with family members, friends, political and social organizations, and, increasingly, religious groups in their countries of origin. For some migrants, dual citizenship and multiple allegiances, including voting in elections in both countries, is possible and encouraged. At a minimum, today's migrants send money home and are able to stay connected through electronic mail and cell phones. The fabric of many migrants' "daily lives becomes transnational" (Vásquez and Marquardt 2003, 42). The geographical site and unit of analysis has changed from what was used in traditional research on immigration to recognize the transnational dynamic of immigration and the multidimensional nature of personal adaptation and societal incorporation (Basch, Schiller, and Szanton-Blanc 1995; Espiritu 2003; Levitt 2001). Comparative research in both countries of origin and host countries, such as that conducted for this volume, is critical in helping us understand the realities of new immigrants.

Religious actors and groups reflect the transnational dynamism characteristic of contemporary migration. This volume directly addresses the need to analyze the role of religion, religiosity, and religious communities as part of the transnational migration paradigm. Gonzalez argues here, for example, that the Spanish and American Christianization of the Philippines also precipitated a Filipinization of American Christian churches, especially in California, which is the adopted home of close to two million Filipino immigrants. Gonzalez's essay clearly demonstrates that when taking a transnational perspective we must address multiple populations, including not only those who migrated but those who remained in the country of origin, and groups and organizations (in this case U.S. Christian churches) affected by new migrants.

Countless examples exist of religious acts and actors reinforcing and complementing transnational connections. Jonathan Lee explores the relationship between transnational identity and transnational religion manifested in the pilgrimage of the U.S. Tianhou/Mazu from the San Francisco Ma-tsu Temple U.S.A. to her mother temple in Beigang, Taiwan. Lee asks what happens when a territorial goddess becomes deterritorialized, suggesting that a paradox of spatiality exists in the transnational veneration of Tianhou/Mazu. Although Tianhou/Mazu is a territorial goddess, her expanding territorial sovereignty is based on a deterritorialization of geographic and temporal space of an imagined community of transnational personalities. In this case, what Peggy Levitt terms a "simultaneity of connection" occurs and "connections are integrated into vertical and horizontal systems of connection that cross borders" (2001, 3).

Levitt defines social remittances as the "ideas, behaviors, identities, and social capital that migrants export to their home communities" (2001, 5). Patricia Fortuny Loret de Mola analyzes the transformation in the *hetzmek* (baptism) ritual of the Maya of Yucatán, Mexico, as they move between Yucatán and San Francisco, California. She also demonstrates that the transnational ties between two Presbyterian churches (one in San Francisco and one in Yucatán) strengthened the respective congregations, facilitated improved communication among family members on both sides, and enabled preservation of rituals such as hetzmek thanks to the receipt of "religious remittances."

Sarah Horton analyzes two lay Catholic movements—the Catholic Ministry of Kerygma and the Catholic Charismatic Renewal—in San Francisco and the transnational connections maintained with their counterparts in El Salvador. She argues that the networklike structure (Castells 2000) paradoxically spurs the Roman Catholic Church to adapt to globalization while also posing a challenge to its hierarchical organization. Lois Ann Lorentzen and Luis Enrique Bazán demonstrate how the transnational social field of gang life in El Salvador and in the United States is perceived as a threat to state actors who then initiate increasingly repressive measures against marginalized youth. Unlike Horton's more optimistic view, gangs reflect the underbelly of "transnationalism from below" and the valiant efforts of religious groups to serve as mediating institutions between youth, the state that hopes to incarcerate or deport them, and the larger society that has failed marginalized youth.

We agree with Manuel Vásquez and Marie Marquardt that religion "is one of the main protagonists in the unbinding of culture from its traditional referents and boundaries and in its reattachment in new space-time configurations. Through this interplay of delocalization and relocalization, religion gives rise to hybrid individual and collective identities that fly in the face of the methodological purity and simplicity sought by modernist sociologies of religion" (2003, 35). We argue in this volume that religion can contribute to transnational flows and consequent formation of multiple identities, challenges to the nation-state, and rejection of assimilationist ideologies.

Civic and Political Engagement

The final essays in this book go beyond the dominant themes in the social and political economies of migration literature that place heavy emphases on the "globalization phenomenon," institutional economics, business-government-society relations, and the capitalization of gender (Chant 1992; Espenshade and King 1994; Halpern 1998). We build on the important writings of Basch, Schiller, and Szanton-Blanc (1995), Choy (2003), Levitt (2001), Parreñas (2001, 2005), Sassen (1998), and Smith and Guarnizo (1998) in recognizing that diasporas are not just static global events caused by "waves of migration" or "push and pull factors" but are dynamically transnational and multidimensional in terms of their capitalization—that is, not just social and cultural.

In part 3, Transnationalism, Gonzalez exposes the relative size and magnitude of the process of reverse colonization occurring in the San Francisco Bay Area due to the inflow of Filipinos and their churches, especially during the more than one hundred years of Philippine–United States relations. The Harvard political scientist Robert Putnam employs a capitalization audit" in his controversial book *Bowling Alone* to argue that in American civil society there is a massive decline in social capital formation and civic culture (Putnam 1993, 1995, 1996, 2000). Undeterred by his many critics, Putnam (2004) further reinforced his U.S. findings when he and his collaborators presented more empirical evidence that this dire situation is also endemic in a number of Western countries. Putnam adds that the decline is evident in both bonding and bridging social capital. Bonding social capital is the inward-focused connections drawing individuals to form a social organization, while bridging social capital is the outward-looking activities linking them to society. However, Putnam and the many others who support his thesis have failed to account for the capital commitments and contributions of new immigrant groups, including Filipino Americans. Hence, in "We Do Not Bowl Alone," Joaquin Gonzalez, Andrea Maison, and Dennis Marzan attempt to rectify Putnam's oversight. They argue that hidden behind the European facades of San Francisco's spiritual spaces "abandoned" by the early Irish, German, English, French, and Italian settlers due to radical sociodemographics shifts are the social, political, organizational, cultural, culinary, and intellectual capitals from new Latino and Asian and Pacific Islander immigrants, particularly Filipinos.

The religion and community-based organizing literature in the United States is dominated by examples and cases of mainstream Caucasian-European and African American religious organizations building bonding social capital (see, among others, Dillon 2003; Harris 1998; Jacobsen 2001; Ramsay 1998; Wood 2002). However, there are few studies about civic engagement among new immigrant religious and spiritual groups. Given that accumulation and accounting of various forms of these bonding capitals exists among new Filipino migrants, as discussed in the preceding paragraph, the question that follows is has this critical mass translated to "bridging capitals" and, more importantly, to civic engagement and societal empowerment? Gonzalez and del Rosario address this question in their essay. They acknowledge that Catholic, Protestant, and independent churches have been utilized as effective hegemonic allies by colonizing states, like Spain and the United States, to pursue their imperialistic political and economic self-interests within their colonies, including the Philippines. Yet colonization and, consequently, globalization may also contain inherent dysfunctions that favor the "colonized" or "marginalized" populations. As discussed in Gonzalez's essay on transnationalism, globalization facilitates a reverse colonization with immigrants moving back and forth through gateway cities like Manila and San Francisco. Philippine Airlines alone flies over the "not so friendly skies" of the trans-Pacific route seven days a week. Just as churches in Manila have been used for Hispanicization and Americanization, Gonzalez and del Rosario assert that in San Francisco the colonized immigrants use Filipinized churches as modern-day counterhegemonic spaces and structures where advocacy, protest, lobbying, and activism tactics are learned and immigrant rights are discussed. Similar to liberation theology and faith-based organizing in Latin America (Cleary and Steigenga 2004; Martin 1990; Smith 1991; Swatos 1995; Torres 1992) as well as the activism of African American churches during the U.S. civil rights movement (Lincoln and Mamiya 2003; Sales 1994; Warren 2001), these contemporary counterhegemonic actions are directed at U.S., Philippine, and international laws and regimes that displace, repress, discriminate, and terrorize not just the global Filipino immigrants but all transnational communities in the post-9/11 era.

EL TEATRO JORNALERO'S FIRST PLAY, *Soldado de arena* (Sand Soldier), tells the story of a young man who crosses the border from Mexico to the United States, watches his brother and parents die at the border, and later finds himself a soldier in Iraq where he is then killed and consequently awarded U.S. citizenship posthumously. Throughout the play the young man (and others) are accompanied by *coyote místico*, a figure who crosses the physical border with the young man and his family and who holds the hands of the dying brother, mother, and father as they cross from life to death. Coyote místico accompanies the young man to Iraq and encourages him to cross cultural borders constructed between Iraqi "sand soldiers" and him. He holds the man as he dies, and mocks the general who "resurrects" him from death to the eternal life of U.S. citizenship. Finally, coyote místico crosses with the soldier from life to death back to life as he is reunited with his family and friends.

We believe that migrants ask us to become academic *coyotes*. In this volume we hope to cross boundaries between the academy and advocacy, and among academic disciplines and ethnic communities. We will be grateful if this book helps us understand the resilience, creativity, and courage of the migrants who have profoundly enriched our lives while conducting research for this volume.

NOTES

1. To protect the privacy of the organization, its name and the address of its website are withheld.

2. Primary funding for this study came from the Pew Charitable Trusts.

3. Copies of the research questions and abbreviated sample questionnaires developed to address aspects of this overarching concern are given in the appendices to this volume.

4. Research staff conducted information sessions on the study's goals, procedures, and timeline for leaders, staff, and congregation at each of the eleven initial study sites. Following these sessions, informed consent was obtained from participants as specified by a University of San Francisco Human Subjects Research protocol. During the first year of the study, requests of signed informed consent were restricted to the religious leaders and staff at each site because data collection solely focused on ethnographic observations. In the second year of the study, informed consent was extended to adults and young people who agreed to participate in interviews.

Acknowledgments

We must first thank the many migrants who opened their homes, lives, and hearts to us. Their courage, resilience, and generosity of spirit moved us deeply. As a team, the Religion and Immigration Project (TRIP) is grateful to the Pew Charitable Trusts for providing the lion's share of the funding for this project; we especially thank Kimon Sargeant who was our program officer at the time. Donald Miller of the Center for Religion and Civic Culture (CRCC) at the University of Southern California merits special thanks for sending Kimon Sargeant our way and for providing initial guidance and moral support. Rebecca King-O'Riain, Russell Jeung, and John Nelson provided invaluable training workshops during the early phase of our research. The Faculty Development Fund and the Jesuit Foundation at the University of San Francisco provided members of the research team with critical support. The USF team members consistently felt the support of President Stephen Privett, S. J., Provost James Wiser, Vice Provost Gerardo Marin, Dean of the College of Arts and Sciences Jennifer Turpin, and Associate Deans Dean Rader and Michael Bloch. We consider ourselves fortunate to be members of an institution that values research for justice.

The Religion and Immigration Project is deeply indebted to the brilliant managerial skills of our initial project manager, Lorrie Ranck. We couldn't have done it without her. We also thank Shelly Tito for so ably continuing to organize us in the last two years of research. We deeply appreciate photographer extraordinaire Jerry Berndt. We benefited from Jerry's friendship and from his creative, insightful, and compassionate way of seeing the world, and we thank him for granting permission for his photographs to appear throughout this book.

Thanks to the editorial team at Duke University Press. We are grateful for our editor Reynolds Smith's interest in our project and for the editorial associate Sharon Torian's graciousness.

From Lois Lorentzen: Thanks to the research assistants of the Salvadoran and Mexican team; their dedication, passion, and energy on behalf of the migrants was truly inspiring. Thanks to Luis Enrique Bazan, Rosalina Mira, Susanna Zayarsky, Liliana Harris, Carlos Torre, and Teresa Mejia. I am also grateful for numerous supportive colleagues at USF including members of the Theology and Religious Studies Department, the Latin American Studies Department, and colleagues too numerous to mention here. The Writing Warriors organized by Tracy Seeley deserve special mention.

I can't thank Roberto Varea enough for founding and continuing to direct El Teatro Jornalero (Day Laborer Theater). Colleagues from the Religion in Latin America and the Caribbean and Latina/o Theology groups of the American Academy of Religion provided support and helpful critiques along the way; thanks to Luis León who pushed me along at a critical stage in my research and to Rudy Busto who consulted early on in the project. I am thankful to supportive friends from the Center for Latin American Studies of the University of Florida where I was privileged to spend a semester as a Rockefeller Fellow. Anna Peterson, Manuel A. Vásquez, Philip Williams, and Milagros Peña provided a true intellectual home and Patricia Fortuny Loret de Mola was the perfect office mate and co-conspirator. The Hispanic Theological Initiative also expressed interest in aspects of this work; thanks especially to Jorge Aquino for organizing a conference at the Graduate Theological Union at Berkeley, and for providing encouragement and friendship.

I am grateful for the Servicio Jesuita Migrantes Norte y Centroamerica (the Jesuit Migrant Service, North and Central America), which has provided a research community across borders. Special thanks to José Luis Rocha, Marcela Ibarra, Vladimiro Valdez, S.J., Maria Vidal de Haymes, Graciela Polanco, Bill Rickle, S.J., Jim Stormes, S.J., Jill Marie Gerschutz, and Victoria Peleaz.

Our team especially thanks the Pentecostal churches, Roman Catholic churches, tattoo removal center, social service agencies, and numerous other groups and religious organizations that we studied in San Francisco as well as in El Salvador and Mexico. We wish we could list in appreciation all of the names of these organization's members and staff for the incredible work they do in migrant communities.

The friends who offered support and a listening ear are too numerous to mention. Special thanks go to Elizabeth Castelli, Jennifer Turpin, Kathryn Poethig, Victoria Rue, the San Francisco "family" (David Batstone, Wendy Brown, Rusty Springer, Bob Whitney, Clark Sorenson, and Brad Berky), Mike Duffy, Gary Erickson, and Kit Crawford. A true gift of TRIP was working with our professional, dedicated, passionate, compassionate, and fun research team.

I admire Joaquin (Jay) Gonzalez, Kevin Chun, and Hien Duc Do greatly and I feel privileged to have been their friend and colleague.

As always, my wonderful family and Gerardo Marín provided the love and support that make doing this work possible. No words adequately express my gratitude.

The Filipino American team, Joaquin Jay Gonzalez, Andrea Maison, Dennis Marzan, and Claudine del Rosario, would like to acknowledge the enthusiastic support and encouragement that was given by leaders, staff, parishioners, members of the Global Church of Christ, Northern California and the Philippines, San Patricio's Catholic Church in San Francisco, and the San Agosto's Catholic Church in South San Francisco. In particular, the wisdom and words of Monsignor B, Sister A, Father R, Father ET, Sister N, Noemi C, and District Minister AC and *mga kapatid sa Iglesia* (brothers and sisters in the church). Thanks to the Gonzalez families in Manila and Laguna as well as Toronto and San Diego, Tito Pete in Cebu, and Tito Dinky in Makati for the food, accommodations, and comfort during our fieldwork.

We could not have conducted our research without the critical funding, staffing, and facilities provided by the Yuchengco Philippine Studies Program, McCarthy Center for Public Service and the Common Good, Politics Department, Asian and Asian American Studies Programs, and the Jesuit Foundation at USF, Mayor George Christopher Professorial Chair at Golden Gate University (GGU), and Faculty Development Funds from USF and GGU. Valuable insights were gathered from colleagues from De La Salle University (Manila), University of the Philippines, Ateneo de Manila University, New Era University, San Francisco State University, City College of San Francisco, the University of California at Davis and Berkeley, Pusod, Westbay, the San Francisco Immigrant Rights Commission, Archdiocese of San Francisco, Graduate Theological Union, *Filipinas Magazine*, Arkipelago Bookstore, Veterans Equity Center, and the Bay Area Organizing Committee. We also thank the wonderful families and friends of Jay, Andrea, Dennis, and Claudine. Special mention goes to Jay's daughter, Elise, who ended up writing field notes while sitting patiently in the pews with dad, Jay's brother, James, who got roped into video recording and survey administration assignments; Michelle Hong who drove, took photos, and created the "Filipino TRIP database"; as well as Claudine's son, Timyas, who did fieldwork with his mom from the time he was in his mother's womb to the days when he could walk. Finally, thanks to New York University Press and USF's Center for the Pacific Rim for kindly allowing us to reprint revised versions of the essays by Joaquin Gonzalez and by Gonzalez, Andrea Maison, and Dennis Marzan.

From Kevin Chun: I would like to thank Selina Lui and Maureen Lin who were key research assistants on the Chinese immigrant team. Their multicultural skills, professionalism, and commitment to serving the Chinese American community greatly contributed to the success of this project. I would also like to thank the organizational leaders, religious members, staff, youth, and families at the Presbyterian Mission and the Buddhist Temple—this project simply would not have happened without their generosity, kindness, and willingness to share their knowledge and personal experiences with us. The Chinese team is especially indebted to the following people: at the Presbyterian Mission, Ms. DDM, executive director, and her predecessor, Pastor HC, Ms. YK, former director of the bilingual after school program and current director of Christian Social Services, Mrs. MQC, case manager, Mrs. VM, counselor, Mrs. MWL, administrative assistant, Pastor EW, former director of Christian Social Services, and his Hong Kong colleagues, Rev. TMK, former General Secretary of the HKCCC, and his wife, Professor T, and Mrs. EL, counselor at the Family Center, Hong Kong; At the Buddhist Temple, Dharma Master HR, Dharma Master HS, Dharma Master HY, Dharma Master HB, Ms. KWF, principal of the Saturday school program, and her fellow teachers, Roger, layperson and staff volunteer, Jenny, layperson and staff volunteer, Ms. SGH, layperson and staff volunteer, the Buddhist youth group members, and Mr. C, layperson and civic leader, at the Taipei Buddhist Books Distribution Association and temple.

Finally, I would like to thank Anthony Ng, his family and friends, and the many talented faculty members in the USF Asian American Studies Program for their support and insights throughout this project.

From Hịen Duc Do: I thank Tommy Luu and Minh Tuan Nguyen who were wonderful research assistants on the Vietnamese team. Their dedication, commitments to long hours, enthusiasm, and participation contributed to the success of the Vietnamese team. A project like this would not have been possible without the support, guidance, dedication, and willingness of the people at the Vietnamese Buddhist Temple and the Vietnamese Catholic Church to open their hearts and to share their life experiences with us. To all of them we are forever grateful for their generosity and time, and for all the things they do to make our community better, stronger, and more compassionate.

I am grateful for the friendship, support, and love that I received throughout this project from Lois, Kevin, and Jay and I will always cherish my friendships with them and our wonderful time together. Finally, I would like to thank my wife Akemi, our children Meiko and Koji, and my family for their love and support during this project.

PART 1

Gender and

Sexualities

Devotional Crossings

Transgender Sex Workers, Santisima Muerte, and Spiritual Solidarity in Guadalajara and San Francisco

CYMENE HOWE, SUSANNA ZARAYSKY, AND
LOIS ANN LORENTZEN

In the early evening hours in the living room of a Guadalajara brothel, "Veronica," a male-to-female transgender sex worker who plies her trade in both Mexico and the United States, rose from her chair to turn up the volume on the stereo. The song, *A quien le importa* (Who Cares?) sung by the Mexican pop diva Thalia, filled the room. Veronica explains that the song echoes the way that many transgender sex workers live their lives: on their own terms, despite condemnation.

> People point me out
> They point at me with their fingers
> They whisper behind my back
> And I don't care at all
>
> I know that they critique me
> They swear that they hate me
> Jealousy tears away at them
> My life overwhelms them
>
> Maybe it's my fault
> For not being mainstream
> It's too late
> To change now
> I will stay firm in my convictions
> I will reinforce my ideas
> My destiny is the one I decide on and choose for myself
> Who cares what I do?
> Who cares what I say?
> I am this way and I will continue to be, I will never change

Veronica's perspective, one that combines defiance with an acute awareness of societal opprobrium, is indicative of much of the devotional practices that are described in this essay. Our focus is on the spiritual practices and religious cosmology crafted by Mexican transgender sex workers who journey between San Francisco, California, and Guadalajara, Mexico. Based on ethnographic research and interviews in both the United States and Mexico, we explore how Mexican male-to-female transgender sex workers craft unique devotional rites and beliefs among one another in order to create spiritual solidarity and confront the often precarious life circumstances that can result from sex work, border crossings, and gender nonconformity.

These religious practices are best placed in cultural and political economic context. Our goal is to better understand how these devotional practices and beliefs coincide with the way Mexican transgender sex workers are, themselves, understood and treated by the state, in Mexico and in the United States, as well as by the social orders of which they are a part. We argue that these devotional practices are not renegade rituals to saints and icons outside of the traditional Catholic pantheon. Rather, the belief systems created by transgender sex workers as they cross geopolitical borders and gendered boundaries, serve to create spiritual agency within structural systems that are hostile to sex work, transgender persons, and border-crossing individuals from the south. Transgender sex workers in Mexico and in the United States, we argue, are acutely aware of the ways in which they are marginalized and thus seek alternative communities and develop spiritual practices that are shared among one another, not to disavow the Catholic traditions they may have learned as children, but to reshape their faith and the meaning they bring to devotion.

Devotions, prayers, and offerings to these saints or "pseudo saints," such as St. Jude and La Santisima Muerte (Saint Death or the Holy Death), might appear to be a way in which marginalized individuals find solace in their difference by embracing the radical fringes of devotion. We argue, however, that the opposite is true. In fact, transgender sex workers in both the United States and Mexico create a mobile, devotional subculture among themselves by sharing, translating, and crossing borders to reevaluate the role of particular saints and religious practices in their lives. In this sense the culturally distinct devotional practices they invent lend further evidence to the deterritorialization of religion, faith, and culture that has followed in the wake of mass migrations and "flows" (Appadurai 1996) of the late-capitalist postcolonial world (Gupta and Ferguson 1997; Hannerz 1989). The border provides a conceptual lens; the border influences the lives of those who traverse it and mediates the unique spiritual practices developed by those who cross it.

A desire to feed one's faith and follow a spiritual path lies at the heart of the religious practices of the transgender sex workers whose voices and experiences are represented here. Migrating from Guadalajara, Mexico, to San Francisco, California, and back again is one factor in the devotions that these women choose—there is an imperative of mobility for religious symbols, easily transported, that "travel well" (Kaplan 1996) on their circular journeys between Mexico and the United States.[1] Coping with what some have called "a generalized condition of homelessness" (Said 1979, 18) entails creative responses. However, the perception that the traditional Catholic Church has rejected them also compels people like Veronica to seek spiritual guidance and faith in particular saints, sanctified virgins, or "unofficial" icons, such as the Holy Death. Mexican transgender sex workers have created a spiritual cosmology that draws from more marginalized icons. In part this reflects their own structurally precarious positions in society, but more than this it reflects their spiritual ingenuity and ability to creatively embrace saints who they believe light their particular way in the world.

To explain the shared spiritual traditions circulated among Mexican transgender sex workers in San Francisco and Guadalajara we first elaborate a definition of transgender and describe the socioeconomic circumstances of the sex workers whose experiences are represented here. Integral to their life dynamics are the conditions of border crossing in both a literal and symbolic sense; we will explain how "the border" provides a key conceptual lens in addition to being a literal geopolitical boundary. Second, we elaborate the historic and migratory ties between San Francisco and Guadalajara, as well as the symbolic significance of each city as particularly tolerant of sexual and gender difference. The cities are linked symbolically as "open," and through word of mouth workers in Guadalajara's *casas* (brothels) are integrated into single residential occupancy (SRO) hotels in San Francisco. We also draw attention to "sexual migration," a process whereby individuals choose to migrate not simply for familial or economic reasons, as much of migration studies and political pundits would have us believe, but for reasons of sexual freedom and expression. Finally, we turn to the social conditions, in particular the social services, available to sex workers in both cities. These structural elements, we argue, must be understood alongside of the religious practices and rearticulations of faith and spirituality that are realized through devotion to St. Jude and to Santisima Muerte.

In both San Francisco and Guadalajara the altars that transgender sex workers construct for the Virgin of Guadalupe (the indigenous virgin of Mexico), Saint Jude (the patron saint of "lost causes"), and Santisima Muerte were adorned with flowers, candles, incense, and money. While all of the sex workers who were interviewed in this research also had relationships with St. Jude and the Virgin of Guadalupe, Santisima Muerte appears to provide a very specific divine intervention in their lives. The Virgin of Guadalupe and St. Jude are both part of the accepted pantheon of viable saints to which one may offer devotions. St. Jude, well known as the saint of lost causes or desperate circumstances, would be an expected source of spiritual sustenance for those who toil in dangerous work like the conditions that confront transgender sex workers on a daily basis. Guadalupe is a national saint, and one's belief in and devotion to her index one's *mexicanidad* or "Mexicaness." Sharing information, tips, images, and techniques of worship to Guadalupe and St. Jude clearly provide a spiritual cohesion among transgender sex workers as they move between San Francisco and Guadalajara.

We will argue, however, that it is Santisima Muerte who reveals the most important axis of spiritual solidarity among Mexican transgender sex workers—it is her feminine form, challenging death, that plays the most dramatic role in their religious lives. Santisima Muerte, who is the most marginalized figure in this trinity, is most like the women themselves and closest to their experience. Most importantly, one learns about Santisima Muerte from friends and fellow sex workers who provide images, statues, and altar-preparation rules.

Santisima Muerte's secrets are circulated among the small network of women who struggle against many odds on a daily basis. She is a shared deity who is condoned by the Church but rather sanctioned through a reciprocal process among transgender sex workers themselves. The Holy Death functions, effectively, to network and knit together transgender sex workers through their shared devotional practices in a spiritual solidarity.

STUDY SCOPE: MOBILITY AND METHODS

Because people, commerce, and discourses now constantly cross borders (Lavie and Swedenburg 1996)—some more easily than others—the research for this essay was mobile rather than situated in a single locale. Interviews with twenty-nine transgender sex workers, all originally from Guadalajara, were conducted in Spanish in both San Francisco and Guadalajara over a course of two years (2002 and 2003). Most participants came from lower socioeconomic backgrounds. However, even those who started working as prostitutes in Mexico when they were teenagers still managed to finish high school, and some spoke with a very sophisticated vocabulary. In Guadalajara the interviews were conducted onsite at the brothels where participants worked, as well as in cafés, parks, restaurants, and private residences. Interviews were conducted with casa managers, as well as with priests, nuns, and other religious workers who work with transgender sex workers and who preferred to remain anonymous.

The interviews in San Francisco were sometimes stalled due to the precarious residency status of the participants; none of whom had legal documentation. These women speak very little English, are sometimes plagued by alcohol and drug abuse, and live in blighted neighborhoods. After more than a year of visiting their homes and speaking with sex workers on the street and in health clinics, the women who participated in the study developed a level of comfort and commitment to the interview and research process. At one time, there were eighteen transgender sex workers from Guadalajara living in the same residence hotel in San Francisco's Tenderloin District. This dynamic fluctuated however, as transgender women went back to Guadalajara and, in turn, came north again.

In addition to individual interviews, countless hours were spent in residence hotels, casas, social service agencies, churches, health clinics, street corners, the occasional bar, and other sites in San Francisco and Guadalajara frequented by transgender sex workers.

GENDER TRANSITIONING AND THE *AMBIENTE GAY*

The term "transgender" is contested territory. "Transgender" was originally understood to designate those who wished to change their biological sex (hormonally and surgically) to match their gender identification. Here we use transgender in a more comprehensive sense in order to include those who live outside the social expectations and norms of gender behavior and comportment (Halberstam 1998; Hooley 1997). Rather than understanding transgenderism as a pathology, our definition focuses on the transcending, or crossing, of culturally defined categories of gender (Bockting, Robins, and Rosser 1998; Nemoto et al. 1999) to include those who wear other-gendered clothing and who may have undergone, or wish to undergo, surgical or hormonal therapy in order to transform their bodies to better suit their perceived gender. In the study conducted in Guadalajara and San Francisco, the majority of participants were male-to-female (or MTF) transgender persons who exchanged sexual services for remuneration (that is, "sex workers"). Three participants identified themselves as "transvestites" and had not had any surgical or hormonal therapy to transform their biological sex to suit their gender. Most commonly, the participants felt that they were born as the wrong gender. They always identified themselves as women and felt attracted to men. Since childhood, they had felt the desire to both act like a girl and wear feminine clothing.

The ability to physically transform one's body was one of the primary reasons that transgender sex workers gave for their decision to migrate North. Earning dollars to pay for gender-transforming surgeries ranked high in their priorities. Cosmetic surgeries that reshape the body (breasts, face, and hips, for example) are of course available in Mexico, but many participants felt that conditions in the facilities there are more dangerous than in those in the United States. News reports in the United States add to this belief, with stories such as the one about a former stripper in Mexico who started her own plastic surgery clinic without any credentials.[2] Instead of injecting citrus blends to burn fat, or bovine collagen to increase the size of hips or lips, she allegedly used a mixture of industrial silicone (for sealing car parts and appliances) and soy oil (a gelatin-like substance). Similar incidents are common in Brazil (Kulick 1998) and in other parts of Mexico (Prieur 1998). In Latin America transgender sex workers have innovated ways to radically alter their physical form, though often not without dire physical consequences and side effects.

A complete sex-change operation, whether in Mexico or in the United States, is highly expensive and very few of the women interviewed can afford the cost, coming as they do from underprivileged backgrounds and having to earn their living in the sex trade.[3] Directly related to their sexual labor is the decision by most to keep their original (male) genitalia. Numerous times they explained that one of their best assets, and one that draws clients to them, is their ability to affect a very feminine appearance—but with male genitalia. Their clients, they explained, prefer them to biological women because many of them desire penetration, or else simply the idea of being with a woman with male genitalia. While these women described their decisions not to undergo genital surgery as one of market strategy or a professionally based decision, there may have been other unspoken reasons that did not emerge through the interviews.

Typically, sex workers had breast implants and surgery to increase the appearance of fat and curves around the hips and buttocks. Lips and eyelids are also made fuller and more "feminine." Alternately, they might use hormonal treatments to increase their body's own production of tissues in strategic locations. Without the benefit of surgery or hormones, some women resorted to street strategies, including injecting themselves with industrial silicone or other ingredients to create more feminine hips. In Mexico, the women reported, there are many transgender women who inject motor oil to create breasts—a very dangerous practice as the oil migrates around the body and into the bloodstream.

Among the transgender sex workers who participated in this study, almost all of them found support for their emerging transgender identity in the *ambiente gay* (gay community or gay scene); in the ambiente they were able to find romantic and sexual partners even if the transgender women themselves did not consider themselves "gay" but rather women who were attracted to men. Being a part of this community, being an *entendida* (someone "in the know") was fundamental to their ability to embrace their gender identity and to be a part of a shared knowledge structure, as one who "understands the significances and nuances of queer subaltern spaces" (Rodríguez 2003, 24).

It is important, however, to point out that in the case of the women who participated in this study, and for other transgender people, there is not a seamless relationship between transgender and "gay" identities. One can be transgender and engage in sexual behavior with the "opposite" sex—or a heterosexual relationship. Alternately, a transgender male-to-female individual might have a sexual and affective relationship with another woman—effectively a "lesbian" relationship. These but two possible configurations make clear how complex gender identification and sexual practices can be—how elusive they are to strict, definitive categorization. Thus a number of scholars have advocated both dissolving the binaries by which we codify gender and sexuality (Altman 2001; Butler 1990; Saldívar 1991; Warner 1999) as well as reconsidering the "classificatory grids" (Donham 1998) that conflate gender and sexual behaviors.[4]

Transgender is a gender category, not necessarily one of sexual behavior or preference, though strict categorizations can often obscure more than they reveal. While transgender identity and gay identity or behavior are not one and the same, it is still critical to recognize that on the street these distinctions may become irrelevant. That is, many of the women whose voices are represented here find themselves marginalized by society because of their gender transgressions and by the sexual labor they do that is seen as "sex for sale"—and that is often coupled with homophobia.

In many cultures there is variability in how individuals enact their gender identity. Anthropologists have found much variation across the spectrum of what individual societies accept in regard to gender behavior (Howe 2002; Herdt 1996; Rosco 1991; Blackwood and Wieringa 1999; Ramírez 1999). However, in most of the United States and in Latin America, both gender and sexuality are generally understood in binary terms (men/women and homosexual/heterosexual).[5] In Latin America since the beginning of the twentieth century men who behaved in an effeminate way or women who wore masculine attire or comported themselves in a masculine manner became symbols of "perverse sexual transgression" (Green and Babb 2002, 6). Research with transgender, MTF persons in Mexico (Higgins and Coen 2000) suggests that social condemnation of gender crossing continues into the present, but at the same time transgender sex workers have also found strategies to protect themselves both on the street and from social stigma by, for example, creating shared households (Prieur 1998). As we will demonstrate here, transgender people have also found spiritual solutions to social opprobrium through their devotional practices.

Becoming a part of the ambiente gay also meant, for some of the women interviewed, that they were shunned by their families and forced to leave their family homes. Typically they began their transformation from men to women as teenagers. They began spending time at gay clubs and incrementally shifted their social networks. Through meeting others who were curious about changing their gender orientation, they learned about hormones and surgeries and everything else that would be required to transform one's self, physically and emotionally, to become a woman. Hormones and surgeries are expensive, and because these women's transgender identity prevented them from working regular jobs, they turned to work in gay clubs as drag performers lip-syncing to pop anthems and dancing into the night bedecked in elaborate, feminine costumes. Working in the clubs was one of the few options for employment open to transgender women in Mexico, but this work also lent a certain glamour, sometimes regional fame, and an opportunity to dress publicly and literally perform as a woman—an opportunity that for many was a first. Prostitution, or sex work, was a convenient way to earn money quickly and steadily. The sex workers in this study hoped to leave sex work eventually and open their own beauty salon or seamstress business.

Despite the often-difficult situations that the sex workers have with their families due to their sexual orientation, gender transformation, or their chosen profession, their ties to their families are usually very strong. Mexican culture places great value on the family, family networks, and collective life (Carrillo 2002). About one quarter of the women interviewed in Mexico continued to live with their natal families or were in close contact with them, visiting regularly. Others had limited contact with their families of origin, only seeing them from time to time. While everyone spoke of the difficulties they had with family relationships as they become more open about their desire to transition genders, some women were able to reestablish the bonds with their natal families more effectively than others. However, regardless of whether they were in the "good graces" of their families or in regular contact with them, all of the sex workers explained that one of the reasons they wanted to earn money in the United States was to help their families back home in Mexico.

For many of the women, leaving their family homes coincided with leaving the Church or attending services less and less frequently. Many of the women had gone to church every week with their families, for mass or confession, and weekly church attendance was essentially a family ritual. Over time as they were drawn in different directions, away from family, to the North, and into sex work, this ritual became more and more remote. However, what transgender sex workers did not leave behind was a sense of themselves as spiritual people able to reinvent iconographies that would fit their new lives as women, as sex workers, and as highly mobile, border-crossing individuals.

Embracing one's transgender identity and choosing to live out one's gender desires disrupts many of the assumptions taken for granted about the relationship between sex and gender and the gender norms that exist in both Mexico and the United States. Distancing one's self from the Church and in some cases from family suggests a further shift away from "tradition." However, the transgender women who lent their voices and thoughts to this study stated that they continued to want to help their families financially, and in fact they have created new kinds of spiritual links with each other based in many ways on reinterpretations of Catholic traditions. Although it may appear as though transgender sex workers are asserting radical difference, they are at the same time creating new forms of ritual practice, communities, and spiritual solidarities vis-à-vis their alterity or difference.

BORDER MOVEMENT AND SEXUAL MIGRATION: TIES THAT BIND GUADALAJARA, JALISCO, AND SAN FRANCISCO, CALIFORNIA

The Mexican transgender sex workers who travel across the border to work in San Francisco, often facing dangerous conditions along the way, come to the United States with very specific goals in mind. Overwhelmingly, the women in this study came to make money for gender-transformative surgeries and to earn start-up capital for businesses they hoped to begin in Mexico. Most stayed in San Francisco for at least a year, traveling back to Mexico to visit their families when they had the funds and freedom to do so. After paying a coyote approximately $2,500 each time they cross the border from Mexico to the United States, they make their way to San Francisco by bus or are picked up at the border by friends. Sometimes sex workers lend money to fellow workers who hope to cross into the United States, and by using inexpensive phone cards they are never far out of contact with their friends who remain in Guadalajara.

Theirs is a circuitous process of traversing the border, which like many crossings is transformative. A shift in status (documented vs. undocumented) and a shift in support mechanisms (language barriers, family networks, social services, and political agency) must be weighed against the net gain of earning dollars in place of pesos. It is partially in response to border crossing, we argue, that transgender sex workers craft the devotional lives that they do; it is not simply their identification as transgender or as sex workers that engenders their interest in unorthodox saints but also their transitions across the border.

In much the same way that gender categories serve to determine one's status as inside or outside of any particular gender system, so too do geopolitical boundaries and borders serve in "the ordering" of identities and citizenship (Kearney 2004, 134–35). The border between Mexico and the United States, while only one of thousands of borders, has become the paradigmatic border. It is here that a "third world" economy and contemporary global military and economic dominance by the United States abut one another and meet at colonial-era lines in the sand. It is this geopolitical barrier, among all others, that signals inequality most readily. At the same time, the U.S.-Mexican border is also the site of multiple possibilities for the exchange and movement of people, capital, and cultural phenomena. The literal geopolitical border between the United States and Mexico demonstrates a host of human interactions including labor and migration (Bustamonte 1983; Chavez 1985; Fernandez-Kelley 1983; Heyman 1990, 1991; Kearney 1991, 1996; Pedraza-Bailey 1985; Salzinger 2003; Villar 1992) where the productive, mobile engagement with wage work becomes visible in a transnational framework. Border policies (Heyman 1995; Weaver 1988) and settlement patterns (Alvarez 1995; Chavez 1989, 1994; Chavez, Flores, and Lopez-Garza 1990; Davis 2001; Rouse 1992; Villar 1990) also demonstrate the multiple ways in which the border conditions the lives of migrants, immigrants, and long-term residents. Environmental and health phenomena (Chavez 1986; Herrera-Sobek 1984; Heyman 1995; Nalven 1982, 1984; Romano 1965; Rubel 1969; Trotter and Chavira 1981) also play a role in the larger border region. What has been less examined are the sexuality and gender dynamics that emerge from border crossing (cf. Gonzalez-Lopez 2003; Hirsch 2003; Hondagneu-Sotelo 1994).

The border is a geopolitical marker and a highly regulated state boundary. But the Mexico-U.S. border can also be understood in less literal terms as a site of shifting identities, conflict, cooperation, and creative responses to a hierarchically organized world. As many authors have demonstrated, the border in many ways magnifies contradictions as well as human accommodation. And "borderlands" as Gloria Anzaldúa (1987, 1990) describes, cannot be simply territorialized in a literal sense but must be understood as an experiential phenomenon for those marginalized by their border-crossing status. The border, more broadly conceived, is both a conceptual and concrete place where identity, practice, and cultural forms are reconfigured. The border crosser is understood to comfortably straddle both worlds, on either side of the border. Feeling completely "at home," though, may be more elusive (Alonso 1995; Calderon and Saldivar 1991; Vila 2000). For transgender sex workers who move back and forth between Mexico and the United States there are complexities of gender, sexuality, illegal work, and lack of documented presence in the United States that impact, in very real terms, their mobility. In more abstract terms, as "so called border people" they "are constantly shifting and renegotiating identities with maneuvers of power and submission" (Alvarez 1995, 452).

The concept of "sexual migration" (Cantú 1999; Parker 1997) is one that draws attention away from strict economistic interpretations of migratory motivations. Instead it focuses on international migration that is partially or fully inspired by the sexuality of those who migrate and their understanding of the role of their sexuality vis-à-vis their future goals. Sexual migration may evolve from the desire to continue a romantic relationship with a foreign national, or it may be connected to hopes of exploring sexual desires or, in some cases, gender identity transformation. Sexual migration may also be necessary to avoid persecution, or simply as a search for more hospitable environs and a higher degree of sexuality equality. In the case of Mexican transgender sex workers, there is a very clear combined dynamic at work that includes economic migration, or crossing the border in order to earn dollars, but also the more subtle sexuality migration, or crossing the border for sexual reasons. In addition to understanding the situation in migrants' home countries—the particular laws and social conventions that may or may not allow for sexual and gender difference, it is also critical to examine the processes that sexual migrants undergo en route, how their perceptions may be transformed, and finally, how they establish their sexuality and identity, in some cases, once they have arrived and then return home once again.

While neither Guadalajara nor San Francisco are literally on the border between the United States and Mexico, the border looms large in the lives of the transgender sex workers with whom we spoke by shaping their sense of who they are, depending on which side of the line they may stand at any given time. Understanding the border as a dialectical entity that influences the lives of those who traverse it allows us to see that the border, as a metaphorical and geopolitical marker, influences the unique spiritual practices developed by those who cross, accommodate, and cross again.

Underscoring the dialectics of the border is the unique relationship between the "sending" and "receiving" states of Jalisco and California, as many of the immigrants and migrants to California come from Jalisco. The cities of San Francisco and Guadalajara also share attributes that distinguish them within their own nation-states. Guadalajara is Mexico's second-largest city (with a population of 3.5 million), and like San Francisco it has a reputation for being a relatively expensive place to live yet also industrious and productive. Guadalajara is also known for its dichotomy and conflicted cultural politics. The Catholic Church heavily influences the city, the capital of Jalisco state. It is known on the one hand for its conservatism and on the other hand as being Mexico's "gay mecca." There are numerous gay bars and nightclubs in the city, many of which are in the Aranzazu area near Plaza San Francisco in central Guadalajara. Gay bars catering to middle-class and upper-middle-class clientele are plentiful; there is even a gay radio station operated out of the University of Guadalajara.

In *The Night Is Young* (2002) Hector Carrillo describes how new generations of Mexicans in Guadalajara negotiate between tradition and changing times vis-à-vis sexuality, in particular heterosexuality and homosexuality. He argues that new public health approaches are required to staunch the spread of AIDS because valuing spontaneity, collective life, and intimacy often clash with the carefully calculated negotiations and planning indicative of global public health policies and epidemiological interventions. Carrillo also described that people in the Guadalajara gay scene romanticize San Francisco because of San Francisco's reputation as an "open" city.[6]

Guadalajara can be understood on one level as a city that lies at the center of sexual politics in Mexico, traversing the line between social and religious conservatism and the liberal ideals of sexual freedom and sexual identity. The city is known to embody the ideal of *mexicanidad*, which valorizes beautiful and attentive women and the strong, *machista* men who protect their virtue. But these notions of nation are being refigured as new generations face new complexities of gender and sexuality in a transnational setting. Guadalajara may be the epicenter of Mexico's version of the "culture wars," if such a thing were to be demarcated in time and space.

In the Guadalajara "gay scene" San Francisco is seen as an ideal city in which to live because of its international reputation for being welcoming to gays, lesbians, and transgender people. Veronica states that it was always her "dream to live in the gay mecca of San Francisco." San Francisco came to be known in the 1950s for its culturally transgressive environment—the beat poets paved the way for the flower children of the next decade. But San Francisco had already seen approximately one hundred years of forging new traditions rather than relying on older, established ones; not the least of which were sexually radical (Boyd 2003; Howe 2001). The University of California at San Francisco was one of the first institutions to undertake transgender (transsexual) surgeries. And the Castro District is globally known as a hub for gay male activity, residences, cafés, and nightlife.

SOCIAL CONTRACTS AND SEX WORKING IN
GUADALAJARA AND SAN FRANCISCO

While San Francisco and Guadalajara share the quality of relative tolerance for sexual and gender difference, the structural conditions that shape the lives of transgender sex workers in the two cities are quite different. While San Francisco provides more state-based services—for example, funding a variety of transgender health and wellness clinics—it is clear that the social networks and sense of "belonging" that these women feel in Guadalajara, along with the community-based support they also receive, effectively outweighs the state-sponsored benefits found in the North.

In Guadalajara, the women worked in three brothels owned and operated by a transgender woman named Patti. All three were located in a lower-middle-class area of the city known for prostitution. Near Patti's brothels or "houses" were other brothels frequented by transgender women and their clients, as well as heterosexual brothels. Every night Patti or her assistant collected a fee for the use of the space—a room in the house where sex workers can see clients. With three brothels total, Patti makes her living from these "use fees." Patti has strict requirements, which she pays an employee to enforce, including a rule that all sex workers must use condoms with their clients. To insure that the rule is enforced she sells condoms onsite. Patti prohibits the use of drugs and alcohol on the premises, though more than a few times women came to work already drunk or high. Only a fraction of the sex workers actually live in Patti's houses; most either live with their families or have their own homes, using the brothels only for work. This proximity to family does not hold true in San Francisco.

Patti is more than simply a bordello madam; she is also the primary community organizer for transgender women in Jalisco. She operates an organization called Contraste (contrast, or difference), which politically represents the transgender community in Jalisco. Patti also described her ties to Mexico's new political party Mexico Posible, which during the time of this research was advocating a political platform based on the decriminalization of abortion, equal pay for women, and gay rights. Patti's position in the community is a powerful one—she is at the center of much of the transgender sexual commerce as well as a major architect of its political profile.

In 1995, Patti described that she was inspired to open the brothels so that "the girls" would have a safe place to work and be able to save money to buy hormones and surgeries. Before her intervention, sex workers were forced to look for clients on the street where they were often assaulted by the police, clients, or ill wishers. As Patti explained,

> In Mexico, like in the United States, prostitution is illegal. So, we have created our own source of funds by opening houses of prostitution where the laws governing prostitution are not valid, because these are private houses. Since these are private houses, the police cannot intercede. They can only arrest someone if they catch someone in the act. We have special accords with the government to allow prostitution. I got my neighbors to agree to allow the brothels to function as long as I didn't bother them. They signed a petition. The brothels are only open from 10 PM to 6 AM when neither children nor old people are on the street. This way, we are not bothering the neighbors. The women are instructed to wear clothes that are not too provocative from 10 PM to 12 AM. After 12 AM, there should not be too many people in the streets and the women can be more scantily clad.[7]

Patti's description shows a complex analysis of the situation: negotiating with legal limits on prostitution by "getting special accords" while at the same time assuaging the neighbors by limiting the working hours and dress of the sex workers. However, Patti's well-considered plans did not always function properly. During the time of this research the police raided two of the houses and hit and arrested some of the sex workers. Later, the police closed one of Patti's houses, and she had to work with police to get it reopened for business.

Patti views her efforts on behalf of the sex workers as a kind of social work for the larger community. By providing a safe place for men to pay for sex with transgender sex workers, Patti explained that she was, in fact, doing a service.

> Our primary job is to fight the discrimination against, and the stigmatization of, transsexuals. Contraste is an organization that works for the transgender, transsexual, and transvestite population. Being a sex worker is a very well-known and valued job. (Here we say "sex worker" and not "prostitute" like in the U.S.) The transsexual sex workers promote health and they are in charge of caring for the health of their clients and couples. They have been invited by the University of Guadalajara to give workshops on HIV/ AIDS. And we have been invited to participate in the radio station from the University of Guadalajara. For the first time the University of Guadalajara took interest in the discrimination against sex workers and transgenders. It's important for transgenders and transsexuals not to feel rejected or cut off from society especially when people that are not part of the community look at them.

As Patti notes, she and the members of Contraste spoke on the University of Guadalajara's Internet gay radio station and Patti made presentations to the local municipality and to the political party Mexico Posible about her work. Patti also planned for members of Contraste to march in Mexico City's International Labor Day parade (May 1) and in Guadalajara's Gay Pride Parade in the summer. None of the sex workers, however, mentioned anything about doing HIV/AIDS presentations at the university.

Patti's successes and those of her colleagues in fighting discrimination and establishing a viable professional presence in Guadalajara suggest that through community-based efforts change happens, even if at a slower pace and more unevenly than Patti might hope for. However, what is critical is the way that Patti and others articulate the work as social service work that serves a greater good. Patti's houses and her investment in the cause of transgender sex workers creates a network of community support, shared struggle, and, importantly, a way of validating the work done by transgender sex workers—who rarely find such validation in the larger society.

While Patti, activist and brothel owner, speaks of social work being performed (and social contracts with the neighbors and the police), the sex workers themselves did not describe their work in this way. In both San Francisco and Guadalajara, interviewees never spoke of their professions as "social work" but rather only as remunerative. Perhaps Patti's description is strategic and legitimizing in a way that does not resonate with those who actually perform the sexual services. Perhaps the transgender sex workers have not been able to conceive of their work in such positive terms. Nonetheless, while in Guadalajara these women do work in a brothel that collects money for political work in favor of the transgender and sex worker community. This is not the case in San Francisco.

Finally, it is notable that during the interviews, none of the sex workers used the Spanish word *bordello* (whorehouse) to describe their places of work in Guadalajara. Rather, they always used the term *casas* (houses), suggesting that they are trying to establish a modicum of respect around their places of work, if not yet around the work itself.

For numerous reasons, in San Francisco the conditions for transgender sex workers are very different from those in Guadalajara. At the beginning of this study (fall 2002) all of the transgender sex workers participating in this project were living in a single residential occupancy (or SRO) hotel in San Francisco's Tenderloin District—a neighborhood known for drugs and prostitution and where most transgender sex workers from Mexico reside. At the Grand Polk Hotel residents are not given a key to the door; rather, both residents and visitors must ring the buzzer downstairs in order to be let in. In a small room at the crest of the dilapidated and dirty staircase, the doorperson monitors all of the comings and goings. Visitors must tell the doorperson whom they are visiting and they are asked to leave a picture ID at the front desk, a requirement that would make many wary. In the evening, visitors must pay $10 to visit any of the residents. Evidently, the building managers are profiting from every client who walks through the door, either to buy drugs or sex. Whereas Patti may have made her living, and perhaps some profit, from the fees she charged for the use of her houses, the taxing of $10 at the SRO speaks to a more blatant profiteering. It is doubtful that any of this money goes to bettering the political and social lives of the women on whose backs these profits are made.

Screaming matches punctuate the hallways of the Grand Polk Hotel as residents and clients unleash some of the effects of amphetamines and alcohol. In the Grand Polk Hotel all of the units share a common bathroom on each floor, but each room has a sink. Many of the sex workers had microwave ovens and refrigerators that they used to prepare food in their room. Over time, some of them were able to move to better residence hotels in the neighborhood,[8] and some even found units with their own kitchenette or bathroom. However, because the women are illegally in the United States and without credit histories, they cannot rent a regular apartment in the city. In most cases, sex workers use their own bedrooms to entertain clients, but some have occasional out-calls.

In San Francisco there is no madam who claims to take care of the transgender community or who acts as a direct political representative for Mexican transgender sex workers. Further, life in the SRO hotels can be isolating. However, there are gathering places such as the Tenderloin's transgender strip club, Divas, where some of the women seek out clients or pass time on the street outside. In the Mission District, where the majority of San Francisco's Latino population lives, the bar Esta Noche (Tonight) hosts transvestite performances by Latinas who lip-sync to pop songs while appreciative fans look on.

There are also political groups in San Francisco who advocate for the rights of sex workers, though they are primarily composed of U.S. nationals or of Latinos and Latinas who have lived in the United States and speak English. The city provides services for sex workers on Wednesday nights at the San Francisco City Clinic in the south of Market Street (SOMA) area. In addition to the Transgender Tuesdays offered by the San Francisco Department of Public Health, the Ark of Refuge provides support services. However, only a small minority of Latina immigrant transgender sex workers actually uses the services. The women involved in this project stayed in the Tenderloin District, worked a lot, and did not take advantage of the free services offered by the city. Transgender outreach workers from the University of California, San Francisco's TRANS program, Proyecto Contra Sida por Vida, City of Refuge Ministries, and the Insituto Familiar de la Raza often visit the sex workers in their places of residence to hand out free condoms and lubricant. They also provide referrals for free English classes, job training, legal help, drug and alcohol treatment, health care, and other services.

Chloe, a former sex worker, is a Latina bilingual transgender outreach worker at the City of Refuge Ministries. She explained why so few transgender sex workers actually go to the free clinics:

> Some go [to the free clinics], but not very regularly. Some get their hormone treatment in the street. If they prostitute themselves during the night, it is hard for them to get up early in the morning. Drug addiction has a lot to do with this as well. I am speaking from my own experience. I don't know why,

I am not one to judge. I am speaking about when I was under the influence of drugs. It is because one doesn't take care of him/herself well. One's self esteem is low because of the prostitution and from taking drugs. Our self-esteem goes down due to the relationships we have and our experiences in life. Because of the type of life we lead, we look for an escape in drugs and alcohol. With this, we are able to medicate, a little bit, the pain we have.

Chloe's words speak to the effects of ostracism and the perpetual cycle of ever-lowering self-esteem that many transgender sex workers experience. Some explained that even in their attempts to "better themselves" they found barriers—like being mocked by other Latinos in their free English classes not because they couldn't speak well but because they dared to express their gender differently than their biological sex.

"I DON'T PRACTICE IT, BUT I'M A BELIEVER IN CATHOLICISM"

In addition to their decision to transition gender and their chosen work, one thing that all of the participants in this study shared was having been raised in what they described as "traditional Catholic Mexican families." They learned the "Ave Maria" (Hail Mary) and the "Padre Nuestro" (Our Father) as children while going to church each week with their families. They celebrated the Catholic holidays of Christmas and Easter in addition to the saints' Holy Days. Following the Mexican and larger Latin American tradition they were baptized, took communion, and confessed at church.

Mexican transgender sex workers often maintained the Catholic traditions they learned as children, despite their sense that they were, or would be, ostracized from the Church because of their gender and sexual identity. According to some interpretations of scripture, homosexual behavior is a sin, as is prostitution. Knowing this, young transgender people are wary of presenting themselves publicly as such, much less showing up at church services in gender-crossing clothes. Entering into the gay community in Guadalajara, they risked being ostracized from the Church, condemned by the priest, or at the very least being whispered about in the pews. Not surprisingly, these fears drive away many transgender people from church services. Instead, as Kristal explained, she would only go to church when there were no services being held in order to be alone and away from scrutiny.

Several women commented that the Church was hypocritical toward what they called "the gay population." Arianna, a transvestite, said that she originally wanted to be a priest but did not feel comfortable with the antihomosexual sentiments of the Church. "I am Catholic because I grew up in the religion. I don't practice it, but I'm a believer in Catholicism . . . but the religion prohibits me from being homosexual. I wanted to be a priest. And I knew that in the seminary there were homosexuals—but the Church wanted to show the outside world that they were against homosexuals. I prefer to get paid for my work. If I work in the seminary, I would be performing sex on others and I would not be paid."

Guadalajara has a gay- and lesbian-supportive church, La Iglesia de Santa Cruz, which is part of the (international) Metropolitan Community Church (or MCC)—a Protestant church begun in the United States that welcomes people of all sexual orientations. However, none of the women interviewed had attended this church. Instead transgender sex workers in Mexico and the United States seem to have developed their own spiritual strategies rather than turning to the religious institutions that already exist, Catholic or otherwise.

Rodolfo Contreras, deacon of the Apostolic Reformed Catholic Church in Guadalajara, was a gay activist and a former Jesuit. Contreras's work with the gay community had provided him with insights on the topic of religion in the transgender community.

> Outreach to the transgender community will be a slow process because transsexuals feel dirty and unworthy and these feelings don't go away with just one talk with them. When people in the community hear the word religion, they automatically close up.
>
> The orthodoxy of the Catholic Church has made them feel like they are unworthy and that they do not have the right to be present at a religious service. The Church has generated guilt, embarrassment, and marginalization. So, it's important to work on their self-esteem and relay the message that God loves them and God is also there for them, even though they are transvestites.[9]

A lack of interest in finding a welcoming church continues when the transgender sex workers migrate to San Francisco. Most explained that they went to mass very infrequently and usually only for the Virgin of Guadalupe holiday (December 12).[10] In addition to having a bilingual transgender outreach worker, the Ark of Refuge has transgender support group meetings on Fridays and a transgender gospel choir.[11] However, there were no transgender sex workers from Mexico who attended the support group meetings or who participated in the gospel choir. The support group meetings are held in English, and the Latinos who do attend the meetings have been in the United States for some time and speak English. Whatever the combined reasons may be for their low usage of these spiritual and support venues, it is clear that transgender sex workers are continuing their spiritual lives by their own means. "All the church I need is with the ones la Santisima selects," declares Blanca.

FINDING FAITH IN THE SROS

Transgender sex workers, who feel ostracized or unwelcome attending church, respond to their spiritual needs by crafting their own devotional practices among themselves. These religious rites are eminently portable, and knowledge about them is shared among friends. While not necessarily sanctioned by the Church, these practices are sacrosanct to those who perform them. Religious practices in Mexico, as in many places, rotate around the repetition of particular rites: going to church every week, saying prayers, making pilgrimages to significant churches, shrines, and sites, and performing specific rituals at celebrations and for the saints' holy days. Likewise, sex workers say their daily prayers, wear pendants and religious symbols, and construct altars to the Virgin of Guadalupe, St. Jude, and Santisima Muerte. Though the objects of their devotion may differ from those found in the churches of their childhoods, they nonetheless continue the practice of worship by maintaining a spiritual element of their lives and looking to each other for guidance on prayer and devotion.

Praying to the Virgin of Guadalupe and going to a church devoted to Guadalupe on her saint's day was important to many of the women in both Guadalajara and San Francisco. Norma, one of the youngest sex workers, described how she trekked to a Church near downtown San Francisco on December 12 to light candles and say a prayer for the Virgin. Since most sex workers rarely venture far from their residences, Norma showed a level of devotion, and fearlessness, in her aims to honor the Virgin.

These women stated that they prayed every day. Many pray before work and once they get home; some chose prayer after each client's visit. Prayer, they explained, gave them strength to face their days and nights on the street. They pray for security and to avoid being harmed as they dodge the dangers of street sex work, including physical attacks by street thugs or abuse by clients. The most common risk to their lives, most agreed, is contracting a sexually transmitted disease because of a broken condom. But there are many threats. As Ninele explains, "I ask God to protect me from anything that can happen. From drugs and from violence." Her prayers are not unwarranted, as transgender sex workers, at least in San Francisco, face much higher rates of HIV, violent attacks, and drug addiction[12]

Sandy, who lives in one of Patti's casas, described her nightly practice of prayer: "Religion is against us, our way of being, our lifestyle. I don't have to be in a church to feel good. I am not very attached to religion. I pray and that's it. I believe in God. When things are not going well for me I speak to the cross that I have on my pendant and I say 'God please help me.'"

Several women wear crosses or pendants with the figure of the Virgin of Guadalupe or the Santisima Muerte around their necks. Some keep their jewelry on when they are with clients; others remove their pendants because they believe it is inappropriate, perhaps even sacrilegious, to wear religious symbols in a brothel. Whether fixed around their necks or stowed in a purse until work is finished, images of saints and icons, crosses, pendants, and figurines all figure heavily in the religiosity of transgender sex workers. Since they are forever on the move, the mobility of their faith symbols is fundamental.[13]

For transgender sex workers in San Francisco and Guadalajara, the iconography of the Virgin of Guadalupe signifies their origins, their culture, and their religious upbringing in Mexico. Many of the sex workers bring religious icons and pendants from Mexico to the United States; these items are chosen among the few things they are able to bring across the border. Both Leila and Maria explained that they were afraid to bring their altars and pendants across the border because they felt that the coyote might steal them. When they were safely settled in San Francisco, their families in Mexico sent to them their altars and pendants. Prizing pendants and fearing their loss suggest that these women place a high value on their religious artifacts, just as these stories underscore the way that border crossing impacts one's sense of vulnerability—down to the stealing of saints. In contrast to the dangers of border crossing is the support that some transgender sex workers received from their families. The transnational shipping of saints is meant to insure the safe passage of their loved ones in their dangerous travels abroad and in life.

In San Francisco, next to the Grand Polk Hotel, is a convenience store that many sex workers frequent to buy food. The store keeps a shelf full of candles and incense, as well as items related to Santisima Muerte and other Catholic saints. Santeria or "Botanica" stores are easily found on the streets of the Mission District, where candles, incense, altar pieces, prayer books, herbs, oils, and other items related to Santisima Muerte as well as more traditional Catholic and non-Catholic items are sold. While some women did travel to the Mission District (a drive of only a few minutes) to find their religious iconography, most did not. The convenience store owner, whose business depends on those who populate the Grand Polk Hotel, must realize, as do the transgender sex workers themselves, that commodities travel well, especially when there are eager buyers on the other side of the border or simply around the corner.

SAINT JUDE THADDEUS: PATRON SAINT OF DESPERATE CAUSES

In San Francisco, a shrine to St. Jude explains that "after the death and resurrection of Jesus, Saint Jude, the brother of James the Less and a cousin of Christ, traveled throughout Mesopotamia for a period of ten years preaching and converting many to Christianity. He died a martyr's death as tradition tells us. He was clubbed to death and his head was then shattered with a broad ax. Sometime after his death, Jude's body was brought to Rome and placed in a crypt in Saint Peter's Basilica." St. Jude, the martyr, is well known as the patron saint of "lost causes," or he who advocates for the most desperate and downtrodden. According to Catholic Online, "His New Testament letter stresses that the faithful should persevere in the environment of harsh, difficult circumstances, just as their forefathers had done before them. Therefore, he is the patron saint of desperate cases."[14] Seeing themselves marginalized in many ways, it is not surprising that transgender sex workers would turn to St. Jude. In San Francisco where they live in dangerous conditions and with no protections of citizenship, and in Mexico where, as in the United States, their work is illegal, transgender sex workers indeed would fit St. Jude's profile of attempting to persevere in "harsh and difficult circumstances."

The notion that St. Jude would help sex workers through their trials is one that spread through word of mouth in the transgender community. Jadira, a sex worker in Guadalajara, described St. Jude as a saint who "helps those who are sex workers. He is the saint of money and he protects people who work on the street." Jadira's faith in St. Jude was clear, as she recommended to many other sex workers that they pray to him. Joanna, a former sex worker in Mexico who visits St. Jude's chapel devoutly once a week,[15] explained why he is so popular with sex workers: "People who are in danger pray to him. There is a lot of popularity for him among drug addicts, delinquents, and prostitutes. Wherever there are addicts, delinquents, and prostitutes, I see him."

Sex workers who have left the trade, like Joanna, or those who still engage in the high-risk work, come to St. Jude in search of protection on the streets, luck with clients, and to pray for money. Joanna's description of seeing St. Jude where there is desperation is telling. In fact many sex workers carried an image of St. Jude or kept one in their rooms readily available. Only three sex workers out of twenty-nine described attending services or visiting church on a regular basis to pray to St. Jude; the emphasis instead was on praying to St. Jude on one's own.

Though some of the sex workers learned about St. Jude from their families, most of them learned about St. Jude from other transgender sex workers. Friends would give altars or icons of St. Jude as gifts—creating a reciprocal relationship between the giver and the recipient. Jadira originally learned about St. Jude from her grandmother. But when she felt comfortable with St. Jude she introduced him to Vanessa in San Francisco as well as to her roommate and fellow sex worker Barbie. Vanessa embraced St. Jude once he was introduced into her life, and even visited the St. Jude Chapel in San Francisco with a Mexican friend.

Some of the altars that sex workers kept were for individual saints, while others were composed of various saints including Jude, Guadalupe, and the Holy Death. Angelica prayed regularly to St. Jude and the altar she had crafted above her bed was devoted to all three figures: Santisima Muerte, St. Jude, and the Virgin of Guadalupe. Her saintly protectors hovering over the bed where she entertained clients were, metaphorically, there to witness all that occurred as well as to oversee her safety. Though she could have, Angelica chose not to remove the altar when clients visited. In Guadalajara sex workers were more apt to have their altars to St. Jude in their homes, not in their workplaces. Because in San Francisco sex workers work and live in the same quarters, it is harder to separate one's devotional life from one's professional activities—a set of circumstances that draws attention to the different structural conditions faced by Mexican transgender sex workers in the United States as opposed to Mexico. This inability to easily separate work from worship also draws attention to the fact that many of the women interviewed felt uncomfortable exposing their saints to the conditions of their lives. There was a desire, overall, to protect their icons from some of the realities of their lives.

Many sex workers expressed that their faith in St. Jude was profound. However, they had little interest in learning about the saint's history, his deeds, and who he was in life during the biblical era. Joanna was the only one who had a prayer book specifically created for St. Jude. Several different types of prayers are included to invoke St. Jude to act as one's intermediary before God. Joanna explained her practice of prayer multiplication as follows: "I pray to him every day. There is a prayer book for St. Jude for a forty-day period. On the first day one has to pray one 'Padre Nuestro.' Every day in the forty-day period, one adds one more prayer. By the fortieth day, one has to recite the 'Padre Nuestro' forty times. I did this." Joanna also noted that a Mexican church had a piece of

St. Jude's bone in the chapel. Deacon Contreras, speculating on what he called a "blind faith," explained that "if people don't have anything sustaining them in their lives, they need to believe in something. They don't care about the history of the person or saint to whom they are praying, they just need to believe in something." While Deacon Contreras's insight underscores the challenges that transgender sex workers face in both Mexico and in the United States and their need to invest faith in "something," it also misses some of the agentive and creative response to marginalization that transgender sex workers appear to be crafting. As a group that is often relegated to the very fringes of social acceptability in both nation-states, the sharing of religious practices, devotions, and "tips" about the most effective ways to worship demonstrate a spiritual solidarity that is hard won among a population that is ever on the move and on the very edge of social and legal legitimacy.

LA SANTISIMA MUERTE: FEARLESS IN THE FACE OF DEATH

The prayer booklet for the Holy Death (*Novena a la Santisima Muerte*) has, on its pink cover, a drawing of the Holy Death. She holds a globe in one hand and a pendulum in the other. She wears a robe covering her arms down to her wrists; there her fingers are exposed as bone. Over her skeletal head rests a halo. The picture is complete with skulls in each corner of the frame. The prayer booklet contains a round of prayers meant to be spoken in a nine-day cycle. Appearing as she does, like the grim reaper, it is not surprising that the Holy Death is an unconventional icon whose presence is not welcome in the traditional Catholic pantheon.

Santisima Muerte, a symbolic representation of death blended with Catholic characteristics, surfaced in Mexico's religious landscape to much popular acclaim. Very little is known about the Holy Death's origins; her followers and scholars promote divergent theories.[16] Some claim that she first appeared to a healer in Veracruz in the nineteenth century and ordered him to create a cult (Quijano 2003, 7; Freese 2005, 10). According to her followers a flood of miracles that continue to the present followed her appearance. Others claim that the cult of death existed in Mexico for three millennia and that Santisima Muerte draws from pre-Hispanic beliefs and practices (Araujo et al. 2002; Freese 2005; Quijana 2003; Aridjis 2003). They point to death figures revered by Maya, Zapotecos, and Totonacas, but especially to the ritual practices of the Aztecs and the Mexicas. The Mexicas worshipped two gods, Miclantecuhtli and Mictecacihuatl, who reigned over the region of the dead. According to these scholars and followers, the strong cult of death practiced among the ancient

Mexicas merged with Catholicism in the form of Santisima Muerte or the Holy Death. Other devotees claim that the Holy Death came from Yoruba traditions brought by African slaves to the Caribbean and passed to Mexico through the Cuban Santería, the Haitian Voodou, or the Brazilian Palo Mayombe; these religions merged with Christian practices to create Santisima Muerte. Other Mexican anthropologists insist that the Holy Death's origins can be traced back to medieval Europe. During plagues and epidemics, European Christians made offerings to skeletal figures and these traditions were brought to the Americas (Freese 2005, 12; Castellanos 2004). Katia Perdigón Castañeda of Mexico's National Institute of Anthropology and History claims that the Santisima Muerte figure is a European archetype of death commonly seen in religious art; statues of the Holy Death opened many Good Friday processions in Spain (cited in Vanguardia 2004; Castellanos 2004). Most scholars do agree however, that Santisima Muerte should not be confused with the Day of the Dead, although it is tempting to make the connection. Although the Holy Death may be venerated on that day, she "appears to be a distinct phenomenon emerging from a separate tradition" (Freese 2005, 4).

Although scholars may find the theoretical debates over Santisima Muerte's origins intriguing, the women in our study didn't know, or seem to care to know, the story behind their beloved saint; instead, her role in the precarious present is what matters. She is called the Holy Death because she looks like the incarnation of death and symbolizes its eventuality. Some of the sex workers explained that Santisima Muerte is the one who first saw Jesus Christ after his death and welcomed him into the world of the dead. Like St. Jude, Santisima Muerte has a following of those in risky professions and those who live on the cusp of danger and death.[17] The transgender sex workers explained how much they valued this "saint" as she helps them dodge death on the streets by evoking through her form the symbolism of death. As Artemia states: "She helps me in the street, to stay away from risks. . . . She exists, she exists, of course; we are all going to die. Death exists and she protects me from all of the dangers around me." In a kind of homeopathic way, Santisima Muerte injects just enough death to ward away its coming.

As with St. Jude, knowledge of Santisima Muerte, and recommendations about how to pray to her and construct an appropriate altar, come via referrals from other sex worker friends. They share with one another their successes and failures in imploring the Holy Death to protect them and, often, do favors for them. Vanessa, who had already been praying to the Virgin of Guadalupe and to St. Jude, began praying to Santisima Muerte in San Francisco on the recommendation of friends. "My friends told me that she does favors like other saints do and that if you ask with faith, she will do the favor. When you ask her for a favor, there is a payment and that is that one has to pray to her." The Holy Death gives, but she expects acknowledgment. She is "like other saints" in her benevolence, but her role in providing spiritual sustenance to transgender sex workers in particular is clear in her popularity and widespread devotion.

Devotees of the Holy Death must first be accepted by her. Pocahontas, who was living and working in Guadalajara at the time, learned about Santisima Muerte from her friend and fellow sex worker Arianna. Pocahontas emphasized that not everyone can enter into the realm of Santisima Muerte. "Sometimes people give statues of Santisima Muerte to their friends thinking that she will help them and it doesn't always work. The candles die out when she doesn't like somebody, she is very selective."

If Santisima Muerte is indeed a fickle and demanding deity who will not allow just anyone to worship her, then it is clear that one must be an "insider" worthy and appropriate to approach her; the logic that Pocahontas puts forward is in stark contrast to what many of her friends and colleagues have experienced in the Church. Santisima Muerte not only accepts you as you are (transgender, sex worker, immigrant, and so on) but she may not even be interested in being worshipped by those who do not dare to live such challenging lives. In this sense, Santisima Muerte is only for the worthy, among a population that has historically been deemed unworthy by religious and social norms.

Those who venerate the Holy Death keep statues to be placed on their altars. They buy Holy Death figurines of different colors with herbs and rice at the bottom to signify good luck. The feminine figurines are draped in a robe, with a skull for a head. Each color signifies a particular desire to be manifested:

Red: destruction as well as passion and love
White: purification
Green: money and legal problems
Orange: protection
Yellow: healing and friendship

To prepare the altar for Santisima Muerte, the devotee lights candles while praying to her. The candles symbolize different effects—white candles for something good, red for love, and black candles for ill wishes.

On both the white and the black candles a prayer is written in both Spanish and English.

"Prayer to the Holy Death"
Oh conquering Jesus Christ, that in the cross were defeated, like you would

tame a ferocious animal, tame the soul of _____. Tame as a lamb and tame as a rosemary flower he shall come to kneel before me and obey my every command. Holy Death I plea of your immortal powers that God has given you towards mortals, place us in a Celestial Sphere where we'll enjoy days without nights for all eternity. In the name of the Father, the Son and the Holy Spirit, I plea for your protection. Grant all your wishes until the last day, hour and moment that your divine majesty orders us to appear before you. Amen.

With prayers that evoke Jesus and God, "in the name of the Father, the Son and the Holy Spirit," it is not surprising that the transgender sex workers who pray to the Holy Death see her as simply another Catholic saint. They do not differentiate between the Holy Death and the more traditional Catholic saints. Rather, she is simply another possible intermediary between themselves and God. Valeria makes no distinction between the Holy Death and Saint Jude for, example, even though the church rejects Santisima Muerte. Artemia wears a pendant and has prayed to Santisima Muerte for nine years. She says, "I started praying to her like to any other normal saint, like to St. Jude or to God . . . I pray every day before I go to work on the street at night." However the Holy Death is not considered by the Church to be a viable saint or divine intermediary; Catholic orthodoxy does not permit the veneration of death (although many symbols, including crucifixion imagery, do just that). Deacon Contreras was clear in his position that "the cult of the Holy Death is one of idolatry. In Catholicism, one is not supposed to adore death."

In spite of this official opposition, devotion to the Holy Death has grown dramatically since 1965; Santisima Muerte now claims over four million followers in Mexico. The rapid growth of the movement over the last decades has led to conflict between devotees of the Holy Death and the official Roman Catholic Church. Although the Catholic Church condemns her veneration, her devotees have declared August 15 to be the Dia de Santisima Muerte, her official day. The Iglesia Católica Tradicional México–Estados Unidos (Traditional Catholic Church, Mexico–United States) founded the Sanctuary of the Holy Death in Mexico City in 2002 and registered as a religious organization in 2003. In April 2005, the government revoked the church's status as a religious organization in a twenty-five page resolution claiming that the group did not meet the qualifications of a religion, citing theological doctrine dating back to the Council of Trent in 1570. The legal action resulted in demonstrations throughout Mexico City and increased press attention, yet it had seemingly little effect on the numbers of people participating in Holy Death religious activities. Fol-

lowing the ruling, David Romo Guillén, founder and archbishop of the Traditional Catholic Church, Mexico–United States, stated, "To the people here,
Death offers friendship, hope, and miracles. We're the church of the people,
down here among the people . . . and that's why the Roman Catholic Church
sees us as a threat" (quoted in Hawley 2004, n.p.).[18]

Most followers see no contradiction between their Catholic religion and
worship of the Holy Death; indeed, they organize practices similar to Christian rituals, including processions, prayers, and altars. There are various rituals
dedicated to the Holy Death; in a brochure provided by one of the sex workers,
the instructions call for devotees to maintain a separate altar for the Holy Death
rather than mixing it with altars for other saints or devotions. The Holy Death,
it seems, is a demanding deity. Most of the sex workers gave offerings to the
Holy Death in order to show their gratitude. Flowers, candles, food, water, and
money were typically placed on her altar. Flowers or money were given when
the Holy Death had fulfilled a specific wish.

Two sex workers, Donna and Paula, explained that for a month they tried
to "work with" Santisima Muerte. They bestowed flowers on her altar every
day and lit candles, yet with no results. None of their wishes were granted
and so they decided not to pray to her any longer. Donna and her boyfriend
both prayed to Santisima Muerte at the same time, but only her boyfriend was
successful in having his wishes answered. Donna decided to stop praying to
Santisima Muerte, but she did not know what to do with her statue. "I was told
that I could not throw away my Santisima Muerte statue and that I could not
abandon it, so I gave it away. I gave it as a gift to a spiritual cleanser. Because
if you throw her away, it is bad. I was told that I had to give her away." Proper
conduct around the Holy Death must be maintained, including a respectful
gifting of her image, not simply tossing her aside. Superstition is likely at work
here, with Donna perhaps fearing that the Holy Death might have retribution
in mind for those who devalue her. But beyond this the belief that Santisima
Muerte must be shared, and exchanged in a reciprocal process, suggests that
the Holy Death functions, in some small way, to network and knit together
transgender sex workers through their shared devotional practices.

In none of the interviews did anyone explain, explicitly, why the Holy Death
is so popular in the sex worker community. Her popularity among these transgender women can in the simplest terms be explained by the fact that the Holy
Death is most useful and most revered by those in risky jobs or those who
constantly operate close to death. The risk of death and violence on the streets,
in sros, and in the brothels of Mexico and the United States are readily clear
to transgender sex workers, and they seek protection. Jajaira, a transgender sex

worker in San Francisco, explained that because Santisima Muerte has such proximity to what they most fear—death—she functions as a strong spiritual force in their lives. "For me, the Holy Death is about a preparation for death, to welcome death. You know that some people are homophobic. Some people are claustrophobic, others are afraid of spiders, closed rooms, darkness, etc. All of humanity is afraid of death. One hundred percent of people are afraid of death and this is a preparation for death. It's about not being afraid of death, about not being so attached to the fear of death. More than anything, it's about not being afraid, to know that there will be something after my spiritual release." Vicky, a sex worker who worked in San Francisco and returned to Guadalajara, explained her faith in this way. "The majority of gay people are in danger and the Santisima Muerte takes care of people in danger, she helps us survive."

Pocahontas and Arianna mirror this sentiment and are unswerving in their faith to Santisima Muerte because, they explained, she saved Arianna from a deadly fire. "One night, I dreamt that I was going to die in a fire. [The fire actually] happened to me after the dream repeated itself several times. And it really happened. I was in the hospital and I was doing really poorly. Pocahontas took the statue of Santisima Muerte to the hospital and that's what saved me. With the help of Santisima Muerte, I recovered very quickly."

Santisima Muerte, is even, for some, a marriageable partner. Vicky, a sex worker who had recently returned from San Francisco, explained that she had "married" the Holy Death because the Holy Death had performed so many miracles for her. And, she further explained, she was not happy with men anymore. Vicky's marriage to the Holy Death appears to have altered the Church's usual domain by transforming the traditional marriage between a nun and Jesus to one of different, though related, intentions. Moreover, Vicky's marriage to the Holy Death is, from one perspective, a first "lesbian" marriage between a human and a deity.

The Holy Death is, according to these tales, a deity more demanding than most. For transgender sex workers in San Francisco and Guadalajara she functioned as any saint would, acting as an intermediary before God and providing favors "in exchange" for prayers. The relationship that each of the women had with St. Jude and the Virgin of Guadalupe clearly fed them, providing different levels of spiritual sustenance. But Santisima Muerte, for those who found her and were accepted by her, provided a very specific divinity to these women. St. Jude and the Virgin both reside in the accepted pantheon of viable saints; they are supported by years of tradition, and millions of mouths have uttered prayers to them. St. Jude, the patron saint of lost causes, would be an obvious choice for religious devotion among those, like the sex workers, who face dangerous work and dangerous lives. The Virgin of Guadalupe, who appeared as a vision in Mexico, suggests one's devotion as specifically Mexican. Exchanging information and techniques of worship to both the Virgin of Guadalupe and St. Jude creates a spiritual community among transgender sex workers as they migrate between Guadalajara and San Francisco.

It is Santisima Muerte that provides the most critical meeting point for spiritual solidarity among Mexican transgender sex workers. She is the most marginal of the three "saints," though by most accounts she is no saint at all. She is closest to their experience and teetering on the edge between the here and the hereafter. Most importantly, Santisima Muerte is in many ways indigenous to the community of sex workers; word of her comes from friends and colleagues, images of her come as gifts from fellow sex workers, her secrets move among the members of a small network of those who struggle against many of the same odds on a daily basis. Santisima Muerte, because she is not easy to please and because she is particular about her devotees, is an icon that makes the chosen ones feel special, wanted, and worthy. Worship of the Holy Death is not a cultish obsession with this mortal coil; rather, devotions to Santisima Muerte reflect a highly mobile spiritual solidarity among the women who pray to her.

CONCLUSIONS: "MORE THAN ANYTHING, IT'S ABOUT NOT BEING AFRAID"

The ways in which people select, perform, and perform again their devotions provides insights into their views of the world and insights into their individual understanding of themselves. Rituals, in other words, "provide a metacommentary on the world" (Bruner 1986, 26) and shine a spotlight on the unique cultural and social dynamics that make up our rapidly shifting global landscape. Our work with Mexican transgender sex workers in Guadalajara and San Francisco has demonstrated that the devotional practices that are shared and circulated among this population are not renegade rituals to marginal icons. Instead the belief systems created and maintained by transgender sex workers as they cross geopolitical borders, as well as gendered borders, create spiritual solidarity among a group of people who often find themselves on the margins within a society that is often hostile toward sex work, transgender persons, and border-crossing individuals from the South.

Establishing alternative spiritual communities is not intended as a way to disavow the Catholic pantheon or the traditions that transgender sex workers learned as children. Rather these communities provide strategic ways to resist marginalization through their faith practices. The novel forms of spirituality that these women create in resistance to their marginalization are drawn from their national and natal traditions, which are circulated among each other as a way of creating a sense of shared practice.[19] Altars to St. Jude and prayers to the Virgin of Guadalupe are key elements of these shared practices. However, their secret weapon against a hostile world is Santisima Muerte. She is a jealous deity who is prone to revenge and discriminating in her choice of devotees; these are precisely the reasons she is so valued. Santisima Muerte is, fundamentally, a shared deity who is not condoned by the Church but rather is legitimated through a reciprocal process among transgender sex workers themselves. The Holy Death effectively works to network and knit together transgender sex workers as they identify with her marginality and embrace her fearlessness in the face of death.

The devotional worldview created by people like Veronica, Chloe, Arianna, and Kristal is incomplete without an understanding of the larger structural, legal, and political economic circumstances that impact their daily lives. We have maintained that the border has many effects, not the least of which is the "ordering" of identities and citizenship. As a paradigmatic geopolitical boundary, the United States–Mexican border, and the larger "borderlands" it engenders, cannot be simply territorialized in a literal sense, but rather should be understood as experiential phenomena for those marginalized by their border-crossing status. While neither Guadalajara nor San Francisco are literally on the border between the United States and Mexico, the border plays a significant role in the lives of Mexican transgender sex workers, impacting them differently depending on which side of the line they may be located. The border, we have argued, is a dialectical entity that influences the lives of those who traverse it by mediating the unique spiritual practices developed by those who cross it. Part of what compels the spiritual solidarity that sex workers create is a "search for a location where one can feel at home, in spite of the obvious foreignness of the space" (George 1992, 79). But also as immigrants they must constantly "straddle competing cultural traditions, memories, and material conditions" (Manalansan 2003, x).

While they cross the border to work in the underground sex industry, thus making their migration a financial one, it is also not coincidental that these women come in particular to San Francisco—a place that they describe as "more open" to people such as themselves. Their migration is multiply motivated rather than simply a search for some gay or transgender nirvana in San Francisco, or purely a matter of an economic "pull" from the north. As Juana Maria Rodríguez describes in *Queer Latinidad*, "practices through which subjects construct identity are never singular" (2003, 8). Instead these women cross the border, often with their *santos* in hand, with very complex goals and strategically laid migratory agendas. Sexual migration—the process of crossing nation-state divides in order to pursue a sexuality-related component of one's life, whether a relationship or a search for more libratory terrain—resonates with the experiences of Mexican transgender sex workers.

Enacting one's gender identity is not, categorically, a practice of sexuality. But in some cases, of course, the two are interrelated. In the case of the transgender sex workers who participated in this study, some saw themselves as part of the *ambiente gay* or identified as homosexuals. At the very least, all of them had found support in gay communities in Guadalajara. The migratory history between California and Jalisco is a long one. It is also not coincidental that transgender sex workers would choose San Francisco as their destination, for in part theirs is a sexual migration. In both Mexico and the United States, each of the participants in this research found themselves socially marginalized because of their gender transgressions or by the sexual labor they do. In addition, they described that homophobia or discrimination against transgender people was also a part of what made their lives so dangerous on the street, and thus part of the reason they turned to Santisima Muerte, St. Jude, and the Virgin of Guadalupe for protection. At the same time, each of the women recognized the limitations of their sexual status and gender identity. The politics of citizenship, legitimacy, and social acceptance are, in both the United States and Mexico, certainly more challenging for those who are outwardly lesbians, gay men, and transgender people than it is for those whose sexuality suits the status quo (Phelan 2001).

In their work lives in both Mexico and the United States, transgender sex workers encountered various levels of state involvement. In Guadalajara, the state intervened with police protection on the one hand and police abuse on the other. In San Francisco, targeted transgender health programs, although underutilized by the women in this study, exist in an attempt to mitigate the political impotency of language barriers and fears of exposure as undocumented migrants. The social networks and political possibilities of the workplace were also quite different in the United States and in Mexico. In Guadalajara "social work" brothels were, according to Patti, owner and transgender activist, an attempt to establish legitimacy for transgender women and their work. In San Francisco's Tenderloin District the women were effectively taxed by the doorperson of the Grand Polk Hotel, a blatant act of profiteering from the work of a vulnerable population. Ironically, perhaps, it was in San Francisco with all of its social services and purported tolerance for difference that transgender sex

workers found, in reality, the least amount of social and psychic support. In Mexico they had home and family nearby, enjoyed status as citizens, and lived in a familiar cultural and social world.

The spiritual solidarity created by the women in this study echoes the idea expressed by Hamid Naficy that "rituals provide the terrain in which the consciousness of communal boundaries is heightened, thereby confirming and strengthening individual location and positionality as well as social identity" (1991, 295). The devotions described by transgender sex workers codify a sense of shared community that emerges from the highly mobile and uncertain circumstances in which they find themselves. By definition, they require religion that travels well. But Santisima Muerte, St. Jude, and the Virgin of Guadalupe are not simply santos easily stowed in luggage but concepts and spiritual ideals. Embracing "lost causes" or acknowledging the inevitability of death creates a spiritual grounding for the uprooted, a sense of solidarity among the ostracized, and a sense of stability for individuals who are always on the move.

NOTES

Portions of this chapter were first published as "Transgender Sex Workers and Sexual Transmigration between Guadalajara and San Francisco," *Latin American Perspectives* 35 (January 2008): 31–50.

1. Because the majority of the transgender individuals who participated in this study identified themselves as "women" rather than "men," we follow their self-identification by using the "emic" or "insider" category, which resonates with the transgender sex workers themselves.
2. Alicia Calderon, "Fake Plastic Surgeon Accused of Harming Hundreds," Associated Press, October 20, 2002. Available at http://www.discussanything.com/forums/showthread.php?t=16839.
3. The price for a breast implant operation in Mexico ranges from $1,200 to $2,000, whereas the same operation in the United States can cost between $5,000 and $6,000.
4. From this perspective not only is the homosexual/heterosexual binary ineffective and minoritizing for those who fall outside the norm at any given historical moment, but further, rigid distinctions around sexuality, sexual behavior, and identification has "a determinative importance in the lives of people across the spectrum of sexualities" (Sedgwick 1990, 1).
5. An exception to the sexual binary of "homosexual" and "heterosexual" is usefully broken down in Lancaster's book, *Life Is Hard* (1992), which considers the Nicaraguan case.
6. Carillo, personal communication with Susanna Zaraysky, December 4, 2002.

7. The ethnographic and interview material here is based on the extended fieldwork and interviews conducted by Susanna Zaraysky over the course of two years in both San Francisco and Guadalajara, and it reflects her excellent rapport with interviewees and her careful observational insights. All names of interviewees have been changed to protect their identities. Interviews with twenty-nine transgender sex workers in both the United States and Mexico were conducted in Spanish and audiotaped unless the interviewee requested that she not be recorded. This research was sponsored by the Pew Charitable Trusts and administered through the University of San Francisco's Religion and Immigration Project (TRIP), under the direction of Lois Lorentzen in the Theology and Religious Studies Department. A key area of investigation in the Religion and Immigration Project was to analyze the role of religion in the lives of recent Mexican immigrants in San Francisco, California.

8. The average rent for SROS in this neighborhood ranged from $800 to $1,000 a month.

9. Contreras interchanges the words "transvestite, transsexual and transgender," but he is referring to the same population.

10. The Virgin of Guadalupe is the well-known and widely revered patron saint of Mexico; according to legend she first appeared to the indigenous peasant, Juan Diego, atop a hill in 1531.

11. The Ark of Refuge developed its "Transcending Program" in 1997 to provide services to transgender individuals. According to their program description posted online, "Transcending provides Practical support, Peer and Treatment Advocacy services for Transgenders of color in San Francisco who are impacted by HIV/AIDS or at risk for HIV infection" (http://www.arkofrefuge.org; visited on September 14, 2004). The Transcending Program is financially supported by the CDC Section of the San Francisco Department of Public Health, AIDS Office.

12. See for example, Clements-Nolle, Marx, Guzman, and Katz 2001; and Lombardi 2001.

13. Deacon Contreras explained the portability of religious icons as a national phenomenon: "Mexican immigrants bring their religion with them. Their Catholicism is very much based in rites, traditions, and customs that are not questioned. In the U.S., there are Mexicans who wear the image of the Virgin of Guadalupe even though they are outside of Mexico."

14. Catholic Online, http://www.catholic.org (site visited December 10, 2003).

15. In Guadalajara there is a special chapel devoted to St. Jude, who is quite popular among Mexicans generally. A special service is held every Wednesday for those who are sick and poor. On hot days the doors of the church are opened wide so that people outside may watch and hear the sermon. Often, all of the pews are full.

16. Surprisingly little academic literature exists in English about the Holy Death movement. The religion and its followers have received attention in the popular press in Mexico, Latin America, and even in the United States, yet scholarly treatments in either English or Spanish are sparse.

17. Santísima Muerte is particularly popular in Mexico among police, drug traffickers,

gang members, prison inmates, and sex workers; in short, those who live close to death. Her larger social base, however, is among very poor people who may be excluded from the formal economy. Although she is popular among some artists, intellectuals, politicians, and actors, the Holy Death's primary constituency is among the marginalized.

18. Archbishop Davíd Romo Guillén and the Traditional Catholic Church, Mexico–United States also promote condom use for men and women, as well as the day-after pill. The doors of the church are open to gays, lesbians, transvestites, and transgendered. Priests are allowed to marry (Romo himself is married with five children), women can become ordained, and divorce is not censured. These practices, in addition to the worship of the Holy Death, place them in opposition with the Mexican Roman Catholic Church.

19. Similarly, Martin Manalansan describes new iterations of a traditional Filipino religious tradition, the Santacruzan, as it has changed in its transnational form: "The combination of secular, profane, and religious imagery as well as the combination of Filipino and American gay/mainstream icons provided an arena where symbols from the two countries were contested, dismantled, and reassembled in a dazzling series of cross-contestatory statements" (2003, 133).

Sexual Borderlands

Lesbian and Gay Migration, Human Rights,
and the Metropolitan Community Church

CYMENE HOWE

Michael and Wuen-lin fell in love, they said, "within hours."[1] Their correspondence began online, with Wuen-lin in Singapore and Michael in California. They met in person for the first time when Michael made the trip to Singapore; since then, they have experienced eight years of affection for one another, as well as the challenges of being a same-sex binational couple (that is, a couple in which the partners come from different countries). Michael, a white gay man, was "in hiding," he said, until he read Armistead Maupin's *Tales of the City* (1976): "My barriers were shattered . . . I was stuck in Bakersfield[2] and I made a decision to commit to either Long Beach or San Francisco. Even though I had been afraid of San Francisco, from what I had heard in the media and what it meant to be gay there, I fell in love with the city after visiting and I made the choice to relocate."

Wuen-lin, who was born and raised in Singapore, identifies himself as Chinese. He describes being raised Taoist "with Buddhism inside," but he became a Christian at thirteen years of age. Looking back, he says that he accepted Christianity because he knew that he was gay then. "[Christianity] was a way of dealing with too much guilt . . . they offered a way out by saying that Jesus forgives of all your sins: Accept Christ and all will be forgiven . . . just pray harder and I will be straight or something." After completing a bachelor's degree at the University of Singapore, Wuen-lin came to the United States to be with Michael and to earn an MBA degree, "because that is the only way I could stay here."

Wuen-lin and Michael's story, although only one among many, demonstrates some of the challenges of migration for same-sex binational couples; the role of religion in meeting those challenges; and the complexities of creating a home when faced with crossing borders, dealing with legal barriers, and living one's sexuality in places where it is not always safe or sanctioned to do so. Wuen-lin's belief in Jesus's forgiveness allowed him to imagine new possibilities for himself as part of a binational same-sex couple. Christianity was a legitimizing framework for his new sense of identity and, following his arrival in the United States, the Metropolitan Community Church (MCC) became an important spiritual and social support for both Wuen-lin and Michael as they worked through the challenges of Wuen-lin's migration and of being a binational gay couple.

Largely unknown to the general population—and even within the lesbian, gay, bisexual, and transgender (LGBT) community—gay and lesbian migrants confront a number of complex challenges as they cross national boundaries. Documented cases of queer[3] migration experiences are relatively rare, and the ones that do exist are often less than positive. Historically, partners in binational same-sex couples and lesbian and gay migrants coming to or already in the United States have been reluctant to disclose their sexuality for fear of being "denied access" (Ranck 2002, 373). Even though the agencies in charge have changed, the current situation is similar to that of earlier years: lesbian and gay migrants may fear revealing their sexual identity to Immigration and Customs Enforcement or U.S. Citizenship and Immigration Services officials.[4] From the point of view of the immigration authorities, migrants' involvement in an ongoing same-sex relationship would constitute a risk of their overstaying their visa, thus making them, in some cases, immediately deportable (Donayre 2002).

In this essay I examine some of the many dynamics surrounding migration for lesbians and gay men and binational couples, and I explore issues of legal precedent, human rights, and how religious communities such as MCC might function as advocacy resources. I argue that MCC's philosophical and epistemological foundations may be especially conducive to addressing the advocacy concerns surrounding migration for partners in same-sex binational couples. First, I wish to suggest that MCC has several conceptual resources and historical antecedents that might prove particularly adept at helping people move beyond the heteronuclear family paradigm that so prevails in immigration law and practice and has, historically, worked to the detriment of lesbian and gay migrants.

Second, I aim to show how MCC as a church—a religious, spiritual, or faith-based organization as opposed to a civil institution—may provide spiritual support for those immigrants who are inclined to attend it. Migration to a new country always involves a radical upheaval from home and is, therefore, a process that more often than not requires networks of social support. Just as family and kin networks have proven critical to nonlesbian and nongay migrants (Menjívar 2000), the spiritual essentialism propounded by MCC may serve as an alternative for people who do not, because of their sexual identity, have the support of their natal kin networks. Given the volatile culture wars in the United States surrounding homosexuality and immigration policies, religious institutions with their socially sanctioned status may be able to draw upon social and spiritual legitimacy in ways that civil institutions may not be able to do. Although I do not want to imply that nonreligious organizations— such as Immigration Equality or Love Sees No Borders, both of which are dedicated to migration concerns for lesbians, gay men, and binational couples— are not capable of or prepared for these challenges, I do want to suggest that religious institutions may be particularly well equipped to address some migration issues for same-sex binational couples in the contemporary political climate. In the context of the embattled discussion over faith-based initiatives and their increased role in providing support to marginalized populations in the United States, this consideration of the overlaps between human rights, MCC, and queer migration seeks to open new areas of dialogue surrounding these dynamics.

I framed this analysis ethnographically through an extended interview with a binational couple, Wuen-lin and Michael.[5] However, this research is not an empirical study of migration for lesbians, gay men, or partners in same-sex couples, nor is it a study centered on MCC's results or pragmatic accomplishments in facilitating such migration. My purpose here, in other words, is not to examine whether MCC's philosophical foundations work for same-sex-attracted migrants but rather to explore how those foundations might be poised to do so. As such, this essay is an exploration of the theoretical dimensions of queer migration, human rights, and the role of spiritual communities: an attempt to link the complexities of material, legal, political, ideological, and personal challenges of migration for partners in same-sex binational couples. I argue that approaching queer migration through a human rights framework offers a critical lens because it draws on transnational moral and humanitarian norms rather than depending solely on the benevolence of sovereign states to liberalize their immigration policies. Through the lens of human rights, humanitarian ethics may be placed at the center; this move may be especially important to lesbian and gay people globally because homosexual relationships are illegal in approximately half of the world's countries. Indeed, as Nancy Wilson, the top-ranking official of MCC, put it, "In many places in the world, it is our humanness as gays and lesbians that is still the issue" (1995, 16).

Binational same-sex couples, as well as individual lesbian and gay migrants,[6] may especially benefit from the support of organizations, both religious and secular, for two key reasons. First, legal migration to the United States has largely depended on norms centered on the nuclear family, with visa regulations privileging family networks and familial ties to the United States. Both historically and at present, U.S. citizens or legal permanent residents have not been able to sponsor their same-sex spouses in the way that partners in heterosexual couples have been able to do in taking advantage of the relatively simple conjugal route to immigration and citizenship in the United States. Second, although lesbians, gay men, and same-sex couples may have family in the United States, they may not have familial support because of their sexuality. Lesbian and gay migrants potentially lack the social and financial support associated with kin networks, both in their countries of origin and in their countries of destination, that proves so critical to nonlesbian and nongay migrants (Hondagneu-Sotelo 1994; Mahler 1995; Menjívar 2000; Perez 2004). Because of these obstacles, lesbian and gay migrants especially may require support from community or religious organizations, or both, to negotiate the many legal requirements for, as well as the social aspects of, migration to the United States.

In the same way that I suggest using a human rights framework as a way to look beyond the nation-state vis-à-vis lesbian and gay migration, so too I believe that it is necessary to think beyond the family as the hegemonic criterion for migration. Instead, I want to highlight the frameworks—practical and conceptual—of community-based and spiritually based collectives as a way to imagine new possibilities surrounding migration for same-sex-attracted individuals.

I begin this essay with a brief exploration of the foundations of human rights as an ideological starting point for the migration of lesbians, gay men, and partners in binational same-sex couples. The issue of human rights, though certainly open to various critiques, does offer ways to think through the many obstacles involved in border crossing, sexuality, and citizenship. I next consider the dynamics of migration—from legal histories of discrimination in U.S. (im)migration law to more recent lesbian and gay asylum claims and the 2005 Uniting American Families Act (UAFA; formerly known as the Permanent Partners Immigration Act)—that attempt to mitigate the exclusion of lesbian and gay people hoping to find sanctuary in the United States. Drawing from the concept of sexual migration—that is, when migration decisions are at least partially based on one's sexuality—I will propose that collective approaches can provide the necessary networks, tools, and ideological resources for migration of lesbians, gay men, and partners in binational same-sex couples. In particular, I consider the conceptual frameworks of the United Fellowship of the Metropolitan Community Church (UFMCC) as a way of examining these complexities. Undoubtedly, other religious communities might serve a similar

purpose, including, potentially, those that are not part of the Christian tradition, such as mosques, temples, and sanghas. However, as the largest spiritual
organization of lesbian and gay people in the world, MCC offers an important
case study.[7] The MCC has promoted an ideological flexibility, maintained transnational aspirations, and oriented its mission toward social justice, all of which
resonate with the needs of binational lesbian and gay couples. Although organized religions are often seen as inflexible, rule-bound institutions that cannot
allow for rights-based advocacy, I will propose that MCC offers a different sort
of model. With its socially legitimatized status as a church, MCC has built a set
of philosophical foundations through which human rights for lesbian and gay
migrants might be effectively addressed.

HUMAN RIGHTS AND LESBIAN AND GAY MIGRATION:
IN SEARCH OF ESSENTIAL TRUTHS

Human rights begin with recognizing and affirming each individual's identity
and value as a human being. Wuen-lin describes how MCC had supported him
and his identity: "What they talk about [at MCC] is essential truths—what it is
to be a human being who happens to be queer. Not that it necessarily has to be
a big deal to us, but because the world makes it a big deal we have to recognize
it for what it is and we also have to deal with that part of it. It is a church that
lets you know you are loved, unconditionally, in a community when we have
been rejected by our family or friends. . . . This is a place where they said no,
you are loved. Period." Michael adds, "What its role for me is to be that spiritual
touchstone to which I can go each week and reconnect with the essential part
of being human."

Following a long tradition in Western political philosophy from Aristotle on,
human rights have provoked questions about what it means to be human and,
ultimately, how one's rights as a human being, as such, are to be configured.
In addressing a group of international lesbian and gay rights advocates, Judith
Butler emphasized that the category "human" is, in fact, redefined through
transnational sexuality rights: "In the context of lesbian and gay human rights
. . . certain kinds of violences are impermissible, certain lives are vulnerable and
worthy of protection, [and] certain deaths are grievable and worthy of public
recognition" (2004, 32). When people begin to take account of sexuality as an
important axis of their humanity—as one of many elements of humanness—
and as the world community recognizes potential violations based on this element of humanity, the often-taken-for-granted framework of human rights is
challenged. As sexual rights gain recognition around the world, how are ap-

proaches to sexuality and lesbian and gay identity rethought or reordered in the international domain? In discourses of rights, how does one place sexuality at the center, not as an all-determining bedrock or essential attribute but rather as one element that piques the question of how the category of human is subject to "redefinition and renegotiation" (Butler 2004, 33). Since the broad outline of the protection of human rights has been put forth,[8] many advocates—those fighting to end, for example, torture or female genital surgeries—have sought to expand the definition of human rights to encompass critical sites of struggle. Scholars have also sought to understand a more stubborn question, one that has existed since the classical age: What does it mean to be human? This question, in turn, leads to another: What is the nature of the rights that are attached to this humanity?

Michael Ignatieff (2001) claimed that the world has been embroiled in a "rights revolution,"[9] one that has been made possible, and necessary, in the wake of the declining power of nation-states and the increased interconnectedness that leads to cross-national moral responsibilities—including, as Olivia Espin notes, a burgeoning "interest in the plight of immigrants and refugees worldwide" (1999, 18). In practice, human rights concerns have recently proliferated in large-scale campaigns around the world. The creation of what have been called "new rights"—women's human rights, children's human rights, indigenous people's rights, lesbian and gay and sexual rights, the right to development, and so on—has occurred in response to human suffering, dispossession, and displacement. The application of new rights in international documents, advocacy campaigns, and nongovernmental institutions has initiated a renaissance surrounding how human rights are to be defined and understood in their most expansive sense without losing sight of how to implement and achieve rights for very specific potential violations. Sexual migration and the legal status of lesbian and gay migrants and same-sex couples suggest several quandaries not only for the pragmatics of immigration law but also for human rights and notions of citizenship.

Perplexities and Paradoxes: Lesbian and Gay Rights Beyond Legalism

In *The Origins of Totalitarianism* (1958), Hannah Arendt posed a profound paradox between the role of governments (or nation-states) and their ability to protect the rights of their citizenry. According to Arendt, the case of refugees—stateless populations that had been deprived of civil and civic rights by virtue of their displacement—presented a breakdown and a fundamental challenge to the principles of human rights. That is, refugees, left with nothing but the "minimum fact of their human origin" (300), should have provided a quintessential embodiment of a pure subject for human rights but instead invited a crisis of meaning. As Arendt put it, "The world found nothing sacred in the abstract nakedness of being human" (299). In the oscillation between the universal nature of human rights and their intended universal applicability, Arendt found that when a human is deprived of her or his sociopolitical identity, she or he ceases to be recognized as human.[10]

Similar to the refugee paradox that Arendt described, undocumented migrants cannot claim full citizenship rights in the country to which they migrate because they are effectively betwixt and between—that is, in a liminal condition of nation-state membership. Lesbian and gay people wishing to migrate, individually or coupled, also mirror the concerns that Arendt noted in the crises of the mid-twentieth century. Neither undocumented migrants nor lesbian and gay migrants can easily achieve full citizenship. Regular migration channels, for undocumented migrants, are largely foreclosed due to migrants' illegal status. Lesbian and gay couples and individuals are additionally barred by their inability to legally marry a U.S. national and establish citizenship through a marital family tie.[11] Many scholars of lesbian and gay and queer politics have argued that homosexuals have constituted a social class that has been legally defined, if incorrectly so, as deviant, criminal, or unworthy of equal legal protections and rights (Phelan 2001; Stychin 1994). This second-class citizenship, as Kathleen Hull called it, thus has become one defining element of gay and lesbian identity—one that challenges human rights to achieve their original proposal to protect "without distinction" (2003, 630). Despite the limitations of universalizing tendencies and legalistic limits, the humanitarian norms of human rights, with a jurisdiction that exceeds the nation-state, are well suited to operate as a set of principles to support lesbian and gay immigration rights.

Legalistic approaches to social change, as both part of and distinct from social or cultural transformation, have their place and their limit. Regular immigration is managed by the federal government and, as a brief review of U.S. immigration law will show, has often sought to control sexuality—usually under the mantle of racial, class, national, and moral considerations, as well as fears. Legal mechanisms and approaches, as well as an ability to think outside of legalism (Halley and Brown 1999), need to be combined to effect lasting social change. Although nonprofit, nongovernmental, or religious organizations may be more precarious partly because their funding may be less secure than that of governments, this positioning may also give them more authority than legislation alone. Religious institutions in particular, given their general social legitimacy and credibility, may offer holistic approaches to questions surrounding migration for lesbian and gay individuals and binational same-sex couples. The challenge is to incorporate the values of human rights without relying solely on legalistic, state-based approaches to social change.

Migration: Surveillance, Sexuality, and Stories of Sanctuary

During the Christmas season following September 11, 2001, Wuen-lin received a notice that he would no longer have a sponsor for his work visa, and thus he would have to either find another job willing to sponsor him or leave the country. As Wuen-lin described, "It's difficult . . . because you get comfortable and then have to change." Michael then added that "[first], it was trying to get Wuen-lin here, then [because he had to be enrolled in a university in order to remain in the United States] it was school—papers, and exams. You are afraid to settle in. I don't even want to get a pet, other than my seventeen-year-old cat, because you don't know what is going to happen. It's just too frightening to allow yourself to settle in." Wuen-lin elaborated: "We are not very interested in a domestic partnership [which is available in the city in which they reside] because it is still a legal tracking . . . As free and open as we are here in San Francisco, in a lot of ways it feels like we are in the closet a lot."

Wuen-lin and Michael are relatively out about their homosexuality in the United States, but they are closeted in regard to Wuen-lin's immigration status. U.S. immigration proceedings are sites where sexuality—as well as race, class, and gender—is placed under surveillance, monitoring, and control. As regulatory statuses, citizenship and immigration are inextricable from the priorities of the nation-state, and they convey implicit value systems affecting those who are allowed or disallowed entry. As Lauren Berlant put it, "Immigration discourse is a central technology for the reproduction of patriotic nationalism" (1997, 195). The 2006 congressional legislation aiming to criminalize assistance to undocumented immigrants, and the massive protests that followed, are recent examples of both the regulatory system of immigration and its implicit values.

Geopolitical concerns and notions of national sovereignty intersect in immigration law. For queer migrants, argued Tomás Almaguer (1993), there are always potential barriers of racial, linguistic, or heteronormative discrimination in the United States. For example, the Mariel boatlifts from Cuba during the 1980s provoked fear in the United States that criminals and homosexuals were invading the country. Particular kinds of Cubans were considered less desirable and perhaps less morally upstanding than those who migrated for anticommunist, political reasons. Ironically, as Lourdes Argüelles and B. Ruby Rich (1985) argued, earlier queer Cuban migrants were used to paint an anti-Castro campaign that overemphasized the persecution of homosexuals in Cuba and was cited to legitimate U.S. policies. In these earlier waves of migration, the fact that homosexuals were being persecuted in Cuba and that some had been granted entry to the United States was used to bolster the image of the United States as being both modern and liberal. The U.S. government, however, continued to maintain several immigration provisions that barred homosexuals' entry to the United States thereafter. More recently, prohibitions against HIV-positive individuals can be seen as more in a long line of legal provisions that have drawn on fears of sexuality, concepts of disease, and issues of safeguarding the nation to impose immigration restrictions. Discourses on immigration also outline the prevailing conceptual borders of gender, sexuality, race, and class as they articulate with notions of the nation.

Martin Manalansan (1997) wrote that queers migrate not only as sexual subjects but also as citizens of nation-states that have a racialized, classed, and geopolitical history with the United States. Furthermore, migration is also conditioned by structural, historical, and military linkages between the United States and other nation-states that often provide bridges for migration (Sassen 1996). The collapse of social support networks and the weakening of welfare states, in both sending and receiving countries, have created a world of relative transience and increases in migration globally. Although neoclassical approaches to the study of migration have emphasized a "rational actor" model (that is, centering analysis on an individual who chooses migration based on very pragmatic, cost-benefit calculations), more recent scholarship (Fernández-Kelley 1983; González-López 2003; Grasmuck and Pessar 1991; Hondagneu-Sotelo 1994; Pedraza-Bailey, 1991; Portes and Rumbaut 1996; Sweetman 1998) has explored the significance of race, gender, and class dynamics within migration. Although sexuality is certainly intertwined with the gender, racial, and class elements of one's identity—and consequently with immigration processes—race, class, and gender perspectives cannot substitute for the explicitly sexual or sexual identity dimensions of migration (Espín 1999; González-López 2005).

Sexual migration (Cantú 1999; Carrillo 2004; Parker 1997) provides a critique of purely economic (push and pull) interpretations of migratory motives. As an analytic framework, sexual migration attends to the role of social support networks that may not be kin based. Building on research specifically focused on gender and migration (Grasmuck and Pessar 1991; Hondagneu-Sotelo 1994; Sweetman 1998), the term "sexual migration" suggests a way to think through sexual desire and life goals related to one's sexuality and attends to the complexities—physical, psychological, and cultural—that arise when sexuality is taken into account. Sexual migration occurs when a person's decision to migrate is motivated by the hope of maintaining or establishing an affective, sexual, and committed relationship with a foreign national (Brennan 2004; Cabezas 1999; Cantú 2002), or it may be linked to an individual's desire to explore her or his sexuality and sexual identity. Sexual migration may also result from people making a move necessary for avoiding persecution or prosecution in their home country based on sexual behavior or status. For example, homosexuality is illegal in eighty-five countries and is punishable by death in eight countries, and other countries impose extended prison terms for homosexual behavior, actual or perceived (Ungar 2001). Sexual migration may involve a search for more hospitable environs and a higher degree of tolerance for individual differences in sexuality and its expression. In the case of binational same-sex relationships, any and all of these elements of sexual migration may be at work. Here I focus on queer migration to the United States and the concerns related to this process.[12] U.S. immigration law, as I will show, has maintained prohibitions related to sexuality throughout its history; however, the specific U.S. case I cite additionally demonstrates the importance of internal migration within the United States for lesbian and gay community building.

Historicizing Lesbian and Gay Migration

Migration, as such, is not all that new to lesbian- and gay-identified people in the United States. In fact, migration at least partially defines gay and lesbian identities in the United States. What Kath Weston (1998, 32) called the Great Gay Migrations following the Second World War were made possible by increased employment opportunities in U.S. cities; the development of enclave communities, also called gay ghettos (Bérube 1990; Chauncey 1995; Kennedy and Davis 1994); and the linked processes of capitalist growth and gay identity (D'Emilio 1983). The internal migration of lesbian and gay people to urban centers within the United States has in many ways defined the contours of many lesbian and gay communities. The contributions of foreign-born migrants to the construction of lesbian and gay communities and culture in the United States, however, have not been well documented (Román 2000). With increased flows of people and capital in today's world, the shifting borders of lesbian and gay identities, politics, and communities need to be considered in an international framework.

The migratory barriers faced by same-sex-attracted individuals and same-sex couples cannot be understood outside the context of historical exclusions around perceived differences, including those of race, national origins, gender, and class.[13] The explicit exclusion of lesbian and gay migrants to the United States began in 1917. At that time, the legal category "constitutional psychopathic inferiors" included "persons with abnormal sexual instincts" as well as "vagrants" and "pathological liars" (Loue 1990, 126, n.11),[14] all of whom were prohibited entry to the United States. In 1952, legislation with provisions to exclude homosexuals was instituted to bar immigrants who had committed "crimes of moral turpitude" (Canaday 2003, 353), a designation based on behavior. It also barred the entry of "homosexuals qua persons," a term used to designate a category of person who was "afflicted with psychopathic personality" (353). The term "psychopathic personality" was sufficiently broad to envelop a number of conditions, including homosexuality as it was defined by the diagnostic norms of the time. In 1965, U.S. immigration law was again reworded and revised to exclude gays and lesbians under the aegis of their being "sexual deviates" (Luibhéid and Cantú 2005, xiii). It was not until 1990 that a ban prohibiting the entry of lesbian and gay immigrants was repealed.

The limitations of immigration law not only restrict individuals as such but also maintain larger conceptual frameworks: in particular, a focus on the family. Shane Phelan (2001) argued that an increasing heterosexualization of U.S. citizenship has occurred throughout the twentieth century. In 1965, revisions to immigration law demonstrated a renascent commitment to the heterosexual nuclear family by mandating that 75 percent of permanent visas would be granted only to those with family ties in the United States. These family provisions—with preferences given to spouses, children under twenty-one, and parents of adult U.S. citizens—also affected the ability of Asians and Africans to migrate to the United States. Because migrants from Asia and Africa had been barred for so long historically, many potential migrants were consequently without the quotient of family ties required by the 1965 codes (Reimers 1992).

Drawing from discourses of protecting the public health of the body politic, in 1987 HIV/AIDS was added to the list of contagious diseases for which immigrants could be excluded entry. Congressional legislation in 1993 amended the Immigration and Nationality Act (1952) to bar "HIV-positive aliens applying for immigrant visas, refugee visas, and adjustment to permanent resident status" (Barta 1998, 336).[15] In 1996, the Immigration and Naturalization Service stated that HIV-positive status could be grounds for seeking asylum, thereby allowing discretionary relief to HIV-positive individuals. In 2008 as part of the President's Emergency Plan for AIDS Relief (PEPFAR), President Bush repealed the statutory ban prohibiting HIV-positive tourists or immigrants' entry into the United States. Although lesbians and gay men comprise only a small percentage of the world's HIV-positive people, the 1987 and 1993 prohibitions—despite the partial remedy through asylum and PEPFAR—have affected queer individuals' ability to migrate.

Nevertheless, even though the United States has allowed openly identified lesbians and gay men to enter only since 1990, the nation continues to figure as a sanctuary for many—particularly those who come from home countries that may have repressive laws against homosexuality. Along with establishing more liberal laws regarding lesbian and gay migration and asylum seeking (McClure, Soloway, and Nugent 1997), the United States appears, to many around the world, to be a haven for sexual minorities and, by extension, for binational or dual-migrant same-sex couples. According to Eithne Luibhéid and Lionel Cantú, lesbian and gay migration narratives tend to be oriented around a movement "from repression to freedom" or a "heroic journey undertaken in search of liberation" (2005, xxv). Although the realities of migration processes and lesbian and gay tolerance in the United States are more complicated than that, it is nevertheless important to recognize that the perception of relative freedom in the United States often provides motivation for same-sex couples' migration.

Strategizing Sexual Migration: Advocacy Organizations and Legislative Interventions

Despite many challenges, lesbian and gay migrants do enter the United States: some are closeted, some are out, some are undocumented, and some are under asylum (Ranck 2002). Because of the inherent complexity of immigration law, advocacy organizations, information centers, and websites have been instrumental to the migration of lesbians, gay men, and same-sex couples to the United States. More recently, the same-sex marriage movement in the United States has sparked congressional legislation that would qualify same-sex couples for visa provisions similar to those of heterosexual couples. In addition to the multiple dimensions of pending law, organizations that educate and advocate on behalf of lesbian and gay migrants also offer perspectives on the concerns of lesbian and gay migrants.

The concerns of lesbian and gay migrants may include not only a fear of disclosing their sexual identity to immigration officials but also a fear of letting their families know about the reasons behind their migration. In response to the question, "Are you out to your family?" Wuen-lin answered: "Well, yes and no . . . my family still thinks I live with a roommate. My sisters know, but my parents don't know. They've been here to visit and they know who Michael is and they ask about him every time they call. But now they are asking when am I going back [to Singapore]. That is another challenge I have to face soon. I don't even know [how to say the word] 'homosexuality' in my language to be able to tell my mother."

Many lesbian and gay individuals and binational same-sex couples are reluctant to reveal their sexual identity to immigration officials for fear of deportation. Therefore, it is very difficult to know exactly how many binational same-sex partners currently live in the United States. Only a handful of organizations in the United States—including Immigration Equality, the Human Rights Campaign, and Love Sees No Borders[16]—address the concerns of binational same-sex couples, as well as issues of lesbian and gay migration more generally. Marta Donayre, cofounder of Love Sees No Borders, claimed that approximately half a million members of same-sex binational couples in the United States had come from a range of social, economic, political, and national origins (2002, 25). In the 2000 U.S. census, according to Immigration Equality, 6 percent of the 594,391 same-sex unmarried partners included one citizen and one noncitizen, making an estimated 35,663 same-sex binational couples in the United States.[17] Furthermore, 27,546 same-sex unmarried partners reported in the 2000 census that both of them were noncitizens. Thus, a total of 63,209 same-sex unmarried couples in the United States include one or both partners who are noncitizens. In other words, of the overall 594,391 total couples who reported as same-sex unmarried partners in the 2000 census, more than 10 percent of them had at least one noncitizen. Because U.S. immigration law recognizes only heterosexual married couples, these same-sex partners cannot file visa applications or register citizenship claims based on their committed relationships. Therefore, same-sex couples may continually face a threat of one or both partners being removed from the United States for a number of different reasons, such as an expired tourist, student, or work visa or lack of initial immigration documentation.

Legislation and Legitimacy of Same-Sex Partnerships in U.S. Immigration Law

Seventeen countries (Australia, Belgium, Brazil, Canada, Denmark, Finland, France, Germany, Iceland, Israel, the Netherlands, New Zealand, Norway, South Africa, Spain, Sweden, and the United Kingdom) currently recognize same-sex couples for immigration purposes,[18] with Belgium, Canada, the Netherlands, and Spain granting the right for same-sex marriages as well. The situation is quite different in the United States.

Most frequently, immigrants to the United States become legal permanent residents through employer sponsorship or direct family ties. Although heterosexual couples can marry and thereby create a direct family tie through a conjugal relationship, the same possibility does not exist for same-sex binational couples. The so-called culture wars in the United States continue to rage over the question of same-sex marriage, from constitutional amendments aimed at prohibiting same-sex marriage to social activism aimed at ensuring same-sex marriage equality. The Defense of Marriage Act (DOMA) legislation, enacted in 1996, continues to prohibit same-sex binational marriage claims because, for immigration purposes, the DOMA legislation defines marriage as a relationship between a man and a woman. At the federal level, the United States neither recognizes the legal legitimacy of same-sex marriage nor allows naturalization claims to be made on the basis of direct family ties through same-sex partnerships. Any state-based rights granted to same-sex couples (such as civil unions or domestic partnerships in California, Hawaii, New Jersey, and Vermont, and marriage in Massachusetts) are ineligible for immigration claims because immigration and citizenship considerations operate at the federal level (through the Department of Homeland Security) and therefore are unaccountable to individual states' definitions of immigration-viable partnerships. However, legislation intended to transform the federal immigration status of same-sex couples has recently been placed before Congress.

Introduced in 2005 as an amendment to the Immigration and Nationality Act,[19] the UAFA (Uniting American Families Act) would allow U.S. citizens and legal permanent residents to sponsor their same-sex partners for immigration purposes. Essentially, the amendment adds the terminology "permanent partnership" after the term "marriage" to the Immigration and Nationality Act. The UAFA outlines detailed parameters intended to ensure that only committed same-sex partners are able to use it. Although the wording of the bill does not explicitly mention same-sex partners, it does specify that the couple must be "unable to contract . . . a marriage [with said partner]." In other words, one cannot immigrate as an opposite-sex unmarried couple, but same-sex partnerships have a unique provision. Resistance to the amendment has included the claim that to legally facilitate same-sex spousal sponsorship would be tantamount to allowing a tide of alleged partners and immigration fraud. Like heterosexual married couples, same-sex partners would need to show financial interdependence as proof of their committed relationship. Violation of the UAFA by fraudulent same-sex partnerships would incur steep fines, just as fraud does for heterosexual marriages that are illegitimately contracted solely for immigration purposes. Passage of the UAFA would constitute an important leap forward for the cause of binational lesbian and gay couples, and would move the United States closer to the norms of similar nation-states such as the seventeen countries listed above that currently recognize same-sex couples for immigration purposes.

The UAFA does continue to rely on the trope of the family, centered as it is on the concept of a couple with a "lifelong commitment," with permanent partnerships serving a symbolic and legal role similar to that of the traditional married couple (Lewin 1998). The UAFA does not, however, make the more profound move of examining the universality of the nuclear family form or, as Doreen Indra put it, "the notion of 'the' household itself" (1999, 14). If it were to be made law, the UAFA would constitute an important victory for lesbian and gay immigration equality but it would not unseat the ideological ideal of the nuclear family that lies at the heart of U.S. immigration law.

Under immigration law, entry into the United States is framed as a privilege—one that may be summarily denied. However, asylum and refugee conventions follow different epistemologies and are linked to broader frameworks, including U.S. foreign policies and international human rights conventions. The refugee and asylum system came into being globally following the Second World War, and the purpose of asylum is an explicitly moral one: attempting to provide people sanctuary from persecution based on race, religion, nationality, political opinion, or membership in a particular social group (following the Universal Declaration of Human Rights, 1948).[20] Although asylum seekers in the United States were initially conceived through a model that assumed a politically persecuted and autonomous male subject, there have been significant changes in recent years. Accounting for the legal category of a social group or a political opinion, particularly as such categories pertain to sexuality and gender, has become a key question in U.S. asylum law. Since the early 1990s, judicial proceedings have considered, in rather profound ways, persecution based on sexual orientation and gender identity; it is in this area that important new precedents have been set.

In 1994, U.S. attorney general Janet Reno declared the *Matter of Toboso-Alfonso* to be precedent. In this case, a Cuban gay man was found to be eligible for withholding of removal (not deportable) from the United States because he was a member of a particular social group—namely, homosexuals. *Toboso-Alfonso* established that a well-founded fear of persecution on the basis of one's sexual orientation is a valid basis for an asylum claim in the United States. Since the *Toboso-Alfonso* case, courts have generally been more likely to expand the definition of what constitutes a social group, including girls and women who have undergone female circumcision (genital surgery or genital mutilation) or are victims of domestic violence. Although there is no clear statutory definition of what counts as membership in a particular social group, the concept has been used generally to designate a group with immutable characteristics— shared qualities that members of the group cannot, or should not, be required to change. Since the *Matter of Toboso-Alfonso*, more than half a dozen precedents have been set regarding gay, lesbian, bisexual, transgender, and HIV-positive asylum cases.[21]

Negotiating the complexities of the legal system and immigration law in the United States, particularly for those who may be undocumented migrants, can be an overwhelming experience as well as a financial and logistical burden. Procuring transportation to the United States, recruiting attorneys, and paying legal fees and living expenses, in addition to spending the enormous amount of time needed to file documents and set up possible trial dates as well as meet with lawyers, judges, and immigration and naturalization officials, can add up to an insurmountable task (Ranck 2002). No matter which route a lesbian or gay migrant or binational couple may choose for legal migration, it is a highly class-dependent proposition. International student visas require the holder to demonstrate that she or he has sufficient funds for tuition (often higher than the rate charged to U.S. residents), and international students are prohibited from working in the United States. Work visas require that the holder have skills that the employer requires, and although the employer may have a stake in retaining the employee, the migrant is also more prone to the vicissitudes of employment. A person with significant financial resources may acquire an investor's green card or create an international corporation, but these options are available to only an elite few. Migration is never free from the very concrete, material realities of adequate funding, time, and informational resources. In other words, the migration process requires a sufficient network of support, knowledge, and commitment.

METROPOLITAN COMMUNITY CHURCH: A SPIRITUAL PHILOSOPHY FOR LESBIAN AND GAY MIGRANTS?

For Wuen-lin and Michael, the community they found through MCC and the Lesbian and Gay Immigration Rights Task Force was very important because it provided a support network.[22] As Wuen-lin explained: "Basically, it is our extended family. I feel they care for me and they listen to me and they worry about me. At the same time, I feel I have a role to play in that relationship. If they need me to do anything and I am able to do it, I'll do it. That is my community." Michael then added: "[Wuen-lin's] spirituality, his identification with Christianity, his faith is such an important and essential part of him . . . even though I wanted nothing to do with Christianity and all of that, I could not *not* be a part of such an important part of him. . . . And so if I am going to go, then the compromise was that this was the church I would feel most comfortable going to because I have been working and living in the Castro [neighborhood in San Francisco] for a few years, enough to know their [MCC's] reputation for social justice and that they are *the* queer church, *the* gay church—they were the gay church when no other church would have us." Wuen-lin interjected: "Actually for me, the first day I walked in, it's like [looking around with elation], 'Oh, wow . . . I'm home.' I really feel very comfortable there. In Singapore, I attended church regularly but I didn't contribute to the church because I didn't see the money going anywhere; they didn't organize anything, not any social justice programs. To them, the money is used for church picnics, barbecues . . . I have never gone to any other church here [in the United States] but MCC."

As Michael states above, MCC was "*the* queer church, *the* gay church." It describes itself as ministering primarily within the lesbian and gay community, although it is open to all. The church is also considered to be one of the largest grassroots organizations of LGBT people in the world, with 230 congregations in more than twenty countries. First and foremost MCC is a religious community, but social action has been part of its agenda from the beginning (Warner 1995). The sheer size and scope of the UFMCC, its locations in numerous countries, and its long-standing commitment to lesbian and gay people and their rights suggest that as an institution, MCC might form an ideal nexus to address migration concerns for lesbians, gay men, and binational same-sex couples from an advocacy point of view.

Queer Community and Border-Crossing Liturgies

The origin story of MCC is one of overcoming discrimination. The founder of MCC, Troy Perry, took the position that the Bible itself does not condemn homosexuality per se. Rather, he explained that "the six clobber passages" derogating homosexuality had been interpreted out of context.[23] Perry asserted that rather than reading these lines in context and accounting for changing historical conditions, people had used these passages to discriminate against lesbian and gay people, who are themselves God's creation. It is upon this unjust paradox that Perry founded his church: "I know that intolerance is an enemy of mine just as it is an enemy of God's. I know that people are intolerant of those—the 'theys'—of the world, and a part of my mission is to eliminate that attitude of 'they.' I have learned that man is alone everywhere, especially homosexuals. . . . The religious feelings of these, my people, are very deep" (1972, 5). Perry's explicit framing of those he calls his people in a struggle against intolerance pointed to the nascent emergence of a larger, collective ethos—a form of lesbian and gay or queer kinship and relatedness that would develop over time in MCC.

The church originated theologically from American Pentecostal roots and

Perry's early spiritual training (Perry 1972; Warner 1995).[24] Since then, MCC has become a much more eclectic mix of liturgical forms that include Catholic, Episcopal, and Lutheran approaches (Dank 1973) as well as, in some congregations, goddess worship, New Age spirituality, and universalism (Warner 1995). The church has also reworked its approach to favor inclusive language. For example, the Lord's Prayer may be spoken using the words "our creator" or "our sustainer" in lieu of "our father" (Warner 1995), thus shifting from a patriarchal, family-based discourse to one that attempts to signal a move beyond the family.

The Reverend Elder Nancy Wilson, a member of MCC since 1972 and the successor to Troy Perry as moderator of the UFMCC, formulated a sense of lesbian and gay or queer collective identity through the trope of the "transnational tribe" when she asked, "Who are gay men and lesbians? Sometimes, in my deepest self, I feel like we are some ancient tribal remnant that has survived and that now appears to be dispersed among every other earthly tribe—a transnational tribe!" (1995, 11–12). Wilson's invocation of a tribal collective sentiment and history is not new to gender and sexuality epistemologies. Indeed, creating a sense of historical legacy and legitimacy associated with tribal origins is a way in which marginalized people, whether gay or not, have historically sought to cement their sense of identity.

Similarly, feminist and postcolonial scholars have described "strategic essentialism" as a way to acknowledge the constructed nature of identity while putting to political use putatively innate differences to invert the oppressive tactics of colonial and positivist essentialism. Strategic essentialism can then serve as a powerful mechanism for social change, albeit one that is limited by its reliance on innate and immutable differences. Lesbian and gay and queer scholarship, as well as queer communities, have shaped similar forms of association, whether through fictive kinships described as families they choose (Weston 1991); as a queer nation (Patton and Sanchez-Eppler 2000; Seidman 1996); or as a queer planet (Warner 1993)—though these claims for community do not necessarily draw from essentialist claims. The kind of strategic essentialism that emerges out of a globalized, tribal conception of lesbian and gay people is also particularly well suited to human rights imperatives. Recall that the United Nations recognized that "membership [in] a particular social group" may lead to a refugee's inability, or unwillingness, "to return to [his or her country]."[25] These tenets have been a central discourse in precedent-setting asylum claims in recent years.

By imagining an innate quality of homosexuality, both Wilson and Perry suggest a form of queer kinship or a tribal ethos that potentially serves the larger social justice concerns of MCC and its members. Although scholarly critiques of essentialist sexuality have prevailed throughout the 1990s, particularly in queer theory, in practice some forms of strategic essentialism might be deployed to achieve reformist political goals. However, whether this ethos of tribal kinship works in practice for all the parishioners of MCC is debatable. Although the epistemological foundations may coincide in important ways with the advocacy goals of migration for people in binational same-sex couples, this sort of spiritual essentialism cannot be expected to work for all potential migrants, at least partially because a religious preference (in this case, Christianity) is involved. Moreover, although MCC may prescribe an essentialist orientation, for myriad reasons many parishioners perhaps cannot, or choose not to, take up this particular mantle.

The essentialist concepts illustrated in both Perry's and Wilson's reckonings of homosexuality and lesbian and gay solidarity provide a formula that might exceed the heteronuclear family models so entrenched in immigration law. And yet, MCC has rather famously been performing same-sex wedding ceremonies since the founding of the church in 1969. According to the MCC website, MCC ministers perform six thousand weddings annually in their churches around the world.[26] More recently, MCC has been a strong supporter of same-sex marriage equality. Although some would argue that same-sex marriages are a recapitulation of heteronormative pair-bonding, by virtue of their same-sex gendering these ceremonies also need to be understood as a challenge to presumed heterosexuality. Beyond same-sex weddings, the larger ideological framework of MCC aims to create a sense of community, one that is to some degree essential and tribal (in Wilson's phrasing)—a kinship extending beyond the heteronuclear family form. Nevertheless, this long-standing commitment to same-sex marriages suggests that MCC may not diverge radically from a family-based model, thereby limiting MCC's ability to argue against these entrenched biases in immigration law.

The church's strategic essentialism and tribal kinship do have the potential to unsettle heterosexual kinship and family models that have so dominated migration law in the United States, though whether this potential would manifest in reality remains an open question. The conceptual frameworks of essentialism and tribal kinship, however, also dovetail well with some of the fundamental principles of human rights epistemologies. In seeming to speak to one of the central questions of human rights political philosophy—what constitutes the human—Wilson asked: "So, do gay and lesbian people identify more with our tribe(s) or more with our humanness? . . . Those in whatever dominant group or culture always want all the rest of us to focus on our generic humanness, on how alike we are, not on our differences" (1995, 15).

As R. Stephen Warner notes, "For Troy Perry," who founded MCC in 1969, "religion had always been a matter of love, not law" (1995, 87). Although love may have come before law, the act of seeking social justice, sometimes through legal channels, has also been central to MCC's work. The church became an institution through one of the momentous political and cultural agendas of the day, the gay liberation movement in the late 1960s and early 1970s. Following a survey of gay rights movements in the early 1980s, Dennis Altman suggested that MCC was in many locales singular in its ability to gather a committed gay constituency: "In many places the church is the only form of the gay movement that exists" (1982, 123). Having established itself as a key site committed to the gay movement, in 1978 MCC went on to help defeat the Briggs Initiative in California, which sought to prohibit gay men and lesbians from being teachers (Perry and Swicegood 1990). More recently, MCC has called for federal legislation on hate crimes and lobbied for antidiscrimination laws to protect lesbian and gay people.

Although undertaking social justice projects runs through the history of MCC, a new emphasis on human rights, as such, pervades current MCC discourses and the ways that MCC frames its social justice work. As UFMCC's Statement of Vision says, "Metropolitan Community Churches are on a bold mission to transform *hearts, lives,* and *history.* . . . Just as Jesus did, we are called to: Do justice, show kindness, and live humbly with God (Micah 6:8)."[27]

The church's social justice projects include achieving the Millennium Goals (the United Nations poverty-reduction campaign), working against the spread of HIV/AIDS and caring for HIV-positive individuals and their families, advocating for marriage equality, and creating online communities (e.g., Living Fusion, which aims to organize social action around the world). Thus, in addition to its inclusive approach to the liturgy and a form of the essentially defined connectedness of lesbian and gay people, MCC continues to emphasize the centrality of social justice and human rights.

The Metropolitan Community Church of San Francisco (MCCSF), the second-oldest lesbian and gay congregation in the United States, was founded in 1970 by Reverend Howard Wells. In its online discussion about values, MCCSF states the following tenet: "We believe that all people are equally deserving of God's love and that all people share inalienable human rights." Following both the human rights framework and the eclectic approach of the larger UFMCC liturgical style, MCCSF goes on to describe that it is "influenced by liberation, inclusive, and feminist as well as traditional theologies . . . various Christian and non-Christian traditions." The congregation strives for inclusive language that avoids gender bias and states a desire to extend church membership to all while providing "a home for queer spirituality."[28]

With MCC's church status, which helps define it as a sanctioned institution for good works,[29] it may also evade some of the volatile politicization that is inherent in the hotly contested issues of both same-sex marriage and immigration. Many churches, mosques, and temples are committed to doing good works in their communities. However, in combination with the church's long-standing support of lesbian and gay people and human rights, MCC is philosophically well suited to meeting the challenges of binational lesbian and gay migration issues. Whether dealing with such concerns can be productively undertaken in practice and not simply in theory remains to be seen. MCC's approach to inclusiveness, which attempts to establish an expansive sense of us-ness without excluding nonlesbian and nongay people from its ministry mission, may also prove politically advantageous. The church makes claims of an overt inclusiveness rather than depending on exclusionary forms of identity politics that might be seen as divisive, perhaps especially by right-wing foes. Embedded in the MCC philosophy are the seeds of a larger transnational lesbian and gay ethos, one that is inclusive and, more important, explicitly global. According to MCCSF, "We build and grow a beloved community of queer people, family, and friends that is local and global, physical and virtual."[30]

The global scope of MCC is critical in an era of pervasive migration and increased interconnectedness; of course, many of the so-called world religions have global scope. The question is how well MCC or other faith-based communities and institutions will be able to rally their globality and commitment to social justice in support of concerns surrounding migration issues for lesbian and gay individuals and binational same-sex couples. The church's focus on lesbian and gay members is a central element suggesting that the MCC could become a logical location through which to address migration issues for lesbian and gay people. The church was conceived out of both spiritual and political commitments, particularly through some of the early work of its founder Troy Perry. His proposal, situated within a varied liturgical style, was that homosexuality is innate (or "essential"),[31] and that as such it is a gift from God (Warner 1995). Using the trope of essentialism and a linked sense of community through the tribe, MCC mirrors many of the political strategies that have proven effective in ethnic, gender, and other sexuality-based struggles for human and civil rights. As the comments of Wuen-lin and Michael made clear, these strategies are more than just political and rhetorical: they are, for many MCC parishioners, deeply felt. Although many members of the church may benefit from and embrace these narratives of kinship, community, and tribal membership, it is not clear whether such tropes work effectively for all of those involved. That is, essentialism has its limits, as the past two decades of identity politics have demonstrated; MCC's inclusiveness may work well as a theoretically rich avenue for lesbian and gay migration, but the proof of its utility in practice remains to be seen.

Beyond its transnational commitment to lesbian and gay issues, since its inception MCC has had at its core four key components that appear, theoretically at least, to situate it as a social and spiritual location that might be particularly suited to the cause of migration issues for lesbians, gay men, and same-sex binational couples. First, in drawing on discourses of a tribal community or kinship among lesbian- and gay-identified people around the world MCC advocates for an expanded sense of relatedness. This sensibility, a larger ethos of queer people, is an ideological position that is poised to reach beyond the parameters of the nuclear, heterosexual family that has been so foundational to the last decades of immigration legislation in the United States. Second, MCC has also held, since its beginnings in the late 1960s, that social justice and, more recently, human rights are central to its mission, vision, and practice. Third, MCC can draw on its putatively apolitical identity as a church, with the legitimating power of churchness, in ways that nonprofit, nongovernmental organizations and groups may not be able to do. Although MCC may not have the explicit approval afforded to some other religious institutions (arguably because it is a so-called queer church), it does nonetheless occupy "the legitimate social space accorded to religion in the United States" (Warner 1995, 82), which may shelter it from some political attacks. Although religion in the United States can hardly be said to be an apolitical arena, the marriage of Christianity and good work—the stuff of most churches, including MCC—may ameliorate some of the political vitriol so infamous in debates about homosexuality and migration. Finally, MCC has been a geographically particular church, one that has evolved out of urban spaces and continues to thrive in them with a relative tolerance for gays and lesbians. That is, it is a church that was largely born through the Great Gay Migrations (Weston 1998). The church was founded in Los Angeles, California (where the primary MCC unit remains), but it has developed other thriving congregations in the United States, many in migration gateway cities in the southwestern and southern United States.

The way that MCC has combined an expanded sense of kinship and family (Weston 1991) with essentialist renderings of homosexuality, commitments to human rights, church legitimacy, and migratory origins suggests that it is well positioned with respect to the issues surrounding the migration of lesbians, gay men, and partners in binational same-sex couples to the United States. The branch MCCSF, which has served as a brief case study here, presents one example of MCC's values and practices in an important gateway city for both international migrants specifically and lesbian and gay people in general. In a recent sermon at MCCSF, then Reverend Dr. G. Penny Nixon underscored the nexus of migration and sexuality when she described Jesus as a border crosser (Nixon 2006). Nixon's emphasis was on the ability of Jesus to transcend the strictures of religious and ethnic boundaries and extend compassion to all. Given that her sermon occurred during the height of the 2006 immigration rights protests, there is an uncanny resonance between MCC's message and the turbulent politics of immigration in the twenty-first century.

CONCLUSIONS

The relationship between U.S. (im)migration and LGBT lives demonstrates both possibilities and prohibitions. For many years, lesbian and gay people were explicitly barred from obtaining the right to immigrate to the United States. Yet many lesbian- and gay-identified people around the world have held out hopes for sanctuary in the United States. In a contemporary context, questions concerning the migration of lesbians, gay men, and partners in binational same-sex couples offer a particular opportunity to revisit the crisis of meaning that has troubled political theorists and human rights advocates alike regarding how human rights, supposedly the most fundamental rights owed to everyone, are distributed — either through state bureaucracies or in the domain of international moral injunctions. As with earlier refugee paradoxes, undocumented migrants and lesbian and gay people each face difficulties in claiming full citizenship, either by virtue of their undocumented status or by virtue of their sexuality (coupled with a refusal to marry someone whom they do not love simply to gain entry to or remain in the United States). Both undocumented and lesbian and gay migrants are potentially legally and epistemologically betwixt and between; that is, they are in a liminal state in a world where belonging to a nation and having the rights of citizenship are crucial to one's well-being. Undocumented migrants, as well as lesbian and gay partnerships and marriages, have been embattled sites for the U.S. culture wars. Historically, sexual minorities have been legally designated as unworthy of legal protections and rights equivalent to those held by the general populace. Although this form of second-class citizenship is receding (albeit slowly), it has served to partially define gay and lesbian people as well as undocumented migrants. Each case

challenges human rights at the level of theory and practice to enact the promise, made in 1948, to defend what Hannah Arendt (1958) called the sacred and
abstract nakedness of being human, without distinction.

The philosophical model of MCC has institutionalized many of the pertinent
questions surrounding human rights, lesbian and gay citizenship, and the challenges of border crossing. In addition to being the largest spiritual and religious
collective of lesbian and gay people in the world, MCC has built conceptual
foundations of social justice and human rights practices corresponding to the
complex concerns that arise regarding the migration of binational lesbian and
gay couples and individual lesbian and gay people. As a religious institution,
MCC may also draw upon its depoliticized legitimacy as a church rather than
being perceived as an advocacy-oriented organization. The juridical struggles
around same-sex marriage and immigration certainly afford space for interventions at the level of Congress, as with the UAFA. But I maintain that moving
beyond a purely legalistic approach is also critical. From an advocacy point of
view, legal interventions aimed at establishing the rights of sexual minorities
are critical — but so too are social, cultural, and, perhaps, spiritually based community interventions. In fact, religious or spiritual communities may have networks, tools, and philosophical resources that are better suited to overcoming
some of the barriers associated with migration issues for lesbian and gay people
and binational same-sex couples.

The case of MCC also allows for a rethinking of the nuclear-family-based
heterosexual model that has been so central to immigration law in the United
States. In particular, MCC offers a lens through which to visualize a kind of lesbian and gay collective that is not solely grounded in notions of the family. The
concept of a tribal kinship can offer a way to think outside the confines of the
family and the household unit. MCC's commitment to a kind of global queer
kinship or a lesbian and gay tribal mentality suggests a way of thinking outside
the predictable legal avenues of consanguine (blood) and affinal (marital) approaches that determine who shall be allowed or denied immigration access.
This variety of queer kinship may use essentialist tropes of immutable difference, but in attempts at reform this approach may be the most realizable.

As Wuen-lin and Michael have voiced throughout this article, parishioners
and the leadership of MCC have a heartfelt commitment to the institution and
the forms of community it provides. Although for this very reason the ideology
underlying MCC may be understood as essentialist and politically useful, this
usefulness does not invalidate the fact that for many the true appeal of MCC
is its phenomenological and spiritual fit, not simply — or even primarily — its
political utility. Although the concept of sexual migration serves as an initial

concept for understanding these dynamics, more research is needed to understand and evaluate both the legal apparatus and the personal dimensions of
migration to a new country as a sexual minority, as well as the place and home
of sexual-minority migrants within migrant communities or lesbian and gay
social networks in the United States.

NOTES

An earlier version of this essay appeared under the same title in *Sexuality Research and
Social Policy* 4.2 (2007): 88–106.

1. The interview with Wuen-Lin and Michael (both pseudonyms) was conducted by
   Lorrie Ranck in July 2003 as part of the Religion and Immigration Project (TRIP),
   directed by Lois Lorentzen at the University of San Francisco with funding provided
   by the Pew Charitable Trusts.

2. Bakersfield, a city in central Southern California, is considered by many to be socially conservative.

3. In this essay I use the terms "lesbian" and "gay"—and, to a lesser extent, "queer"—to
   designate individuals in same-sex affective and sexual relationships. Though these
   terms cannot fully provide the nuance required to capture same-sex relationships
   from a variety of cultures, I rely on these categories as a form of shorthand in this
   discussion. The term queer is used more advisedly in this discussion because despite
   the popularity of queer identity among activists and (largely) urban and (largely)
   youth populations in the United States, many sexual minorities in the developing
   world hope to normalize their status rather than index their queer nonconformity.
   Finally, although many of the migration concerns covered in this essay could be
   applicable to bisexual or transgender individuals or couples, I am not able to fully
   address those complexities here.

4. Formerly, functions related to (im)migration were carried out by the Immigration
   and Naturalization Service (INS). Under the aegis of Homeland Security, the procedures formerly undertaken by the INS are now the responsibility of Immigration
   and Customs Enforcement, U.S. Citizenship and Immigration Services, and U.S.
   Customs and Border Protection.

5. Wuen-Lin and Michael's narrative history is simply one example of many potential intersections between sexual migration and the racial, ethnic, class, and geographic origins that invariably affect the dynamics of binational same-sex couple
   migration. As men from relatively economically privileged origins (in the global
   scheme of things), their experience cannot be taken as a representative case study.
   However, Wuen-Lin and Michael's case does illustrate several of the central themes
   of the Metropolitan Community Church, human rights, and the potential pitfalls
   of migration. Their story serves as a guidepost for the discussion—it is not meant
   to insinuate that the migration of binational same-sex couples is an issue limited to
   gay men or citizens of the developed world.

6. Throughout this essay, the term "migrant" designates a person who has crossed a U.S. border to seek permanent or temporary residence, either with or without legal documentation.

7. A number of the political advocacy organizations aimed at lobbying for lesbian, gay, bisexual, and transgender rights, both in the United States and internationally, also have significant membership bases. The National Gay and Lesbian Task Force, which has been in existence for more than three decades, has approximately twenty thousand members in the United States, and the Human Rights Campaign, founded in 1980, has had approximately six hundred thousand U.S. members over the course of its tenure. Two prominent organizations working toward establishing lesbian and gay rights internationally are the International Gay and Lesbian Human Rights Commission and the International Lesbian and Gay Association, which forms a network of four hundred member organizations (or affiliates) from ninety countries.

8. The 1948 Universal Declaration of Human Rights (UDHR), developed largely in response to the Holocaust, maintained that citizens must be protected from potential abuses exercised by nation-states; to this end, the UDHR has sought to codify international norms of equality, moral standards, and humanitarian principles. The UDHR has also drawn attention to the facets of human life that had, historically, been used by states to deny people's rights. These included "race, colour, sex, language, religion, political or other opinion, national or social origin, property, birth or other status" (Universal Declaration of Human Rights, December 10, 1948, United Nations General Assembly Resolution 217 A III, United Nations Document A 1810 at 71, article 2, para. 1. United Nations, http://www.un.org [site visited February 26, 2007]).

9. For a trenchant critique of Ignatieff's celebratory position on human rights, see Brown 2004. Although many would support the egalitarian aims of human rights in practice, there are also a number of well-founded critiques regarding the theoretical foundations of human rights and their current implementation. In brief, human rights, as I point out here, are overly reliant on nation-states and military intervention for their implementation (Agamben 1998; Chomsky cited in Feher, 2000); they are often part of neocolonial regimes, thereby ensuring complicity with a putative civilizing mission that has its roots in European colonial hegemony. Formulations of which rights in particular (such as choice) are most worthy of protecting are also historically and culturally contingent entities (Žižek 2005). In this essay, though I emphasize the usefulness of human rights as a political framework, I am also aware that rights are historically contingent, and in their application they may erase cultural particularities in the service of universal rights (see Nagengast and Turner 1997).

10. It is not that human rights are prior to the political rights guaranteed by the nation-state, but rather the other way around. This situation creates a perplexity because human rights are essentially entrusted to states, which are also, ironically, the primary violators of human rights. This situation also creates "contradictions, [for] if

they are supposed to be inalienable and universal, free from the determinations of any particular nation or state, [human rights] are also dependent on the sovereignty of that nation or state for their definition, protection and realization" (Balfour and Cadava 2004, 281).

11. Of course, lesbian, gay, bisexual, and transgender people are allowed to marry an individual of the opposite sex in the United States and establish citizenship through a conjugal tie. Indeed, many do. However, this method has its price. First, such a marriage is arguably illegitimate because it is based not on sexual affections and romantic commitments but on the desire to migrate; were such a marriage found to be a fraud, it would be grounds for deportation. Second, many LGBT people would argue that marrying someone simply to match a heterosexual paradigm and overcome legal immigration restrictions would be a betrayal of themselves and their sexuality.

12. This process is limited, of course, because it cannot account for the particularities of migrants' countries of origin, nor can it fully consider the lives of people in same-sex affective relationships around the world more generally (e.g., Blackwood and Wieringa 1999; Boellstorff and Leap 2004; Carrillo 2002; Gevisser and Cameron 1995; Howe 2002, in press; Manalansan 2003; Ratti 1993; Rofel 1999; Sinnott 2004).

13. The migratory barriers faced by same-sex-attracted individuals and same-sex couples cannot be understood outside the context of historical exclusions around perceived differences, including those of race, national origin, gender, and class. In 1790, U.S. law mandated that naturalization was reserved for whites only. In the late nineteenth century, the Page Law (1875) prohibited Asian women from entering the United States because they were thought to be migrating for putatively lewd reasons. Chinese women in particular were singled out for immigration exclusion because they were marked as likely prostitutes. The Page Law was a harbinger of a yet more expansive Chinese Exclusion Act (1882) and the barring of southern European immigrants in the 1920s for similarly racialized reasons. Immigration law in the early twentieth century included prohibitions against women entering the United States for prostitution and forbade entry of so-called immoral women and polygamists (Hutchinson 1981). Only in 1952 were all formal, explicit racial barriers removed from U.S. citizenship law.

14. According to a 1918 Public Health Service manual for alien examination, "the moral imbeciles, the pathological swindlers, the defective delinquents, many of the vagrants and cranks, and persons with abnormal sexual instincts" (cited in Canaday 2003, 359) were to be excluded.

15. Though legal details change, an HIV waiver is available to foreign nationals who have qualifying relatives in the United States and can demonstrate that they will cover the costs of any medical treatment associated with the disease. Refugees and those seeking asylum may apply for an HIV waiver even without a qualifying relative.

16. Immigration Equality (formerly the Lesbian and Gay Immigration Rights Task Force), the only such national organization in the United States, has nineteen chapters across the country and provides outreach, advocacy, and education about

lesbian and gay and HIV-positive migration to the United States. As a grassroots organization, Immigration Equality aims to establish legal equality for lesbian and gay and HIV-positive individuals under U.S. immigration law. Founded in 1994, with national headquarters in New York City, it has grown to a membership of ten thousand. It is funded by private foundations such as the Ford Foundation, George Soros's Open Society, and the lesbian and gay foundation Horizons, among others, as well as by member donations. The Human Rights Campaign (HRC), a large, well-known national lesbian and gay rights organization that has been a strong supporter of marriage equality (or same-sex marriage), also supports the cause of binational same-sex couple migration. Though migration is not one of their central issues, the HRC website directs visitors to the Immigration Equality website. One link on the site has a prompt titled, "If your partner is about to be deported." The HRC also features information about the Uniting American Families Act. The HRC's approach to the question of lesbian and gay or same-sex couple migration follows in step with the organization's more general orientation to normalize (Warner 1999) homosexuality and gay and lesbian relationships within larger social frameworks through the models of family and long-term monogamous partnering. Love Sees No Borders is a much smaller organization that focuses solely on binational same-sex couple migration. The organization defined itself as "dedicated to disseminating information about the injustices suffered by gay Americans and their foreign-born partners." More recently, the organization has defined itself as advocating "on behalf of binational same-sex couples in trying to live in the United States" (Love Sees No Borders, "About Us," 2005, http://www.loveseesnoborders.org [site visited February 22, 2007]). Love Sees No Borders does not consider itself a political or advocacy organization per se but rather an educational resource for binational same-sex couples.

17. Immigration Equality, "Frequently Asked Questions about the Uniting American Families Act: How Many Couples in the U.S. Are in Binational Same Sex Relationships?" http://www.immigrationequality.org (site visited May 8, 2006).

18. In 2003, Brazil's National Immigration Council instituted Administrative Resolution No. 3, which recognized legal same-sex unions performed abroad for immigration purposes. Following an earlier finding in favor of a binational (British and Brazilian) gay male couple residing in Brazil, the resolution effectively "disposes of the criteria for the concession of temporary or permanent visa, or of definitive permanence to the male or female partner, without distinction of sex (*Diário Oficial da União*, cited in Immigration Equality, "Brazil Clarifies Its Same-Sex Immigration Policy," May 11, 2004, http://www.immigrationequality.org [site visited Feburary 14, 2007]). Same-sex couples who have been legally married (in Belgium, the Netherlands, or Canada), or are in a civil union or domestic partnership (in Vermont or California, for example), or registered as partners in a city registry (in San Francisco or Buenos Aires, for example), can use their certificate to apply for immigration benefits in Brazil—making it the first country in Latin America to extend such an opportunity.

19. The UAFA was submitted to the 109th Congress as S. 1278 and H.R. 3006, formerly

called the Permanent Partners Immigration Act (S. 1510 and H.R. 832). In 2005, the
UAFA was introduced by Representative Jerrold Nadler (D-NY) and Senator Patrick
Leahy (D-VT), though it was not enacted. The wording from Section 2, "Defini-
tions," is as follows:

Section 101(a) (8 U.S.C. 1101(a)) is amended—
(1) in paragraph (15)(K)(ii), by inserting "or permanent partnership" after "mar-
    riage"; and
(2) by adding at the end the following:

The term "permanent partner" means an individual 18 years of age or older who—
  (A) is in a committed, intimate relationship with another individual 18 years of
      age or older in which both parties intend a lifelong commitment;
  (B) is financially interdependent with the individual described in subparagraph
      (A);
  (C) is not married to or in a permanent partnership with anyone other than the
      individual described in subparagraph (A);
  (D) is unable to contract, with the individual described in subparagraph (A), a
      marriage cognizable under this Act; and
  (E) is not a first-, second-, or third-degree blood relation of the individual de-
      scribed in subparagraph (A).

20. The 1951 U.N. Convention on the Status of Refugees, as well as the later incorpora-
    tion of the Refugee Act into U.S. law in 1980, created the legal structure and system
    of settlement to ensure the rights of asylum seekers.
21. Immigration Equality, "LGBT/HIV Asylum Manual: Asylum Law Basics—Brief His-
    tory of Lesbian, Gay, Bisexual, Transgender and HIV LGBT/H Asylum Law," http://
    www.immigrationequality.org (site visited March 27, 2007).
22. As previously noted, the Lesbian and Gay Immigration Rights Task Force (LGIRTF)
    is now Immigration Equality. However, Wuen-lin and Michael referred to the orga-
    nization as LGIRTF, so I have preserved that phrasing here.
23. Troy Perry, message to the author, April 18, 2002.
24. R. Stephen Warner (1995) argued that MCC has depended on what he called con-
    servative foundations of Pentecostalism and essentialism in order to advance its
    rather progressive cause: a lesbian and gay church that challenges homophobia and
    provides a spiritual home for gays and lesbians in contrast to the hostility of many
    mainstream churches. Central to MCC's effectiveness, in his formulation, is the fact
    that it is an American church growing out of Pentecostal vitality and scriptural inter-
    pretation, which has allowed for liturgical flexibility. Warner described the history
    of MCC as one that has followed a conventional teleology of development, growing
    from a congregation to a denomination (the Universal Fellowship of Metropoli-
    tan Community Churches) and ultimately aspiring to become part of the National
    Council of Churches (also see Warner 2005; Wilcox 2003).
25. United Nations General Assembly, "Convention Relating to the Status of Refugees,"

article 1a, sec. 2, para. 1, July 28, 1951, http://www.ohchr.org (site visited March 20, 2007)

26. Metropolitan Community Churches, "MCC Marriage Equality Valentine's Day 2006: Resources, Activities, and Partnerships," http://www.mcchurch.org (site visited March 26, 2007).

27. Metropolitan Community Churches, "Human Rights/Social Justice," n.d., http://www.mcchurch.org (site visited June 18, 2006).

28. Metropolitan Community Church of San Francisco, "About MCC San Francisco: History," n.d., http://www.mccsf.org (site visited February 7, 2007). ·

29. Through outreach and voluntarism, the Metropolitan Community Church of San Francisco (MCCSF) seeks to transform the larger social world. The congregation has a shower project aimed primarily at San Francisco's homeless population, a meal program, cancer support groups, and a program to provide foster children with suitcases so they need not use garbage bags to move from one home to another. The congregation has worked with the San Francisco Department of Public Health to provide HIV testing on location in the church building. The church also created the Harvey Milk Civil Rights Academy (named for the gay member of the San Francisco Board of Supervisors who was murdered in 1978).

30. Metropolitan Community Church of San Francisco, "About MCC San Francisco: History," http://www.mccsf.org (site visited February 7, 2007).

31. See, for example, Dennis Altman's *Homosexual: Oppression and Liberation* (1993 [1973]) for an ideological overview of the gay liberationist struggle that aimed, not unlike a later iteration in queer movements in the United States, to point to the bisexual and latent homosexual potential in everyone rather than centering dialogue on an exclusive homosexuality among a minority population. Using Herbert Marcuse's *Eros and Civilization: A Philosophical Inquiry into Freud* (1966) and Alfred Kinsey and his colleagues' survey work (1948, 1953), gay liberation (in broad strokes) underscored both the centrality of sexuality as a social site of repression (following Marcuse) and the continuum of homoerotic experience (following Kinsey).

El Mílagro Está en Casa

Gender and Private and Public Empowerment in a Migrant Pentecostal Church

LOIS ANN LORENTZEN WITH ROSALINA MIRA

Stenciled on the side of an apartment building in the Mission District of San Francisco are the words "Buen Samaritano." On any given day a visitor, after pressing a buzzer by the front door, might enter to the sound of a woman sobbing and praying the words "Gracias a Dios, Gracias por el poder y la voz," or "Thanks to God, thanks for empowerment and voice," words that are music to any feminist's ears. Yet the setting is a Pentecostal church, one of a type that is scorned by many for its alleged reactionary ways and conservative politics. In this essay, with the help of Rosalina, I explore the appeal of Pentecostalism for new migrants to the San Francisco Bay Area, the seemingly paradoxical characteristics of Pentecostalism as both countercultural and an upholder of the status quo, and the ways in which the church approaches questions of identity. I also examine the conflation of the religious and theological with migrant identity; the church's approach to the collective and individual identity of being "American"; and the shifts in gender roles that occur in this Pentecostal space. This essay reflects findings from three years of fieldwork conducted with Rosalina Mira in Buen Samaritano,[1] a storefront Pentecostal church with a working-class, Spanish-speaking congregation—a high percentage of which are new migrants.

The rapid expansion of Pentecostalism in Latin America has been well documented by numerous scholars, and André Corten has called it "the most important religious transnationalism of the twentieth century" (1999, 44). Nearly one quarter of U.S. Latinos call themselves Protestants, and most of them are Pentecostals (Espinosa, Elizondo, and Miranda, 2003, 14). Scholars of Pentecostalism in Latin America agree that its growth does not reflect a North American invasion, or as Karla Poewe writes, "inventions foisted upon the poor of the world by the Christian right" (1994, xi), as was once widely assumed. The classic hotly contested explanatory models for the rapid growth of Pentecostalism include anomie in the face of rapid social change, class differences with attendant alien-ation, failed modernization, personal uprooting, economic marginalization, and globalization (Cox 1995; Droogers 1998, 2001; Lalive d'Epinay 1970, 1983; Martin 1990; McDonnel 1980; Willems 1967; Williams 1981). Numerous recent scholarly works on Pentecostalism caution against generalizations given the variety of forms it takes. The Pentecostal Study Group is correct in arguing that "the global trend of Pentecostal expansion . . . like all processes of globalization . . . should be studied in its local manifestations" (Boudewijinse, Droogers, and Kamsteeg 1998, viii).

Pentecostalism in the United States arose from U.S. Methodist and Bap-tist sanctification or holiness circles at the end of the nineteenth century and then rapidly spread to Latin America. Whether it owes its founding to white ministers such as Charles F. Parkham and the Assemblies of God or to the African American William Joseph Seymour and the Church of God in Christ, the spread of the Azusa Street Mission between 1905 and 1909 quickly gave Pentecostalism what Corten terms a "third world flavor" (1997, 314). Begin-ning in California, early Pentecostalism attracted Latino converts; Juan Lugo, Francisco Olazabal, Antonio Nava, and others became influential in its spread. Thus, new migrants to the United States who join Pentecostal churches become part of a homegrown ethnic religious movement.

Buen Samaritano is affiliated with one of the largest and oldest Pentecostal groups, a denomination founded at the turn of the century that now has more than nine million members worldwide. The region it belongs to encompasses Nevada, California, Arizona, and Oregon and contains over two hundred His-panic churches, with twenty in the San Francisco Bay Area alone. In the past de-cade the denomination has established churches in every city with new Latino populations, and the Mission District has five affiliated congregations. Rather than competing with each other, these neighborhood churches serving simi-lar populations congregate frequently.[2] With roughly three hundred members, Buen Samaritano is a small branch of a denomination with a reach throughout the Americas.

DIASPORA THEOLOGY

Although the church has a long history in the Mission District and has always been Spanish speaking, the current congregation is made up almost exclu-sively (90 percent) of migrants who have come to the United States within the past fifteen years. All services are conducted in Spanish. Members come from Mexico, El Salvador, Guatemala, Nicaragua, Puerto Rico, Argentina, and

Peru. Most would be considered low-to-middle working class. Women work as housekeepers, nannies, and sometimes as teachers, and the men work as cooks, dishwashers, gardeners, and day laborers. A privileged few (the handful who went to a university or a college in the United States) work in corporate America. Before migration, congregants held a range of occupations, from merchant to teacher to guerrilla.

Church doctrine is based on a literal interpretation of the Bible and mirrors that of other Pentecostal or fundamentalist churches: personal conversion and sanctification, the baptism of the Holy Spirit (including speaking in tongues), baptism by immersion in water, bodily resurrection following final judgment, and belief in the verbal inspiration of the Bible, original sin, and the doctrine of the Trinity. Religious practices include the sharing of testimonies, the laying on of hands to heal the sick, speaking in tongues, interpretation of tongues, and prophecy. Yet, Buen Samaritano expands upon traditional doctrine in the light of the migrant experience.

The church self-consciously uses the language of migration and displacement in its religious symbolism and theology. "God brought you here for a reason," Pastor Manuel announces. "God brought you miles away because you could not accept God in your country. You could not leave the life that you were living."[3] Testimonies, prayers, bible readings, and preaching all reflect a theme of struggle—particularly the struggle faced by uprooted peoples in a new land. Hermana (Sister) Isabel testifies that God has finally answered her prayers about her immigration status. A visiting pastor from Tennessee uses the experience of discrimination and mistreatment to exhort congregants to become "exemplary immigrants," thus defying stereotypes. The congregation has sent financial assistance to sister churches in El Salvador following earthquakes.

Three states of mind exist simultaneously in congregants and are reflected in religious practice and discourse: first, *la vida cotidiana* (daily life) in the United States, with concerns over employment, immigration status, housing, crime, drugs, and gangs; second, life in migrants' countries of origin and ongoing concern with family members left behind; and third, heaven. These states of mind correspond to Fernando Segovia's notion of the diaspora theology of migrants, which includes myths or narratives of origin, recollection, reconstruction, and retelling: "For those who entered the country as immigrants, the status of exile is likely to prove a primordial reality" (1996, 202). Pentecostal theology embraces discontinuity and in this sense fits well with the migrant experience. As John Burdick argues, "the transformative discourse inherent in Pentecostalism, in contrast to Catholicism, forges new possibility for suspending, questioning, inverting, and re-creating secular identities" (1993, 66). The pastor frequently uses the analogy of the discontinuity of migration as a metaphor for spiritual transformation.

Segovia is correct that migrant churches such as Buen Samaritano create diaspora theologies, but these are generally overshadowed by the demands of everyday life; testimonials, prayers, and sermons reflect these daily struggles. This is not an otherworldly movement. The concerns expressed in church are about jobs, visas, physical health, drugs, gangs, violence, housing, food, education, and so on. Each service devotes time to *testimonios*; a woman gives thanks to God for a safe return from Guatemala, a man is happy because he found a job after months of looking. Buen Samaritano counts among its members people who claim to be former drug addicts, gang members, guerrillas, and drug dealers. Juan, a former gang member, tells his Sunday school class how his life was saved by meeting the pastor of the church: "Pastor Manuel went to the streets and invited me and my gang friends to the church; my whole life changed after that." As Waldo Cesar writes, "The experience of the sacred reveals itself in concrete situations in everyday life" (2001, 27).

QUESTIONS OF IDENTITY

Questions of ethnic and national identity both are and are not important at Buen Samaritano. Church music sounds similar to cumbia, merengue, rancheros, and samba. For fundraisers people cook food from their countries of origin—tostadas, bistec encebollado, and pupusas. Yet members also believe that "culture" is secondary to a culture of Christianity. Burdick writes that a "tension exists between Pentecostalism and the development of strong social identities . . . pentecostalism encourages believers to see themselves as belonging to a transcendent worldwide brotherhood of the saved. Such a view is at odds with the ethnic project, for the universalizing insistence that before Christ every human being is the same is in tension with a focus on group-centered discourse" (1998, 123). The church sends money and video greetings to other churches in Mexico and Central America because they consider them linked through religious kinship. After the earthquakes in El Salvador, the church collected money, prayed, and videotaped messages, and an official from the main office in Tennessee visited congregations and denomination members at sister churches. Guest pastors from El Salvador, Mexico, and Guatemala frequently preach during Sunday services at Buen Samaritano. These ongoing contacts are not tight transnational pairings but rather create a sense of participation in a larger network. Members may visit a church in their country of origin, but they also feel connected with congregations in Mexico, Guatemala, Puerto Rico, or Tennessee through visits, the exchange of pastors, videos, mission projects, and other means. The intent of the videos, for example, is to show that "all Christians pray the same and are joyous in God." Information technologies allow members to participate in global flows of information and practices within their multisited church. In this and other ways Buen Samaritano contributes to globalization as well as emerges from it, made up as it is of migrant members.

Burdick, who studies Brazilian Pentecostalism, suggests that messages of self-valorization serve to promote feelings of self-worth for black women. He writes that there are "few places where a dark skinned black evangelical feels treated more equally than in a Pentecostal church" (1998, 127). At Buen Samaritano explicit messages of valorization focus more on migrant and class than on ethnic identity. People are certainly proud to be from El Salvador, Nicaragua, Mexico, and Guatemala, but explicit emphasis on identity, whether from the pulpit, in people's conversations, or in self-identification, revolves around religious identity and migrant and class identity. As Ruth Marshall-Feratani writes, "conversion does not necessarily imply rejection of other identities, but . . . their assimilation with a complex of discourses and practices governing all aspects of social, cultural, economic, and political life: . . . one is always born again first" (2001, 86). Members of Buen Samaritano may be born-again women, janitors, Latinos, Mexicanos, or Salvadorans, but they are first of all born again.

Many scholars point to (and often criticize) neo-Pentecostalism's "theology of prosperity," yet at Buen Samaritano far more preaching time is spent in harsh criticism of U.S. consumerism. Pastor Manuel consistently attacks the belief that God is the provider of cars, televisions, and homes: "You can buy just about anything in this country and have millions of credit cards, Visa, American Express, *la tarjeta de aluminio*—God does not care how much you have, that is all trash in his eyes." At a local Pentecostal congress the "American dream" was explicitly and frequently criticized as slavery. Worshippers were warned about becoming slaves to material possessions and were told that they must not pray to God for material possessions or rely on them. Pastor Manuel said that he had actually prayed that a certain individual would lose his big new house. Church members seem to share the pastor's concern. As Juan tells his Sunday school class, "If you have three cars we need to give one of those cars to some of our brothers and sisters that do not have any. That is the way, it is not easy and against everything that this world teaches, but we are no longer part of the *mundo*, we are part of the family of God, we have been rescued and paid for in blood." Another member of the congregation, José, complains about life in the United States, saying, "In the U.S. the values are money and power. The one who has money can do things [but not] the one who doesn't. . . . There is nothing more important than power in the U.S. to have, to have and to have."

References to television also occur, at times mirroring social science research concerning violence's effects on children, and decrying the passivity that excessive television watching engenders. Criticisms of the dominant culture in which migrants find themselves are common. Paradoxically, however, members also strive to be "exemplary migrants"; that is, "perfect participants in a world they are supposed to detest" (Droogers 1998, 7). Although they may profess antimaterialism, they also need to prosper for very concrete reasons. Many support families both in the United States and in their countries of origin, and being "exemplary immigrants" is seen as helpful for other migrants; if others see you as exemplary, they will want others like you as tenants and workers and will change immigration laws to allow more like you into the country. Being exemplary is viewed as a social and political tool by opening space for greater participation of those who also criticize the values of the dominant order.

During the presidential elections in 2000 the church voted as a bloc. The members' moral codes and religious beliefs made them feel that they had much in common with George Bush, but after church discussions and political sermons they decided to vote for Al Gore. The vote was based on immigration policies and their assessment that Gore and the Democrats were more likely to look out for the needs of the least privileged. This decision made sense. Relatively few congregants were actually eligible to vote, and a vote for Gore was seen as a vote on their behalf.

I witnessed the tension between being an "American" and being a social critic most dramatically when I attended Sunday services at Buen Samaritano on the day that the first bombs were dropped on Afghanistan by the U.S. military. In the parking lot, U.S. flags were flying from all the car antennas. The pastor began his sermon by telling the congregation how thankful they should be to the United States: "This country has given you refuge, given you jobs, allowed you to support your families here and at home. We must be grateful and proud to live here." He then asked, "Was Jerry Falwell right when he said that the World Trade Center was hit to punish America for its sins such as homosexuality, feminism, abortion, adultery, and so on?" To my surprise, he said no and proceeded to read passages from the Old Testament about trusting in horses, chariots, and gold. The rest of the sermon was a scathing critique of the reliance by the U.S. on economic and military power. The pastor harshly criticized the country for its sin of arrogance in "going it alone" and for relying on its own "horses, chariots, and gold." A member of the congregation rose and stated that "people in the United States think money is God. The twin towers symbolized money; our satisfaction should come from higher values." Others agreed, interpreting the attack on the World Trade Center as an attack on materialism.

The pastor and the congregants powerfully articulated the tension between being a faithful citizen or resident as well as a scathing social critic. According to church literature, "Our goal is to fulfill the obligations we have to society, being good citizens, correcting social injustices, and protecting the sanctity of life." The official statement holds in tension both exemplary citizenship and social critique.

Although criticisms of the U.S. government are made from the pulpit, the government is part of members' daily lives—they pray for a change in immigration laws so that they can bring relatives to the United States; they offer testimonies of success at the Immigration and Naturalization Service[4] office; and they use government social services. They take a critical stance on government and political practices, but they also believe in the government and when possible they attempt to manipulate it for individual and collective ends. And, understandably, they have minimal expectations of receiving government services. As Pastor Manuel says, "Remember social services were invented not by the government but by people like you and me who feed the hungry." Churches like Buen Samaritano provide food programs and other needed services.

Numerous paradoxes exist at Buen Samaritano: there are the simultaneous egalitarian and hierarchical orientations (members participate with relative equality in congregational life yet submission to a literal interpretation of the Bible is expected); there is a dialectic of emphasis both on intense change and on order (the discourse on intense change is common in both conversion and migration narratives, yet upholding societal norms and strict moral codes is also emphasized); and there is symbolic social and political protest coupled with exemplary participation in the dominant system. Many of these paradoxes are particularly evident in the gender roles at Buen Samaritano.

EL MILAGRO ESTÁ EN CASA

At a service at Buen Samaritano Pastor Sammy reads a Bible passage about a widow who is in debt and is trying to provide for her children; in response to it he states, "Women, you need to believe that the miracle is at home." As he repeats the exhortation, people raise their hands, reaching up and crying, "El milagro está en casa, el milagro está en casa." The congregants' chant calls to mind Carlos Monsiváis's claim that "among the most extraordinary cultural migrations in female identity is the great change that occurs in the space of

historic subjugation (the household)" (quoted in Guttman 2003, 1). For a feminist researcher, gender relations at Buen Samaritano are complicated terrain.
The church has many strong women, most of whom do not see themselves as
victims or pawns of patriarchy. Indeed, many feel that they have power and
a voice. As Patricia Fortuny Loret de Mola writes of women in a Pentecostal
church in Mexico, "converted women feel stronger" (1998, 2). The women at
Buen Samaritano are grateful for the church community. They receive social
support from it, including childcare. Many who are married emphasize how
responsible their men are. And, through testimonies, prayers, praise, speaking, and occasional preaching, their voices are frequently heard. Carol Drogus
suggests that whereas "the real intention of most Pentecostal groups is to promote conservative gender relations and morality," it is important to distinguish
between "what Pentecostalism sets out to do (reinforce male domination) and
what it actually does (equalizing some male-female relations)" (1997, 58, 63).
In the case of Buen Samaritano, there is little evidence that reinforcing male
domination is a particularly important goal.

Numerous studies have explored the "feminization of machismo," as Elizabeth Brusco (1995) describes it, or the male "domestication" that occurs in
some Pentecostal groups, especially in Latin America (see, e.g., Slootweg 1998;
Peterson 2001). At the same time, Matthew Guttman correctly warns scholars against the assumption that machismo is ubiquitous in Latin America,
and he suggests that the term is "one whose etymology derives as much from
international political and social currents as from cultural artifacts peculiar
to Latin America" (2003, 18). Researchers do, however, frequently point to an
improvement in the overall position of the family following male conversion.
According to testimonies at Buen Samaritano, husbands after conversion are
less likely to be unfaithful, use drugs, abuse alcohol, or physically abuse their
wives. Testimonials by both men and women frequently refer to being delivered
from these vices, and much preaching is devoted to these problems. Indeed,
Pastor Manuel notes, "I have seen many women come through this door, and
I ask them why they stay with someone so savage." Divorce or separation is
encouraged if physical abuse is present. The pastor asks, "If you love your wife,
the mother of your children, then why do you hit her? If you value your family
and children then, why don't you spend more time with them? If you want
your children to love you, why are you not a good parent?" As the congregation member Juan states, "If you think you rule in your home, but your rule is
through hitting and punching, then you are corrupting the instinct that God
has given you."

Paradoxically, men are held responsible for the abuse of drugs, physical

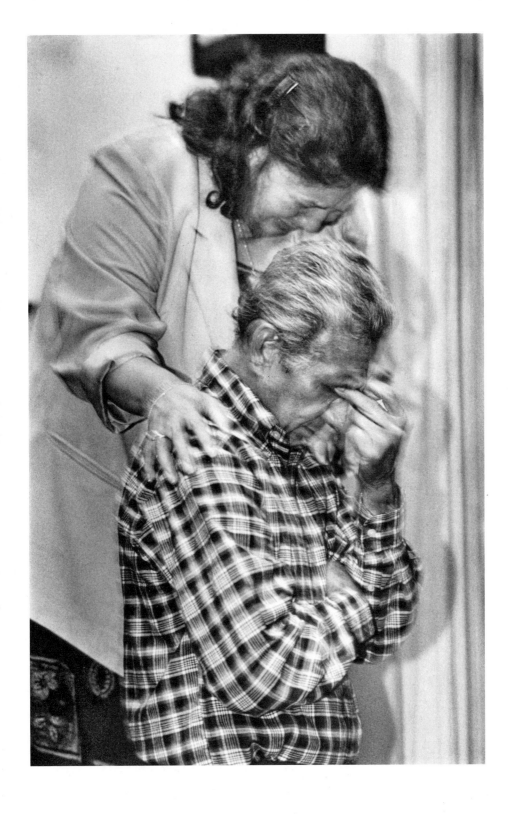

abuse, family neglect, spending, alcohol abuse, and infidelity, yet they are also viewed as victims. Wives may view their men as "easy prey for the devil" (Das Dores Campos Machado 1998, 47). Reconciliation with wife, children, church, and community becomes possible when the husband is "freed" from the devil or other human or spiritual enemies. In cases of domestic abuse, this allows the church to commiserate with the victims and confront the abusers, as the pastor does quite explicitly, while also providing a mechanism for reconciliation, since blame for domestic abuse is shifted away from the individual.

Men at Buen Samaritano are also encouraged to be more involved in the nurturing aspects of child rearing, and indeed one sees men taking care of children, pushing strollers, and taking on such "female" tasks as teaching in the Sunday school and cooking for church fundraisers. At Buen Samaritano gender roles are not dismantled—instead, the church provides opportunities for them to be rearranged. Members seem more willing to cross gender lines, at least in terms of task assignment. In addition, because of financial constraints that require both men and women to work outside the home to survive, the church often acts as a surrogate family—for example, by providing childcare during church events and services. In all these ways a slippage of roles occurs, and gender lines, while affirmed ideologically, become blurred in fact. Official ideology, according to the church website, proclaims that a wife owes submission to both Christ and her husband. It quickly goes on to state, however, that submission doesn't mean that the husband can "lord" it over his wife. Submission is "easy" if each partner is "supporting the mission, goal, and objective of the other." The husband's role as "head" is to support his wife's goals and objectives. The ideological affirmation of a gendered dualism of leadership and submission is quickly softened by redefining the dualism as mutual support and by blurring gender lines in practice.

Buen Samaritano also explicitly challenges the double standard in sexual behavior. As Maria das Dores Campos Machado (1998) has reported of Pentecostal churches in Rio de Janeiro, conversion seems to lead to greater preoccupation with sex education for children. Expectations concerning youth and sexuality are broadcast both publicly during sermons and in Sunday school. While a conservative sexual ethic is promoted, the emphasis is equally on young men and women—both sexes are pressured equally to remain "morally pure." The objectification of women on television is also criticized, and respect for sexual partners emphasized. Juan encourages his fellow church members to "talk about sex to our boys and girls . . . We need to eliminate the taboos about talking about sex and share our perspective with our children."

Buen Samaritano provides some surprises regarding sexual ethics. As Marco, a church elder and a recent migrant from Nicaragua, told me, "Before I moved here and joined the church, I hated homosexuals. Now the pastor has convinced me to love gays. I now have homosexual colleagues and friends." This is surprising because the church is affiliated with a denomination known for its fundamentalism. This adaptability to the context of San Francisco speaks to the fluidity of the church's practices and beliefs. According to the church website, the official teaching is that "sinful practices which are made prominent and condemned in these scriptures include homosexuality, adultery, worldly attitudes (such as hatred, envy, jealousy), corrupt communication (such as gossip, angry outbursts, filthy words), stealing, murder, drunkenness, and witchcraft." Placing homosexuality on the same level as gossip, for example, may give the pastor and congregants room to "love gays" while staying true to church teaching. Pastor Manuel also used the example of the gay experience to encourage people to "come out of the closet" about being Pentecostals; as he states, "If you drive on Castro Street you see large flags with many colors. Why can't we be happy and proud and out about being Pentecostals also?" At gatherings of Bay Area churches, and at larger regional conferences, Buen Samaritano did not seem to be ostracized for the pastor's stance.

Women take active and public leadership roles at Buen Samaritano. They are frequent speakers, leaders of prayer and praise, teachers, and evangelists. They belong to the vestry, the church body responsible for decisions related to membership, money, services, expansion, recruitment, etc. They learn to see themselves as leaders and, most important, as public leaders. Drogus (1997) asserts that Pentecostalism may offer lower-class women access to public space typically denied to them, and this is the case at Buen Samaritano. Although the pastor is male, church flyers refer to the pastor and his wife as *pastores*, and ordained female pastors were introduced at a regional church convention. Hermana Concha's bookmark proclaims that the first prophet was a woman. In fact Buen Samaritano, although proclaiming an ideology of traditional family values, also redefines the relation between gender and public and private space by encouraging the increased participation of men in the domestic sphere and the increased participation by women in the public realm. This description fits Brusco's (1995) analysis of Pentecostalism as a "strategic women's movement." As David Smilde writes, however, "while empirically describing the simultaneous presence of such opposing tendencies (the coexistence of patriarchal and egalitarian gender relations) has become commonplace, theorizing it has remained problematic" (1997, 343). What is going on at Buen Samaritano is even deeper than the "strategic" or the coexistence of patriarchal and egalitarian practices, and it challenges the conceptual constructions that many feminists are fond of interrogating.

Religious is experienced physically and viscerally at Buen Samaritano. People dance, lift their arms, move their hips, sway back and forth, cry, shake, move to the front of the room, and lay their hands on the bodies of others for healing. Luis León writes that in Pentecostal worship both "women and men give their bodies to God" (2004, 233). Women and men are both mediums for what they interpret to be the presence of God in them; God manifests in their bodies. Mind, body, and spirit become one for both women and men. Andre Droogers argues that Pentecostalism's sense of individual wholeness represents a critique of Western culture that is familiar to feminist ears—a critique of conceptual dualism that favors reason over emotion, mind over body: "Pentecostals want to unite what others have divided" (1994, 34). The Pentecostal theologian Samuel Solivan claims that Pentecostalism is not a reversal of modernity but rather a critique, in that it is suspicious of the objective, rational, scientific priesthood of the dominant culture (1996, 141). He writes, "Our theology . . . stands as a sign of hope that not everyone has sold out to the god of reason and the priesthood of atomistic scientism" (148).

A woman finishes praying and tells the congregation that she feels God's presence in the room. She then leads the group in praise, shifting the mood from sad cries for help to happiness and ecstatic joy. A man cries for the mem-

ory of a father who got close to his children only to punish and hit them. Corten describes Pentecostal discourse as a discourse of emotion. What is striking about Buen Samaritano is that emotion seems genderless. While in some denominations women are the carriers and receivers of faith and spirituality, at Buen Samaritano men and women are overtaken by the presence of the Holy Spirit in the same way. Both men and women cry and raise their hands in the air in collective emotional prayer. One might analyze this emotional expression as a movement in which oppressed men and women are both feminized and privatized, escaping to a "haven of emotions in a rationalized and bureaucratized world" in a dominant culture in which they have little voice. The vitality and social engagement of Buen Samaritano, however, leads me to concur with Corten that affective Pentecostalism is "inarticulate protest." Pentecostal piety is a medium of collective identity that is unacceptable in its very operation as a sect. If it is true that there is privatization in the sect, it is a way of providing a frame of circulation for the "inarticulate utterance of praise and for the plausibility of divine healing which is unacceptable elsewhere," allowing "the accumulation of proto-political attitudes and categories" (Corten 1999, 125). Yet here, as Solivan writes, "the disempowered and voiceless exercise their power and share their insights . . . the maid and the dishwasher are given respect and opportunities to exercise their gifts and talents" (1996, 143). At Buen Samaritano a nanny teaches scripture and a hotel maid leads public prayer, thus embodying the highest authority. Although they hold some of society's most undervalued jobs, in the church they assume valued roles and identities.

Pentecostalism as practiced at Buen Samaritano challenges dualisms of mind and body as well as affectivity and reason, assigns valued roles and identities to women and other disempowered peoples, and increases male involvement in the domestic arena.

CHALLENGE TO THEORY

When I presented a version of this essay at the American Academy of Religion meeting in November 2002, members of the audience challenged my conclusion that Pentecostal enclaves like Buen Samaritano do not produce political pressure and larger social transformation. Perhaps rather than judging Buen Samaritano on the basis of social movement or feminist theory, we should use observations about Buen Samaritano to rethink those theories. Burdick offers a similar challenge when he writes that if we insist on privileging social movement organizations we risk missing other fields of social action:

It remains an open question and one that calls for careful analysis and debate, whether, for example, women's participation in Pentecostal churches in Latin America represents on its own a more effective challenge to patriarchy than the effort of Latin American women to organize themselves into groups expressly with this as a goal . . . in analyzing the cultural field of religion in Rio de Janeiro, I have been moved to reflect on the limitations of the Gramscian position that hegemonic and counterhegemonic beliefs coexist simultaneously within the subaltern's contradictory consciousness. The problem here is the assumption that we can always distinguish which is which. (1998, 201)

Rey Chow (1993) relates this concern to feminist discourse by warning feminist theorists against focusing on certain notions of feminism at the expense of discourses that try to resist domination in other, less obvious ways. Feminist speech risks the "double disappearance" of dominance and othering if it remains a prescriptive speech and practice of overt resistance. Pentecostal women are multiple and contradictory, as are Pentecostal men, and they encourage multiple and frequently contradictory "feminist knowings" (Harding 1993, 147).

Heidi Hartmann looks to the family as the primary locus of gender, class, and political struggle: "Changes in people's household behavior can be understood as response to conflicts both within and outside households" and are therefore political, feminist acts (1994, 190). If Pentecostalism yields changed household behavior with regard to gender roles, then it does indeed perform political, feminist acts. (I say "if" because, although we have observed male versus female task assignment at the church, we did not conduct similar studies at the individual household level.) If we define a social movement in Cynthia Cockburn's terms as "the non-powerful, non-wealthy, and non-famous using both civil and confrontational means to transform the social world radically" (1998, 46), then efforts at Buen Samaritano to reshape gender roles qualify it for membership in the worldwide women's movement.

As mentioned earlier, Buen Samaritano also promotes increased civic engagement. Members who are citizens are encouraged to vote, political and social issues are addressed from the pulpit, political developments directly affecting immigrants are followed carefully, and, as noted earlier, the church voted as a bloc for the Democratic candidate in the 2000 presidential election. These civic and political behaviors confirm David Smilde's conclusion that evangelical political culture is no more contradictory, syncretic, or paradoxical than that of other religions; rather, its actors "can lend themselves to both individual variety and collective unity depending on the features of the context and social processes" (2004, 95). In Buen Samaritano's case, increased engagement in civil society may result from encouragement by the pastor to become "exemplary migrants" in both civic and political ways.

It could be that the Pentecostalism of Buen Samaritano is uniquely well suited to the migrant experience. James Beckford claims that "one of the marks of globalization is that it puts all ideologies and belief systems under pressure to clarify their place in relation to the new circumstance" (1998, 13). As Pentecostalism negotiates the tension between universalization (promoting stability) and particularization (helping migrants adapt to new contexts), it takes on this task. Migration is obviously a time of great change, and the theology of Buen Samaritano embraces change. Migrants, possibly more than most people, are aware of "being involved in global flows," and Pentecostalism embodies both the openness of a global network as well as a "stable collection of narrative formulae and well organized structures which provide an anchor for individuals" (Corten and Marshall-Feratani 2001, 3). Buen Samaritano provides a safe place for change for people in flux. It offers support for the preservation of families, a social life and community, and networks for assistance with daily life—finding an apartment, a job, childcare, and so forth.

As the church assists migrants through these changes, the San Francisco context may also help newly arrived immigrants to see their gender construction as just that—a construction like many others. Some may argue that this context makes it possible for Buen Samaritano to adopt more tolerant and progressive attitudes concerning gender roles, childrearing practices, and sexual preference than is generally the case for Pentecostal churches. The relative tolerance of Buen Samaritano cannot be generalized to Pentecostalism or neo-Pentecostalism as a whole, but it does demonstrate the plasticity of its theology and its adaptability to context. As Beckford writes, "Social movements will play an increasingly important role in influencing national and regional 'refraction' of global forces because many of the most perplexing issues will concern identity, solidarity and meaning. Religious movements are also likely to remain important for the intellectual, ideological and emotional resources with which they seek to frame and resolve these issues" (1998, 183).

With issues such as the increased participation of men in the home, public roles for women, challenges to conceptual dualisms, harsh criticisms of U.S. consumerism and hyperindividualism, and help with childcare, we might think we have stumbled onto a feminist utopia. Pentecostalism is not a religion that self-consciously attempts to dismantle patriarchy; instead, it promotes a patriarchy that emphasizes full responsibility for the family. Is it possible that this reinvention and transformation threatens patriarchy? As Drogus writes, Pentecostal churches may "provide women with social spaces which they lack in secular society. Church constitutes a space where women find security, moral support and spiritual and material aid" (1997, 19). Will Pentecostal enclaves translate their actions into political pressure and larger social transformations? Will social movement and feminist theorists rethink their formulations on the basis of this rapidly growing movement?

There are two questions that are helpful in thinking in terms of theory. The first can be framed as follows: What constitutes political pressure and larger social transformation? Some might argue that the transformations noted at Buen Samaritano remain "en la casa," whether literally in the individual household or in the "home" of the church. As such, some might claim that they do not translate into larger political or social transformation. Given that marriage and religion remain society's primary institutions, however, one could argue that Buen Samaritano has indeed encouraged larger social transformation. The Roman Catholic Church down the street from Buen Samaritano may be grounded in liberation theology, but a female priest will not perform mass in the near future. Buen Samaritano, on the other hand, is part of a denomination that ordains women, and several of its Bay Area counterparts boast ordained women pastors. The denomination's website makes its inclusive stance explicit: "Love for others and the recognition of the equal worth of all men in the sight of God (Acts 10:34; 17:26) should compel us to take steps to improve the situation of those who are underprivileged, neglected, hungry, homeless and victimized by prejudice, persecution and oppression (Matthew 22:39; Romans 13:8-10; 1 John 3:17). In all of our dealings, we must be sensitive to human needs (Luke 10:30-37; James 1:17) and guard against racial and economic discrimination. Every person should have freedom to worship and participate in the life of the church regardless of race, color, sex, social class or nationality."[5] The church links large-scale structural transformation with the internal life of the church. People at Buen Samaritano pray "for those rich people who have so much money that they do not know what to do, help them see how they can help and make them give up their jets to take food to those brothers and sisters of El Salvador."

The second question that can be posed for theorists asks, What can be learned from comparative studies? It is beyond the scope of this study to make large claims about the household participation of Pentecostal men. A fruitful study might compare the household participation of Pentecostal men with that of other male cohorts. Other studies might explicitly address the claims concerning the prevalence of domestic violence in Pentecostal households. If the claims are true that Pentecostal men change their behavior and that levels of domestic violence are significantly less for this cohort, then feminist theory must take this into account. As an indicator of decreased patriarchy or, at a minimum, of Brusco's strategic women's movement methods, radically diminished domestic violence reflects significant structural change.

Buen samaritano demonstrates that Pentecostalism possesses neither monolithic political nor gender tendencies and strategies. Rather, Pentecostalism is a "repertoire of multiple, often countervailing schemas that are transposed by actors, schemas that can lend themselves to both individual variety and collective unity depending on the context and social processes" (Smilde 2004, 95). When we look at this particular migrant church in its context, rather than relying solely on doctrinal and theological formulations we find a church that opposes consumerism, works for favorable immigration laws, votes as a bloc for Democratic candidates, encourages female leadership in public church roles, applauds male participation in the domestic realm, challenges dualistic constructions, and explicitly encourages its members to become more gay friendly. The casa may indeed shelter under a large roof.

NOTES

Portions of this chapter were first published as "El milagro esta en casa," *Latin American Perspectives* 32 (January 2005): 57–71.

1. Buen Samaritano is a pseudonym. Throughout this essay all names of individuals and organizations have been changed to protect their anonymity.
2. It is worth noting here that the collaboration among religious institutions seems to challenge new paradigm and rational choice theories. For analyses of the inadequacy of rational choice theories to explain the growth of Pentecostalism and contemporary religious pluralism, see Vásquez and Friedman Marquardt 2003; and Peterson, Vásquez, and Williams 2001.
3. The interviews with members of the Buen Samaritano congregation were conducted by Rosalind Mira with additional fieldwork by Lois Lorentzen. All interviews were conducted in person in San Francisco from 2001–2003. All quotations are from these interviews unless otherwise noted.
4. The former Immigration and Naturalization Service (ins) is now three agencies: Immigration and Customs Enforcement (ice), Citizenship and Immigration Services (cis), and Border Patrol (bp), all of which are under the jurisdiction of the Department of Homeland Security.
5. Website of Buen Samaritano, visited on March 12, 2003.

PART 2

Acculturation

Religious Organizations in San Francisco Chinatown

Sites of Acculturation for Chinese Immigrant Youth

KEVIN M. CHUN

The fields of religious studies, history, sociology, and literature offer rich accounts of the religious lives and histories of new immigrants in the United States. Of particular note is the growing body of religious scholarship on Chinese immigrants, who represent the largest and historically oldest Asian American immigrant community. Still, a conspicuous gap exists between this body of scholarship and the wealth of psychology literature on Chinese and other Asian American immigrant groups. This is surprising given that both literatures address issues of transformation, adaptation, and adjustment during immigration. As religious scholars have noted, many Chinese immigrants rely on their religious belief systems, faith communities, and cultural resources when attempting to relocate "home" and negotiate new individual and collective identities (see, e.g., Matsuoka 1995; Prebish and Tanaka 1998; Yang 1999). Such issues are directly related to the burgeoning psychology literature on immigration and acculturation. At its most basic level, acculturation is a dynamic and multidimensional process of cultural acquisition and maintenance during sustained contact between distinct cultural groups. Psychologists have highlighted a number of important linkages between acculturation and psychological adjustment for Asian Americans and other ethnic communities (see, e.g., Balls Organista, Organista, and Kurasaki 2003; Chun et al. 1998; Kuo 1984; Uba 1994). However, the underlying factors that mediate these linkages have yet to be fully articulated, and fundamental questions concerning the actual nature and characteristics of acculturation still need to be addressed; for example, why would new immigrants feel compelled to alter or preserve their cultural and ethnic practices, beliefs, and identities in a new cultural environment? How do environments and the background characteristics of immigrants influence their acculturation experiences and outcomes? Or, more pointedly, how does acculturation actually unfold in a given cultural setting? Finding answers to these questions has been complicated by the widespread use of self-report paper-and-pencil measures that provide important snapshots of acculturation but often fall short of capturing its multifaceted and fluctuating nature.

One of my primary goals in this essay is to expand the psychological discourse on acculturation by illustrating the significance of religion and religious organizations to cultural acquisition and maintenance for Chinese American immigrants. I also aim to illustrate the utility of ethnographic research methods in uncovering the multidimensional and dynamic properties of acculturation. Finally, I strive to introduce key concepts from the psychological literature on acculturation to a new audience of religious studies scholars with the hope of offering new perspectives on the lives of immigrants in faith communities. This essay is thus organized into four main sections that are intended for a diverse audience of scholars and students from religious studies, sociology, psychology, migration studies, and other allied disciplines. The first section introduces key concepts and tenets from acculturation theory, which serves as the overarching conceptual framework for the essay. New developments in psychology research on acculturation are also presented in this first section. The next section outlines the central role that religious organizations play in the lives of many immigrants and why these organizations should be considered as important sites of acculturation. This second section also discusses how the distinct contexts and settings of religious organizations open new avenues to observe and analyze the multidimensional and dynamic properties of cultural acquisition and maintenance, including specific conditions and circumstances that can elicit variations in acculturation patterns. The third section presents ethnographic study findings on youth acculturation processes at two religious organizations in San Francisco Chinatown. These study findings illustrate how contextual factors at these religious organizations ultimately inform the acculturation experiences of their youth membership. For the purposes of this essay, contextual factors are broadly defined as environmental, social, and organizational influences on acculturation. Youth acculturation was deliberately selected as an investigative topic because the vast majority of acculturation studies rely on adult samples and overlook important developmental issues in cultural acquisition and maintenance. Finally, the conclusion section provides a synopsis of ethnographic findings on youth acculturation and discusses their relevance to our current understanding of acculturation processes and future investigative endeavors.

ACCULTURATION: RECENT DEVELOPMENTS
IN PSYCHOLOGY RESEARCH

The growth in acculturation research has coincided with remarkable demographic shifts in the United States over the past two decades, which especially can be seen in the rapid rise of Asian American and Latino populations. Although many definitions of acculturation exist, psychologists have conceptualized it as a multidimensional and dynamic construct that encompasses continuous and long-term contact with different cultures or sub-cultures; maintenance or alterations to attitudes and behaviors along multiple cultural and ethnic dimensions; a fluid process such that individuals are in constant movement along these cultural and ethnic dimensions; and various strategies and varied outcomes including conflict and adaptation (Marin, Balls Organista, and Chun 2003). Acculturation can be manifested in numerous ways, including in the acquisition of new cultural information, skills, and attitudes, and even in the adoption or transformation of religious values, beliefs, and practices.

Notions of assimilation, ethnic identity formation, and experiences of racial discrimination are often equated with acculturation; however, psychology research has highlighted a number of important distinctions between these constructs. For instance, researchers have noted that assimilation, with its historical references to the "melting pot theory," represents only one type of adaptation strategy or "mode" of acculturation. In this case, assimilation refers to a situation in which immigrants essentially lose their original cultural identification and identify with another cultural group, typically the dominant group in a new country. However, immigrants may also exhibit the acculturation modes of "integration," "separation" and "marginalization." All of these modes, including that of assimilation, are based on the degree to which individuals maintain their original cultural identity and also maintain a relationship with the dominant group in the host society (Berry 1980, 2003, 2006). Integration, for example, represents a bicultural strategy in which new immigrants maintain their cultural heritage and likewise participate in, or establish a relationship with, dominant society. For ethnic minority immigrants who reside in racially stratified societies, this can entail community empowerment through political advocacy and civic activism. Separation, another mode of acculturation, occurs when immigrants do not have any ties to dominant society, but nonetheless exhibit strong cultural identification and participation. This is seen for Chinese immigrants who maintain strong ties to Chinese family or regional organizations in the United States that often supercede their affiliations with dominant society. Marginalization may also be witnessed among immigrants when they essentially do not identify with or participate in dominant society and in their own cultural group. Individuals who exhibit marginalization are typically socially disenfranchised and are lacking economic, political, and psychological ties to dominant society and their own cultural group. Acculturation modes are not exclusively a matter of individual choice, but are also shaped by prevailing sociopolitical attitudes and forces as seen in societies where dominant groups enforce assimilation, marginalization, or separation through physical force and coercion (e.g., the internment of Japanese Americans during the Second World War, the physical removal of American Indians to reservations, and discriminatory immigration legislation targeting Asian and Latino groups). Alternatively, integration can be facilitated through national policy that is typically forged from civil protest.

Psychologists also have noted that although acculturation is a distinct construct it is related to ethnic identity. Specific dimensions of ethnic identity have been empirically identified across different ethnic groups in the United States. These include ethnic self-identification or the ethnic labels that people assign to themselves; a subjective sense of belonging to an ethnic group and attitudes or feelings about group membership; and the level of ethnic identity development or the degree to which one has examined and resolved identity issues (including conflicts and crises in identity) leading to an "achieved ethnic identity" (Phinney 1990). These dimensions covary in different ways with acculturation by reflecting their close links with cultural acquisition and maintenance. For instance, in regard to self-identification research shows that first-generation immigrants to America often use a singular ethnic or national label to describe themselves (e.g., Chinese or Korean) while subsequent generations are more likely to use compound or bicultural labels (e.g., Chinese American or Korean American) (Phinney 2003). However, acculturation does not necessarily attenuate ethnic identification or affiliation as might be expected. Fourth- or fifth-generation ethnic minorities might report high levels of acculturation on a number of indices (e.g., socialization to American culture or high English proficiency) yet still report strong affiliations with their ethnic groups. Researchers have commented that contextual factors such as the presence of racism and discrimination often compel ethnic minorities to retain strong identification with their culture of origin (Phinney 2003). This experience is typically not witnessed for European Americans because they are more likely to relinquish their original ethnic identities across generations as a function of gaining dominant group membership.

Finally, psychologists have found that experiences of discrimination and prejudice are also distinct from acculturation. In this case, researchers have found that perceived discrimination has an independent effect on levels of depression for new immigrants (Finch, Kolody, and Vega 2000). This finding suggests that new immigrants must not only deal with adaptation pressures during acculturation but also with the added and distinct stressor of racial discrimination. The importance of developing culturally appropriate coping resources for new immigrants like those found in many religious organizations becomes all the more apparent in such circumstances.

Much acculturation research has focused on "acculturation stress" or stress associated with adaptation pressures and adjustment problems in a new cultural setting. Acculturation stress arises when adaptation demands exceed individuals' abilities and resources to meet their goals and expectations for resettlement in a new cultural environment. Adaptation demands are manifested in numerous ways and center on pressures to learn new cultural skills, behaviors, beliefs, and attitudes such as demands to learn or acquire a new language, interpersonal skills, and normative social and political beliefs in a new country. Acculturation stress is likely to occur when the new cultural behaviors, beliefs, and attitudes are incongruent with those from one's culture of origin—a situation popularly known as a "culture conflict." Adaptation demands can also be manifested in the transformation, weakening, loss, or maintenance of cultural behaviors, beliefs, and attitudes. In the context of religion, immigrants may find it difficult to maintain their religious practices and identities when confronted by cultural and institutional barriers and when lacking social and financial support. Acculturation stress can especially result from such circumstances if an immigrant's faith traditions and religion lie at the core of his or her personal and collective identities.

Researchers typically measure acculturation stress using self-report psychological measures of anxiety and depressive symptoms. Such symptoms are then analyzed in relation to a number of background variables (e.g., English-language proficiency, years spent in the host society, or generational status) that serve as indirect or proxy measures of acculturation levels. Research with Asian American immigrants indicates that low levels of acculturation (e.g., having poor English proficiency, being a new or first-generation immigrant, or having little knowledge of the United States prior to migration) in conjunction with certain personal characteristics (e.g., being older in age, having less formal education, or lacking social and financial support) are associated with higher levels of acculturation stress (Chun 2006). Researchers have also noted that families can experience acculturation stress in multiple ways. Parent-child or intergenerational conflicts and marital problems associated with differences in acculturation levels between family members have been particularly well documented (Chun and Akutsu 2003). Recently, researchers have called for greater attention to contextual or environmental factors that can potentially affect one's risk for experiencing acculturation stress (Chun, Balls Organista, and Marin 2003). Studying the relationship between acculturation stress and the characteristics of communities and cultural settings where immigrants resettle is one example in which more investigation is needed. Certain environmental characteristics (e.g., ethnic enclaves or pluralistic and multicultural neighborhoods) potentially buffer or minimize acculturation stress whereas others (e.g., segregated and ethnically homogenous neighborhoods) may exacerbate it (Sue 2003). To date, this notion of "environmental fit" and its relationship to experiences of acculturation stress have not been fully addressed for immigrants and their religious communities.

Religious organizations offer rich opportunities to study the multidimensionality and process of acculturation. In regard to multidimensionality, acculturation can transpire along numerous indices at these organizations as witnessed by the acquisition or maintenance of religious beliefs and practices, organizational and social roles, interpersonal relations, and daily activities and rituals. Considering these multiple dimensions allows for a more comprehensive portrait of acculturation than that offered by any one single dimension or acculturation index. A multidimensional evaluation also speaks to the fact that immigrants in faith communities often face multiple adaptation demands such as learning a new language, communication rules, and cultural practices and, in some cases, they face pressures to relinquish or alter their religious practices and beliefs.

Treating religious practices and beliefs as potentially important acculturation indices for investigation would represent an important new development in acculturation research. The lack of study data on these indices is somewhat perplexing given their immense importance to those immigrants who routinely reference their faiths to construct meaning in their lives when faced with the challenges and uncertainties that come with living in an unfamiliar land. For refugees, religion can inform their experiences of and responses to traumatic episodes and upheavals in their lives. Personal accounts from Southeast Asian refugees suggest that Buddhist beliefs of fate or karma lessen the negative effects of trauma and acculturative stress on mental health (Rumbaut 1985). A relatively modest and somewhat mixed set of findings on religion and mental health likewise points to the beneficial effects of religion on psychological well-being. There is some evidence that "religiosity" or one's attitude about the importance or salience of religious experience in one's life is associated with longevity, abstinence from drugs, and lower risk for depression (Gartner 1996). Still, the significance of these findings to ethnic minority faith communities and the effects of acculturation on religious beliefs and practices have not received their due attention in the psychology literature. Compared to other widely studied acculturation indices (e.g., food, clothing, and music preferences or ethnic composition of social networks), religious beliefs and practices are plausibly more resilient to change because they are salient aspects of one's core identity and may be construed as essential coping resources that necessitate their maintenance. Thus, potential variations in rates of acculturation can be explored when changes to religious beliefs and practices are compared with changes that occur along other acculturation indices. Often, religious beliefs and practices are codified and clearly outlined by religious organizations, thus making it possible to identify a "baseline" or normative set of beliefs and practices from which acculturation effects can be assessed.

Religious sites also present an opportunity to investigate the directionality of acculturation. Some researchers still examine acculturation along a unidimensional continuum, thus suggesting that movement toward a new culture (i.e., acquisition of new cultural behaviors and beliefs) invariably leads to movement away from one's culture of origin (i.e., loss of culture of origin behaviors and beliefs). This study approach, however, overlooks other possible adaptation outcomes as previously noted. Many immigrants possess bicultural competencies that allow them to maintain meaningful relationships with their new cultural environments and their countries of origin. Such competencies can be facilitated by religious sites that actively promote ties to an immigrant's culture of origin (e.g., through the incorporation of cultural symbols and rituals) while supporting their integration to a new society (e.g., through language instruction and employment assistance). The directionality of acculturation can thus be informed by the religious practices, belief systems, and characteristics of programs and services at religious sites.

Fundamental questions concerning acculturation can also be explored at religious sites: How does adaptation and adjustment occur among their immigrant members? What are the circumstances and situational contingencies that underlie these processes? Why do certain patterns of acculturation emerge at these sites? These questions are pertinent to identifying underlying factors that drive acculturation processes. It would also be valuable to know how new immigrants cope with acculturation stress in the context of their religious communities. For instance, certain religious teachings might help some new immigrants cognitively reframe their experience of acculturation stress, or religious teachings might be transformed or tailored to effectively address different acculturation challenges.

Religious sites also present an opportunity to understand the effects of contextual or social and environmental factors on acculturation. Religious organizations provide a specific context for human interaction that is comprised of unique social and cultural demands, expectations, and norms, as well as official roles and responsibilities that can generate diverse acculturation patterns. For instance, a layperson and a church leader from the same generational cohort might have altogether different acculturation experiences at their religious organization—experiences that stem from their distinct organizational roles, social status, and duties. The histories of religious organizations, internal politics, and even the way in which organizations are structured also lay the groundwork for distinct acculturation patterns. Given the dynamic nature of acculturation, these contextual factors can be theoretically modified or altered over time by organization members, thus further adding to variations in acculturation patterns at these sites.

The ethnographic findings described in the following sections were gathered by the Chinese research team (headed by the author of this essay) for the University of San Francisco (USF) Religion and Immigration Project. This project investigated the role of religious organizations in the civic participation and incorporation of new immigrants in the San Francisco Bay Area. The Chinese research team specifically selected acculturation theory to study the experiences of Chinese youth at two religious organizations in San Francisco Chinatown with the aim of exploring and identifying the distinct contexts and characteristics of youth acculturation at both sites. As previously noted, this included identifying contextual factors, which were broadly defined as environmental, social, and organizational influences on acculturation. The two religious organizations in this study were selected from a larger pool of potential study sites based on their historical and religious ties to the Chinese immigrant community in San Francisco and on recommendations from local Chinese American community leaders and residents. For purposes of confidentiality, these two religious organizations are hereafter referred to as the "Presbyterian Mission" and the "Buddhist Temple." Data were gathered using participant-observation methods during weekly field site visits lasting approximately two to three hours over a one-year period. Both the Presbyterian Mission and the Buddhist Temple offered a multitude of programs and services that presented unique opportunities for comparative analyses of acculturation experiences. An important historical feature of these programs and services is their shared goal of mentoring and educating Chinese youth. With this in mind, two specific youth programs were selected for study—the Presbyterian Mission's after-school program (hereafter referred to as the Presbyterian Mission Program) and the Buddhist Temple's Saturday school program (hereafter referred to as the Buddhist Temple Program). Both programs offered academic tutorials, didactic instruction, social activities and, to varying degrees, religious instruction for Chinese American youth. Moreover, the goals and contents of both youth programs were intimately tied to the missions and histories of their larger organizations as outlined in this essay. The Presbyterian Mission Program mainly targeted low-income, first-generation Chinese immigrant youth ranging from seven to thirteen years of age residing in San Francisco Chinatown and in outlying city districts mostly populated by Chinese Americans. The majority of Presbyterian Mission Program youth claimed family origins in Hong Kong and in Guangdong Province in southern China. The Buddhist Temple Program youth ranged from five to sixteen years of age and primarily were second-generation Chinese Americans who belonged to families of middle to upper-middle socioeconomic status. The preponderance of Buddhist Temple Program youth resided outside of San Francisco Chinatown and in outlying Bay Area suburbs, and they claimed family origins in Taiwan, mainland China, and to a lesser extent Hong Kong.

The contextual factors identified as key influences on observed acculturation processes at the Presbyterian Mission, Buddhist Temple, and in their respective

youth programs are as follows: their institutional histories and missions; the characteristics of their leadership and staffing; and the contents and emphases of their youth programs and activities. All of these key contextual factors were interrelated and responsive to the unique characteristics of their youth membership. The following sections describe these contextual factors in detail and outline their significance to the acculturation goals and youth acculturation experiences at each study site.

SIGNIFICANCE OF INSTITUTIONAL HISTORIES, MISSIONS, AND STAFF TO ACCULTURATION GOALS AT STUDY SITES

The Presbyterian Mission: Evolution from Foreign Mission to "Home" Institution

The Presbyterian Mission is centrally located in Chinatown near a major commercial thoroughfare, where it has served new Chinese immigrants for over 130 years. The genesis of the Presbyterian Mission can be traced back to the late nineteenth century when American Presbyterian church women were organizing foreign missions across the globe (Wilson 1974). In 1873, Presbyterian women in San Francisco formed the Presbyterian Woman's Occidental Board of Foreign Missions, which at the time was distinguished as the only Presbyterian foreign mission within the confines of the United States. Originally, this board of Presbyterian women wanted to establish an orphanage in Shanghai, China, but geopolitical barriers discouraged them from pursuing this project. They subsequently redirected their attention to the Chinese population in San Francisco Chinatown where they saw the need to combat "yellow slavery," or the forced prostitution and indentured servitude of Chinese immigrant girls. The Presbyterian Mission is currently named after its second superintendent, a missionary woman of Scottish descent who was born in New Zealand. She was originally hired as a sewing teacher at the Presbyterian Mission but eventually became an admired organizational leader and caregiver to the mission youth throughout her forty years of service. The mission statement of the Presbyterian Mission as posted on their official website reads as follows: "Our mission is to empower people to fully participate in and contribute positively toward a healthy society. We create a safe and nurturing environment by providing counseling, peer group support, and crisis intervention, and we enable active involvement in the community through leadership development, education, and advocacy."

Social services and advocacy work at the Presbyterian Mission are organized into Christian Social Services and Youth Programs branches. Over the course of its long history, the Presbyterian Mission has established multiple civic and religious ties to the city and county government of San Francisco and the surrounding Bay Area communities. The Presbyterian Mission also possesses historical ties to China through its former residents and, more recently, through some of its staff and members who maintain informal transnational family and social links to Hong Kong.

According to one historical account, the Presbyterian Mission originally set out to "build up a haven for the stranded and friendless among the pathetic waifs, bereft of all except evil ties in this strange new land" (Wilson 1974, 10). This early institutional goal was formulated during a time of global Protestant missionary projects to proselytize and Westernize the "unassimilable Oriental" and thereby test the limits of the "melting pot theory" (Yu 2001). This complex racial zeitgeist in the late nineteenth century—which cast Chinese Americans as "inherently foreign and exotic Orientals" (Lee 1999)—provides some insight into the Presbyterian Mission's founding status as the only foreign mission in the United States, and it suggests that the mission had an initial acculturation goal of assimilation for its youth members. This soon changed, however, as sociopolitical, cultural, and economic forces (e.g., the cessation of "yellow slavery" in 1930, the revocation of the Chinese Exclusion Act in 1943, and the passage of the Immigration Act of 1965) gradually transformed San Francisco Chinatown (Chen 2000; Zhao 2002) and the Presbyterian Mission itself. In particular, the Presbyterian Mission began to develop new services for a growing number of Chinese American families in Chinatown during the 1940s, which led to the creation of its youth program in 1945 to train local Chinese youth to become leaders in the Chinese American community. Over the years, this youth program has generated an impressive corps of Chinese American alumni who have maintained long-lasting ties with the Presbyterian Mission through capital contributions, volunteer activities, and by filling its staff positions. Perhaps most significantly, returning alumni have transformed the leadership structure of this organization. The executive director and her predecessor, both of whom are alumni of this youth program, were the first and second Chinese Americans, respectively, to hold the leadership post at the mission. Their Chinese American cultural heritage, deep family roots in San Francisco Chinatown, extensive personal ties to the mission, and progressive political views opened a new chapter in the organization's history. Specifically, their presence spawned a new Asian American and emergent pan-ethnic minority consciousness in the organization that promotes integration and multicultural competencies. The executive director's strategic vision of fostering inter-ethnic collaboration with different Asian groups and other ethnic minority communities attests to this fact. Additionally, many of its current staff members are first-generation Asian immigrants who share a firsthand understanding of the need for social and political advocacy across all marginalized immigrant groups. For instance, the former director of the mission's Christian Social Services branch is a first-generation Chinese immigrant who has an impressive record of social justice activities and immigrant rights advocacy in San Francisco and in his native home of Hong Kong. These significant changes to the leadership and staff have radically shifted the Presbyterian Mission's orientation to San Francisco Chinatown and its people—the once foreign and exotic Oriental space of San Francisco Chinatown is now the familiar and kindred, an embodiment of "home" and family. Racial and cultural boundaries that once differentiated the Presbyterian Mission from the Chinatown community have largely dissipated. The Presbyterian Mission leadership and staff have become mirror images of the Chinatown community that it serves, both ethnically and culturally, through its own lengthy macro-level or organizational acculturation process. This process continues as intergenerational ties between local Chinese American families and the Presbyterian Mission expand. Many of the Presbyterian Mission's parents and their offspring walk the same halls as their forebears, reminding them of a shared family and community history and place. This point was echoed by the leadership and many of the staff and alumni who fondly recalled how they and other family members "grew up" at the Presbyterian Mission, which they considered their "second home." Such intergenerational ties to the Presbyterian Mission have laid the groundwork for a unique and dynamic acculturation setting that sustains the acculturation mode of integration. As alumni and new immigrant clients come together, cultural information and skills are exchanged and enacted across a broad continuum of cultural acquisition and maintenance. On one level, this process renews and regenerates the Presbyterian Mission's historical narrative of assisting new Chinese immigrants. On another level, this process produces a new collective and multifaceted organizational identity that incorporates multiple cultural, national, linguistic, religious, and class identities from an increasingly diverse Asian American community. This is highlighted by the growth of new immigrant groups in San Francisco Chinatown (e.g., refugees from Southeast Asia and immigrants from across mainland China) who are reshaping and renewing the character of the Presbyterian Mission as clients, members, and staff. This dynamic process and its promotion of integration are enacted and sustained in its youth programs.

*The Buddhist Temple: Propagating the Buddha
Dharma from East to West*

The Buddhist Temple is located in a former large-scale restaurant along a main historical commercial and residential corridor of Chinatown that now mostly serves a tourist clientele. Unlike the Presbyterian Mission, the Buddhist Temple claims its origins in mainland China. Its founder and venerable master was born in northern China in 1918 and is recognized as the forty-fifth Patriarch from Shakyamuni Buddha and the ninth Patriarch of the Wei Yang Sect. He founded the San Francisco Buddhist Temple in 1970 "as a place of practice of orthodox Dharma." His journey to San Francisco was preceded by years of austere Buddhist training and cultivation at a number of renowned sacred sites and monasteries throughout China from the late 1930s to the early 1960s. In 1959 the venerable master laid the organizational groundwork for his current worldwide Buddhist association; in 1962 he arrived in San Francisco and established a Buddhist lecture hall and then, eight years later, the Buddhist Temple and monastery. Although the Buddhist Temple congregants are predominantly first-generation elderly Chinese American women, the organization still actively maintains a Saturday Chinese school and academic tutorial program for Chinese youth. The Buddhist Temple is part of a worldwide network of monasteries, schools, and Buddhist book publication and distribution centers that were founded by the venerable master across Asia, the United States, and Canada. The acknowledged hub of this worldwide association is a large campus in northern California that houses a number of religious, instructional, monastic, and administrative buildings. As the mission of this worldwide Buddhist association, including that of the Buddhist Temple, officially states: "Taking the Dharma Realm as its scope, the Association aims to disseminate the genuine teachings of the Buddha throughout the world. The Association is dedicated to translating the Buddhist canon, propagating the Orthodox Dharma, promoting ethical education, and bringing benefit and happiness to all beings. Its hope is that individuals, families, the society, the nation and the entire world will, under the transforming influence of the Buddha dharma, gradually reach the state of ultimate truth and goodness" (Buddhist Text Translation Society 1995a, 25).

Similar to the Presbyterian Mission, the Buddhist Temple was born from a religious vision that was global in scope. However, the vision for the Buddhist Temple is unique not only in its Buddhist themes but also in its messenger and in its general orientation to America and to San Francisco Chinatown in particular. These factors, in addition to the temple's relative brief presence in

San Francisco Chinatown, have contributed to varied acculturation goals that include features of separation, integration, and "reverse" assimilation.

An official memorial biography provides extensive details of the life history and events of the venerable master and his worldwide Buddhist organization (Buddhist Text Translation Society 1995a). According to this text, the genesis of this worldwide Buddhist organization can be traced back to 1936 when its founder was a nineteen year-old novice monk who was mourning the passing of his mother. At that time, he initiated the Chinese filial practice of three years of mourning in an austere Buddhist fashion in a graveside hut. The story follows that the Sixth Patriarch in China of the Chan (Zen) Lineage walked into his hut one day and spoke with him at length. The patriarch told the venerable master the following: "In the future you will go to the West, where you will meet limitless and boundless numbers of people. The living beings you teach and transform will be as countless as the sands of the Ganges River. That will mark the beginning of the Buddha dharma in the West" (3). When the patriarch left the hut, the venerable master realized that the patriarch had entered Nirvana in AD 713. The venerable master gradually received widespread recognition for his filial piety, "pure" Buddhist lifestyle, and compassionate acts of healing. His reputation as an extraordinary monk was enhanced by a number of auspicious signs and miracles beginning at birth that were "too numerous to count." After a lengthy religious sojourn through China, the venerable master eventually "saw that conditions were ripe in the West." He thus journeyed to San Francisco and established the Buddhist Temple in 1970. The temple has been at its current location in the heart of San Francisco Chinatown since 1986. The Buddhist Temple and its larger worldwide Buddhist association represent the culmination of the venerable master's life work, which encapsulated the following goals: bringing the true and proper teachings of the Buddha to the West and establishing a proper monastic community of fully ordained monks and nuns (Sangha); organizing and supporting the translation of the entire Buddhist canon into English and other Western languages; and promoting wholesome education through the establishment of schools and universities. With the explicit purpose of addressing this latter goal, the venerable master established the Buddhist Temple's Saturday school program in 1976.

This story of the venerable master and his religious vision and mission in America set specific contexts for acculturation at the Buddhist Temple along the following lines: first, a new orthodox Buddhist tradition and identity was to be established and maintained around the world; second, cultural and religious contact and exchange and the propagation of the dharma was to move along an "East to West" axis. The significance and importance of these two organizational goals are reinforced by the legendary character and stature of the venerable master. His reported preternatural Buddhist cultivation skills (e.g., he could recite and teach complicated sutras from memory) and supernatural powers (e.g., he had the power to stop typhoons and earthquakes and to discover water in arid lands) suggest that as a living incarnation of Buddha his vision and message have the imprimatur of heaven. Thus one might argue that the Buddhist Temple's goals and expectations for cultural and religious contact and exchange—in this case, the maintenance of an orthodox Chinese-Buddhist identity across the globe—would be more resilient to change and alteration because of its ascribed religious and spiritual authority.

The resiliency of the goals and expectations of the venerable master's vision was witnessed in the Buddhist Temple's official religious and cultural teachings and practices. This was best illustrated by the nuns, monks, and to some extent the laity who adhered to the venerable master's prescriptions for daily Buddhist practices that he formulated in China. This included observing a strict dietary regimen of one vegetarian meal a day, wearing specified holy garments, sleeping upright for a restricted time period, and following specific gender role prescriptions. In this latter case, men and women in the Buddhist Temple were divided into different sections during worship, and nuns and monks had limited supervised contact with members of the opposite sex. Temple followers also upheld certain Confucian cultural values and practices during formal events and in their daily interactions. Filial piety and respect for elders were promoted throughout the Buddhist Temple's official texts and during its worship services as an essential characteristic of their Buddhist tradition. Thus, the Buddhist Temple's formal teachings, practices, and activities emphasized the maintenance of the venerable master's original religious and cultural prescriptions in America. According to some of the nuns, maintaining their religious and cultural traditions required considerable effort in the crowded urban setting of San Francisco Chinatown. They explained that the speed and "temptations" of American culture presented considerable challenges to their orthodox Buddhist identity and lifestyle. The very fact that they did not alter their Buddhist practices and lifestyle under these reportedly stressful conditions spoke to the resiliency of the venerable master's religious vision across the Pacific Ocean as he had originally intended.

The Buddhist Temple's religious and cultural practices, organizational identity and character, and stance toward its Chinatown environs pointed to an acculturation mode of separation. Dominant group discourse often mischaracterizes this mode of acculturation as a form of ethnic isolationism, civic disengagement, or hostility toward a "host society" whenever it is witnessed in ethnic minority immigrant communities. However, a careful reading of the venerable master's vision and teachings indicated that instances of separation at the Buddhist Temple are more accurately framed as cultural and religious preservation in what is perceived to be a Western religious "frontier" by the temple founder and his followers. In this case, the temple's core identity was based on strict observance of orthodox Buddhist practices and principles; thus, constructing new and alternative religious identities would potentially undermine the temple's existence and divinely inspired mandate. As the venerable master once stated, "Precepts are the pulse of the Buddha dharma. Without precepts, the Buddha dharma dies" (Buddhist Text Translation Society 1995a, 94). Additionally, the directionality of the vision—movement from "East to West"—situates religious and cultural authority in the "East" (China) while delineating the "West" (the United States) as an inchoate religious and cultural frontier. In his memorial biography, the venerable master characterized America as a spiritually underdeveloped territory where Buddhist tenets and practices are frequently confused with folklore and superstition (Buddhist Text Translation Society 1995b). A nun highlighted this point by noting that congregants often focus on improper notions of evil spirits and ancestor worship rather than concentrating their efforts on Buddhist cultivation. Many visitors to the main temple in northern California also appeared to be unaware of "proper" Buddhist teachings and practices. At this main temple site, visitor's brochures displayed in the foyer of the main prayer hall provided instruction, tailored for an American audience, on sanctioned areas for lighting incense and respectful methods of worship. Such instances again framed the "East" as religious and cultural center, and the "West" as distal religious and cultural terrain. Thus, the acculturation mode of separation—which primarily focuses on cultural maintenance rather than on cultural acquisition—reflects this propagation of the Buddha dharma.

Features of separation were also partly observed in the temple's orientation to San Francisco Chinatown. As previously noted, some nuns did not necessarily view San Francisco Chinatown as their home, especially in light of the many challenges that it presented to their Buddhist cultivation. The temple's nuns and monks were given rotating assignments to other sites in their global association, thereby further complicating their ability to form extensive personal ties to the Chinatown community. Additionally, the Buddhist Temple lacked broad intergenerational links with its local congregants due to its relatively brief presence in San Francisco Chinatown. Buddhist teachings on attachment provide additional insights to the temple's orientation to San Francisco Chinatown. The Buddhist tenet of nonattachment posits that spiritual enlightenment and well-being are independent of life conditions and circumstances (Smith 1991). This coincides with the temple's stance that its Buddhist tradition, practices, and mission transcend time and space, including attachments to place. In fact, its Buddhist teachings suggest that attachments, including attachment to place, can actually interfere with cultivation, the propagation of the dharma, and spiritual growth. Separation can thus be viewed as an embodiment of this Buddhist principle of nonattachment, which is practiced on an organizational level at the temple.

Still, aspects of integration were likewise seen at the Buddhist Temple and its larger association when other acculturation domains were considered. This was most evident in the larger association's impressive record of civic and political participation on citywide, statewide, and national levels. Most of this work involved the application or promotion of Buddhist teachings for the betterment of different religious, cultural, and ethnic communities. For his religious, civic, and philanthropic work the venerable master received widespread official recognition from a number of government officials including former San Francisco Mayor Frank Jordan, former Governor Pete Wilson, and former President George H. W. Bush (Buddhist Text Translation Society 1995a). Additionally, the temple and its larger association offered a wide array of educational assistance and instruction programs to their youth members that integrated their American academic curriculum with the Buddhist religious canon. According to the temple nuns and their staff, a primary aim of these educational services was to place their students in prestigious American universities so that they could actively participate in contemporary American society.

Integration at the Buddhist Temple and at its larger association was likewise exhibited by a movement toward other religious traditions and Buddhist sects in the form of interfaith collaboration and dialogue. For instance, the larger Buddhist association maintains a world religions organization that is located in the San Francisco Bay Area. The venerable master established this site to "study the truths of religion in harmony with other religious groups, without rejecting or opposing any religion . . . and to propagate the spirit of [the main temple] with expansive open-mindedness" (Buddhist Text Translation Society 1995a, 29). The venerable master appointed his friend, a Catholic cardinal from Taiwan, as the first director of this organization. The venerable master once invited the same cardinal to be "a Buddhist among the Catholics" while he promised to be a "Catholic among the Buddhists." In a similar spirit, the venerable master once encouraged his followers to join the "younger" Catholic Church if they felt that Buddhism was "too old-fashioned" (Buddhist Text Translation Society 1995b, 142). These instances of interfaith dialogue and collaboration presented a paradox when juxtaposed with concurrent features of separation in the temple. Adding to the complexity of the temple's acculturation goals were instances of "reverse" assimilation in which European American congregants adopted a Chinese Buddhist religious and cultural identity. Some of the master's early disciples in the 1960s were young European Americans who were interested in meditation and sutra lectures. Many adopted the temple's orthodox Chinese Mahayana Buddhist tradition and a few entered monastic life largely relinquishing their European American cultural identities. Such instances problematize the popular belief that over time ethnic minorities invariably move toward the dominant group. These examples of reverse assimilation may stem from the temple's resilient acculturation goals and expectations as previously noted. Also, reverse assimilation might simply be one facet of highly variable and evolving acculturation patterns at the Buddhist Temple and in its larger organization that mirror the multidimensional and dynamic properties of acculturation. In this context, different modes and rates of acculturation might be witnessed across different areas of the temple's organizational identity and activities. Likewise, the apparent variability in the temple's acculturation goals may simply represent different snapshots of an ongoing, dynamic, and multilayered process of cultural change and maintenance. As the temple maintains its core religious and cultural beliefs, a simultaneous and gradual shift in its orientation to American society and culture may be occurring. This is highlighted by the creation of its sister world religions organization (established twenty-four years after the temple's founding), which was specifically designed to provide a contemporary "American" setting for interfaith dialogue with ethnically diverse English-speaking locals in mind. Given the sustained contact with other religious and cultural traditions this interfaith site may perhaps serve as an important catalyst for transformation in the larger Buddhist association and in the San Francisco Buddhist Temple. This transformative process is speculative, however, in light of the Buddhist Temple's resilient orthodox Buddhist identity and the enduring presence of the venerable master and his religious mission in the collective memory of his followers. Furthermore, shifts in acculturation goals and related transformations to organizational identity typically transpire over protracted periods of time, as demonstrated by the over one-hundred-year transformation process at the Presbyterian Mission. Thus it is difficult to fully anticipate the evolution of the temple and its worldwide organizational network.

In summary, the different acculturation modes and goals that were observed at the Presbyterian Mission and at the Buddhist Temple were forged from their unique and rich organizational histories and missions and from the distinct characteristics of their leadership and staff. Their organizational histories and missions encompass broad religious and cultural themes and diverse immigrant narratives that framed and contextualized the acculturation experiences of their members and congregants. In the next section I focus on how the histories and missions of these two religious organizations are manifested in the emphases and contents of their youth programs, which in turn directly shape the acculturation experiences of their youth members.

EMPHASES AND CONTENTS OF YOUTH PROGRAMS: SETTING THE STAGE FOR VARIED ACCULTURATION EXPERIENCES

The Presbyterian Mission Program: "For Many of These Kids, It's the First Time That They've Experienced or Come into Contact with These Types of Things."

The Presbyterian Mission Program was structured as a weekday after-school mentoring, tutorial, and recreational program that operated between the hours of 3:00 PM to 5:30 PM. It was staffed by six Chinese American youth mentors (three females and three males), ranging from eighteen to twenty-one years of age, who were individually responsible for four different groups divided by grade levels two through eight. According to the program director, a twenty-six-year-old Chinese American woman, the staff title of "mentor" was selected over "tutor" because their primary role was serving as "big brothers and big sisters" to the youth. The typical weekday session began with group and one-on-one academic tutoring followed by supervised recreational games and activities. The special social and recreational activities that were scheduled on Fridays included arts and crafts, group meal and snack preparations, movie presentations, and group games. The program also had internal clubs and committees for its youth members (e.g., festivities committee, yearbook committee, and chess club) and field trips and holiday celebrations throughout the academic school year. Additionally, the Presbyterian Mission Program offered an anger management group to help its youth members manage their anger, express their feelings in constructive ways, and strengthen their social skills. The leader of this group, a middle-aged Chinese Vietnamese woman, was a full-time case manager in the Christian Social Service branch of the Presbyterian Mission.

Ethnographic observations and solicited feedback from select youth members, their parents, and program staff indicated that the Presbyterian Mission Program effectively promoted integration and fostered bicultural competencies among its immigrant Chinese American youth by affirming their ethnic and cultural heritage, facilitating their acquisition of new cultural knowledge and skills, providing academic support that contributed to their educational advancement and integration in their schools, and establishing a culturally appropriate setting that minimized acculturation stress.

The Presbyterian Mission Program affirmed its youth members' ethnic and cultural heritage by programming activities and events that incorporated their cultural practices and traditions and their preferred dialect of Cantonese. For instance, youth members celebrated the Chinese New Year with Chinese food and candies, and they participated in games that incorporated cultural themes and symbols (e.g., a hidden picture game called "Find the Chinese Zodiac"). The youth members were also allowed to freely communicate in both Cantonese and English with their mentors, volunteers, and peers throughout the daily activities and during special events. This was particularly important to the younger program members who mainly came from monolingual Cantonese households and preferred to speak Cantonese with their program peers and mentors. Finally, youth members from all grade levels routinely brought Chinese food items for snacks and light meals, which they ate during the program's tutoring and study sessions. It was not uncommon to see the youth members focusing on their homework assignments while eating dried cuttlefish, Chinese fruit jelly candies, steamed rice tamales, and pork buns, and such activity was not questioned by their peers or by the staff.

The Presbyterian Mission Program's activities and events also presented its youth members with multiple opportunities to acquire new cultural knowledge and skills that facilitate integration. Following a special field trip to the San Francisco Chinatown branch of the San Francisco Public Library, a group of second and third graders spoke enthusiastically about learning how to borrow materials and how to utilize library facilities for the first time. Youth members also learned popular children's games for the first time (e.g., bingo, hot potato, and musical chairs) along with new trends in popular music (e.g., hip hop and rap music) from their older peers and youth mentors during special recreational sessions. The Presbyterian Mission Program also promoted cultural acquisition and learning during its annual holiday celebrations. For the program's annual Easter celebration, older youths volunteered for the festivities committee, which provided opportunities to learn valuable leadership and organizational skills while planning the special holiday activities and meal. Youth members were also encouraged to support their peers' acquisition of new cultural knowledge and skills. For instance, a fifth-grade youth offered instructions to his third-grade peers for an Easter egg hunt while a sixth grader demonstrated egg-dying procedures using a readymade color set to a group of second graders. The younger children in both of these instances initially appeared confused and hesitant because they were unfamiliar with the American Easter holiday traditions, but they soon became highly engaged with these new opportunities for cultural acquisition primarily because they were being led by another youth member. Cultural acquisition and learning were also observed during a group discussion on the significance of Easter. The program director initiated this discussion by posing a question to the youth, "Does anyone know why bunnies are a part of Easter?" In response, one of the six-year-olds replied, "Because it's the Year of the Bunny?" The director, youth mentors, and the other students in the group did not appear surprised or bewildered by this boy's response because they implicitly understood that he was referring to the Chinese zodiac calendar, which marks different years with different representations of animals. As a result, this boy did not encounter ridicule or questions from the group. Instead, the students listened attentively as the program director gently corrected him and explained that rabbits symbolized the rebirth of Christ. This Easter celebration came to a close with a communal meal of chow mein and deep-fried miniature chicken legs from a neighborhood Chinese deli along with potato chips and red fruitpunch.

Additional observations of cultural acquisition were seen during the Presbyterian Mission Program's annual Christmas party. A first-generation third-grade boy approached the former executive director of the Presbyterian Mission and remarked that he "felt a little funny" because his stomach was warm and he felt a little sleepy. The former director proceeded to check the child's temperature and, after a series of questions, could not detect anything unusual. He soon discovered that this child had never tasted hot chocolate before and was therefore unfamiliar with its soothing physical effects. The former executive director noted the significance of this episode: "For many of these kids, it's the first time that they've experienced or come into contact with these types of things."

Although these illustrations of cultural acquisition and learning might appear inconsequential at first glance, they have important implications for the youths' socialization, development of friendships, self-esteem, and sense of belonging in their peer groups, all of which affect their acculturation. Exposure to various elements of American culture, or more specifically elements of popular American youth culture, strengthens their ability to communicate and bond with their more acculturated peers in meaningful and age-appropriate ways. This may be a particularly salient concern for immigrant youths who, unlike their adult counterparts, face pressing developmental demands to establish friendships, build their self-esteem, and formulate their identities. In this context, acquiring information on popular youth culture might be equally important to acquiring formal academic knowledge and skills for the youths' daily functioning. This was underscored by numerous observations of informal peer discussions between youth members in which their social acceptance and social status rested on their skillful ability to converse about popular youth trends in music, television shows, cartoons, fashion, foods, and video games. The Chinese American mentors in this program were integral to the youths' acquisition of new cultural knowledge and skills because they served as their cultural brokers and interpreters of popular youth culture. In this capacity, the mentors helped the youths identify and discuss popular trends in youth culture that were part of their daily experience but were outside the purview of the youths' immigrant parents and adult family members. Youth mentors also modeled how to navigate American culture because most were first-generation immigrants themselves. A majority of mentors noted that their own early memories of struggling with competing cultural demands (e.g., seeking autonomy in their lives while respecting the collectivistic values of their families) compelled them to help other immigrant youths at the Presbyterian Mission Program. The relatively young age and Chinese immigrant backgrounds of the program mentors enhanced their credibility as cultural brokers in the eyes of their students. From a social learning perspective (Bandura 1977), these factors positioned the mentors as culturally competent role models who could effectively show their students how to enact an integration mode of acculturation in their daily lives.

The acquisition of new cultural knowledge and skills was also witnessed in the anger management group. Illustrated group workbooks explained the nature and causes of anger (e.g., "Everyone becomes angry now and then — young people, old people, tall people, short people"; "People can become angry quicker and easier when they don't feel well or when they are in a grumpy mood") and outlined age-appropriate anger management strategies (e.g., "Give yourself time to calm down by counting to ten slowly"; "Breathe deeply and take a time out"). In addition to reviewing these workbooks, the youths practiced breathing exercises and were encouraged to identify and share their feelings using a pictorial feelings chart. The group leader mostly conducted these exercises and lessons in English, but she turned to Cantonese whenever she wanted to emphasize certain lesson points or needed to provide added examples. These group activities and lessons were significant opportunities to acquire new cultural knowledge and skills because immigrant Chinese children are often socialized around collectivistic values that discourage overt or public expression of negative emotions such as anger and sadness that might upset others or disrupt group harmony (Markus and Kitayama 1991; Shon and Ja 1982). There was some evidence that the youths successfully retained and effectively applied the coping strategies and lessons that they learned from this group. For instance, members of the fifth-grade group successfully recalled a long list of coping methods to deal with their anger that they had learned three weeks earlier. In another situation, a second-grade boy discussed how he applied his group lessons to deal with a child who stole a basketball from him during recess at his school. He acknowledged that his anger made him feel like punching the child, but that he refrained from doing so after remembering the guiding principle of "Don't hit."

The Presbyterian Mission Program also fostered integration by providing academic assistance and support to its youth members. As noted earlier, an integration mode of acculturation requires establishing meaningful relationships with other cultural groups while retaining ties to one's culture of origin. Given that the youths in this program closely identified with their Chinese cultural heritage, integration thus required mastering the academic skills that would enable their engagement in a multicultural society. The Presbyterian Mission Program supported academic skills development through its individual and group tutoring sessions, which were conducted in a quiet and focused study environment. During these sessions, the majority of the youth members in all grade levels worked diligently on their homework assignments and routinely asked their mentors and fellow peers for assistance. This designated time and space for their homework was essential to their academic success because most came from multigenerational immigrant households where quiet and focused conditions for study were not always available. Additionally, many first-generation Chinese parents had little formal education and limited English skills and thus often were not able to provide assistance to their children. This point was expressed by a first-generation Chinese mother who said that she was highly appreciative of the youth program's tutoring because she could not understand the English-language assignments given to her junior high school daughter. Some of the immigrant parents also spoke about having little time to actively participate in their children's school activities and events due to their demanding work hours. A father of two elementary school students expressed his appreciation for the academic and emotional support that was offered by the program because his extended workshifts only afforded him a few hours in the evening with his children. The low cost of these tutoring services, the availability of program scholarships, and the central location of this program enhanced the accessibility of the tutoring services for these Chinese immigrant families. According to the program director, the youth members relied on these low-cost tutoring services because she estimated that roughly 95 percent of them came from economically disadvantaged families and approximately 90 percent experienced academic difficulties in their schools. A Chinese mother of a second grader offered praise for the program's tutorials by proudly remarking in Cantonese that her daughter was now ranked second in her class after being ranked at the bottom prior to her enrollment in the mission program.

The Presbyterian Mission Program also helped its youth members acquire important English-language skills. Acculturation research has identified limited English-language proficiencies as one of the most consistent predictors of depression and anxiety symptoms for new Asian immigrants and refugees (Chun, Eastman, Wang, and Sue 1998). Thus, English proficiency was not only essential for the youths' academic success but also for their overall psychological well-being during acculturation. The significance of the program's English-language tutoring was demonstrated for a fifth-grade girl who requested assistance on an English homework assignment. This particular assignment involved translating a variety of anachronistic English sayings (e.g., "A stitch in time saves nine," and "Birds of a feather stick together") that would have presented difficulties for American-born, monolingual English-language speakers. The assignment was especially challenging for this particular first-generation Chinese American girl because she had limited exposure to American colloquialisms. Also, the nature of the assignment precluded her from soliciting assistance from her first-generation immigrant parents at home because their English skills were less proficient than hers. Her youth mentor intervened in the situation by providing individual assistance for each phrase and offering brief grammatical instruction on difficult verb tenses and personal pronouns that are absent in the Chinese language. The significance of such tutorial assistance for this student is multifold; it not only provided her with requisite English-language skills for academic success but also equipped her with new cultural knowledge (i.e., American sayings and expressions) that potentially facilitate integration.

The program's goal of integration was also achieved by providing a culturally appropriate environment that minimized acculturation stress. The bilingual and cultural competencies of the staff along with the program's bicultural environment offset a number of acculturation demands (e.g., demands to become monolingual English speakers, to attenuate ethnic and cultural ties, and to modify cultural practices and beliefs). The bicultural skills of the program director and her staff were displayed in a difficult situation involving a first-generation mother who publicly ridiculed her son whenever he made mistakes on his homework. The director and the youth mentors first gathered together to discuss this situation, noting the underlying cultural dynamics of punitive parenting practices and their own experiences with their parents on this matter. Eventually they developed a culturally appropriate plan that involved validating the mother's concern over her son's academic success (thus preventing the mother from losing face) and offering alternate parenting styles (e.g., patience, support, and encouragement) that were more effective in American educational settings. The program's culturally supportive environment was also sustained by the youths themselves. For instance, fifth graders in the anger management group invariably came to each other's aid whenever someone struggled to pronounce a particular word during group readings. These types of student interactions illustrated the reciprocal nature of cultural acquisition and learning that was seen throughout the mission program—youth members used their newly acquired cultural skills and knowledge to facilitate each other's cultural acquisition and learning so that building bicultural competencies and movement toward integration became a shared and mutually supported endeavor.

The Buddhist Temple Program: "We Are Not Only Teaching the Students How to Write and Speak Chinese. We Are Teaching the Chinese Culture!"
The Buddhist Temple Program was structured as a Saturday morning school held from 8:30 AM to 12:00 PM for elementary, middle, and high school youths. Its staff consisted of a volunteer principal and four volunteer teachers, all con-

gregants of the temple, whose ages ranged from the mid-twenties to the late fifties. Formal Mandarin language instruction was taught in kindergarten, elementary, intermediate, and advanced class sections at the beginning of the program session. Other program activities included a group meditation session, group storytime sessions that incorporated classical Chinese and Buddhist narratives, instruction on Buddhist religious rites and practices, and a communal vegetarian lunch with temple congregants. Youth members also participated in special Buddhist holiday celebrations and annual temple events that promoted traditional Chinese and Buddhist values.

The Buddhist Temple Program was primarily focused on strengthening the youth members' ties to their Chinese cultural heritage and Buddhist traditions. As noted above, at the temple the terms "Chinese" and "Buddhist" appeared to be synonymous—fused together by a designated spiritual and cultural center that was situated in China, the homeland of their founder and venerable master. Ethnographic observations and solicited feedback from select youths, their parents, and staff indicated that the temple program provided multiple opportunities for cultural and religious maintenance through its Mandarin coursework and lessons, its formal teachings on Chinese cultural values focusing on filial piety and respect for elders, and its formal instruction on Buddhist principles and practices. In general, the first-generation parents expressed highly favorable opinions of these cultural and religious maintenance opportunities while their second-generation offspring expressed both favorable and somewhat unfavorable opinions. Parent-child disagreements over cultural and religious maintenance at times led to intergenerational tensions that were a potential source of acculturative stress.

The temple's Mandarin language instruction consisted of group and individual reading sessions, writing and speech lessons, and special Chinese calligraphy instruction for older youth members. Language lessons often incorporated Chinese cultural values and classical Chinese literary narratives. During their language instruction, all of the youths, including the five-year-olds in the kindergarten section, generally sat attentively in their chairs with little conversation or disturbances for the entire one-hour didactic session. The teachers maintained a somewhat strict but caring stance toward their students, and much of their communication was unidirectional (speaking to the students) rather than bidirectional (engaging in mutual dialogue with the students). One of the resident nuns commented that this teaching style represented a "traditional Chinese" way of teaching. Most of the parents concurred and stated that this type of instruction actually compelled them to enroll their children in this program. A first-generation Chinese mother said that she woke up at 6 AM every Saturday in order to make the approximate hour-long trip to the temple from her home in a neighboring suburb. She initially enrolled her five-year-old daughter in a Taiwanese language school that was closer to her home and held at a more convenient time, but she eventually became dissatisfied with this school because it "didn't teach Chinese" and its teachers "only wanted to socialize with the students." She was pleased to have found the Buddhist Temple Program because it had "a better culture" and was "more traditional." Furthermore, she was hopeful that the temple program would help her daughter become fluent in Mandarin (her daughter currently prefers to speak English) so that she would feel more comfortable in forming friendships with other Chinese children.

Another mother offered her views on the cultural significance of the temple's Mandarin lessons: "It is important for my children to speak Chinese because they *are* Chinese." This mother's statement suggests that speaking Chinese is equivalent to being Chinese. Parents might therefore consider Mandarin instruction to be an important method to socialize their children to Chinese culture, and they might view proficiency in this language as a marker of their children's ethnic and cultural authenticity. In the field of psychology, this process of socialization to one's culture of origin is called "enculturation," which is often portrayed as a less challenging and less stressful experience than acculturation to a new culture. However, the youth's responses to their Mandarin instruction were quite varied; some were engaged with the lessons, readily responded to the teachers' questions, and showed enthusiasm for the didactic activities. Others, however, seemed to struggle through the lesson plans and viewed them as externally imposed tasks from their parents. One kindergarten boy, for example, said that he didn't want to go to this Chinese school but that he relented because his parents wanted him to attend. Still, some of the older youths had favorable responses to their language instruction and viewed it as an important component of their Chinese ethnic group membership and a source of ethnic and cultural pride. A middle-school student who self-identified as Chinese American said that he felt proud to be Chinese "because [he] could speak Chinese" and that he felt attached to the Chinese American community because he attended the temple program "where [they] chanted and spoke in Mandarin." However, he "didn't know what it [meant] to be Chinese American," thus indicating that the intended effect of these language lessons—to strengthen ethnic and cultural identity—was contingent upon the youths' developmental abilities and their stage of ethnic identity formation. According to psychology research, an individual's understanding, knowledge, and appreciation of his or her ethnic background depends on a whole host of factors such as cognitive skills, age, family environment, neighborhood characteristics, and access to cultural resources (Phinney 1990, 2006).

The Buddhist Temple also supported cultural maintenance in its formal teachings on Chinese cultural values such as filial piety and respect for elders. Filial piety basically refers to fulfilling family obligations and duties, especially those related to caring for one's parents, and a general responsibility to place family concerns and needs over one's own (Shon and Ja 1982). During a story-time session with the elementary school children, the teacher read a famous Chinese tale about two brothers who were in the possession of two pears, which ends with the older brother giving his little brother the larger pear of the two. This tale thus highlighted Confucian teachings on filial piety and the culturally prescribed role and duties of the older brother. The elementary school children appeared to grasp these underlying themes on some level; when asked by their teacher whether they would take the large or small pear, they uniformly responded by saying the smaller. The significance of filial piety in this youth program and in the larger temple itself is intertwined with the venerable master's legendary reputation as "Filial Son Bai" (Buddhist Text Translation Society 1995b). Thus, the youths in this program are not only maintaining their cultural traditions when they practice filial piety but also they are re-creating and honoring the life of their temple founder. The youths in this regard provide living testimony to the venerable master's holy vision of bringing the "proper" dharma to the West. By embracing his values and those of the Buddha's in their daily lives, their acculturation process is imbued with religious and cultural significance.

The youth program and the larger temple also promoted respect for elders by instructing their students to respectfully greet their principal and teachers in the morning, to serve meals to the elderly congregants before eating their own meals during the lunch hour, and to follow adult congregants in prayer procession. The youths are also encouraged to participate in the annual Respect Elders Day when the elderly congregants of the temple are publicly honored for their wisdom and lifetime contributions. Other Chinese cultural values were taught in the youth program as well—in a reading of the Chinese classical tale of the monkey king, the teacher instructed her kindergarten class on the virtues of wisdom, brave leadership, and discipline.

These teachings on "traditional" Chinese values were central to the Buddhist Temple Program's curriculum, as noted by the principal: "We are not only teaching the students how to write and speak Chinese, we are teaching the Chinese culture!" This sentiment was shared by all of the teachers and volunteers who viewed themselves as stewards of the Chinese culture for their mostly

second-generation students. One of the resident nuns explained that most of the parents were first-generation Taiwanese immigrants who were concerned that their children were becoming too "Americanized." This was expressed by a mother of a five-year-old girl who believed that her daughter's "Americanization" was the root cause of her increasingly rebellious and disrespectful behavior. Moreover, this mother enrolled her daughter in the temple program with the explicit hope of instilling her with Chinese and Buddhist values to stem the tide of assimilation. Another mother similarly framed the temple program as a countervailing cultural weight against the omnipresent influence of American culture. She explained that the children's schools "always teach American values" whereas the temple program provided a special occasion to learn "Chinese values." Again, the parents in this youth program responded to the temple's cultural instruction in a highly favorable manner and believed that it produced tangible benefits in their children's lives. A mother reported that as a function of the temple's instruction her two elementary school-aged children were more polite, more willing to help others, more thoughtful and considerate toward elders, and less likely to talk back. She acknowledged that her children were still young and that she "didn't expect them to be perfect," but she was nonetheless "quite satisfied" with the program's results. Some of the youths also responded favorably to the program's cultural instruction. A second-generation junior high school student said that he was proud to be Chinese and felt that he was a part of the Chinese American community because he attended this program where he "learned to respect [his] elders and to be responsible."

Finally, the Buddhist Temple Program created opportunities for religious maintenance through Buddhist mantra recitation practice, Buddhist story sessions, group meditation sessions, vegetarian meal-offering ceremonies with adult congregants, special Buddhist holiday celebrations, and, on the second Saturday of each month, formal worship with the temple congregation in the main prayer hall. A story session with elementary school children included an illustrated children's book on the sins of eating meat. Following this story, the teacher encouraged her students to be vigilant vegetarians by reminding their parents to cook vegetarian meals at home. Another story session focused on the Buddhist principles of speaking "good" words, doing good deeds, and thinking in good ways, after which the students offered their own examples of good deeds (e.g., "Finishing homework, asking mom about what I can help her with, don't speak when the teacher is teaching"). During the daily group meditation sessions (led by a resident nun), the teachers and volunteers assisted the youth in meditation posture and techniques as they sat silently on individual pillows facing walls lined with Buddhist meditation sayings. One of the temple's nuns explained that rather than having a recreational hour "where children ran around wildly," it was important to teach the children "to quiet their minds" as espoused by their Chinese Mahayana Buddhist tradition. The impact of these meditation sessions on the younger students' Buddhist practices and identity were somewhat difficult to ascertain because they couldn't fully articulate their experience. Still, the majority of kindergarteners sat silently on their individual pillows throughout the twenty-minute session with some closing their eyes tightly in an attempt to focus their concentration while others appeared somewhat restless. Older youths showed varied responses to these meditation sessions and to the other Buddhist practices and teachings in this program. A middle-school boy said that he "kind of liked going to the temple" because it helped him feel less irritable and angry toward his older brother and he learned to be more patient, peaceful, and to have less desire. He contrasted this with his early childhood experiences of "going more crazy" and "flipping chairs and throwing things" out of anger and frustration. A second-generation high school student, however, expressed mixed feelings about Buddhist practices and his attendance in the temple program. He said that he meditated at home because he "had to" and that he "didn't necessarily feel anything" possibly because he lacked concentration. He said that he followed some Buddhist rules in his daily life and that he studied Buddhism "a little bit" on his own, but he lamented that Buddhism required him to follow a lot of rules — unlike his non-Buddhist friends who "had more freedom." He elaborated on this latter point by describing how his parents favored a strict "Asian way" of parenting, which to his dismay restricted his social life and growing need for autonomy. Finally, he said it was difficult to explain to his teenage friends why he still listened to his parents and attended the temple program rather than socializing with them. He said that he typically dealt with these circumstances by "making up something" so that he didn't have to offer any explanations to them.

The temple program's curriculum and teaching methods, which were characterized as "traditional" by the Chinese staff, parents and students alike, reflect Chinese "child training" practices that involve an amalgam of strict, controlling, supportive, and caring parenting behaviors. A basic aim of these child training practices is to teach children culturally appropriate behaviors and skills so that they can achieve academic success and meet societal and family expectations (Chao 1994). As such, it would be inaccurate to characterize the temple's instructional methods as being overly rigid or restrictive because the first-generation Chinese parents and staff in this program might view them from an entirely different cultural perspective. Still, some of the second-generation youths in this program had mixed responses to these instructional methods and the program's overarching goal of cultural and religious maintenance mostly because they felt that they were parental demands. Also, the temple's Mandarin lessons and cultural and religious instruction might not have been vital to their daily functioning in their predominantly English-speaking suburban neighborhoods, peer circles, and schools. Therefore, some of the second-generation Chinese youths might have lacked a personal stake in cultural and religious maintenance because it was not a necessary condition for their academic success and their ability to form friendships. Their first-generation parents, however, tended to believe that maintaining a Chinese-Buddhist identity was vital to their children's moral development and overall character, fearing what they perceived to be the corrupting effects of "becoming Americanized." Matters were complicated for the adolescent youths in this program who faced normative developmental demands for autonomy, which tended to exacerbate conflict with their parents over cultural and religious maintenance.

CONCLUSION

Although the significance of environmental variables to acculturation patterns and outcomes has been highlighted in the acculturation literature, few studies illustrate how specific characteristics and features of different cultural settings actually influence acculturation processes. As such, the fundamental question that was raised at the beginning of this essay—How does acculturation actually unfold in a given cultural setting?—is often left unanswered. This essay attempted to systematically address this question. At face value, parallel youth acculturation patterns might have been expected across the Presbyterian Mission and the Buddhist Temple given their central locations in San Francisco Chinatown and the similar ethnic background and age ranges of their youth members. Ethnographic observations, however, uncovered important contextual factors that contributed to varied youth acculturation experiences at both sites. The distinct histories and missions of each religious site, the novel visions of their leadership, and the unique characteristics of their staff influenced the types of acculturation goals that they promoted to their members on an organizational level. The Presbyterian Mission began with a goal of assimilation at its founding in the late nineteenth century, but eventually it moved toward its current goal of integration. In contrast, the Buddhist Temple showed features of separation, integration, and "reverse assimilation," which are somewhat difficult to interpret as a whole, but were fundamentally part of an overarching goal of maintaining a Chinese-Buddhist identity. These organizational goals were in turn manifested in the unique structures, curricula, activities, and events of their respective youth programs, all of which set specific conditions and parameters for acculturation among their youth members. The youths' responses to these contextual factors and conditions were influenced by their different motives and goals for attending these programs and by their distinct developmental abilities that further contributed to variations in their acculturation experiences and outcomes.

The first-generation Chinese American youth in the Presbyterian Mission Program showed evidence of integration in their acquisition of new cultural knowledge and skills, including the requisite English skills for academic success as well as the knowledge of popular American youth culture essential for establishing friendships with their peers. Also, integration was facilitated through program activities and events that affirmed the youths' cultural practices and Cantonese dialect and through a culturally supportive learning environment that was staffed by Chinese American mentors who acted as credible cultural brokers and biculturally competent role models for the youth members. In general, the youth in this program exhibited positive responses to the programs' goal of integration because it responded to their own needs and concerns as first-generation Chinese American youth. Furthermore, the nature and structure of the program's activities and events matched their own developmental interests and abilities.

In the Buddhist Temple Program, the primarily second-generation Chinese youth members were afforded opportunities to maintain a Chinese-Buddhist identity through Mandarin language lessons and formal instruction on traditional Chinese values and Buddhist principles and practices. The youth members responded to these opportunities for cultural and religious maintenance in varied ways. At times they endorsed Chinese-Buddhist values and practices and were engaged in the program's lessons and activities, while on other occasions they felt at odds with cultural and religious maintenance because they perceived it as being imposed on them by their first-generation Chinese parents. For some youths this resulted in intergenerational tension with their parents, especially for those who desired greater autonomy in their adolescent years, and perhaps also for those who did not view cultural and religious maintenance as a necessary condition for their overall adjustment and well-being in their schools and social settings.

There were a number of limitations to the ethnographic observations at the Presbyterian Mission and the Buddhist Temple. First, field site visits were for practical reasons limited to the settings and activities of these two religious organizations and their youth programs. Thus, the nature and characteristics of the youths' acculturation experiences in other settings (e.g., their households, schools, and peer groups) deserve further exploration. It would be interesting to investigate whether the acculturation goals and activities of the youth programs bear upon the youths' acculturation and adjustment in the other spheres of their daily lives. It is entirely possible that the unique conditions of these daily settings, each with their own set of acculturation demands and cultural resources, contribute to even greater variations in youth acculturation. Also, it would be important to solicit reports and feedback from additional youth members, family members, and staff and to consider studying other religious sites to more fully comprehend the range of acculturation experiences at religious organizations. Finally, the effects of transnational activities on youth acculturation at these study sites deserve in-depth discussion. For immigrant communities transnational activities can take many forms, such as the sharing of religious and cultural information or maintaining dual residences or citizenship as a function of increasing globalization (Smith and Guarnizo 1998). An effort to examine the historical context and complexity of transnationalism at the Buddhist Temple and Presbyterian Mission is well beyond the scope of this essay. Nonetheless, both study sites have formal and informal transnational links with various regions in Asia. Some of the Presbyterian Mission staff and its members maintain informal transnational family and social ties with the Hong Kong community. To some extent, these transnational ties have sustained the Presbyterian Mission's historical position as a site of cultural exchange and communication, which ultimately enhances its culturally supportive environment and programs for new Chinese immigrants. The Buddhist Temple and its larger worldwide organization conduct transnational activities that span across Asia and North America. There is some evidence that these transnational activities support the Buddhist Temple's goal of cultural and religious maintenance. Most notably, the rotating assignment of the nuns and monks and the production of religious texts and materials within its transnational religious network remind the venerable master's followers of his holy vision to teach and promote Chinese and Buddhist traditions in cultures across the globe.

As both sites continue to evolve, new contexts for acculturation will emerge that potentially expand opportunities for their members to develop new and more complex cultural skills and knowledge. This becomes all the more apparent when considering that the immigrants who enter these sites have the capacity to act as active agents in the reformulation and regeneration of their cultural environs. Future studies might examine organizational characteristics that support individual agency and how this subsequently impacts an organization's acculturation goals and outcomes over time. Additionally, future research can further explore the relationship of religion and spirituality to acculturation by articulating how new immigrants actually construct meaning in their lives during resettlement, the manner in which religious organizations participate in this process, and how this affects the overall adjustment of immigrant congregants and their families. This investigative endeavor assumes added complexity when considering the developmental context of religious identity formation and faith practices for immigrant children and adolescents. Do immigrant youth comprehend and experience in different ways from adults the world, the transcendental, and life changes and upheavals? Again, scholars who study the lives of new immigrants must initiate a new interdisciplinary dialogue that incorporates and synthesizes conceptual models and research methods from multiple fields in order to comprehensively address these issues. This essay has attempted to initiate this dialogue by illustrating how acculturation theory from psychology and ethnographic research methods traditionally associated with other disciplines can be brought together to provide new insights to immigrant experiences in religious organizations.

Immigrant Religious Adaptation

Vietnamese American Buddhists at
Chua Viet Nam (Vietnamese Buddhist Temple)

HIEN DUC DO AND MIMI KHÚC

Beginning in the 1960s major waves of new groups of immigrants arrived in the United States. This phenomenon inspired great scholarly interest in immigrant life, with immigrant religious life in particular providing a rich area for exploring the many dimensions of immigrant experience, especially that of adaptation and acculturation. Vietnamese American religiosity is no exception. However, while scholarship on Vietnamese Americans has focused largely on issues of immigration, social and economic adjustment, acculturation, and the second generation—all major themes in the study of Asian America more broadly—it has only begun to explore Vietnamese American religious life and to use religion as a lens through which to examine these major issues. In this essay we will explore Chua Viet Nam, or Vietnamese Buddhist Temple, in San Jose, California, to investigate issues of adaptation and acculturation for Vietnamese Americans.

IMMIGRANT ADAPTATION: CONCEPTS AND CONSTRUCTS

Immigrants have traditionally been approached as people between two cultures, namely that of the "home" and that of the "host." And these two cultures are seen as competing with one another within the immigrant as an individual as well as in the immigrant community as a whole. To discuss this process of competition and change, scholars have used terms such as "acculturation" and "assimilation"—though their usage differs from discipline to discipline. These terms come from the social sciences and related interdisciplinary fields such as ethnic studies, and they range in exact definition and relationship to other concepts depending on the field (and even on the scholar within a field). In an essay in this volume, Kevin Chun defines these terms by drawing on the field of psychology. Contemporary psychology uses the term "acculturation" as an umbrella term to discuss the ways in which different cultures in contact affect changes along multiple dimensions within one another, particularly in terms of a minority group negotiating between its culture and that of the dominant culture. "Assimilation," then, is one possible type or result of acculturation and acculturating processes, along with "integration," "separation," and "marginalization" (Chun, Balls Organista, and Marin 2003).

The sociologists Alejandro Portes and Ruben G. Rumbaut (1996) utilize similar but slightly different definitions. For them, "adaptation" is the larger umbrella term, and "acculturation" and "assimilation" are stages along the adaptation process. Here, acculturation is the beginning step while assimilation is the final stage. While there is a kind of trajectory in this model, Portes and Rumbaut see this process as complex and acknowledge its multidimensionality. Particularly for the post-1965 immigrants, acculturation and assimilation are not simple: what Portes and Rumbaut find is that a kind of selective acculturation results in "segmented assimilation"—that is, assimilation that is partial and not "uniform," in contrast with previous immigration in the United States.

Notions of acculturation and assimilation must also be understood in a larger context, particularly in discussions about diversity within the United States. The central question is how a new immigrant group is going to be incorporated into our society. To address this question two perspectives, assimilation and pluralism, offer major approaches to diversity. Assimilation models are prescriptive, unidirectional models in which one result is the goal: for cultural minorities to fully assimilate to the host culture by relinquishing all cultural ties and markers of the past. The sociologist Robert E. Park's (1950) classic "race relations cycle" demonstrates this conceptual and normative model: contact, competition, accommodation, assimilation. This notion that immigrants must fully assimilate in order to participate and succeed in American society is part of a larger narrative about the United States, its history, and its future. Underlying this assimilation perspective is a narrative of a unified American people who together create and achieve the American project, or the "American experiment." Samuel Huntington (1996) is an example of a strong voice for this perspective, notably in his view of diversity and change as a problem to be overcome in order to realize the potential of the West. Portes and Rumbaut, while far from agreeing with Huntington politically, come somewhat from this assimilationist perspective: while they care about immigrant communities, ultimately they are still interested in "successful" assimilation, particularly for the second generation. "Segmented assimilation" is a problematic result of selective acculturation—a result that creates problems for the immigrant communities.

The major opposition to the assimilationist perspective is the pluralistic, or multicultural, perspective, which is also a prescriptive stance. Here, it becomes acceptable—even celebrated—to keep cultural markers of difference. Different cultures bring their own "flavor" to the "salad bowl" of American society: we are a nation of immigrants, and we all have something to contribute. Major proponents of this stance, particularly in the study of religion, include the sociologist of religion Robert Wuthnow and the religion scholar Diana Eck, who is the head of the Harvard Pluralism Project on religious diversity in the United States. These scholars have clearly demonstrated that, at least with respect to religious diversity, America is one of the most diverse countries in the world. Since 1965 the United States has shifted from being a predominantly Protestant nation to one that includes Roman Catholics, Jews, Buddhists, Muslims, Hindus, Sikhs, and other religions. Proponents of a pluralistic or multicultural perspective argue that growing religious diversity is the current landscape of America and that this diversity only helps to strengthen the nation.

Although the descriptive models differ from the prescriptive—and the prescriptive from one another—at the foundation of these constructs lies a shared binary. As mentioned above, immigrants are traditionally seen as caught between two cultures, and models of adaptation view immigrants as moving along a kind of spectrum between the cultures. Contemporary scholars attempt to nuance the model by emphasizing the multidimensionality and multidirectionality of adaptation, thereby allowing for biculturalism within different aspects of identity. Even taking a neutral stance in which neither assimilation to the host culture nor maintenance of the home culture is preferred, we are still operating with a spectrum that has only two ends and allows only two options for immigrants: assimilate or maintain. While these concepts can be useful, they may be too limiting for understanding the complexity involved in the process of immigrant adaptation. The following case study of Chua Viet Nam provides examples of adaptation that fit in this "host-versus-home" paradigm, but it also provides examples that do not, which will allow us to expand our understanding of adaptation, acculturation, and assimilation. In sum, this case study will allow us to better understand the complexity involved as well as some of the ways in which a group of recent immigrants have used their cultural knowledge and religion to navigate and negotiate this difficult and challenging process.

VIETNAMESE IMMIGRATION

While some Vietnamese were in the United States before and during the war in Vietnam, the majority of Vietnamese immigration occurred after the fall of Saigon in 1975. Vietnamese immigration has been divided into two phases: refugee and immigrant. The refugee phase consists of three groups: exiles in 1975; boat people, peaking in 1978 and 1982; and later refugees between 1988 and 1992. After the mid-1990s, most Vietnamese entering the United States were immigrants reuniting with family members (Zhou and Bankston 1998).

In order to minimize the social impact of the large influx of Vietnamese refugees on an American public that was unfavorable to the Vietnam War, the United States government adopted the Refugee Dispersion Policy. This policy served four purposes: to relocate the Vietnamese refugees as quickly as possible so that they could achieve financial independence; to ease the impact of a large group of refugees on a given community that might otherwise increase the competition for jobs; to make it logistically easier to find sponsors; and to prevent the development of an ethnic ghetto (Liu, Lamanna, and Murata 1979). The goal of this policy was to encourage the Vietnamese refugees to quickly assimilate into the American society by working as soon as possible upon their exit from the refugee camps. This was primarily done through contracting nine voluntary agencies to help recruit sponsors willing to provide some assistance.

After living for a period of time with their sponsors, many Vietnamese refugees began to relocate to different locations throughout the United States—what scholars call secondary migration. They did not remain in the original resettlement place for a variety of reasons, the most important of which include family reunification, job availability, the desire to live close to people similar to them, and climate conditions. Over the years, they have gathered and developed communities across the country, with census data from 2000 indicating that the states with the greatest Vietnamese populations include California, Texas, Louisiana, Virginia, Washington, Pennsylvania, and Florida.

Like immigrants before them, Vietnamese immigrants and refugees brought with them their religions. The two major religions in Vietnam are Buddhism and Catholicism, but Vietnamese assert that there is also an underlying religious culture called Tam Giao, or the Three Religions: Buddhism, Confucianism, and Taoism. While Catholics make up only about 10 percent of the population in Vietnam, they make up 30 percent of the Vietnamese in the United States because the first group of refugee exiles in 1975 consisted mainly of Catholics that had experienced persecution from their refugee experience in 1954 and continued to fear persecution from the communist government. Most Vietnamese Americans are Buddhist, however, and they mainly follow a form of Mahayana Buddhism received through Chinese influence (unlike their Theravada Buddhist neighbors throughout Southeast Asia) (Do 1999).

Vietnamese American Buddhists and Catholics have had different experiences in the United States, particularly in terms of their religious organizations. While Catholics could rely upon the American Catholic structure (albeit with difficulties, of course), Buddhists had no existing organizational structure in 1975. As a result, even with language and cultural differences Catholics were able to resume their religious practices more quickly after their initial resettlement period because the structure of the Catholic Church was already in place for them to continue to attend their religious ceremonies and services. Catholics also have more access to resources, especially since the American Catholic Church was one of the nine voluntary agencies that helped in the initial resettlement of Vietnamese refugees in 1975, and with their extensive network it was able to provide more support.

Despite the lack of an existing structure, Vietnamese American Buddhists were able to rebuild their religious communities—often in creative ways. One major example is the "home temples," or the residential buildings purchased for Buddhist monks and transformed into small neighborhood temples. In 1993 Orange County in Southern California, with the largest Vietnamese American community in the country, was home to nearly thirty home temples (Breyer 1993). These home temples resonate with earlier Buddhist immigrant strategies such as creating small temples and worship spaces in their garages and homes.

The base location for our research work—San Jose, California—is home to the second-largest concentration of Vietnamese Americans in the United States. While San Jose is more generally known as the heart of Silicon Valley, where the majority of the high-tech industries originated in the 1970s and 1980s, the city also has had a long history of farming, agriculture, and other industries that require unskilled and semi-skilled labor. In 1975 it was also one of the major cities where Vietnamese refugees were initially sponsored by churches, congregations, families, and individuals as a result of the Federal Government Dispersal Policy. The development of this Vietnamese American community therefore began with the arrival of the initial refugees to San Jose and the surrounding areas to fill the demand for unskilled and semi-skilled labor in those already established industries, and it also coincided with the rise of the high-tech industry that required a more educated labor force. The formation of this community is therefore typical of the resettlement patterns of Vietnamese American communities seen throughout the United States. In short, in most cases of sponsored immigrant settlement there is an initial small group of refugees that is sent to a specific location. Once the group establishes itself and is able economically to survive, they began to reconstruct and reestablish the family and friendship networks that were temporarily severed because of the exodus and refugee experiences. Additionally, since San Jose was at the time just starting its high-tech industry, the refugees benefited from the relatively large number of available unskilled jobs that required little English as well as from other jobs in the agriculture industry. They were able to enter the job market as a result of the strong demand for a specific type of labor—in many ways, they were at the right place at the right time. However, unlike many racial and ethnic communities in the United States, one of the noticeable characteristics of this specific community is that there is no single concentrated geographical area that visitors can point to as the center of the community; rather, it is spread out over a large area with smaller pockets of mini-malls that cater to the needs of this community.

As a result of the recent arrival of Vietnamese refugees and immigrants to the United States as well as the sensitive history of this community, from the very beginning of this project our team was assembled in such a way that required the researchers to be members of the community, to have the necessary language proficiency, understanding of cultural knowledge and traditions, and most importantly, the trust of the community and the participants. To that end, all of the researchers were refugees themselves and all came to the United States either as young children, as teenagers, or as unaccompanied minors. Members of the team all live, work, and participate in the community in various capacities. They work as social workers and teachers; they help organize a number of cultural celebrations throughout the year; and they attend Catholic masses and Buddhist services.

Finally, since the community was spread out over a large area, so were all the temples and churches. The Buddhist temples ranged from home temples to more elaborate and established temples. The Catholic churches varied in their location and to the level of their "ownership" by the Vietnamese Catholic and community leaders. As a result, before choosing Chua Viet Nam as our research site, we conducted preliminary fieldwork in all of the Catholic churches and Buddhist temples that served the Vietnamese American community in San Jose and in the larger surrounding areas. We spent time conducting preliminary fieldwork (guided by the overall research questions) and examined a number of churches and temples to determine which Buddhist temple and Catholic church would best represent our research questions as well as provide us with

access to the structure, the leadership, and the congregations for our three-year participation observation project.

Chua Viet Nam (Vietnamese Buddhist Temple)

On a Sunday in May 2001 over a thousand Vietnamese Americans celebrated Buddha's birthday at Chua Viet Nam in San Jose. On a cold and windy Saturday about two years earlier, over four thousand people came to the temple to pay their final respects to and celebrate the extraordinary life of Venerable Dam Luu, a Vietnamese American Buddhist nun and the abbess and founder of the temple.

Venerable Dam Luu, or Thich Dieu Thanh (her Buddhist name), lived an unusual life even before coming to Northern California as a refugee from Vietnam in 1980. At sixteen years of age she had been one of the first Buddhist nuns in Vietnam to be ordained. During that time, a formal education was not required to enter the monastic life. However, her teacher wanted her students to have a deeper understanding of Buddhism and thus encouraged all of her disciples to become more educated. As a result, Dam Luu was not only one of the first nuns in Vietnam to be ordained but also one of the first to be educated and to pass the very difficult national exam for a high school diploma (Thich 2000).

During the war in Vietnam, Dam Luu participated in political demonstrations against the South Vietnam government for its persecution of Buddhists, and she was jailed in 1963. She was released later that year when President Ngo Dinh Diem of South Vietnam was overthrown. As a result of the many societal changes caused by the war, in 1964 the United Vietnamese Buddhist Church recognized the need for its members to participate in more secular professional fields. Consequently, Dam Luu was among a handful of people sent abroad to obtain the necessary education and skills. She studied for five years in Germany where she received a master of arts degree in social work. She returned to Viet Nam in 1969 to become the director of a newly established orphanage, Lam Ty Ni. With the help of the local Buddhist community she operated the orphanage to care for the children who were victims of the war as well as those who could not be cared for by their families. The orphanage was dissolved after the North Vietnamese communist victory in 1975. In 1976, Dam Luu was pressured to make false accusations against a monastic friend, and when she refused she was threatened and harassed by the government. After four failed attempts to leave Vietnam, she finally managed to escape in a small fishing boat in late 1978 (Thich 2000).

Dam Luu arrived in the United States as a refugee in 1980 when she was forty-eight years old. She had less than twenty dollars in funds to start her new life. Thanh Cat, a Vietnamese Buddhist monk in East Palo Alto, California, sponsored her resettlement in the United States, and she was later assigned to San Jose where she eventually founded Chua Viet Nam. At present the temple, located at a busy intersection of an urban residential area, is over nine thousand square feet in area and as such is one of the largest Vietnamese American Buddhist temples in the nation. It is also one of the few temples in the United States that is run by nuns. But the temple began on a very modest scale. After her arrival in 1980 Dam Luu rented a small house on the east side of San Jose and started a "home temple" with the help of another Buddhist monk. As with all home temples, the entire house became different representations of a larger temple: for example, Dam Luu used the living room as Buddha's hall while a tent erected in the backyard served as a dining hall, a lecture hall for dharma lessons, a classroom for children to learn Vietnamese, and on occasions even a space for overnight guests. Following the tradition for temples in Vietnam, Dam Luu received donations from the small Buddhist following in the immediate community. These donations were not, however, enough to cover the rent and other expenses, so Dam Luu used her free time to collect aluminum cans and newspapers. Although she did this quietly and without fanfare, word began to spread in the community about the Buddhist nun who collected recyclables, and women and children in the area began to join her. During the duration of this effort—from the late 1980s to the mid-1990s—Dam Luu managed to save a large sum of money that, when combined with community donations from the larger Bay Area, totaled to $400,000 (about 30 percent of which was raised through the recycling work). The construction of the temple began in 1995, the majority of which was completed three years later. Its present configuration consists of a recently completed main hall in addition to a dining hall, kitchen, eating areas, classrooms, sleeping quarters for the thirteen resident nuns, and two small parking lots (Thich 2000).

As the current abbess notes, "the Venerable Dam Luu chose this location for its convenience, in terms of transportation. Students of all ages can attend and the seniors can take the bus. Parents can also drop off the children on Sunday. There are those that can just walk here because they live nearby."[1] The temple was designed and furnished in the traditional Vietnamese architecture and symbols that distinguish it from Chinese temples. Dam Luu wanted the temple to reflect the traditional architecture of ancient temples that she knew in Vietnam, and she worked with a Vietnamese architect specifically to assure that many of the elements were included in the final design. Since the preparations for the temple had to be made before the actual buildings were constructed, a special challenge was faced in importing the necessary statues and other Buddhist relics from Vietnam. The temple was planned during the time when the United States imposed a trade embargo against Vietnam, and a large majority of the statues and religious figures were ordered from Vietnam before the embargo was lifted in late 1994. To assure that the statues arrived during the construction period, they had to be shipped first to Thailand before being shipped to the United States. While the temple's location was chosen based on specifications as an area with a large Vietnamese population and with easy access to public transportation, the temple itself is designed with a peaceful garden and lush greenery in order to provide a quiet retreat from a busy urban life upon entering the grounds.

Chua Viet Nam was the first Vietnamese Buddhist nunnery in the United States. As part of her work Dam Luu trained fifteen to twenty nuns, and several resident nuns lived at the temple year round.[2] In more recent years, nuns have been sent from Vietnam by sister temples to study with Dam Luu. Upon completion of their studies, the nuns are expected to return to Vietnam to assume leadership roles there.

The temple also occupies an important position in the Vietnamese American Buddhist monastery community. Due to a lack of resources there is no monastery for monks, so Dam Luu opened her temple to provide for their training. Many of those who have been trained by Dam Luu are nuns, monks, or dharma teachers working throughout the United States, Europe, and Vietnam. As a result of this position within the Vietnamese Buddhist community, Chua Viet Nam receives many visiting monks and nuns who provide dharma talks for the temple.

Religious Responses to Immigrant Life in the United States

The leaders, members, and activities of Chua Viet Nam express certain responses to the Vietnamese immigrant situation in the United States. First are the examples of the attempt to preserve aspects of the home culture. Like its counterparts in other Asian American religious communities the temple provides Vietnamese language classes for the younger generation—a service that Dam Luu has provided from the very beginning. Further, when parents stated that they did not have enough time to bring their children to the temple for the classes, Dam Luu solicited help from volunteers and began offering free lunches for the students. Thus, the desire to preserve aspects of the home culture prompted not only the usual language courses but also creative changes such as a lunch system to support those language courses.

According to the coordinator of the language classes, the curriculum is developed to reflect the age of the students and to attract them by providing activities relevant to their lives in the United States. In order to accomplish this, the temple conducts services that are age specific. They also have created live performances of music, dance, and ritual celebrations because, as the coordinator notes, "most temples do not have live performances, but we put that together because we want to include children, adolescents, and teenagers at Chua Viet Nam. Whenever they have a chance to help Chua Viet Nam in their performances, they feel proud and want to come more often. Also, if they want to perform, they must learn and understand the entire story in order for them to perform."

The language courses and performances not only serve as ways to transmit religious knowledge but also as a place where students can interact with the teachers and the nuns and to share the struggles they face at school and at home. During the dharma classes it is customary for all of the students to report to their teachers how they are doing in school and to be reminded to focus on their education. While the students benefit from attending these classes, the teachers also benefit because it allows them to apply their technical skills and knowledge to help build a stronger Buddhist and Vietnamese American community as well as a way to interact with those similar to them. The community and the students also see the teachers as role models because of how they exercise their commitment to the temple while balancing their professional lives, family obligations, and religious beliefs. The leadership of the temple also encourages the nuns to continue their higher education by enrolling at the local community colleges and universities as well as to continue their graduate studies.

Another way in which home culture is preserved is through rituals and celebrations. One example can be seen in the events on May 6, 2001, at the annual celebration of Buddha's birthday. The day began early with volunteers and nuns busily setting up for this important occasion. Before the formal ceremony, parents, grandparents, and children dressed in their best clothes lined up to burn incense in honor of Buddha and their ancestors. The nuns and monks, dressed in their traditional formal Buddhist attire, began the day at 10:00 AM with an hour-long session of chanting and reciting sutras, which was followed by a dharma talk by the Venerable Thich Minh Duc. After the formal ceremony, the temple was transformed into a stage where the students and teachers of the Vietnamese-language classes performed an hour-long musical celebration of Buddha's birth—a performance that had been months in creation. The day ended with many members sharing the free and for-purchase vegetarian food in the eating areas and others congregating outside the temple to socialize and to share two cakes served to all the participants. This annual Buddhist festival underlines the desire for Vietnamese Americans to maintain and practice as much of their cultural heritage and religious customs as possible. During the three-hour celebration, very little English was spoken; the chanting, sutras recitation, and songs were all performed in Vietnamese.

Chua Viet Nam also provides examples of assimilative changes toward the dominant American culture. Like earlier Buddhist organizations in America, this temple arranged its activities around the American work week, making Sunday the major day of religious activity. The language courses were also on Sunday, thus acting as a kind of "Sunday school." When Dam Luu noticed that one of the most pressing issues of the community was the growing generation gap, she advised the older generation of Vietnamese to learn English. In order to address the generation issue, the temple organizes activities that encourage interactions between the different generations, including the English classes for the elderly. Additionally, the temple is open regularly during the weekdays and weekends to allow opportunities for the older generation to volunteer their service as well as providing a place for them to socialize with other people in similar circumstances. This is an adaptive strategy to life in the United States and it reflects the deliberate decision by the temple to help alleviate some of the stresses faced by the older generation. These activities also increase opportunities for social and personal interactions between the different generations in order to minimize the generation gap. This is a new responsibility for the nuns at Chua Viet Nam. Although they are committed to their work, they clearly understand how this relationship has shifted. One of the nuns we interviewed reflected on this shift as follows: "Here in the U.S., when our members come to the temple, they need us to be family, to be blood. In Viet Nam, that demand is not very much because in the family, the people are closer, [and so when] the people come to the temple it is mostly to pray and talk to the teachers a little bit before heading home. But here, the difficulties seem to be very stressful. It seems that we need more time . . . I don't know why but the work in the U.S. is very rushing. That's why we have all those programs, and one that says to people, breathe in, breathe out, slow down."

Another way in which this community could be said to assimilate is in terms of the application of technology. Since San Jose is located in the heart of Silicon Valley, many community members had acquired technical skills that allowed them to provide technology and technical support at the temple. Members helped to record and duplicate important lectures, videotape and edit important celebrations, and record and distribute cassettes and CDs to the congregation at no cost. The use of technology enables individuals to listen to the Buddhist teachings in the privacy of their home or car while also providing an opportunity for people to donate funds to help maintain the temple. The temple

has even created its own website, with community volunteers responsible for the site's maintenance. The temple has utilized its location as well as the skills and knowledge of its members to provide different tools for people to use to maintain their religious practices even if they are not able to attend the services provided at the temple. Furthermore, technology not only enables the temple to provide materials to people in the area but also allows Buddhist teachings to be spread throughout the country and even overseas. Although all of this application of technology is strictly voluntary, those who volunteer have to have the "right attitude and the willingness to share these things" and believe in the mission of the temple.

Although Dam Luu's creative fundraising methods might be considered an example of assimilation, the efforts might also be considered a kind of innovation. Her idea to raise money through recycling employs an American concept and activity, but its application to religious fundraising is probably something not encountered in either host or home cultures. This is an example of Dam Luu's use of her religious teachings—in this case to not waste anything and to live simply, combined with the American concept of environmentalism—to help raise money for a temple. This fundraising tradition has continued through the many volunteer groups who provide service and expertise to address the many needs of the temple, and doing so in an environmentally responsible manner. One such effort is made by the "the fix-it crew," a group of middle-age men responsible not only for building repair but also mending broken items given as donations. Another group of volunteers is responsible for picking up and transporting heavy items donated to the temple from individual homes and other temples.

Like the fundraising, many other aspects of Dam Luu's activities are neither clearly assimilative nor preservative but instead are innovative—a creative response to a new environment with its new stressors. One example is Dam Luu's decision to open her temple to train both nuns and monks. In Vietnam nuns and monks live in separate temples and are trained in different ways. This act is thus a creative adaptation to solve the problem of the lack of facilities for monks to practice Buddhism in the United States. Another creative response is Dam Luu's openness to, even encouragement of, establishing relationships with other Buddhist sects. For several months during the summer, the nuns are required to visit, live, and learn at different temples in order to enhance their knowledge and to understand the many varieties of Buddhist practices. Other events support this effort, including, for example, visits and dharma talks by Tibetan monks; an exhibit of rare Buddhist artifacts from Tibet; a service performed by the Venerable Ribur Rinpoche, a well-known Tibetan yogi and scholar; an annual dharma talk by the Zen monk Thich Nhat Hanh, arguably the most recognizable Vietnamese Buddhist monk in the world; and dharma talks by monks from Vietnam as part of their visits to the United States. The temple has also taken part in the annual pilgrimage to the Land of Ten Thousand Buddhas, a significant event attended by many different Buddhist temples in Northern and Central California representing different ethnic groups as well as Buddhist sects. This kind of pan-Buddhist organizing and interaction is different from Buddhist activities in the home culture of Vietnam, but clearly it is not part of a kind of assimilation to white American culture. Perhaps it is a result of understanding oneself as a part of a religious minority that needs to build alliances with others under a larger religious identity. On an ethnic and racial level, Asian Americans have seen this kind of panethnic organizing as a result of racial experiences in the United States over the last forty years (Espiritu 1992).

A final example of Dam Luu's innovation is also paradoxically an example of preservation and maintenance: namely her creation of her own Vietnamese prayer book. While Dam Luu was living in a refugee camp in Malaysia, she observed that many Vietnamese who claimed to be Buddhists did not seem to behave in ways that reflected Buddhist teachings. She wanted to provide people with the opportunity to truly understand, learn, and practice Buddhist principles. As a result of China's influence, Vietnamese chanting books were written in Chinese and passed down for generations. Thus most of those reciting the chants did not understand the meaning of the words and therefore simply recited what was in the book. Dam Luu decided to translate the chanting books into Vietnamese so that people could understand the texts on their own. Additionally, she wanted the chanting books to include passages that were applicable to people's daily lives, especially their current experiences in the United States. These changes were not met without controversy within the temple. Although the changes were generally welcomed by the younger generation, many older members felt that Dam Luu was deviating too much from tradition and from Buddhism as they knew and practiced it. Although they threatened to withhold their financial support to the temple, this threat did not deter Dam Luu from executing her plans. Her decision to translate Buddhist scripture into Vietnamese has gained wide support at many Vietnamese Buddhist temples throughout the United States—so much support, in fact, that many are now using Dam Luu's translated text at their own temples (Thich 2000). Dam Luu's decision, and the wider community's acceptance of these changes, is particularly interesting here because they it is a seemingly paradoxical combination of preservation and innovation. The translation of the Buddhist text into Vietnamese was a significant break with Vietnamese tradition, but it was not a move toward assimilation in any way. In fact, by choosing Vietnamese as the language of translation, Dam Luu actually helped to preserve the Vietnamese language in the community, just as she did by sponsoring the Vietnamese language classes for the younger generation. Dam Luu's translation work is an important innovation that challenges the traditional model of assimilation because it reinforces Vietnamese Americans' religious and ethnic identity.

CONCLUSION

Chua Viet Nam is, first, an example of the significant role of religion in immigrant life. But it also serves as an example of the many changes that have occurred as a result of immigration and the displacement of a religious community. Like other immigrant religious organizations, this temple has taken on roles in the community that it did not have in the home culture. The temple performs many of the same functions of a temple in Vietnam while also changing and adapting to address the issues that arise specifically for the community in the United States. These changes, however, are not simply assimilative or preservative. As we have seen, immigrant religion also reacts to its environment in innovative ways by creating new elements in its structure to respond to the new needs of the community. The case of Chua Viet Nam and the abbess Dam Luu allow us to rethink and expand notions of adaptation and acculturation in ways to encompass a more complex picture of not only immigrant religion but also immigrant experience more generally.

NOTES

Portions of this chapter were first published as "Reproducing Viet Nam in America: San Jose's Perfect Harmony Temple," in S. Prothero, ed., *A Nation of Religions: Pluralism in the American Public Square* (Chapel Hill: University of North Carolina Press, 2006).

1. Abbess Suco, interview with Hien Duc Do and Tommy Lu, October 18, 2001.
2. An exception to this is the period of several months during the summer when they are sent on extended visits to learn other Buddhist doctrines and practices around the world.

PART 3

Transnationalism

Americanizing Philippine Churches and Filipinizing American Congregations

JOAQUIN JAY GONZALEZ III

In my interview with Professor Leny Mendoza Strobel of Sonoma State University I asked her about how her family in the Philippines experienced the missionary presence there. In response, she offered the following anecdote: "The first American Methodist missionary in the Philippines converted my grandfather at the turn of the twentieth century. Never mind that the Spanish came there first and that my grandfather's first choice was to become a Catholic priest. But the white man who stood on his soapbox at the town square charmed my grandfather and seduced him to becoming one of the first Filipino Methodist pastors in the region."[1] Strobel added that her father eventually came to the United States, and as a Methodist pastor he became a volunteer chaplain for Friends House, a Quaker retirement community in Sonoma, California. I believe that this transmigration connection is not unusual between a former mother country and a colony. After all, not only has more than a century of transnational relations (from 1898 to 2006) between the Philippines and the United States seriously affected both countries economically, militarily, environmentally, and politically, but also cross-cultural exchanges and social influences between the two countries have been quite evident during their long colonial, neocolonial, and postcolonial experiences.

Unlike other studies that have concentrated heavily on the broad sociocultural outcomes that emerged from immigration (Pido 1986; Posadas 1999; San Juan 1998), this essay revisits the historical roots of intersecting American and Filipino spirituality. In so doing it moves away from the unidirectional emphasis on America's contributions to religious life in the Philippines, especially the Protestant churches (see, e.g., Apilado 1999; Kwantes 1998; Maggay 1989; Miller 1982), by focusing on Filipino historical, sociological, and political influences on a broad range of church denominations in the United States.

The turn of the millennium brought a plethora of scholarly works exploring the contemporary effects and issues associated with Filipino transnational migration and globalization (see Choy 2003; Espiritu 2003; Ignacio 2005; Manalansan 2003; McKay 2006; Parreñas 2001, 2005). But ironically none have ventured into the Filipino religious contextualization and their trans-Pacific societal implications, even though churches are be the space where they would have been most visible ethnographically. The Filipinization of faith locations as a transnational cultural phenomenon gained greater relevance as waves of Filipino immigrants started flowing into the major gateway cities of the United States beginning in the early 1900s. And yet while a number of recent scholarly compilations on Asian Americans and their religious spaces and encounters have emerged from the academy (Carnes and Yang 2004; Jeung 2004; Min and Kim 2002; Yang 2000), the Filipino American spiritual transnationalism has remained understudied.

Although modern-day Filipino sojourners are known largely for their economic contributions into their new homelands, I argue that they automatically bring with them their Hispanic, Anglo-Saxon, and indigenously inspired religious belief systems and spiritual practices. Through the church, a societal institution in which they are culturally comfortable, new Filipino immigrants and their American counterparts are able to deal effectively with acculturative stress, to assimilate politically, and to contribute social energy to their host societies. But at the same time their Filipinized American churches have become safe spaces for negotiating and challenging identity, ethnicity, and nationalism (see Cordova 1983; San Buenaventura 1999). Filipinized locations are where Filipino immigrants are able to express and voice Filipino-style Catholic, Charismatic, Protestant, Masonic, and independent as well as indigenous (*baybaylan*) spiritual practices. Conversely, I argue that Filipino immigrants have shaped American faith and changed the spiritual contours of the United States not only through their presence here (e.g., taking over empty churches) but also through their influence on how America does religion. In this essay I use acute transnational and diasporic lenses to historicize the "second comings of Christianity": first, as manifested in the American Christianization of the Philippines starting with the bustling city of Manila, and second, as illustrated by the growing Filipinization of churches in the United States through the gateway city of San Francisco, California.

THE AMERICAN CHRISTIANIZATION OF MANILA

The emergence of the United States as the new global hegemon at the end of the nineteenth century has brought forward international economics and security as key starting points for balance-of-power relations among nation-states. Many scholars have noted that the tenor of Philippine-American relations was no exception (Banlaoi 2002; Baviera and Yu-Jose 1998; Delmendo 1998; Fast and Richardson 1982; Schirmer and Shalom 1987; Williams 1926). The quotes that I cite below from high-ranking Washington political and military officials reinforce these overriding themes as the basis for transnational links between the two countries.

In a stirring speech to Congress in 1900 the American Senator Albert Beveridge outlined the economic imperative for the United States in colonizing the Philippines: "The Philippines are ours forever. . . . and just beyond the Philippines are China's illimitable markets. . . . The Pacific is our Ocean. Where shall we turn for consumers of our surplus? Geography answers the question. China is our natural customer. The Philippines will give us a base at the door of all the East. No land in America surpasses in fertility the plains and valleys of Luzon: rice, coffee, sugar and coconuts, hemps and tobacco. The wood of the Philippines can supply the furniture of the world for a century to come" (quoted in Lyon and Wilson 1987, 62). Meanwhile, from a military standpoint, General Douglas MacArthur justified the strategic security importance of the country by stating:

> The Philippines are the finest group of islands in the world. Its strategic location is unexcelled by that of any other position in the globe. The China Sea, which separates it by something like 750 miles from the continent, is nothing more nor less than a safety moat. It lies on the flank of what might be called a position of several thousand miles of coastline: it is in the center of that position. It is therefore relatively better placed than Japan, which is on a flank, and therefore remote from the other extremity; likewise India, on another flank. It affords a means of protecting American interests, which with the very least output of physical power has the effect of a commanding position in itself to retard hostile action (quoted in Bello 1983, 3).

Hence, Scholarly critical analyses of the relations have placed a heavy emphasis on these key areas, especially the dysfunctional economic and political effects of the colonial and postcolonial linkages (Brands 1992; Delmendo 1998; Golay 1998; Pomeroy 1970; Shalom 1981). As the relationship deepened, many researchers from both sides of the Pacific also began to discuss the converging sociocultural experiences between the two countries (see Shaw and Francia 2003). However, very few scholars actually mention that the transnational links that developed between colony and former colony also had an interesting religious dimension—one that would actually usher in the "second coming of Christianity" into the Philippines.

Just like the economic and security imperatives for colonizing the Philippines, which were trumpeted by leaders from Washington, the religious "calling" was announced from the highest political pulpit in the land. In 1899 President William McKinley, a devout Methodist, proclaimed that there was a burning need for the "benevolent assimilation" of the Philippines. McKinley elaborated on this political revelation with the following remarks to a delegation of Methodist Church leaders who called on him at the White House: "I walked the floor of the White House night after night until midnight, and I am not ashamed to tell you, gentlemen, that I went down on my knees and prayed to Almighty God for light and guidance more than one night. And one late night it came to me this way—I don't know how it was, but it came . . . *that there was nothing left for us to do but to take them all, and to educate the Filipinos, and uplift and civilize and Christianize them, and by God's grace do the very best we could by them, as our fellowmen for whom Christ also died"* (quoted in Schirmer and Shalom 1983, 22 [emphasis mine]). To many of his astonished guests, it seemed that someone forgot to brief the president that the country he was referring to was already very Christian after more than three hundred years of evangelization by Spanish Catholic religious orders. Nonetheless, as his tirade continued it became apparent that what McKinley really meant was that his fellow Methodists should spread the word of an American brand of Christianity to what he perceived as wayward Filipino Christians. The Methodist visitors left the White House with McKinley's civilization-Christianization mantra still ringing in their ears—the church must go where America chooses to go!

THE ARRIVAL OF AMERICAN PROTESTANT CHURCHES

Like their European colonial predecessors, the United States needed to use the church to effectively and efficiently make the Filipinos embrace the patterns of behavior for an Anglo-Saxon civilization. Although church leaders were at first hesitant to provide support to what seemed to them the beginning of American imperialism, church leaders would eventually stand behind their beloved president's appeal. In the years to follow, many American Christian missionaries boarded the same ships that carried businessmen, civil servants, teachers, and military officers who were going to the Philippines for commercial, public administration, educational, and security concerns. By initially concentrating their religious activities in the gateway city of Manila, American Methodists, Congregationalists, Presbyterians, Lutherans, Baptists, Adventists, Episcopalians, Mormons, Jehovah's Witnesses, and other Christian missionaries came to convince Filipinos to embrace American Protestant teachings. They also ministered to the thousands of American Protestants who had gone with them to the Philippines to work.

The Protestants were very effective because unlike their Spanish religious counterparts who discouraged the masses to learn Spanish and banned the reading of the Bible, American Protestant Christian missionaries immediately began teaching English and set up many mission schools, especially for the poor. They also encouraged the translation of the Bible into the various Philippine languages and dialects. The American Protestants believed that there was a need to reform the Spanish-style practice of Christianity, which was not strongly based in the Bible and was tainted with folk beliefs, idolatry, and the veneration of saints and the Virgin Mary.[2]

Historically, even before America's turn-of-the-century annexation of the Philippines, the first missionaries had already arrived as soldiers deployed to fight in the Spanish-American War of 1898. For instance, the first Protestant service was held in August 1898 by the Methodist chaplain George C. Stull of the First Montana Volunteers. At the same time two American YMCA workers, Charles A. Glunz and Frank A. Jackson, were already actively ministering to U.S. soldiers in downtown Manila. Additionally, two artillery batteries arrived from Utah with the Mormon missionaries William Call and George Seaman.[3] On two Sundays in March 1899 Bishop James M. Thoburn of the Methodist Episcopal Church ministered at a rented theater in Manila. In April 1899 the Reverend James Burton Rodgers established the Philippine Presbyterian Mission. This was the first permanent American Protestant mission in the country. Reverend Burton stayed for forty years to help guide the work of the Presbyterians. Following the lead of the Presbyterians came the numerous American Bible Societies in the same year. Men and women working for the American Bible Societies put themselves to the task of translating the Bible into the local dialects and printing and distributing thousands of copies.

America's insistence on its "manifest destiny" of colonizing the country led to the Philippine-American War, a struggle that continued beyond the capture of Philippine General Emilio Aguinaldo in 1902. During the war, Filipinos were literally "baptized with fire." Instead of water over their heads, their bodies were immersed in pools of their own blood. Many Philippine towns were burned to the ground, and individuals who collaborated with the Filipino revolutionaries were tortured. Churches were not spared the destructive wrath of the American army. More than half a million Filipinos died in the conflict. These rites of war were performed by American troops both "in the name of God" and "as part of the white man's burden"(Agoncillo 1990; Constantino 1989). While these wanton acts were being done in areas outside of Manila, American church planters proceeded with their conversion work in the capital city as if nothing unusual were happening.

In January 1900 the Methodist Church formally established its Philippine presence when the Reverend Thomas H. Martin of Helena, Montana, started missionary work in Manila. By March of the same year Nicolas Zamora, the first Filipino Methodist deacon, was ordained with authority from the South Kansas Conference. Concentrating largely in Manila and its environs, the Methodists held regular meetings at Rosario, Pandacan, San Sebastian, and Trozo. Following the ordination of Reverend Zamora was the establishment of the first Methodist Church in Pandacan, Manila. On May 9 a second American Methodist missionary arrived.

At the beginning of the twentieth century the American Northern Baptist Church established a mission in the country. Then, encouraged by the positive reports from the Foreign Missions of the first batch of American Protestant Churches, an annual influx of other Christian congregations arrived to claim a share of the evangelical bounty in the new colony, including the United Brethren in 1901, the Disciples of Christ in 1901, the Protestant Episcopals in 1901, and the Congregationalists in 1902. Harassment from local Catholic clergy and their staunch supporters did not deter these missionary pioneers from their work.

After the Philippine-American War, the Seventh-Day Adventist Church sent its first mission to the Philippines in 1905.[4] The following year the Adventists J. L. McElhany and his wife arrived to work among the American soldiers, businessmen, and teachers who were sent to Manila. Founded in 1870, the work of the Jehovah's Witnesses also began in the Philippines when the American Charles T. Russell, president of the Watch Tower Bible and Tract Society in New York, gave an intriguing talk entitled "Where Are the Dead?" at the Manila Grand Opera House on January 12, 1912. Russell's evangelical talk was presented to an audience of nearly one thousand, which included General J. Franklin Bell, the commander in chief of the twenty thousand American troops stationed in the Philippines at that time. To spread the gospel, organized missionary work followed in the years to come, with Bible literature being provided by the headquarters in Brooklyn, New York. More than two decades after Russell's pioneering visit a Philippine branch was formally established in Manila.

In October 1914, more than thirty years before the founding of the ecumenical World Council of Churches, Philippine-based Presbyterians, Methodists, and Disciples of Christ decided to form the Union Church of Manila. The union of these Protestant churches was formally established at a liturgical service officiated by Bishop Charles Henry Brent of the Episcopal Church, Reverend George W. Wright of the Presbyterian Church, and Reverend Edwin F. Lee of the Methodist Church. The Union Church of Manila congregation eventually grew to include twenty-two denominations representing Baptists, Congregationalists, Disciples of Christ, Lutherans, Episcopalians, Federated churches, United Brethren, Church of God, Latter-Day Saints, Greek Orthodox, Hebrew, Dutch Reformed, Evangelical, Mennonite, Nazarene, and some Roman Catholics. Union Church has historically been the premier place of worship for expatriate Americans and Europeans based in Manila. At this church they are able to interact with individuals from their hometowns, organize picnics and socials, and maintain a predominantly Western atmosphere while living in the Philippines. They are also able to use the church to contribute to local social charities as well as to work toward the alleviation of poverty both domestically and internationally.

The early Filipino converts from Catholicism and other Christian faiths were very helpful with spreading the gospel. But many lay expatriate American citizens—those who were simply serving in official military and civilian functions, setting up businesses, or teaching classes in Manila and other parts of the Philippines—were also responsible for promoting Protestant Bible and gospel teachings. Canadian and European Protestant missions also supplemented the work of the Americans. In the decades to come, Protestant missionaries would spread the word to all the regions of the country. They would not only build churches but also seminaries, schools, hospitals, publishing houses, shelters, and social services in Manila and in all of the major cities and towns, even reaching hinterland areas that the Spanish Catholic friars were not able to cover.

THE AMERICANIZATION OF THE HISPANIC CATHOLIC CHURCH REGIME

Many scholarly works have been written about the systematic conversion of the native Filipinos by Spanish Catholic religious orders, or friars. The Order of Saint Augustine sent the first Catholic priests to the Philippines. They came

with the conquistador Legazpi expedition of 1564. The Augustinians were followed by the Franciscans in 1577, the Jesuits in 1581, the Dominicans in 1587,
and the Recollects in 1606. In the second half of the nineteenth century, the first
batch of Spanish religious groups was joined by the Sons of Saint Vincent de
Paul in 1862, the Sisters of Charity in 1862, the Capuchins in 1886, and the Bene-
dictines in 1895. For more than three centuries, these religious orders facilitated
the conversion of more than 85 percent of the population (or 6.5 million out of
an estimated 8 million) into Catholicism.

The new American political administrators had no choice but to get involved early on in the religious situation in the Philippines because the 1896
Philippine revolution released the anger and fury of the Filipinos not only
against Spain's provincial government in the islands but also against the entrenched friar establishment. At the outbreak of hostilities, thousands of friars
were able to flee to the safe confines of Manila. But some who were not lucky
enough to reach the capital city were taken prisoners, while others were beaten
or killed. Fearing for their lives and the sequestration of their vast properties, the friar leadership ensured that the terms of surrender between Admiral
George Dewey and the Spanish authorities, as well as the Treaty of Paris (which
formally ceded the Philippines to the United States), included provisions that
guaranteed American army protection for their churches and "ecclesiastical
lands." The Vatican had no objection to this arrangement. The American military governor, General Elwell Otis, created additional controversy when he
allowed Spanish Archbishop Nozaleda, a hated friar, to replace the Filipino pastor at Paco Church in Manila. Made without their involvement, these policies
and actions angered many Filipinos, especially the clergy, who began to suspect
that their battle to gain control and influence over both church and state had
not ended with the ousting of their Spanish conquistadors. Their new enemies
were now the American religious authorities and the American government.

The changeover to American rule in 1898 and the end of Philippine-
American hostilities brought many American and other non-Spanish, European Catholic orders and congregations to the Philippines. These included in
1906 the Redemptorists, the Benedictine Sisters, and the Congregations of San
Jose, and in 1907 the Fathers of the Divine Word and the Missionaries of the
Immaculate Heart. The Franciscans, Jesuits, and Dominicans also made adjustments in their Philippine congregations by sending more Americans priests.
Because of the resentment by local Filipinos against the abuses and excesses of
the Spanish friars, the American religious orders tried to create a new image of
the Roman Catholic clergy. The American religious orders also tried very hard

to show to the local populace that even though they were Catholic priests they were different from the Spanish friar stereotypes that the Filipinos disliked. They also opened public schools to everyone in order to appease their apprehensions. Not surprisingly, the person who was put in charge of educational initiatives was a Catholic priest, Reverend Father William D. McKinnon, the chaplain of the First California Volunteers. He was directed by Governor General Otis to begin the organization and construction of primary and secondary institutions in Manila. Father McKinnon's rapport with the Catholic laity, the predominantly Catholic population, and knowledge of Spanish contributed heavily to his initial successes at setting up an American educational system in the capital city.

Some changes were also implemented in the Catholic Church hierarchy in the Philippines. Spanish priests were not expelled, unlike the Spanish military personnel and government officials. However, given the resentment against them by the Filipinos, many had decided to go back to Spain or get reassigned. Immediately after the takeover, the high-ranking positions held by the Spanish clergy were assumed by American priests, many of whom were of Irish American descent. In 1903, the Missouri native Reverend Father Jeremiah James Hart became the first American archbishop of Manila. Many parishes with Spanish pastors were redistributed to diocesan priests from Ireland, Germany, Belgium, and France. Religious societies of monks, brothers, and sisters from America and Europe also established missions, monasteries, convents, and schools all over the country. By the end of the year, the number of Spanish friars in the Philippines was reduced from a peak of more than 1,100 in 1896 to a mere 246 five years after the American takeover. In 1904 the last Spanish bishop had left the Philippines and almost all of the high positions in the Catholic Church were occupied by American bishops.

These new Christian leaders tried to create an American-style church regime beginning with a firm promotion of the principle of separation of church and state and the freedom to believe in any religion. These attempts to promote American liberal democracy in the religious aspect of Filipino society were actively supported by both American Catholic and Protestant church leaders. Many Filipinos also warmly received this change after experiencing centuries of intervention by the Spanish Catholic Church in running the government and even their personal lives.

Dogmatically, the American Roman Catholic orders agreed with some of the observations by American Protestant Christians that there was a need to reform the Spanish-style practice of Christianity, which was not strongly based in the bible and also was tainted with idolatry. Apparently, both American Catholic and Protestant missionaries were after the creation of a more Anglo-Saxon–Teutonic culture in the practice of religion. English became the language of education, the government, the military, business, and of course, the church.

THE FOUNDING OF FILIPINO INDEPENDENT CONGREGATIONS

If the Spaniards used the Catholic Church to effectively conquer the hearts of the Filipinos, the Americans used the Protestant Church to uplift their kindred spirits. Many Filipino nationalists noticed this and concluded that the American modus operandi for colonizing the country was no different from that of Spain. For instance, just as in the running of government, very few Filipino religious leaders were granted positions of influence and leadership in the early American period of Protestant and Catholic Church hierarchies. Besides, Americans controlled the military and American firms received monopolies, subsidies, and preferential treatment. Tired of this same colonial socioeconomic situation, many Filipino leaders decided to lobby and fight for their political, social, and economic rights and freedom while Filipino spiritual leaders were emboldened to organize their own indigenous and independent Christian churches.

The most serious breakaway group from the Catholic Church was the Philippine Independent Church (PIC; also popularly known as the Iglesia Filipina Independiente, or the Aglipayan Church). Although founded largely as a response to the total dominance of Spanish friars in the Catholic Church hierarchy, the PIC did not anticipate any serious organizational changes to happen with the arrival of American Catholic clergy. Hence, one month after President Theodore Roosevelt declared the end of the Philippine-American War in July 1902, in the meeting of the General Council of the Union Obrera Democratica (UOD), its head, Isabelo de los Reyes Sr., announced the establishment of the Philippine Independent Church with Reverend Gregorio Aglipay as obisbo maximo (supreme bishop). De los Reyes and Aglipay convinced many Filipino priests to join their cause-oriented religious sect and they sequestered the Roman Catholic Churches in the "name of Filipinos." A year after the founding of the PIC, it was believed to have amassed one and a half million members, which at the time was roughly one quarter of the population of the Philippines. Rejected by the Vatican, the PIC still did not see fit to align with the Protestant churches despite numerous talks with Methodist, Presbyterian, and American Bible Society leaders and missionaries. The American-controlled Catholic Church in the Philippines took more than four decades before Monsignor

Gabriel Reyes, a Filipino, was finally appointed Roman Catholic archbishop of Cebu in 1934. But the damage had already been done. The PIC had grown in significance.[5]

An indigenous Filipino Christian Church that emerged during the American occupation was the Global Church of Christ (GCC).[6] This independent church was founded by Brother Edmundo G. Albano,[7] who was born and baptized a Catholic. As a teenager, Albano left the Catholic Church and was fascinated by the Bible interpretations preached by the various American Protestant Christian denominations who arrived in the Philippines at the turn of the century. In order to learn more about their view of the gospel, Albano joined the Methodist Episcopal Church and studied at the Presbyterian Ellinwood Bible Training School. He later ventured to the American-inspired Christian Mission and the Seventh-Day Adventist Church. His exposure to the various Bible teachings made Albano dissatisfied with the doctrinal contradictions and inconsistencies in the teachings and interpretations of these American-inspired Protestant faiths. In 1913, after praying, fasting, meditating, and seeking the guidance of God, he began the work of forming a new and independent Church of Christ. Based on a Filipino perspective of God's word, Albano developed an integrated set of teachings and church organization based on the various American Christian faiths he had attended. In 1919, he also went to the United States to study and reflect on his new church. Albano is seen by GCC members as God's chosen messenger, having received spiritual enlightenment in order to reestablish the Church of Christ beginning from the East (Reed 1990; Tuggy 1978).

Attempts by Filipino Protestant and independent church leaders to "challenge" the administrative powers of their American counterparts contributed to the creation of the United Evangelical Church in 1929, the Philippine Methodist Church in 1933, and the Evangelical Church in 1943. These loose alliances of Filipino-led independent Protestant churches became the precursors to the establishment of an umbrella organization, called the United Church of Christ of the Philippines, in 1948—four years after the granting of independence by the United States.

Other Filipino indigenous Christian sects and Masonic organizations that blossomed during the American period were Ruben Ecleo and his Benevolent Missionaries Association, Apolinario de la Cruz and his Confradia de San Jose, Felipe Salvador and his Santa Iglesia Guardia de Honor de Maria, and the Rizalistas (including the Samahang Rizal, Iglesiang Pilipinas, Watawat ng Lahi, and Iglesia Sagrada Filipina ng Sinco Vulcanes).

THE FILIPINIZATION OF SAN FRANCISCO'S CHURCHES

Unknown to President McKinley, a parallel "second coming of Christianity" was already underway even before the Philippines became a U.S. colony in 1898. Unlike the Americans who needed to build battleships and start a bloody war to civilize and Christianize the inhabitants of the Philippine islands, Filipinos were able to reach the shores of the United States through quiet and peaceful means. They accomplished this by crossing the Pacific Ocean as crewmembers of the famous Spanish commercial galleons that went back and forth from Manila to the North American continent bringing precious commodities to Spanish settlements in what is now California and Mexico and as far east as Louisiana. Because of the harsh treatment and low pay they received in service of the Spanish crown, many of the Filipino seamen jumped ship and settled in the pueblos of Acapulco and in the bayous of Louisiana. Mostly Catholics, these men blended with the Mexican and American Christian church congregations wherever they went. In the Louisiana bayous they set up Filipino settlements on stilts and introduced shrimp processing techniques. They also brought with them to these new lands their religious faith, devotions, and prayers as part of their Filipino heritage.

While many Americans were busy administering, developing, and Christianizing their one and only prized colony in the Far East, successive waves of Filipinos left the Philippines for the United States during the period from 1910 to 1930. While most of these immigrants were hired to work in the farm areas as agricultural workers, many also stayed in the cities and worked as domestic helpers, hotel and restaurant cooks, dishwashers, bellhops, elevator boys, and busboys in Hawaii, California, Alaska, Washington, Oregon, and New York. There was also a large group of *pensionados* or U.S. government scholars who came to study at American universities. After the Second World War, many Filipinos who served in the U.S. military also decided to try out greener pastures away from their native land. Immigration increased further with the passage of the Immigration Act of 1965, which encouraged a new wave of highly skilled professionals (i.e., doctors, nurses, engineers, and accountants) to move to the United States. Their families were allowed to join them soon afterward (Bonus 2000; Choy 2003; Cordova 1983; Takaki 1987).

Through the course of several decades, San Francisco was the popular gateway city for most of these Filipino immigrants. They brought with them rich and distinctive cultures that eventually blended with the diverse cultural mix that characterizes the Bay Area. Filipino food, dances, music, art, languages, and literature were slowly integrated into the local scenery. But probably the biggest and most obvious cultural contributions of generations of Filipino immigrants to San Francisco are the active roles they play in the city's churches—roles that range from pastors to brethren. Given the mass exodus from their motherland, perhaps the "second coming of Christianity" was really destined to be from the East to the West, or from the Philippines to the United States.

After all, before 1965 many San Francisco Catholic and Protestant churches had been experiencing serious declines in active memberships. Low attendance rates led to low financial contributions. With rising maintenance bills, many of these churches had to rent out space to other interested religious congregations. Some were simply forced to close and sell their property. Heavy commercialization in the downtown neighborhoods reduced the number of residential homes in the areas around churches. Moreover, earthquakes and fires also contributed to closures and human movements away from cities and into suburban areas. Interestingly, many of the religious centers affected by these natural and man-made tragedies have been "saved" by new immigrant groups, including, not surprisingly, Filipino Christians. Nowhere is the Filipino Christianization in the United States felt more than in California, which is home to close to a million Filipino immigrants of Catholic, Protestant, and independent church backgrounds.

RECONSTUCTING SAN FRANCISCO'S CATHOLIC INSTITUTIONS

Most new Filipino immigrants, coming from the only predominantly Catholic country in Asia, are likely to be socialized in the Roman Catholic faith and traditions. Indeed, beginning in the first decade of the twentieth century the growing number of Filipino immigrants to the United States increased church attendance rates, especially in the Catholic Churches, in the major gateway cities of San Francisco, Honolulu, Los Angeles, Seattle, New York, and Chicago. According to U.S. government records between 1920 and 1929, 31,092 Filipinos entered California, of which more than 80 percent went through the port of San Francisco (California Department of Industrial Relations 1930). The biggest beneficiaries of the Filipino inflow were the Catholic Churches in the area of San Francisco then known as "Happy Valley." Some of these historic churches include San Patricio[8] (founded in 1851), Saint Joseph (founded in 1861), and Saint Rose (founded in 1878). Another favorite among the Manilatown and Chinatown Filipino residents was Old Saint Mary's Cathedral (founded in 1854).

During this period, close to 90 percent of Filipino migrants were single males between eighteen and thirty-four years of age. Family building was difficult since there were few women from the Philippines. The 1930 census estimated that in the entire United States there were only 1,640 women of Filipino descent — 309 single, 1,258 married, 53 widowed, and 16 divorced. To complicate matters, Filipino men were "discouraged" from marrying European American (Caucasian) women by the antimiscegenation laws. This was not the case for Caucasian men who wanted to marry Filipino women. One of the first recorded baptisms in San Francisco was held on November 8, 1914, when Isaac Braan, originally from Raleigh, North Carolina, and his Filipina wife, Gregoria Pena, brought their infant daughter, Erminda Celeste, to San Patricio's church. The Braans would later bring to the same church their two other children, born in 1916 and 1917, to receive the same religious sacrament. Church records also indicate that a few other Filipino children's baptisms also followed during the years to come.

To combat the restlessness of the largely male Filipino immigrant group and to encourage them to channel their socio-emotional energies toward morally appropriate activities, the diocese leaders of Seattle and San Francisco sponsored the creation in 1922 of a Catholic Filipino Club in each city (Burns 2000). Around six hundred workers from Seattle registered and availed of the services of their club. While in San Francisco, Archbishop Edward J. Hanna and the Community Chest became active supporters of the popular Catholic Filipino Club, which soon became the hub of social activities for the estimated five thousand Filipino residents of the city. Aside from the Catholic Filipino Club, there were two other Filipino Catholic organizations — the Catholic Filipino Glee Club and the Catholic Filipino Tennis Club. Other Filipino groups availed of club space posted activities and recruited members from those who went to the central club space.[9]

During the mid-1920s, the Caballeros de Dimas Alang, a religious brotherhood in the style of the Masons, was also established in San Francisco by Pedro Loreto. Four years later another fraternity, the Legionarios del Trabajo, was formed in Stockton and San Francisco. Other famous fraternal groupings were the Gran Oriente Filipino and the Knights of Rizal. Many Filipino Catholics joined these quasi-Masonic Filipino organizations because they continued to feel discriminated against in the Caucasian-dominated Catholic churches. Besides, some of the new immigrants still had brought with them to America their negative experiences and corresponding revolutionary thoughts about the Catholic Church.

As noted earlier, the end of the Second World War and the passage of the 1965 Immigration Act further increased immigration to the United States, thus further filling Catholic churches in the vast Archdiocese of San Francisco (which encompasses the counties of San Francisco, San Mateo, and Marin). By the 1960 census, there were 12,327 Filipinos in the city of San Francisco alone. This figure more than tripled by the 1990 census. According to official estimates in 2000, out of an estimated population of more than 150,000 Filipinos there are more than 90,000 registered Catholic parishioners in the archdiocese. Statistically, one out of every four Catholics in the area is of Filipino descent.[10]

One example of a church that has been influenced by Filipinos is San Patricio's Catholic Church, once a favorite place of worship for Irish Americans. Its dynamic Filipino pastor, Monsignor Ferdinand Santos,[11] has proudly proclaimed that "Filipino parishioners practically saved the historic church from serious demise." San Patricio's is presently staffed by Filipino priests, Filipino nuns, Filipino deacons, and Filipino lay workers. Daily noon services are popular among Filipino workers in the surrounding downtown area, while Sunday services draw loyal parishioners not just from the city but from all over the Bay Area.

New Filipino immigrants to San Francisco usually attend services at San Patricio's and then move on to other Catholic Churches once they feel comfortable with American life and can start affording homes outside the city. Some continue to go to San Patricio's even after moving out of the area, especially to attend the 2:00 PM Tagalog mass every first Sunday of the month. The noon daily mass is also a favorite among Filipino immigrants who live outside the city but work in San Francisco.

The inside of San Patricio's generally resembles the decor of typical Irish churches, although it has been slightly Filipinized with statues and images of saints and the Virgin Mary. Some of the images are of indigenous Filipino folk figures like the Santo Nino (or Christ Child) and San Lorenzo Ruiz (the first Filipino saint). Visiting statues of the Virgin Mary from the Philippines are also accorded a special place in the church. For instance, the statue of Our Lady of the Most Holy Rosary from Manila was a recent visitor. Filipino American parishioners, like their peers in the Philippines, line up to touch, kiss, and wipe their handkerchief on the statue of the Virgin Mary. Many non-Filipino parishioners and visitors have also learned to venerate in this "Filipino way" in order to conform to the culture of praise and worship that they encounter. They have also heard from many Filipino parishioners that their way works because they have had "miracles" happen in their lives.

Many other Catholic churches have filled up with devoted Filipino parishioners, especially south of San Francisco and across the bay in the neighboring Diocese of Oakland. Both Saint Andrew's Church and Our Lady of Perpetual Help Church in Daly City, along with Saint Augustine Church in South San Francisco, have Filipino priests preaching to memberships that are more than

80 percent Filipino. Tagalog masses are held at San Patricio's Church and Saint Boniface Church in San Francisco as well as at Holy Angels Church in Colma. Filipino American choirs, devotions to the Santo Nino, San Lorenzo Ruiz, and Mother Mary are very common. Seven parishes celebrate the Simbang Gabi while Flores de Mayo and the Easter Salubong are slowly being integrated into regular church activities. Popular Filipino Catholic groups such as the El Shaddai, the Jesus Is Lord movement, Bukod Loob sa Dios, Couples for Christ, and Divine Mercy have also gone forth and multiplied rapidly among Filipino brothers and sisters. The El Shaddai group, headed by the charismatic Brother Mike Velarde, which claims millions of active members in the Philippines, meets regularly at the Cathedral of Saint Mary of the Assumption and other Catholic churches in the Archdiocese of San Francisco.

The Reverend Fathers Bantigue (Mission Dolores Basilica), Antonio Rey (Our Lady of Perpetual Help Church), Max Villanueva (Holy Angels Church), and Ferdinand Santos (Saint Joseph and San Patricio Churches) are some of the first Filipino Catholic priests in the archdiocese. Father Bantigue began his pastoral work in San Francisco as early as the 1950s. Since then, fourteen Philippine-based religious congregations of men including diocesan priests have sent members to serve in San Francisco parishes and dioceses all over the United States. The demand for Filipino priests continues to increase as the number of Caucasian Americans entering the priesthood decreases and as more Filipinos immigrate to the United States. American theological seminaries have also started recruiting students from the Philippines to replenish the diminishing ministerial pool. Currently, Filipinos already make up a significant part of the leadership of San Francisco Bay Area Catholic churches. In 2002, there were thirty-nine priests, twelve full-time deacons, five sisters, and thirty lay workers of Filipino descent in the fifty-two parishes of San Francisco. The Council of Priests in the archdiocese was once chaired by Reverend Father Eugene D. Tungol—a Filipino pastor.[12]

Surprisingly, some of the earliest Filipino Catholic missionary congregations to work in San Francisco and in other parts of the United States were religious organizations of Filipino women. In December 1955 the Benedictine Sisters of Ilocos Sur arrived to help with the needs of Filipino families in the Salinas area. The Sisters opened a religious class for preschoolers, and they were also instrumental in the creation of the Legion of Mary and the Our Lady of Antipolo Society—the popular devotions to the Virgin Mary practiced in the Philippines. In 1959 the Manila-based Religious of the Virgin Mary started its overseas mission in the Sacramento area, followed by Honolulu in 1972 and then San Francisco in 1982. Members of this group assist in the spiritual needs of parishioners in San Patricio's Church and in Our Lady of Mercy Church. Starting with an overseas mission in Hawaii in 1964, the Dominican Sisters of the Most Holy Rosary from Molo in Iloilo Province in the Philippines then moved to the mainland with a San Francisco presence beginning in 1982. The Dominican Sisters have made an impact by helping to run Catholic schools and by assisting in devotions and services at Saint Charles Borromeo Church and at Holy Angels Church. By the late 1990s, thirty-two Philippine-based congregations had religious sisters working in the United States.[13]

Aside from Catholic churches, Catholic clubs, and Catholic religious organizations of men and women, another major beneficiary of the Filipino inflow to San Francisco were the archdiocese's many Catholic schools. As early as September 1963, thirty-eight of the forty-five elementary schools in the city reported a total of 680 Filipino children in attendance. The schools with the largest numbers were Sacred Heart Elementary (78), Saint Paul (42), Star of the Sea (41), Saint Peter (38), and Saint Monica (28).[14] By the 1980s and the 1990s San Francisco's elementary and high schools experienced a surge in Filipino enrollment growth as immigrants from the 1960s and 1970s began sending their children to religious schools. New arrivals and their families also contributed to the increase. By 2000 Corpus Christi Elementary School had become more than 75 percent Filipino in terms of its student body. Aside from Corpus Christi, elementary schools at the Church of the Epiphany, the Church of the Visitacion, Saint Elizabeth, Saint Emydius, Saint Finn Barr, Saint John the Evangelist, Saint Kevin, Holy Angels, and Our Lady of Perpetual Help have student populations that are close to 50 percent Filipino.

Some of the Catholic high schools in the San Francisco Bay Area currently have between 20 and 25 percent Filipino student populations, including Saint Ignatius College Prep, Archbishop Riordan, Mercy High, Bishop O'Dowd, and Sacred Heart Cathedral Prep. Furthermore, Catholic tertiary institutions like the University of San Francisco and Santa Clara University have also experienced rapid growth in Filipino student enrollment. Saint Patrick's Seminary and University in Menlo Park also reported a significant number of students of Filipino descent training for the priesthood and taking graduate theological and religious programs.[15]

PROTESTANTISM RETURNS TO AMERICA

McKinley's "prophesy of a second coming of Christianity" to the Philippines brought many American Protestant groups to "build churches and save the Filipinos." Little did Americans know that the same Filipinos they would "save and baptize" would bring back Protestantism to America and in so doing precipitate a "second coming of Christianity"—this time to the United States. Although this group is smaller in size and distribution compared to their Filipino Catholic counterparts, their presence and growth is still worth examining. Filipino Protestant agricultural workers in the United States began attending services and Bible studies with the various American Christian Protestant churches in Hawaii and California. As their size grew, they also began to establish their own Filipino American Christian Protestant congregations. Just as in the Philippines, many Filipino American Catholics have also converted and joined Protestant congregations.

Following the pioneering efforts of their American Methodist counterparts, who blazed the trail in Manila as a response to President McKinley's 1899 call, Filipino Methodist immigrants started arriving in San Francisco early in the century. In 1920, with their growing numbers, they established the Filipino Wesley Methodist Church—only two decades after the beginning of the American occupation and "Christianization" of their homeland. These Filipino Protestant pilgrims gathered together regularly for fellowship and a sense of belonging to the new and strange land. Later in the year, Dr. J. Stanley was appointed pastor. The congregation went on to change its name to the Filipino Fellowship Church. By the 1930s, around one hundred Filipino Protestant Christians in San Francisco were registered with the Filipino Christian Fellowship and with the YMCA's Filipino Christian Endeavor.

Outside of San Francisco, the Presbyterian pastor Pedro F. Royola began evangelical work among Salinas-based Filipino farm workers in 1924. He formed the Filipino Community Church (which later became Saint Philip's Church). Trained in Manila, Reverend Royola was greatly influenced by none other than the American Presbyterian Dr. James B. Rodgers. He received his formal education from the American-established Ellinwood Malate Church, the Silliman Institute, and the Union Theological Seminary. Prior to moving to California he was successfully ministering to Filipino plantation workers in Hawaii (Solis 2000).

In the Pacific islands between the Philippines and California, Hilario Camino Moncado, one of the early Filipino labor migrants working the sugar plantations of Hawaii, founded the Filipino Federation of America in 1925. The charismatic Moncado eventually transformed this labor organization of U.S.-based Filipino workers into the Equifrilibricum World Religion, popularly known as the Moncadistas. Moncado claimed to be the reincarnated Jesus Christ, and he was seen by his fellow workers and religious followers as the person who would deliver them from the economic exploitation, unfair treatment, and racial discrimination that they were experiencing in American society. Unlike other social organizations during those times, which were notorious for their gambling, dancing, and drinking, Moncado's group claimed to promote a clean and upright lifestyle. Equifrilibricum also gained a foothold among the Filipino workers in San Francisco (Mercado 1982).

Joining forces with tired, oppressed Mexican and other Asian migrant workers, Filipinos started many labor mobilization activities. In 1928, protesting Filipino workers were driven out of the agricultural fields in Yakima Valley in Washington as well as in Hood River and Banks in Oregon. This was not the first time they had instigated strikes. Fighting for the rights of thousands of migrant workers, Filipinos began to earn the reputation of being "radicals." During that same year, however, down the long Pacific coast, another group of Filipino agricultural laborers working in Southern California were also determined to organize. But this time it was for a less confrontational objective—the establishment of the first Filipino American Christian Fellowship Church of Los Angeles. Peaceful religious worship services did not placate the restless Filipino farm workers, especially in rural California. They organized socials and invited white women, to the chagrin of many white rural men. Filipino migrant workers were also accused of stealing agricultural jobs from white Americans. Tensions ran high and in January 1930, violent anti-Filipino riots erupted at Watsonville in Monterey County. Six years later, the larger American labor unions took notice of their plight.

Because of successive waves of immigration starting from the 1920s, Filipino Methodists, Presbyterians, Baptists, Adventists, Episcopalians, Mormons, and Jehovah's Witnesses have successfully established flourishing congregations all over the San Francisco Bay Area. Many of these Filipino religious congregations have taken over houses of prayer and worship that used to be attended primarily by Caucasians. Peter Burnett, California's first governor, would probably never have expected that Saint James Presbyterian Church in Visitacion Valley, where his family attended services and taught Sunday school, would one day be transformed into a church led and participated in by brown-skinned Filipinos from across the Pacific Ocean. Similar changes have taken place at Saint Francis and Grace United Methodist Church in the Sunset District, which has become predominantly Filipino.

Members of the all-Filipino Faith Bible Church of San Francisco purchased the former Salvation Army Church on Broad Street, while the San Francisco Filipino American Seventh-Day Adventist Church in Pacifica as well as Holy

Cross and Our Lady of Peace Episcopal Church in Sunnyvale converted former Lutheran churches. In 1968 the largest non-Catholic denomination in the Philippines, the Global Church of Christ, began its overseas mission when it formally established locales in Honolulu and San Francisco. In less than forty years it has expanded to twenty-four American states and seventy countries in the world. Beginning with two Bay Area congregations in the early 1970s, the Filipino American Jehovah's Witnesses have increased to twelve congregations, and members need to be versed in Tagalog to attend their Filipino services.

Meanwhile, the Filipino ward of the Church of Jesus Christ of Latter-Day Saints in Daly City, which also began in the 1970s, has grown to more than 350 members. The Mormon Church has members who have been former missionaries in the Philippines, and some have Filipino spouses. Because of their language training and exposure to mission work in many parts of the Philippines, members are able to sing Tagalog hymns and attend Tagalog services when they return to the United States. Some know a number of Philippine dialects in addition to Tagalog and thus they are able to participate in the Visayan and Ilocano Bible study sessions.

From the date of their establishment, it took the American Protestant Churches more than a hundred years to cross the Pacific Ocean and establish themselves in the Philippines. In comparison, the independent Global Church of Christ (GCC) only needed approximately half this time to set up formal missions in the United States and then proclaim the Bible to the rest of the world. As early as 1967, GCC migrants to Hawaii began gathering other brethren on the island of Oahu, and in 1968 the GCC began its overseas work in Honolulu. After a month in Hawaii, Brother Edilberto Albano[16] proceeded to San Francisco and officially proclaimed the establishment of a GCC congregation in the continental United States (Reed 1990). Some of the largest GCC congregations in the United States are found in San Francisco and in nearby Daly City. The GCC offers both Tagalog and English services, and it has more than fifteen hundred members in Honolulu and San Francisco alone. In addition, some Caucasian members have learned Tagalog and join in the singing and Bible readings.

The first Filipino Jehovah's Witness congregations were established in Stockton in 1974 and in Salinas in 1975. Most of the members were the early Filipino farm workers and their families. In the 1980s and 1990s, the number of Filipino Jehovah's Witnesses increased rapidly, and now there are twelve Filipino American congregations in the San Francisco Bay area, twelve in the Los Angeles area, and four in the Washington-Oregon area. Each of these Filipino American congregations has around 100 active members. All twenty-eight

Filipino American congregations are a closely-knit group and meet regularly throughout the year. The San Francisco area congregations are found in Alameda, Daly City, El Cerritos, Hayward, Milpitas, Salinas, San Francisco, San Jose, Stockton, Sunnyvale, Vallejo, and West Sacramento.[17]

Organized in 1967, the San Francisco Filipino American Seventh-Day Adventist Church is part of the sisterhood of churches of the Central California Conference of Seventh-Day Adventists. It is committed to proclaiming the Gospel to its community, training and equipping its members for Christian service, and preparing believers for the second coming of Jesus. While the Seventh-Day Adventist Church exists primarily to reach individuals of Filipino background, it also endeavors to minister to people of different cultures. As a result there are active African American, Caucasian American, and Asian American members of the church. It offers two Tagalog Bible classes, one Kapampangan Bible class, and one English Bible class every Saturday.[18]

The first service of the Faith Bible Church of San Francisco (FBC) was in April 1971 at the Twenty-first Avenue Baptist Church. The Filipino group stayed there until 1973 when the church was formally organized in the home of Pastor Leo Calica. In 1975 the group moved to Saint James Presbyterian Church, with Pastor Calica as the full-time pastor. In both places they shared the facilities with other congregations, but two years later the FBC group found a permanent home when they purchased the Salvation Army chapel on Broad Street. In 1989 a Tagalog service was started in FBC San Francisco. With Pastor Calica's able leadership FBC grew in membership and in activities, and it now proudly supports missionaries all over the world. Other Faith Bible Churches have also emerged in Oakland, Vallejo, and Pittsburg. Pastor Calica's son has followed in his father's footsteps, and he is now the pastor of Faith Bible Church in Vallejo.[19]

Reverend Arturo Capuli is the third Filipino American pastor of the Saint Francis and Grace United Methodist Church (San Francisco). His two predecessors, Reverend Leonard Autajay and Reverend Juan Ancheta, were originally trained as Baptist ministers. All three started their training in the Philippines and then moved to the United States for their advanced theological studies. The present congregation was a merger between the Filipino Wesley Methodist Church and Parkside Methodist Church, a predominantly Caucasian congregation whose membership was rapidly declining. Over the years, the Caucasian congregation diminished rapidly and it became an almost all-Filipino group. Saint Francis and Grace United Methodist Church is one of three UMC churches that has a Filipino ministry. The other two UMC churches

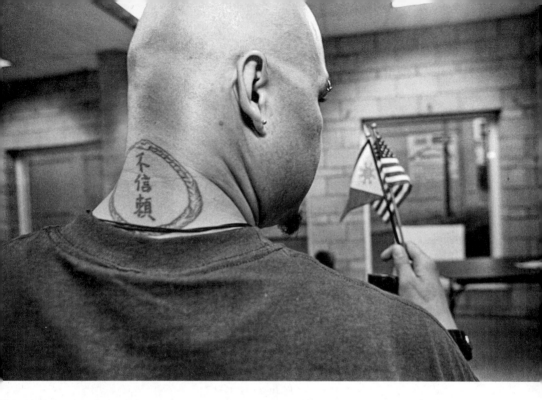

are on Geneva Avenue in San Francisco and in Southgate in Daly City. There are a total of twenty-two UMC churches in the Bay Area, and all of them have Filipino members.[20]

CONCLUSION

The second coming of Christianity to the Philippines has helped build the country's social infrastructure with the development of a mass-based English-language educational system. This move not only increased the educational levels of Filipinos but also facilitated the reading and understanding of the Christian Bible, which the Spanish friars banned for more than three hundred years. The cost was literally baptism by fire, however, with the eruption of the Philippine-American War. While Catholic churches sought to refurbish their tainted image among the Filipinos through newly installed American clergy, American Protestant churches and their missionaries came and spread a different brand of Christianity throughout the country. A group of nationalist leaders, unconvinced of any changes in the political, economic, and most especially the religious leadership in the Philippines, were inspired to deviate from the Western-dominated church hierarchy and establish the Philippine Independent Church. The shortcomings in the teachings of independent, Protestant, and Catholic churches from the West inspired the establishment of the GCC from the east. Filipino Protestant church leaders also challenged the centralized authority of their American counterparts—an effort that contributed to the creation of Filipino-led independent Protestant churches, which later came under the umbrella organization called the United Church of Christ of the Philippines.

The "second coming of Christianity" to the colonized also precipitated a "second coming of Christianity" to the colonizer, a phenomenon that occurred through successive waves of Filipino immigration to the United States beginning in the early 1900s. Interestingly, unlike President McKinley's benevolent assimilation policy, which did not have any scriptural basis, there are many Filipinos who believe that the second coming of Christianity to America, as manifested in the rise of Filipino American churches, is foretold in the Bible—"From the far east will I bring your offspring, from the far west will I gather you" (Isaiah 43:5).

Filipino Christian congregations have blossomed in San Francisco and in many other gateway cities in America since the 1920s. They have taken over places of worship that were previously occupied by predominantly European American congregations. Asian American, African American, Caucasian American, and Latino American attendees of Filipino places of worship have learned to accept the rituals, beliefs, and nuances of Filipino Catholicism, Protestantism, and Christianity. They have learned to pray to San Lorenzo Ruiz and to say their confessions to priests with heavy Filipino accents. Non-Filipino congregants have even learned to appreciate the Filipino humor and anecdotes of their ministers and pastors. They have learned to sing English compositions from the Philippines as well as Tagalog hymns. Hence, the influx of Filipino clergy and congregations into San Francisco's churches has also created a reverse situation of "benevolent assimilation" for non-Filipino congregants who are now into Filipino Catholicism, Protestantism, and Christianity.

Aside from the Filipinization of churches as illustrated in their attendees, many Filipino church leaders, ministers, administrators, and religious workers are also becoming more visible in American communities. Besides churches, immigration has increased the number of Filipino students at San Francisco's Catholic educational institutions, from the elementary to the tertiary levels. Through their churches, Filipino immigrants have been making significant contributions not only to the cultural fabric of San Francisco but the larger American society as well. Over the years, a number of second- and third-generation Filipino American Methodist, Baptist, Catholic, Global Church of

Christ, and Presbyterian missionaries, lay workers, evangelists, ministers, and pastors have gone back to the land of their ancestors, some as short-term visitors and others as long-term religious workers.

The historical analysis demonstrates that the scope and magnitude of the transnational movements (i.e., the Americanization of Philippine congregations and the Filipininization of American churches) has intensified over the years. Globalization and the Filipino exodus of eight million in 120 countries has transformed the phenomenon into a diasporic one. Filipino culture and religious life is being mainstreamed into a borderless global society. Not surprisingly, Filipino immigrant pastors and parishioners in Catholic churches in Madrid and Barcelona have also brought forth a "second coming" to Spain and many other cities of Europe. It is magnified even further because of advances and continuing innovations in technology, transportation, communications, and education that are facilitating preaching and conversion across physical and spatial boundaries. Based on their migratory pattern Filipinos continue to flock and to multiply, bringing their strong faith and traditions with them to the "promised land," wherever it may be. As this study has shown, the churches and religious spaces that these migrants Filipinize have become major instruments that help facilitate their acculturation, assimilation, and incorporation into their new home. At the same time, their churches will always be used as a safe space for negotiating and challenging identity, ethnicity, and nationalism.

NOTES

Portions of this chapter were first published as "Transnationalization of Faith: The Americanization of Christianity in the Philippines and the Filipinization of Christianity in the United States," *Asia Pacific Perspectives* 2.1 (2002): 9–20.

1. Interview with Professor Leny Mendoza Strobel, Sonoma State University, April 9, 2005.
2. The first Protestant missionaries to the Philippines, including the Dominican priest turned Protestant missionary Manrique Alonso Lallave, came from Spain during the period of Spanish occupation (see Apilado 1999; Kwantes 1998).
3. There was no Mormon missionary activity in the Philippines until the end of the Second World War, when Maxine Grimm, the wife of a U.S. Army colonel and also a worker serving the American Red Cross in the Philippines, introduced the gospel to Aniceta Pabilona Fajardo, the first Filipino to join the Church of Jesus Christ of Latter-day Saints in the islands. Sister Fajardo was baptized in 1945.
4. Doctrinally, Seventh-Day Adventists are heirs of the interfaith Millerite movement

of the 1840s. Although the name "Seventh-Day Adventist" was chosen in 1860, the denomination was not officially organized until May 21, 1863, when the movement included some 125 churches and 3,500 members.

5. Serious schisms would later reduce PIC membership significantly. In 1947, relations with the Episcopal Church of the United States of America (ECUSA) were formally laid down in two documents: the Declaration of Faith and Articles of Religion and the Constitution and Canons.

6. "Global Church of Christ" is a pseudonym used to preserve anonymity.

7. Pseudonym used to preserve anonymity.

8. "San Patricio" is a pseudonym used to preserve anonymity.

9. Edward B. Lenane, "Survey Catholic Filipino Club, 1421 Sutter Street, San Francisco, California." Unpublished pamphlet, March 25, 1935.

10. Based on the author's interviews with Noemi Castillo, director of the Office of Ethnic Ministries, Archdiocese of San Francisco, May and June 2001.

11. Pseudonym used to preserve anonymity.

12. The information on Philippine leadership is from the official directory of the Archdiocese of San Francisco (various years); and the Catholic Directory of the Philippines (various years).

13. Information from the official directory of the Archdiocese of San Francisco (various years) and the Catholic Directory of the Philippines (various years), supplemented with the author's interviews with Sister Avelina Macalam and Sister Gloria Burganoy, Religious of the Virgin Mary, May and June 2001.

14. Memo from Monsignor Foudy to Most Reverend Joseph T. McGucken, S.T.D. regarding "Minority Group Students in Catholic Elementary Schools, City of San Francisco," September 30, 1963.

15. Based on the author's interviews with Noemi Castillo, director of the Office of Ethnic Ministries, Archdiocese of San Francisco, May and June 2001.

16. Pseudonym used to preserve anonymity.

17. From the author's interviews with Brother Ismael Laguardia, San Francisco Filipino Jehovah's Witness, March 2001.

18. From the author's interviews with Reverend Gerry Ebora, pastor, San Francisco Seventh-Day Adventist Church, March 2001.

19. From the author's interviews with Reverend Leo Calica, pastor, Faith Bible Church of San Francisco, March 2001.

20. From the author's interviews with Reverend Arturo Capuli, pastor, Grace United Methodist Church, San Francisco, March 2001.

Creating a Transnational Religious Community

The Empress of Heaven and Goddess of the Sea, Tianhou/Mazu, from Beigang to San Francisco

JONATHAN H. X. LEE

In recent decades, within the context of an accelerated globalization, Chinese America has experienced unprecedented demographic changes, which in turn have originated a new diversity—along class, language, political, economic, and religious lines—within ethnic Chinese American communities across the United States. This accelerated globalization, fueled by rapid advances in telecommunications and Internet technology, as well as by growing financial, commercial, and cultural-religious global ties, has concretized existing transnational connections and forged new ones in ways previously not imagined.

In this essay I propose to examine this process as it is unfolding by examining the transnational veneration of a goddess from the vast Chinese folk pantheon. She is known both by her imperial title, Tianhou, and her more familial name, Mazu/Mazupo, and she is the Empress of Heaven and Goddess of the Sea. I use Vivian-Lee Nyitray's probing and critical inquiry as a guide on the reconfiguration of Tianhou/Mazu's religio-cultural and political sovereignty: "The multiple and powerful forces of modernization and shifting world populations have redrawn the boundaries of Tianhou/Mazu's concern. What remains to be seen is the final map of the goddess's sovereignty: Will it be so localized that Chinese people worship Chinese Mazu, Taiwanese people worship Taiwanese Mazu, and North American devotees worship a Canadian or American or Mexican Mazu? Or will Tianhou/Mazu's sovereignty shift from the identity politics of nation-states and ethnic origins to a conceptual realm of common culture?" (2000, 175–76).

In the following pages I give a brief introduction to the goddess and I survey the history of her veneration in the United States. I follow this survey with a discussion of the relevant trends in transnational Chinese immigration and its relation to the creation of a transnational community and, by extension, a transnational goddess. I then discuss some preliminary observations on the transnational veneration of Tianhou/Mazu in the United States as manifested in the pilgrimage of the Tianhou/Mazu from San Francisco's Ma-tsu Temple U.S.A. to her mother temple in Beigang, Taiwan.

THE EMPRESS OF HEAVEN AND GODDESS OF THE SEA

In the cities and villages of China's coastal provinces the goddess Tianhou/Mazu ranks second only to the Buddhist Bodhisattva Guanyin as a female object of popular devotion (Nyitray 2000, 165). Although in this essay I focus on the United States, specifically San Francisco and Sacramento, Tianhou/Mazu is also popular in the Chinese diaspora in places as disparate as Brazil, Burma, France, India, Indonesia, Japan, Malaysia, Mexico, the Philippines, Singapore, Thailand, and Vietnam.[1]

The cult of Tianhou/Mazu is based on the worship of a maiden named Lin Moniang ("Miss Lin, the Silent One") who is said to have lived from 960 to 987 CE on the island of Meizhou in the Minnanese Putian District of Fujian Province. There are numerous myths and legends surrounding her life, but the most widely held beliefs conform to the following outline. Miss Lin was born on the twenty-third day of the third lunar month in 960 CE into a pious family, variously described as humble fisherfolk or as local gentry. Her father is frequently identified as a virtuous but low-ranking Confucian scholar and official. Miss Lin is described as having as many as four brothers and as many as five sisters. The Bodhisattva Guanyin made Miss Lin's conception possible by giving her mother a magic pill. In another version, Guanyin of the South Sea (Nanhai Guanyin) visited Tianhou/Mazu's mother in a dream and gave her an *utpala*, or blue lotus, to eat; fourteen months later she gave birth to Lin Moniang. The process by which Miss Lin transformed from mortal girl to goddess to the Empress of Heaven is straightforward. Miss Lin's dedication to helping her family and others in perilous situations, especially while at sea, coupled with her many magical powers, brought about the respect, support, and dedication of her early devotees.

Settlers from coastal Fujian, the original home of the Tianhou/Mazu cult, brought the goddess with them when they immigrated to Taiwan. In Taipei and in the port city of Lugang, Mazu's cult was well established by the time the Qing authorities (1644–1911) made their presence felt. The Mazu temples in Taiwan were thus identified with the political and cultural interests of indigenous Taiwan. Accordingly, in Taiwan the goddess is known by her kin name, "Mazu/Mazupo," and not by her imperial title, "Tianhou."[2]

Tianhou/Mazu is a fluid and flexible goddess who adapts to meet the needs

of her devotees. The first wave of Chinese immigrants sought her protection as the "goddess of the sea" because they traveled across the Pacific Ocean. In other words, it is her role as "protector" that made her invaluable to the first wave. In light of this, we can pose a number of questions: Has she continued in the role of protector as immigration laws and cultural trends have changed? What role does she play in the various and complex ethnically Chinese American communities? Is her role limited to helping new immigrants make their transition to the United States? What role does she play in the established Chinese American communities? What part does she play in the construction and continuation of Chinese identity in Chinese American society? Is she a common denominator in the various generational, regional, and diverse ethnically Chinese American communities, honoring linguistic and other local differences, while simultaneously unifying them as Chinese-cum-Chinese American? I address these questions beginning with an examination of how the first wave of Chinese immigrants to San Francisco brought Tianhou/Mazu with them and incorporated her into their new lives.

The First Tianhou Temple in the United States

In San Francisco's Chinatown it is easy to miss the temples on Waverly Place unless one looks upward toward the heavens. The street level is occupied with restaurants, salons, florists, bakeries, and cafés, but on the upper level there are several Chinese associations and temples housing the gods and goddesses of "Chinese popular religions."[3] The Chinese temple is a unique physical setting in which mythology, folklore, legend, and great figures out of China's past are brought into the present. It is a realm symbolically created by the fusion between earth and heaven; geographical space and position are transformed into symbolic space and time in accordance with the practice of feng shui.

The Tien Hau Temple is located in the upper realms of Waverly Place. The temple, dedicated to Tianhou, is one of the oldest operating Chinese temples in the United States, having opened its doors in 1852. The Sanyi District Association appears to have been the original owner of the temple, but sometime later (before 1906) the ownership of the temple switched to the Sue Hing Benevolent Association.[4] Its present address at 125 Waverly Place is thought to be its original location; however, the original structure was destroyed during the 1906 earthquake and fire.[5]

After 1906, the Sue Hing Benevolent Association built a new multistory building on the original site and placed the temple on the fourth floor. Although the original Tien Hau Temple was destroyed in the earthquake and fire, the image of Tianhou and part of the altar were saved. The temple bell was buried in the ruins, but was uncovered during the construction project and re-installed in the new temple. All other furnishings in the temple were imported from China in 1910 (Wells 1962, 26).

Prior to the 1860s Waverly Place was called Pike Street and was known for its brothels filled with prostitutes brought from China. It deserved its nickname as the place of "homes of ill repute."[6] In fact, the first recorded Chinese resident in what became San Francisco's Chinatown was a prostitute named Ah Toy who emigrated from Hong Kong in 1849. She settled first in an alley of shanties off Clay Street and then moved to Pike Street to establish a brothel with immigrant Chinese prostitutes. It is said that Chinese miners from the Sacramento Valley would travel by boat to the city just to get a glance at the alluring beauty of Ah Toy (Pan 1995, 6). Later on, in the times when the Tien Hau Temple was estab-lished, the street's reputation changed, and a new nickname circulated among the Chinese citizenry: Tien Hau Miu Gai, or Tianhou Temple Street.

For reasons that are unclear the temple was closed in 1955, but it reopened twenty years later on May 4, 1975—the twenty-third of the third moon, Tian-hou's birthday.[7] A possible explanation for the temple's closure may be that it happened as a result of the Chinese Exclusion Law of 1882. As Bill Ong Hing notes: "In the 1880s cities and towns with a Chinatown were scattered through-out the West, though the Chinatown might consist of only a street or a few stores and its inhabitants might number only a few hundred. Eventually, these enclaves disappeared altogether. By 1940 only twenty-eight cities with China-towns could be identified; by 1955, only sixteen" (1993, 50). The temple eventu-ally closed its doors to the public and reopened when Chinese immigration to the United States was reestablished with the passage of the 1965 Immigration Law. As Hing states: "Since 1965 immigrants have contributed to the rejuvena-tion of Chinatowns in San Francisco, New York, Los Angeles, and Chicago. One need only walk along Grant Avenue or Stockton Street in San Francisco at noon . . . to feel the vibrant intensity of these resilient enclaves. After World War II these Chinatowns began to shrink and even disappear as the older immigrants died. The first signs of their revival appeared in the early 1960s with the admis-sion of refugees from Mainland China. . . . Chinatowns endure because, as the second and third generations leave, immigrants replace them and because the larger community sustains them" (84–85).

Chinatowns in San Francisco and elsewhere are historical reminders of anti-Chinese discrimination, so it is ironic that the temples also serve as tourist attractions for sightseers visiting Chinatown.[8] The Tien Hau Temple, now cele-brated as part of the multireligious fabric of the American religious landscape, was viewed not too long ago as "idolatrous" and "pagan." The reintroduction of Chinese emigrants from China, Hong Kong, Taiwan, Southeast Asia, and elsewhere has rejuvenated Chinatowns in major cities across North America. When the Tien Hau Temple reopened in 1975, this rejuvenation was reflected in the addition of new deities popular among the incoming Chinese immigrants (e.g. "the legendary Han dynasty physician" Shenyi Hua Tuo; "the Twelve model mothers" Shier nainiang; the Daoist Immortal Lü Dongbin; the Daoist Immortal Han Zhongli; and the Great Immortal Sage Huang, Huang daxian). As San Francisco's Chinatown endures, so too does the Tien Hau Temple.

Today the temple continues to serve a small group of Cantonese-speaking Chinese and newer ethnically Chinese Vietnamese who also speak Cantonese. The current positive attitudes toward religious pluralism, coupled with changes in immigration policies and the increasingly global economy, have created a favorable environment for the establishment of a new Tianhou/Mazu community, this time by emigrants from Taiwan instead of Mainland China.

A New Temple to Tinahou/Mazu

In San Francisco on March 14, 1986, Taiwanese-Chinese immigrants established a second temple to Tianhou/Mazu—the Ma-tsu Temple U.S.A.—as a branch of the Chaotian Temple located in Beigang, Taiwan.[9] After ten years on Grant Street, the temple relocated to 30 Beckett Street. The temple's stated mission is to advocate the virtues of Mazu, teach benevolence, uphold the Buddhist dharma, teach the principles of human kindness, and promote social morality.

If the Ma-tsu Temple U.S.A. reflects the changing geography and demographics of Chinese America in the wake of the 1965 Immigration Reform Act,[10] it also heralds something new: the appearance of transnational individuals who live both in Taiwan and in the United States. The existence of transnational Taiwanese is made possible by the rising economic status of East and Southeast Asia. Throughout the 1980s, Taiwan's economy was characterized by some as a "miracle," attested to by its successful development from a poor peripheral country to the world's thirteenth-largest trading economy and a producer-exporter of high-tech products (Harrell and Huang 1994). There has been an enormous increase in the standard of living among all sectors of the population on the island. As a result there are Taiwanese—new transnational citizens—participating significantly in creating new transnational communities alongside Taiwanese-Chinese Americans.

The joining of Taiwanese and Taiwanese-Chinese Americans in a transnational community between the island and the United States is symbolized by the establishment of the Ma-tsu Temple U.S.A. Mazu becomes a transcontinental deity in the deterritorialized space of this new transnational community composed of diverse individual devotees who share not only a common Chinese heritage but also a new American identity. Tianhou/Mazu's identity—cultural and national—mirrors the multiple identities that her devotees possess: they are simultaneously Chinese, Taiwanese, and American.

Tianhou/Mazu is a territorial goddess. The territorial nature of her religiosity is manifest in her celestial inspection tour, a ritual procession during which she views the state of her religious realm and the territory in which she is sovereign. A key question posed by Vivian-Lee Nyitray concerns the localization and identity of Tianhou/Mazu, who finds her Chinese devotees worshipping a Chinese Tianhou/Mazu, her Taiwanese devotees worshipping a Taiwanese goddess, and her U.S. devotees worshipping an American goddess. The differences between these identities are evident in small ways, such as the prefix to their titles Meiguo (America) versus Beigang (Taiwan). Beigang Mazu is one and the same as American Mazu; at the same time she is understood to be different entities, as mother versus daughter, or as Taiwanese versus American.

The American Mazu is enshrined at the Ma-tsu Temple U.S.A. and is referred to as Meiguo Mazu in all religious rituals. In the Ma-tsu Temple U.S.A., Beigang Mazu's honorary shrine is placed in front of Meiguo Mazu's main shrine, indicating Meiguo Mazu's origins and connection to Taiwan. As daughter temple to the original Beigang Mazu temple in Taiwan, all statues of Mazu housed in the Ma-tsu Temple U.S.A. are from the Beigang temple, including the ones donated to the temple by Taiwanese American devotees. The name Ma-tsu Temple U.S.A. in contrast to the name Beigang Mazu Temple reflects unity and diversity; they are both Mazu temples but are located in different places. There are slight differences in religious functions resulting from the different needs and concerns of Taiwanese communities versus Chinese American communities. Immigrant Taiwanese Americans confront cultural, linguistic, social, and political issues that their Taiwanese relatives back home do not. Taiwanese American parents tackle issues of moral and familial education as their children negotiate their identities and attempts to fit into the United States. How has the Ma-tsu Temple U.S.A. been able to negotiate traditional religious duties while creating new ritual traditions that cross cultural and national boundaries?

TRANSNATIONAL DIMENSIONS OF TIANHOU/MAZU'S VENERATION

Every few years, Taiwanese-Chinese American members of the Ma-tsu Temple U.S.A., along with transnational Taiwanese Americans, journey back to Beigang, Taiwan. This journey to the mother temple is made in order to replenish the spiritual *qi* of Meiguo Mazu (American Mazu). The pilgrims' return to Taiwan reestablishes community ties with other Mazu devotees while reaffirming their identity as Taiwanese-Chinese, a dual identity. Meiguo Mazu is a symbolic manifestation of this dual identity. On the one hand she is the daughter of Beigang Mazu and thus is Taiwanese. On the other hand she is Meiguo Mazu, the American daughter who lives and works in San Francisco and whose sovereignty is in America. Meiguo Mazu returns to the Beigang Mazu Temple because she needs to do so: at the mother's temple she acquires and assimilates her spiritual energy, her spiritual efficaciousness, or *ling qi*. The pilgrimage home reestablishes the American daughter with her powerful Taiwanese mother, as well as with all of her sisters, thus reaffirming Meiguo Mazu's status and power. Beigang has been the center of the Mazu cult in Taiwan for over one hundred years.[11] The history of the Beigang Temple is the source of Meiguo Mazu's ling-qi, her efficacious qi:[12] the older the temple, the more powerful the deity. Hence, Beigang Mazu's qi is very powerful, and Beigang Mazu gives her daughter Meiguo Mazu power when she returns home to Taiwan for a visit.

It is important to be aware of the social-communal dimension of the pilgrimage. The Beigang community members expressively inform their American relatives of their roots and origins. They inform Meiguo Mazu that she is their Mazu too. From October 3 to October 17, 2002, fifteen Taiwanese Americans journeyed home to Taiwan on a Meiguo Mazu pilgrimage to the Beigang Mazu Temple. The group of fifteen joined with a group of devotees who were already in Taiwan. During this time, Meiguo Mazu was paraded in the streets and alleys of Beigang, her hometown, thereby symbolically claiming the territory of her religious realm. As noted above, Mazu is a territorial goddess, and this parade demarcates her religious realm. Meiguo Mazu symbolically shares this religious realm with her Beigang Mazu mother because in a sense they are one and the same. The communities of worshippers from America and the local people venerate the same goddess and accept her religious sovereignty. There is a dual understanding: Meiguo Mazu is different from Beigang Mazu, just as Taiwanese Americans are different from native Taiwanese, but she is still one and the same, just as the returning pilgrims are still in some measure Taiwanese. Members of both communities create a sense of collective identity based on a shared conception of their common culture whose object of devotion is Mazu.

The Taiwanese American community understands the importance of the direct link to Beigang Mazu because through the mother's power the daughter is powerful. American Mazu will become powerful in her own right as she flourishes in the United States, as her devotees thrive as new American immigrants, and as their descendents prosper. Only the future can say if she will break the matrilineal line of power and become a "mother" herself, with American daughters scattered across the American religious landscape. The local dimension of Tianhou/Mazu's veneration will clue us in on the future as new ritual traditions are established in the diaspora.

The Local Dimension of Tianhou/Mazu's Veneration

In traditional Chinese settings the birthday celebration for Tianhou/Mazu features huge bonfires, firecrackers, big banquets, continuous religious rituals performed in the temple by Daoist masters, and performances of Chinese operas—all to honor and entertain the goddess. This type of traditional celebration is still practiced in Hong Kong, Taiwan, Fujian, and other major Tianhou/Mazu temples in East Asia (Savidge 1977). The Tien Hau Temple and the Ma-tsu Temple U.S.A. celebrate her birthday on a smaller scale, however, and there is no celestial inspection tour—at least not during her birthday celebrations.[13]

On Sunday May 5, 2002, I attended Tianhou/Mazu's birthday celebration at the Tien Hau Temple in San Francisco's Chinatown. By 11:00 AM, large numbers of worshippers were visiting the temple to make offerings to Tianhou/Mazu. By noon there were dragon dances outside the temple punctuated by the blasts of hundreds of firecrackers. The offering table was full of fruits, flowers, cookies, cakes, Chinese pastries, roast duck, chicken, pork, and other foods. Many devotees were engaged in Chinese divination practices, and the temple offered visitors and worshippers a vegetarian meal and a souvenir.[14] In addition, the Sue Hing Benevolent Association used the occasion to bring its members together, and a band playing Chinese folk music had been hired to entertain the senior members of the association. By 2:00 PM the activities outside the temple had ended, and within the temple the heavy traffic had slowed. Men, women, and children of all ages had attended the festivities, just as they do during Chinese New Year.

On the same day at the Ma-tsu Temple U.S.A. there also was a ritual invocation and offering for Meiguo Mazu. And, just like the Tien Hau Temple, the offering tables were filled with fruits, flowers, candies, traditional Chinese pastries, vegetarian dishes, and, in this case, some meat dishes. All of those who came to wish Mazu well and to ask for her blessings and continuing protection were offered a large vegetarian meal and a gift of "good luck" noodles from the temple.

As noted above, neither the Tien Hau Temple nor the Ma-tsu Temple U.S.A. includes a celestial inspection tour as part of the birthday celebration.[15] Instead, the Ma-tsu Temple U.S.A. takes advantage of its participation in the Chinese New Year parade, two to three months before the birthday, to provide the goddess with an opportunity to make her celestial inspection tour.[16] During this American version of Mazu's inspection tour she views the state of the world and extends her protection to the community by joining the large New Year parade, thus adapting to both Chinese and non-Chinese culture while expanding the parameters of her religious sovereignty (Nyitray 2000, 176). One of the main functions of Mazu's tour is to unify the community.[17] As a symbol of Chinese religious culture, she brings to both the Chinese and non-Chinese viewers something that is essentially Chinese.[18]

In events like the New Year celestial inspection tour the Ma-tsu Temple U.S.A. sought avenues to publicly announce its presence in America by taking advantage of civic celebrations and community events. To further this end, the temple also has participated in another Chinese American festival in the historic gold-rush town of Maryville, California.

Expanding Locality: Tianhou/Mazu in the Sacramento Valley

Maryville honors its Chinese American community with the annual civic festival honoring Bei Di, known locally as "Bok Kai," a Chinese god enshrined in the Beixi Temple (North Creek Temple, or "Bok Kai Temple" in the local Cantonese dialect).[19] Chinese immigrants built the temple in 1879 because Bei Di protects his devotees from floods and provides them with bountiful water for farming. The highlight of the annual community festival is the Bok Kai Parade. Tianhou/Mazu has a place in these devotions and festivities. This parade, produced annually for 121 years, is the oldest continuing parade in California. Paul G. Chace (1992) suggests that despite its beginnings as a yearly religious celebration, the parade's 121 years in Marysville have, over time, deemphasized the religious nature of the parade. Instead, he says, two American threads have risen to the fore — commercialism and coping with ethnic and cultural diversity.

Chace considers the present-day Bok Kai parade to be nonreligious, and he explains this secularization as due to what he terms "interpretive restraint" (1992, 3–6). Interpretive restraint is the purposeful withholding of symbolic meaning for traditional ritual performance. Chace suggests that with interpretive restraints, the rites of Chinese popular religions could serve to celebrate the larger community and to promote interethnic and intercultural relations. In this example, interpretive restraint suggests that Chinese Americans have politely concealed or downplayed the original reasons for the parade, thus allowing it to take on a new emphasis in the United States. I find Chace's interpretation interesting, but I question his hasty conclusion regarding the "nonreligious" nature of the parade. While the parade itself may have become a community-wide celebration, it is only one part of the festival. The religious dimensions of the festival occur away from the parade, at the Bok Kai Temple proper, and they are by no means invisible. Thousands of Chinese Americans, including both recent immigrants as well as second and subsequent generations, visit the temple with offerings of whole-roasted pigs and an array of other foods. Every inch of the temple is taken as people perform their food offerings and rituals. Afterward, they adjourn to the adjacent lawn with friends and family, whole-roasted pigs in hand, for a picnic. Clearly the celebration is a dual one: one religious and one civic. Whereas the non-Chinese visitors may be there for the parade, the Chinese visitors, with their whole-roasted pigs, are not there just for the parade but to share a meal.

This dual dynamic is also at work at San Francisco's Chinese New Year parade. The case of Tianhou/Mazu and her participation in both the San Francisco Chinese New Year and Bok Kai parades demonstrates multiple levels of understanding and symbolism. First, participation in Tianhou/Mazu's celestial inspection tour is a religious ritual to the immigrant Chinese Americans. Second, an increasing number of second-, third-, and fourth-generation Chinese Americans attending the parades are aware of its religious significance. Third, to the non-Chinese and fully Americanized Chinese viewers of the parades, Tianhou/Mazu is a symbol of Chinese religious culture, even if the ritual dimension of the religious activities may not be as visible to all because they occur in the temple. This doesn't mean that the ritual dimension lies outside the public domain: it is in the public domain because it is not exclusive to Chinese worshippers. Anyone who comes to the Bok Kai festival can visit the temple and its surroundings and see religious activities. What this suggests is that the religious dimension of these two civic celebrations is visible, invisible, or partially (in)visible to Chinese immigrants, various generations of Chinese Americans, and non-Chinese.

Many viewers of the palanquin carrying Mazu in the New Year parade see her two attendants walking in front of her exploding firecrackers and they understand this to be an aspect of Chinese American culture, just as are dragon dances and young Chinese American children dressed up in folk Chinese clothes. They may not know that from the religious standpoint the firecrackers are used to scare away demons as Mazu inspects her precinct. To Mazu's devotees, her participation in the parade extends far beyond an expression of secular cultural exchange; it is Mazu's birthday celestial tour, with all of its rich religious meaning. This American version of her inspection tour is an example of adaptation by Mazu and her adherents: it serves a dual function, religious and secular. Each year, during the parade, Mazu is an honored symbol of Chinese religious culture for both Chinese American and non-Chinese viewers.

Chace's theory of "interpretive restraint" is informing but limited. New generations of Chinese Americans who watch Mazu on her palanquin with her attendants go by in the parade will not know that what they are seeing is a celestial inspection tour. They will see the nonreligious side of this activity, which is a civic expression. Some leaders of the Ma-tsu Temple U.S.A. want to assimilate Meiguo Mazu more into the civic aspect of this ritual and parade because participation in the annual festival secures them a space in the San Francisco community, and, by extension, in American society. However, the "pilgrims," the devotees, are not concealing the symbols or rituals of their religious act; they are acting religiously in a civic forum, which is public to the point of being televised. What we have here is a religious transformation that results from a fundamental restructuring as a new religious community situates itself on new soil.

Jonathan Z. Smith posits that we must consider two issues when imagining religion—namely that we note what takes place in ritual and what place is to ritual experience. Smith explores the relational dynamics between place and ritual as the determining category for understanding ritual itself and thus as a possible avenue for the reformulation of ritual theory. To this end, Smith posits that "place [is] a fundamental component of ritual" and that "ritual demonstrates that we know 'what is the case'" (1987, 103, 109). Hence, distinguishing the place, for instance, "within the Bok Kai Parade" or "within the San Francisco Chinese New Year parade" versus outside the actual parades, communicates the performance of a religious versus nonreligious "ritual." Within the Bok Kai parade the religious ritual expression may have taken a back seat to civic cultural celebration; however, around the Bok Kai Temple religious life and meaning take a front seat, especially among the Chinese American visitors. In contrast, Mazu's participation in the San Francisco Chinese New Year parade blurs the distinction between religious and civic ritual. Depending on the perspectival limitations of the subject, it is a deep religious ritual expression, a civic celebration, or both.

Civil society is created through the Ma-tsu Temple U.S.A.'s active invitation of non-Chinese participants as a form of cultural exchange. For example, during the Chinese New Year parade, members of the temple warmly invited non-Taiwanese/Chinese volunteers to be flag carriers, horn blowers, and incense holders. They even went so far as to let volunteers wear the costumes of Mazu's two generals. After the parade, they invited all of the volunteers to participate in the ritual return of Meiguo Mazu to her celestial throne, followed by a meal. They invited everyone to visit the temple on any occasion. Their hospitality was matched by the enthusiasm of the volunteers who made it clear that, although they were not devotees, they were excited to show their support for the Chinese American community while having fun by participating in the parade, especially with the possibility of being televised.

The dynamics of transformation vis-à-vis Tianhou/Mazu's celestial inspection tour are still unfolding. Unlike the historic Bok Kai festival, American Mazu continues to return to her native homeland, Taiwan, just like the many new immigrants who live transnational lives. America's civil society and Chinese America's common culture confront each other as a result of global forces, and both have been altered by the encounter. This is nothing new. What is new is the possibility for "transnational culture" to be localized and naturalized. To be American is not to be settled and fixed like Bok Kai and the first wave of Chinese immigrants; rather it is to be like American Mazu, moving back and fourth, to and from, here and there.

A PROVISIONAL CONCLUSION

There is a spatial paradox in the transnational veneration of Tianhou/Mazu.[20] She is a territorial goddess, yet her expanding territorial sovereignty is based on a deterritorialization of the geographic and temporal space of a community of transnational personalities.[21] The new transnational citizen is a citizen with multiple nationalities, and even though the transnational nature of recent and current immigration to the United States is nothing new it has intensified and accelerated as a result of changing immigration laws, economic developments in East Asia, and new understandings of nationality and ethnicity. The first wave of Chinese immigrants in the mid-1800s arrived in America with no intentions of staying; they were sojourners pushed by famine and economic hardships and pulled by the allure of the gold rush. As Erika Lee explains, "A successful sojourn involved not only the accumulation of wealth but also the maintenance of transnational economic and familial ties between the sojourner and his family and village back home" (2003, 120). Today's Taiwanese sojourners are not laborers or gold seekers but rather the children and housewives of newly rich businessmen who send reverse remittances to their loved ones' bank accounts overseas.[22] They maintain active, ongoing interconnections with their home country (Taiwan) and their host (United States) and perhaps with other diasporic Chinese communities as well. These relationships may be political, economic, social, cultural, or religious; more often than not they are all of these simultaneously. Even though the transnational citizen may take up permanent residence and achieve legal citizenship within the host country, this does not imply a break with the homeland. Transnationalism as a way of life and a condition of being is thus a matter of degree. It may be intense, involving constant transcontinental economic exchange, communication, and travel, or it may be relatively restrained, involving only occasional contacts.

Living across borders, transnational migrants break down the identification of nation and state and give rise to the paradoxical concept of a deterritorialized state or, more accurately, deterritorialized space. Geographic boundaries are no longer the sole definition of citizenship, nationality, and identity. Tianhou/Mazu's expanding religious sovereignty and celestial realm are based on her expanding territorial domain. Symbolically illustrated by her celestial inspection tour in San Francisco's Chinese New Year parade, her vitality is predicated on deterritorialized transnational Taiwanese-Chinese American citizens. Tianhou/Mazu's religious sovereignty is not defined by fixed geographic boundaries, just as transnational Chinese identity is increasingly defined less by nation-state and more by culture.

NOTES

1. As I write this essay, plans by Taiwanese Americans are being made to establish a second Beigang Mazu temple in the New York area.
2. Recently Lin Meirong of the Academia Sinica in Taiwan has posited that Mazu has become an important symbol for people attempting to establish different forms of identity. On one level, the Mazu cult has been promoted by local leaders as a source of local pride and used as a means to attract tourists and pilgrims. On the other hand, Mazu has become a symbol for Chinese communist officials who advocate the reunification of China and Taiwan. Lin Meirong examines Mazu's association with Taiwanese folk religion and national identity, as well as her forming role as "national deity." See "AAS Abstracts: China Session 25: Popular Religion and the Problem of Taiwanese Identity," 1996, http://www.aasianst.org [visited on March 3, 2002]); see also Sangren 1983.
3. *Sanjiao*, which refers to the "three teachings," has sometimes been used to describe the notion of Chinese popular religion but fails because it ignores an entire dimension of folk traditions. *Minjian zongjiao* is often translated as "popular religion" as

well, but it is better translated as "religion among the peoples." Traditionally, the term Chinese popular religion has been used to characterize the religious landscape of China and that of culturally Chinese areas. Scholars usually distinguish among at least four Chinese religious traditions: Confucianism, Daoism, Buddhism, and "folk traditions." The term "popular religion" was created as a catchall term for the ideas, actions, and rituals that failed to conform to the fundamental teachings of the three institutional traditions. Therefore, it is important to understand "popular religion" as the religious life, ritual practices, beliefs, values, and ethics among the Chinese peoples. See Teiser 1995 for an overview of definitions of and approaches to the study of Chinese popular religion. Note that the current building architecture of Waverly Place emerged after the earthquake and fire of 1906; for more information, see Choy 1980, 129.

4. See Wells 1962, 25. Unfortunately it is now impossible to determine whether or not the Sanyi District Association was the original owner, because the city documents were destroyed in the 1906 earthquake and fire.

5. Wells (1962, 25–26, 28–29) mentions that it is possible that the "Temple of Ah Ching" that existed in San Francisco located in the sand dunes near Union Square (what is now the corner of Mason and Post Streets) may have been the "original" temple dedicated to Tianhou/Mazu. The owner of the temple was a man named Ah Ching who established it supposedly with an eye for his own profit. Wells's reference for Ah Ching's temple is from "Our Heathen Temples," an article by A. W. Loomis published in November 1868 in *The Overland Monthly*. Besides this article there is no other document or record that this temple ever existed, because most of the city records were destroyed in the earthquake and fire of 1906.

6. See Loewenstein 1984 for a detailed history of San Francisco's street names.

7. Note that Wells visited the Tien Hau Temple in 1962 while she was researching and writing her thesis. At that time, she mentioned that the temple was "closed to the public," but she was able to get a private personal tour from Dr. Peter Kwan (26).

8. According to the temple keepers at the Tien Hau Temple, the majority of worshippers visiting the temple are Cantonese-speaking Chinese, but over the last decade there has been increased participation by Chinese Americans who are Cantonese-speaking ethnic Chinese Vietnamese. Although the number of devotees visiting Tianhou/Mazu at the Tien Hau Temple is small, the overall percentage of devotees to the goddess remains large. This is suggested by Tianhou/Mazu's enshrinement at other Chinese temples throughout Chinatown (e.g., the Ma-tsu Temple U.S.A., the Kong Chow Temple, the Chi Sin Buddhist and Taoist Association, and the Ching Chung Taoist Association of America) where devotees may go to venerate the goddess, ask for protection, and so on.

9. Before moving to the Grant Avenue location, the temple was located in the Latino Mission District. The Ma-tsu Temple U.S.A. does not keep detailed demographic data. However, my informant and friend Dino Tsai tells me that there are approximately fifteen hundred fee-paying lifelong members and roughly eight hundred reg-

istered members. About 60 percent are multilingual speakers of Mandarin Chinese, Taiwanese, and English; about 30 percent speak only Mandarin Chinese; and about 7 percent speak Cantonese Chinese. Devotees speaking other languages (e.g., Vietnamese) often visit the temple as well. In terms of age range, 60 percent are fifty years or older, 30 percent are between thirty and fifty, and 5 percent are under thirty years old.

10. The 1965 Immigration Act abolished the 1924 discriminatory national origins provision favoring immigrants of Western European origin, which was retained in the Immigration and Nationality Act of 1952. The subsequent series of amendments in 1990 of the 1952 act, collectively referred to as the Immigration Act of 1990, provides for an overall increase in worldwide immigration. The 1990 act increases the allocation for both family-related and employment-related immigration and further creates a separate basis by which "diversity immigrants" (nationals of countries previously underrepresented since 1965 due to visa issuance) can enter the United States. Amendments of the 1952 act that were directed toward the increase of Chinese immigrants entering the United States are as follows: the 1981 amendment created a separate quota of twenty thousand for Taiwan, which Taiwan previously shared with China and Hong Kong; in 1987, the annual quota for Hong Kong was increased from six hundred to five thousand, then to ten thousand from 1990 to 1993, and subsequently to twenty thousand; and finally, thousands of people from Taiwan, Hong Kong, the People's Republic of China, and Southeast Asia were admitted to the United States as students.

11. This is a contested center, there is a sense in Taiwan that Beigang may be second to Dajia Mazu (located in Central Taiwan) due to a recent usurpation of power.

12. Qi is generally defined as "life force," "energy," "pneuma," "atom," "breath," and "vapor." The concept of qi underlies all religious traditions in China. Qi is believed to originate from the original primordial Dao. Qi undergoes recurrent cycles of transformation, with its unfolding based on yin and yang, the five phrases, or the eight trigrams. For more on qi, see Bokenkamp 1997, 15–20. Lingqi refers to the efficacy of a deity or a temple's "potency," "power," or "magical power." The intensity of lingqi commonly resides in the incense burner; its ashes may be used for medicinal cures and talismans or for the establishment of new temples. For more on lingqi and its relationship to local temple associations and cults, see Feuchtwang 2001, 86–89.

13. There are some key characteristic differences between the historic Tien Hau Temple founded in 1852 and the Mazu Temple U.S.A. founded in the 1980s. First, the Tien Hau Temple was founded by immigrant Chinese whose primary spoken dialect is Cantonese and the Taishan dialect. The language of preference at the Mazu Temple U.S.A. is primarily Taiwanese and secondarily Mandarin Chinese. The majority of visitors at the Mazu Temple U.S.A. are recent Taiwanese Americans, while the Tien Hau Temple has seen an increase in the number of Sino-Vietnamese Americans who arrived in the United States as a result of the Vietnam War. In addition, the Sino-Vietnamese Americans tend to speak Cantonese.

14. The temple also continues to sponsor regular vegetarian meals, open to the public, based on events in the Chinese lunar calendar (e.g., Guanyin's birthday, Chinese New Year, and other traditional Chinese festivals).

15. Feuchtwang, in *Popular Religion in China: The Imperial Metaphor* (2001, ch. 3) has highlighted the "imperial metaphor" of the "celestial inspection tour." In short, he suggests that because local temples are the centers of territorial cults and deities, they are used imperially as "imperial police" and for "local control."

16. There is a temple dedicated to another Chinese water deity in the Sacramento Valley town of Marysville, where Tianhou/Mazu is enshrined along with several other celestial deities. During the annual Bok Kai Festival and celebration, Tianhou/Mazu along with Bok Kai make their "inspection tour" (see Nyitray 2000, 175–76). The Mazu from the Ma-tsu Temple U.S.A. had been taken out of the temple and driven over to Marysville to participate in the annual Bok Kai Temple festival. The last time they did this was in 2000. It is Mazu from the Ma-tsu Temple U.S.A. who participates in the parade, not the Tien Hau Temple.

17. This effort to unify occurs on several fronts. First, the Taiwanese American community at the Mazu Temple U.S.A. uses the opportunity to gather and visit with old friends and family. Second, Mazu's participation in the Chinese New Year provides a platform for "civic unity." The leadership within the Mazu Temple U.S.A. has been preoccupied with "Americanizing" Mazu since the temple's inception. They offer bilingual newsletters in Chinese and English, openly welcome non-Chinese visitors, provide Dharma classes in English, and since 1986 have established themselves as regulars in the Chinese New Year Parade. On the idea of "unity" Sangren (1983, 4–25) has posited that female deities occupy prominent positions in the Chinese religious pantheon in that, unlike male deities, they are not tied to a territory, they are not bureaucrats, and they are not hierarchical because their gender disqualifies them from being considered "officials." Nyitray (n.d.) has also explored the symbolic nature of Chinese female goddesses in terms of "unity" in advancing the notion of a "collective divine feminine," where syncretic chains of association link local river sprites (e.g., Lingshui furen) to an increasingly powerful maritime deity (e.g., Tianhou/Mazu) and to chaste virgin "mothers" such as Tianhou/Mazu and Guanyin.

18. There are many symbols of Chinese culture publicly on display at the Chinese New Year Parade. However, not all symbols are Chinese (e.g., the corporate sponsors, the various school bands, and the children's organization). On the other hand, the Mazu Temple U.S.A.'s entourage in the parade, carrying incense sticks and wearing yellow vests and straw hats, surround her brightly lighted palanquin, do bespeak something Chinese. Furthermore, the announcers on the televised version of the parade highlight Mazu's Chinese heritage. In the 2003 parade, both the Chinese announcers and the non-Chinese pointed out that she is a "Chinese goddess" who is popular with "Chinese people" from Taiwan and Hong Kong.

19. The Bok Kai Temple is a name designating a location. Bok (Cantonese for north, properly pronounced "Bak"), Kai (meaning creek or stream), and Miu (temple) was originally located at the northern section of a creek before the levees of the Yuba

River were constructed. The deity known as Bok Kai is actually Xuantian Shangdi, also known as Bei Di, meaning the Northern Emperor, whose origin stems from the Chinese classic *Journey to the North*. A snake and turtle, two demons the emperor subdued and took into his service, iconographically accompany Bei Di. He is popularly known in Daoism and popular religion as a powerful exorcist. His association with floods and droughts and his concerns with water are regional adaptations that developed in Marysville, California, as times of drought, floods, and natural disasters are often associated with being possessed by demons and inauspicious spirits. See Stevens 2001 for more information on Bei Di; for a detailed account of his biography, see Seaman 1987. The Bok Kai Festival and parade occur annually on the first weekend of March.

20. My phrase "spatial paradox" is informed by Appadurai's *Modernity at Large: Cultural Dimensions of Globalization* (1996, 48). Appadurai insists on a need for a new type of ethnography due to the changing social, territorial, and cultural reproduction of group identity. As groups migrate, regroup in new locations, reconstruct their histories, and reconfigure their ethnic projects, the *ethno* in ethnography takes on a slippery, nonlocalized quality, to which the descriptive practices of anthropology will have to respond. The landscapes of group identity—the ethnoscapes—around the world are no longer familiar anthropological objects insofar as groups are no longer tightly territorialized, spatially bounded, historically unselfconscious, or culturally homogeneous. We have fewer cultures in the world and more internal cultural debates . . . the ethnoscapes of today's world are profoundly interactive.

21. These landscapes thus are the building blocks of what (extending Benedict Anderson) he would like to call *imagined worlds*—that is, the multiple worlds that are constituted by the historically situated imaginations of individuals and groups spread around the globe. An important fact of the world we live in today is that many individuals live in such imagined worlds (and not just in imagined communities) and thus are able to contest and sometimes even subvert the imagined worlds of the official mind and of the entrepreneurial mentality that surround them (Appadurai 1996, 32). See also Yang 2000, 332.

22. See Ong 1999 for a complete study of the characteristics of new transnational citizens.

Ahora la Luz

Transnational Gangs, the State, and Religion

LOIS ANN LORENTZEN WITH LUIS ENRIQUE BAZAN

Carlos sits in the hospital lobby, waiting for the last in a yearlong series of painful laser treatments to remove his tattoos. Signifiers of gang member-ship—names and images on his neck, chest, and arms, including a tear under his left eye—no longer mark his body. Carlos looks toward the window and seems uncomfortable when asked the difference between his life before and now. Turning back, he says, "Mira, todo lo que te puedo decir es que antes todo era obscuridad y ahora, luz" (Look, all I can tell you is that before, everything was dark and now it is light).[1]

This essay explores a tattoo removal program in San Francisco; the relatively recent phenomenon of transnational gang activity, especially that between San Francisco and El Salvador; the economic and political conditions that form the larger world in which gangs operate; why gangs provide an attractive option for migrant youth; the increased "privatization of violence" and consequent state intervention in both El Salvador and the United States; and the role of reli-gion in encouraging young people to leave gangs. Our concern is for migrant and deported youths who must cope with their marginalized and increasingly criminalized status. Survival strategies such as gang membership help margin-alized youths negotiate a world of global inequalities, cultures of violence, and geographical and cultural displacement.

As researchers from the Religion and Immigration Project we conducted fieldwork in San Francisco, California, and in San Salvador, El Salvador.[2] We spent numerous hours in the lobby of a San Francisco hospital talking to former gang members who were having tattoos removed, doctors and nurses who administered the laser treatments, case workers at Juvenile Hall, police in San Francisco's Mission District, gang members on the streets of San Francisco, and staff members of CASI, a self-help organization that initiated and runs the tattoo removal program.[3] We are appreciative of the gang members and their

families who graciously invited us into their homes. In San Salvador, a group of ex-gang members who had been deported from the United States generously shared their time and wisdom. We also spoke with gang members on the streets of San Salvador, in their homes, and in prison, with researchers from the University of Central America, and with the staff of organizations that work with gangs and other marginalized youths.

THE CONTEXT

El Salvador suffered a brutal civil war from 1981 to 1992, in which over eighty thousand people were killed, most of them civilians. The war also yielded a massive dislocation of Salvadorans as they fled escalating violence, the destruction of their homes and villages, and severe economic hardship. The war resulted from material and political conditions rooted in the centuries-long economic and political domination by a small group of local elites. The Salvadoran government conducted the infamous La Matanza (the massacre) in 1932 after a failed rebellion sought to redress economic inequities. Over thirty thousand people died in La Matanza, and for the next fifty years the military ruled while a tiny oligarchy maintained economic control, their economic dominance guaranteed by military rule. Years of repression, economic and political marginalization, military domination, and violation of human rights convinced many Salvadorans that violence was the only mechanism for social change. The civil war that began in the early 1980s, although a reaction to a local (national) military and government, quickly assumed global dimensions. President Reagan framed the war as a geopolitical and ideological struggle against communism, and he pumped over three billion dollars into El Salvador to aid the military and government. By the time the United Nations negotiated peace accords in 1992, more than two million Salvadorans were living outside their home country—with the majority in the United States. These migrants arrived in places like the Mission District in San Francisco traumatized by the radical rupture of family and community bonds due to the violence of war.

El Salvador continues to report a net loss of well over ten thousand individuals per year. These more recent migrants leave home for economic reasons or to reunite with families. Given that over 50 percent of adults in San Salvador are unemployed or underemployed, and that 36 percent live below the poverty line, the motivations for migrating are strong (Johnson 2006). Poverty, unemployment, disrupted families, and endemic violence are legacies of war, of centuries old socioeconomic marginalization, and of current global economic forces that are represented in part by the rapid growth of the *maquila* industry in the countryside surrounding San Salvador.[4]

Many migrants are young people, a fact that has led Monsignor Gregorio Rosa Chávez, the president of Caritas for Latin America, to call El Salvador a country "that expels its children," and he adds that "rather than giving the opportunities necessary for development, it encourages them to abandon their homes and consider the possibilities of success in other countries, principally the United States" (2002, 3). Given that remittances to El Salvador comprise 13 percent of the gross domestic product, the largest single component, it is no surprise that El Salvador's children are "expelled" in light of global pressures and domestic need.

The Streets of San Francisco

The U.S. Department of Justice claims that 750,000 youths belong to gangs in the United States.[5] The late 1970s and early 1980s witnessed the growth of Mexican gangs such as Calle 18 (18th Street gang). As Central American immigrants moved to poor neighborhoods such as the Pico Union District of Los Angeles, they became both a target for gangs and a source of recruits and vulnerable youths quickly joined gangs for self-protection. The 18th Street gang now boasts twenty thousand members, and although it is panethnic it is predominantly Salvadoran. Mara Salvatrucha (MS) began in Los Angeles as a Salvadoran gang. Members describe the name choice by saying that *mara* stands for gang, *salva* for El Salvador, and *trucha* as slang for "watch out" or for a trout swimming upstream, thus symbolizing survival against great odds (Vigil 2002, 142). The MS gang boasts a reputation for being especially violent, which has led the Federal Bureau of Investigation to name dismantling MS as a top priority for its organized crime unit.

Recent migrants to San Francisco's Mission District enter a predominantly Latino low-income working-class neighborhood. Although the Mission District experienced accelerated gentrification from 1998 to 2000 due to the dot-com boom, it remains predominantly Latino. Recent Salvadoran migrants hold various forms of employment; women generally work as housekeepers, nannies, or cooks, and men as restaurant workers, gardeners, construction workers, or day laborers. The economic downturn in San Francisco following the burst of the dot-com bubble, as well as the decrease in tourism following September 11, 2001, meant that more and more Salvadoran men lined the streets of San Francisco looking for work.

The appeal of gangs is not surprising in a context of economic deprivation, geographical displacement, and discrimination. Some scholars look to the "multiple marginalities" faced by migrant youth to explain the growth of gangs (Vigil 2002, 1998; Vásquez and Marquardt 2003), claiming that gangs serve as a "form of local level social structuration in the face of broader conditions of high crime, insecurity, and, socio-political breakdown" (Rodgers 2006, 267). We often find ourselves reluctant to talk about our work with gangs, given the tendency of the media in both the United States and El Salvador to criminalize poor and marginalized youth. Yet, gang life is a reality both in San Francisco and in El Salvador. Understanding the multiple pressures that make gang life appealing can hopefully be part of the process of de-demonizing these youths. Based on our interviews with past and present gang members we can suggest reasons that young people join gangs, yet we must caution against oversimplifying the complex reasons that any individual may have for joining a gang.

Maria, an ex-gang member, said that she didn't know to which ethnic group she really belonged. Born in the United States, her American friends considered her Salvadoran because she "thought like one." Maria's family, on the other hand, accused her of "behaving like an American girl." First- and second-generation migrant children often face difficulties shaping their identities. As they struggle to construct their identities in the United States, others assign identities to them that may not reflect their own choices.

Susana's story is unfortunately far too common. Susana came to San Francisco when she was very young. Her father abandoned her mother shortly after arriving in San Francisco; she now lives in a family group that has gone through multiple permutations. She says that for years the gang was her "real" family and that it provided an alternative to the disintegration and lack of stability she found in her loosely biological family.

Lupita liked belonging to a gang because people recognized her "power" and they respected her. She said it felt good to walk down streets and have people know to which gang she belonged. A tattoo on her hand displays the name of her gang, Natoma, the street where her gang congregates.

Triste describes his situation as follows: "For my parents it was hard. They argued a lot; there wasn't a lot of money. My dad had sold the house in El Salvador so we could leave; they sold everything, even their wedding rings. My parents always tried to do what was best for us. But as I grew up, I started hanging around with gang members, and I got into it, the gang life."[6]

Many gang members reported that they were recruited in school. Cesar, a former gang member and now a social worker involved with gangs, says, "You know, they recruit, like the army recruiting potential gang members. If they see a kid who is tough looking or looks cool, they will try to court him to get him." Every gang member told us that they had trouble fitting in at school. If schools do not serve as places for young people to find their place in society then it makes sense that gangs would fill this function for them.

Increasingly, young men and women without families or relatives come to the United States to work and send money home. These fourteen and fifteen year olds often can't find work and thus quickly realize that the easiest way to make money is to sell drugs. As Cesar notes, "When you sell drugs you sell them in an area where there are gangs . . . You are going to need protection so you got to join a gang to get protection. So you sell your drugs to make money and send back home. It is a vicious circle."

A sense of belonging, a surrogate family, an ethnic or national identity, being "cool," a way to make money, having fun—any number of these elements could easily appeal to a fourteen-year-old migrant youth, the most common age for gang recruitment. Many gang members left school, faced discrimination, experienced conflicts in ethnic and cultural identity, and reported problems with their families. Manuel Vásquez and Marie Marquardt note that as a response to "multiple marginality" and social conflict, gangs affirm the "self, family (as an extended community) and place," and also that "gangs offer disenfranchised and dislocated Salvadoran youths discourses, practices, and forms of organization that allow them to reterritorialize their lives, that is to re-assert locality against global forces that have torn asunder their communities and families. Gangs also provide a context where the self can be re-centered in an intimate setting, where loyalty and collective identity are central" (2003, 128, 119).

Our interviews, fieldwork, and findings corroborate Vásquez and Marquardt's insight. What surprised us was that virtually none of our San Francisco respondents reported being intimidated to join. Most claimed that they were not coerced into joining gangs, not forced to get tattoos, and were not threatened on leaving the gangs; instead, it was economic marginalization, ethnic and cultural discrimination, and social exclusion that "forced" these youths to join gangs.

The Streets of San Salvador, El Salvador

Some researchers claim that gangs existed in El Salvador as early as the 1950s (Vásquez and Marquardt 2003; Smutt and Miranda 1998), while others link them to the increased violence of the 1970s. No researcher, however, disputes the fact that the rapid growth of gangs in El Salvador began in 1992 when what was then called the Immigration and Naturalization Services (INS) began deporting gang members. Only several thousand gang members existed in El Salvador in 1994; estimates now state that membership ranges from 30,000 to 35,000. The United States deported some 18,000 criminals to El Salvador between 1999 and 2004 and the country received 1,900 deported gang members in 2005 alone (Johnson, 2006). In a study conducted by Marcela Smutt and Jenny Miranda, three out of ten gang members interviewed in El Salvador were deportees from the United States (1998, 154). New gang members arrive weekly, contributing to a transcultural, transnational gang circuit.

These youths land on the streets of San Salvador, speaking no Spanish and with little knowledge of Salvadoran culture or realities. Triste relates his experience as follows: "I had my papers and was a permanent resident (of the United States). After three and a half years in the penitentiary (for a robbery), I was released and spent two months in the immigration detention center. The public defender told me to say I wanted to get deported, and that as soon as I got to El Salvador I could work out my papers and be back within a year. So I listened to her, and they sent me to El Salvador. When it was time to leave, the immigration officials told me they had lost all my paperwork. I hadn't been in El Salvador for ten years, so when I came back I was lost. The only way I knew how to survive was hanging around with the gangs. I wasn't into doing all the gang stuff. I just needed to know where I could sleep and not be alone." The sad fact is that many deported youths die on the streets of San Salvador. Every week during our research in summer 2003 a recently deported youth was killed because he or she wasn't familiar with street and gang life in San Salvador. Although many deported youths hope to change their lives when reaching El Salvador, given their marginalized status, lack of opportunity, poor knowledge of their own country, and little knowledge of Spanish, they often return to the only life they know—that of gangs. These youths suffer a triple process of social exclusion: the poverty and lack of opportunities that forced their families to leave El Salvador in the first place; arrival in a society, the United States, where they suffer discrimination, social exclusion, poverty and few opportunities; and return to a country where they again experience social exclusion.

Deportation alone, however, cannot account for the rapid growth of gangs in El Salvador, or for that matter throughout Central America. As Gustavo Adolfo Guerra Vásquez writes: "Those who claim that U.S. deportees are solely responsible for the current wave of violence ignore the structural problems in Salvadoran society that prevent deported youths from integrating themselves into a country that has been negatively affected by twelve years of civil war. The conditions for young people in El Salvador are so difficult that they alienate youths who act like their Los Angeles counterparts despite having never left El Salvador" (2005, 108).

Gangs in El Salvador appeal especially to extremely poor youths who may be abandoned and already living on the streets. In a study conducted in 2000 by the University of Central America (UCA), 82.9 percent of gang members come from families who live in conditions of poverty (Eastman 2001, 13). Gang leaders often feel responsible for their group. As Mauricio, a gang leader, states, "Look at them, they have no shoes. How am I going to get them shoes?" Given social and economic marginalization, high levels of unemployment, the trans-culturation of violence introduced by U.S. gang members, family difficulties, the privatization of public space, accelerated processes of urbanization, on-going effects of the armed conflict, the absence of alternative groups, and the stigmatization of youth itself, these youths are drawn to gangs to reconstruct their identities through gang membership and as a means to survive life in the streets. Gangs offer them stability, family, identity, status, and protection.

Theories to explain the growth of youth gangs view these gangs as surrogate structures to replace families made dysfunctional by poverty and social mar-ginalization; mirrors of lower-class subcultures; resistance to marginalization and stigmatization; collective strategies for reterritorialization in the face of globalization; informal business ventures; opportunities for maturation and identity construction; or reflections of the deviant personality traits of indi-vidual members (Papachristos 2005; Rocha 2000b; Rodgers 2006, 282; Vásquez and Marquardt 2003; Vigil 2002, 1998; Zilberg 2004). Undoubtedly a combina-tion of these theories explains the recent growth of youth gangs. Most theories incorporate some aspects of the multiple marginalization lens offered by J. D. Vigil and agree that "gangs take over where others have failed" (1998, 35). As Vigil writes, "This multiple marginality derives from various interwoven situa-tions and conditions that tend to act and react upon one another. Although interrelated, the unfolding and interpretation of these ecological, economic, social, cultural, and psychological features of the street gang suggest a develop-mental sequence. All of these considerations are integral to the relationship between multiple marginality and gang patterns" (1998, 1).

Gang experience, whether in San Francisco or in El Salvador, is "shaped by the way in which the particular history and culture of each ethnic group and family interact with the overriding economic and psychosocial forces in the larger society (Vigil 2002, 7). Structural causes must be the starting point for analyses of gang growth, as well as for prevention strategies. Public discourse rarely considers the reasons why impoverished youths find themselves drawn to gangs. Street gangs, whether in the United States or in El Salvador, reflect the "relegation of certain persons or groups to the fringes where social and economic conditions result in powerlessness"; urban youth are forced to the "margins of society in practically every sense" (Vigil 2002, 7).

THE LIFE

Gangs have clear and strict norms and rules concerning member behavior, thus providing an alternative "street socialization" process for young people (Vigil 2002, 10). The gang provides a way for youths to "participate in the production of norms, albeit in a local, informal sphere" (Rocha 2005) rather than adhere to those of mainstream culture. Members must obey the gang's decisions even if they don't agree with them. Loyalty to the group is of ultimate importance and each member must always help other members. Members are, on the other hand, absolutely forbidden to interact with rival gang members because they are sworn enemies. Rituals of entrance and initiation are obligatory, and most new members must go through a "ceremony" in which they are beaten. Each gang proscribes very specific ways of dressing and behaving that might include tattoos with specific letters or numbers, gang-specific language, gang colors and clothing, hand gestures and signs, and the creation of murals or graffiti. These identifiers mark a moral code and the "creation of their own order" (Rocha 2005, n.p.).

Norms of loyalty and support hold an understandable appeal. Interviewees in the UCA study rated friendship, respect, and support as the primary benefits of gang membership. Interestingly, the most common reason that youths in El Salvador listed for joining a gang was the desire to "have fun" (*vacilar*). Having fun is a simple and understandable motive, yet this fun comes with a price; members cite fear of death, going to prison, and the police as the primary disadvantages of their gang life. Finding employment is virtually impossible for the 80 percent of gang members whose bodies display tattoos, and roughly 85 percent of both male and female youths in the UCA study hoped to leave gang life.

Gang membership helps young people construct identity. Members share common narratives, relational bonds, dress, gestures, codes, symbols, language, ways of walking, and public space. In a world where he or she is nobody, the gang offers identity. This identity construction occurs in "a reduced environment, the territory of the barrio, that island in the midst of nowhere in the globalized world. . . . [It is] the base for new identities, more local when the globalized world culture is less accessible for the poor. The domination and defense of a territory gives identities" (Rocha 2000a n.p.).

Women in Gangs

Women's experience in gangs differs from that of their male counterparts. Young men are drawn to gangs for numerous reasons, including desires for belonging, respect, and power. A young woman may join for similar reasons, but she may also seek spaces of freedom in cultures that devalue women. Women from the UCA study reported that they sought friendship, a sense of belonging, the tattoos that marked gang membership and identity, and an end to the discrimination faced by poor youths (Guerra Vásquez 2005, 114). Yet within the gang, young women find themselves excluded and marginalized from spheres of power. Young women are treated as peripheral and as sex objects; some male gang members interviewed didn't think women should be allowed into gangs since they are too "distracting." Female gang members have high rates of teenage pregnancy and abortion (Guerra Vásquez, 2005, 114).Entrance rituals for women generally involve having sex with male gang members. Gang norms tend to "perpetuate a state of male dominance, and females, with few exceptions, largely follow these rules and regulations" (Vigil 2002, 11).

Male gang members experience violence at the hands of rival gangs, but rarely from their own gang. Women, on the other hand, may be raped or beaten by both rival gang members and members of their own gang, thus leaving them no safe place and no protection. The streets of San Salvador "are far more dangerous, both physically and psychologically, for adolescent females than they are for adolescent males" (Vigil 2002, 2). Joining a gang increases a young woman's vulnerability. As Maria Santacruz Giralt and Alberto Concha Eastman write: "The gang reproduces the values and forms of perceiving women that it has learned from society. The most tragic and paradoxical is that, in many cases, the gang is considered by many of the young women as a means of leaving another violent context, whether that is the neighborhood, the school or the home . . . the women then finds herself in a violent and machisto group, where the price to pay for gaining a certain stability, identity, and belonging is very high, joining the gang increases a young woman's victimization and marginalization" (2001, 141–42). Gang involvement structures young women's risk of marginalization and victimization in gendered ways (Miller 1998). Gangs, paradoxically, offer both "protection" and risk; women in gangs exacerbate their state of "multiple marginalities" in ways not experienced by young men. Young women in gangs violate gender norms that relegate them to the domestic sphere by venturing into the public world of the gang. They also violate street norms by bringing the "wrong" gender into the street (Vigil 2002, 2). Paradoxically, their gender-transgressing behavior places them in a context that replicates the norms and values of mainstream culture.

VIOLENCE AND THE STATE

Concern over surviving the streets of El Salvador is real. The death rate due to violent crime during the 1990s was 40 percent higher than the wartime rate; much of this increase is attributed to gang violence (Rodgers 2006, 268). In the UCA study 23 percent of the gang members had killed someone in the year before the interview and 63 percent of these violent acts were inflicted on rival gang members (Santacruz Giralt and Concha-Eastman 2001, 127). Needless to say, it is dangerous and possibly even fatal to be a gang member.

On the surface, the upsurge in the death rate seems to reflect the privatization or democratization of violence in which "broad ideological struggles are increasingly replaced by local identity struggles or simply fragmented interests of an economic or political nature" (Friedman 2003a, 21; see also Rodgers 2006; Wieviorka 2003). We contend that gang violence reflects a response to prior violence, whether that of the state, the family, or economic and social structures. As Michael Wieviorka writes, "It [violence] expresses the distance or time lag between the subjective demands of people or groups and the political, economic, institutional, or symbolic responses. In these instances it characterizes a subjectivity that is denied, broken, crushed, unhappy, and frustrated" (2003, 134).

The best-known gangs in El Salvador—Mara Salvatrucha (MS13), the 18th Street Gang, and Mao Mao—mark their territory by graffiti on walls, fences, and doors to show their zones of domination. Gang members benefit from the nearly half a million guns left from the civil war: "The problem is that the war left the civilian population heavily armed" (Cruz 1998, 93). A project researcher, visiting a gang member's apartment in San Salvador, entered a room full of machine guns, hand grenades, and other arms, all made in the United States. The United States, by providing a million dollars a day during the civil war, effectively armed El Salvador's postwar population, including its gangs.

Guillermo, a former gang member, fled the violence of El Salvador's civil war with his family. As he recalls: "I went to San Francisco in 1980 after Romero's death. I used to go with my mom to mass on weekends, so when Romero was killed, we went to his funeral. We had a little business in the market so my brother stayed in the stand during the funeral. My mom and I were in the plaza when all the shooting started. We are survivors of the 80s massacre during Romero's funeral." Guillermo left a violent environment for a new context of social and economic marginalization; he quickly sought gang protection in this new and frightening world. The structural violence that shaped his life preceded his particular "random" acts of violence. Neither the United States nor El Salvador "acknowledge that these youth are products of a cycle of violence that has fed upon itself due to U.S. foreign and domestic policy, allowing for a compounding of violence that the deportation of gang-involved youth is also promoting" (Guerra Vásquez 2004, 104–5).

Salvadorans express concern over their personal safety. In a 1998 study conducted by the UCA, over 40 percent of the adult population cited gang violence as El Salvador's worst problem (Santacruz Giralt and Cruz 2001, 19). This perception has several implications. Young people in general become stereotyped as public security risks. According to Marcela Smutt and Jenny Miranda, "a large part of the Salvadoran population perceives the binary 'youth and violence' as a synonym for juvenile delinquence" (1998, 23). Youth, especially poor, marginalized youth, become identified as violent. This stigmatization damages both gang and nongang youth (47 percent of the population). Young people with tattoos, for example, find it nearly impossible to obtain jobs. As one gang member says, "I am not who people say I am. . . . I'm not bad like I appear to people, people say I commit crimes, they think I'm an addict. I don't like that people stereotype me, I wanted to be seen as any 'brother' who is on the street" (quoted in Smutt 1998, 152).

Public opinion tends to favor drastic and often repressive, authoritative, and violent means to eliminate gangs. Vigilante groups have killed gang members in a tacitly approved "social cleansing." The police and judicial system have opted to "solve" the gang problem through incarceration, control, and violation of gang members' rights. El Salvador initiated its Super Mano Dura (super heavy hand) antigang measures in 2004, which allowed soldiers to assist police in targeting gang members. The initiative resulted in the arrests of thousands of gang members who were moved to dangerously overcrowded jails (El Salvador's prison population has doubled since 2001). The solution favored by the Salvadoran state (and many of its citizenry) applies the same means that it seeks to resolve: violence. Such remedies do nothing to address a "culture of violence" shaped by a history of repression as a form of social control, the trivialization of the basic rights of the majority by minority interests, the war as a form of conflict resolution, the prevalent use of arms, and the current bowing to global economic and political forces (Santacruz Giralt and Cruz 2001, 25). The UCA study in 2000 found that gang members who had spent time in jail were more likely to commit violent acts than were members of the same gang who had never been imprisoned. A punitive, zero-tolerance approach to gangs both increases the cycle of violence and criminalizes poor youth in general.

The response by the United States mirrors that of El Salvador in emphasizing aggressive, zero-tolerance, antigang strategies. The 1996 Illegal Immigration Reform and Immigrant Responsibility Act included provisions that expanded the definition of "aggravated felony" and applied the definition retroactively; it also changed the seriousness of crimes considered deportable offenses. More gang youths went to prison with longer sentences for lesser crimes. The Bureau of Immigration and Customs Enforcement (ICE) initiated Operation Community Shield in 2005 to increase the deportation of foreign-born gang members.[7] By March 2006, ICE had apprehended 2,388 foreign gang members, 922 of whom were from El Salvador's Mara Salvatrucha (Johnson 2006, 7). Many of the deported are legal residents; yet in the logic of the state they pose national security threats. Officer Frank Flores, a gang expert with the Los Angeles Police Department, told a *New York Times* reporter that "MS is not a gang, it's an army. . . . Within the United States, these guys pose as much a threat to the well being of ordinary citizens as any foreign terrorist group."[8] National identity (security) is thus performed through the expulsion of these "semilegal" residents. Drugs and terrorists (and migrants) come from without, thus deportation is preferred to incarceration in order to preserve the myth of national purity and the danger that comes from outside the "homeland." As Elana Zilberg writes, "It is on the streets of the urban barrio that the United States is most effectively policing the boundaries of its nation-state. . . . Moreover, the emergent transnational identities of these youths are, in fact, created by the very forces of nationalism directed at them through the collusion between local law and federal immigration enforcement bodies" (2004, 759). Paradoxically, the nationalistic impulse that expels foreign-born gang members fosters transnational gang identity and action.

El Salvador, via the media, government, and popular perception, also employs a nationalistic ideology; it scapegoats deported youths as the source of the country's street crime. As Guerra Vásquez writes, "It is easier to scapegoat deportees and former guerilla fighters than to expose the roots of economic and social problems that ravage El Salvador. It is the material and political conditions that led to civil war in El Salvador and to the gang wars in Los Angeles that are responsible for the participation of Salvadoran youth in street gangs both in El Salvador and in Los Angeles" (2004, 107). The reproduction of violence among disenfranchised youth raised in cultures of violence, whether in the United States or El Salvador, is not surprising. Gangs are a reaction by young people to the daily violence in which they are enmeshed. Immigration and gang policies in the United States and in El Salvador criminalize marginalized youth while ignoring social, economic, and political factors.

The perceived privatization of violence serves the state. If citizens live in fear, they are more likely to vote for authoritarian rule. Increased state violence, repression, and the erosion of human rights occur with the citizenry's consent. The protection from privatized violence, the gang member, who also represents the threat from without (as migrant or deportee), serves as a distraction from structural and state-sponsored violence.

Transnationalism from Below

El Salvador is arguably one of the world's most "transnational" countries. Currently, six million people live in El Salvador, and 20 percent of the total global Salvadoran population resides in the United States—which has been dubbed Departamento 15, or the nation's fifteenth province. As Ana Patricia Rodríguez notes, it is the *los hermanos lejanos* (distant relatives) who "maintain material, affective and symbolic connections to their homeland and produce significant social networks, cultures and identities in their new home sites" (2005, 22). Deported gang members become double hermanos lejanos; after living in the United States for most of their lives they are "returned home to a place, where in their memory, they have never been" (Zilberg 2004, 760). Most deported gang members return to the United States, or at least try to do so. They have landed in a country where they may have minimal family ties, few options for employment, and limited Spanish-language proficiency. As noted above, aggressive antigang strategies employed by the state in service of homeland protection (national sovereignty) increase transnational flows and connections. Saskia Sassen writes that "in the interest of protecting the nation," in this case the United States, pollutants are expelled—in contributing to the transnationalization of violence, these trends "signal not only a deterritorializing of citizenship practices and identities, as is usually argued, but also their partial denationalizing" (Sassen 2006, 147).

Forced into constructing transnational identities, youth deported to El Salvador, marginalized youth in El Salvador, and new migrant youth in the United States face complex relationships between space and identity. As Zilberg writes, "Youth deported . . . are the shock effects of globalization as it clashes with nationalism. . . . These narratives of deported immigrant youth speak eloquently to the need for interpretive maps which interrogate the relationship between space and identity and the blurred boundaries between the local and the global" (2004, 762).

Literature on "transnationalism from below" often celebrates grassroots transnational social movements for providing oppositional practices and hybrid identities in the face of globalization (Guarnizo and Smith 1998). Gangs may provide "creative cultural responses to the pressures of immigrant life. Indeed, gang culture contributes to Central American's literary, artistic, and musical expression across borders" (Mahler and Ugrina 2006, 13). Yet, as Vásquez and Marquardt note, "Salvadoran gangs reveal that transnationalism does not always result in the formation of transgressive, counter-hegemonic subjects" (2003, 130).

Our research reflects this paradox. Gangs often function as decentralized criminal networks, yet their crimes rarely have political aims or explicit message. Members, in spite of their carefully constructed transgressive identities, stand "at the end of a long and familiar global commodity chain" (Papachristos 2005, 49). The aim of gangs is often unapologetically consumeristic. Gang members may rob or sell drugs simply to survive; yet they may also use resources to pursue more conspicuous consumption. As transgressive subjects "from below" transnational Salvadoran gangs "simultaneously deterritorialize and reterritorialize, producing local and global spaces that have contradictory consequences . . . Gangs reterritoralize, creating hybrid subcultures anchored in geographically bounded spaces (the street or the neighborhood). While these local spaces may serve to nurture hybrid cartographies of resistance (with these cartographies literally marked on bodies) . . . they can also become isolated islands of expressivism, mirroring the globalized culture of immediate gratification" (Vásquez and Marquardt 2003, 142).

Gangs do not reflect a "rupture with the established order"; rather, "gang members insert themselves with their own style in that order" (Rocha 2000a, n.p.). Gangs share the exclusionary tendencies, sexism, racism, hedonism, obsession with image, and consumerism of the dominant culture. They reinforce the status quo and contribute to further self-marginalization as they drive "members toward the criminal justice system" (Moore 2002, xi). Given that gangs actually "betray the desires of their members for self recognition and for solidarity and intimacy in the face of globalization by re-inscribing global processes at the heart of gang life," it makes sense that religion would provide an alternative way, although not an unproblematic one, for Salvadoran youth to "negotiate the tensions between the local and the global" (Vásquez and Marquardt 2003, 132).

THE TATTOO AS TEXT

Mission District gangs in San Francisco locate themselves by streets, street corners, parks, and other public spaces. Vásquez and Marquardt write that this insertion of the gang into public space allows them "to respond to disloca- tion and multiple marginalities by reasserting territory . . . gangs reconstruct local geographies in response to the deterritorializing processes they confront" (2003, 128). What is significant for our study is that these geographies are em- bodied (e.g., as noted above in the case of Lupita's Natoma tattoo?). As Cesar says of gang tattoos, "They describe their barrios. People used to put their bar- rios to show or whatever their name was. Mine was Folsom." Vásquez and Marquardt write that "scars and *mara* tattoos inscribe locality in the bodies of gang members, making the self part of the landscape. Just as graffiti marks the territory the gang controls, so do tattoos map a certain way of life and a certain sense of belonging and group control onto the body of the gangbanger" (2003, 128). This view implies a sense of agency; the gang member has "placed" him- self or herself on this street or on that corner. They have also "placed" them- selves socially. As Hugo says, "my tattoos show who I am and also honors our martyrs . . . they show the streets that my gang controls." More accurately, the gang members have acknowledged, through their tattoos, that society has both ejected them *from* a place and relegated them *to* a highly localized and "small" space (the street corner and the margins). The gang member enables society to "keep them in their place"; they have now clearly identified where they be- long through the physical marking of the tattoo. As José Luis Rocha writes, "If the body serves as a site where gender, ethnicity and class are marked, tattoos create a cultural body and maintain specific social limits. They express a social position that the body occupies" (2003, n.p.).[9] The subversive act of tattooing "provokes a dialogue" and serves to exacerbate the marginalization already experienced by poor youth; the tattoo "becomes the provocation that brings to light latent social prejudices" (n.p.).

Tattoos tell stories. These narratives of the skin speak of gang membership, killings, love, neighborhood, national origin, and the death of loved ones. The hermeneutic manipulation of this tattoo text "molds not just the body, but the dialogue with others and within the psyche" (Rocha 2003, n.p.). Tattoos mark both pride and stigma. The tattooed body reflects how society perceived marginalized youths *before* they colluded in making visible the "invisible" so- cial markings. The tattoo becomes a "mediator between being and appearing," physically exhibiting the person you want to be, but also marking the body as

stigmatized (n.p.). Given the importance of the tattoo for gang identity and social positioning, it makes sense that the Salvadoran self-help group CASI would
provide tattoo removal as a way to mark the departure from a gang locality and
way of life.

NO TENGO DONDE IR

Nearly half of the gang members interviewed in the UCA study in 2000 wanted
to leave gangs or at least *calmar* (to remain a member but be freed from com-
mitting violent acts—this option is generally reserved for older members who
in a sense "retire"). Leaving a gang is difficult, however. Many are afraid to leave
because they will lose the protection from rival gang members that the gang
provides to them; others are afraid that they might be beaten or even killed
because their own gang may view their departure as a betrayal. Still others feel
a sense of responsibility to the group. There are few perceived advantages to
leaving a gang; the retired gangbanger faces unemployment or low-wage work,
the loss of a social network, potential displacement from home or neighborhood, and the threat of death from his or her own gang or another. As one gang
member said, "no tengo donde ir" (I have nowhere to go).

Pentecostal churches offer one alternative for Salvadoran youth (Vásquez
and Marquardt 2003; León 2004; Rodgers 2006). Salvadoran gang members
who claim to be evangelical or Pentecostal have very low levels of violence compared to other members. A born-again lifestyle offers a way out of the world
of the gang as well as an alternative to it. As Rodgers writes, "The totalizing
nature of evangelical Protestantism means that churches often tended to provide a complete organizational framework for their members . . . and thereby
constituted an alternative institutional form to the gang for youth" (2006, 274).
A "universe of monolithic truths" (Rocha 2000a, n.p.) and seeming stability
replaces a fragmented and fragile world; the gang member has quite literally
gained a place to go. Gangs and Pentecostal or evangelical groups share the
logic of identity creation through exclusion. They redefine values and confer
significance in a world that marginalizes gang youth and entire social sectors.

Although Pentecostal groups are understandably well known for their work
with gangs, they are not the focus of this essay. Instead, we have studied a tattoo removal program in San Francisco that is sponsored by a self-help group
in the Mission District known as CASI. Central American refugees founded
CASI in 1981 with a great deal of support from the church-based Sanctuary
Movement. Many religious organizations helped build CASI, including the Roman Catholic Church, and the Lutheran, Methodist, Presbyterian, and Jewish

communities. The claim by CASI is that its work is inspired by the courage and vision of the assassinated Salvadoran Archbishop Monsignor Oscar Romero, and CASI is arguably the most highly regarded organization in San Francisco working with migrants. In 1998 CASI was asked to restructure and lead the tattoo removal program (another agency started the program in 1996). The program, in conjunction with a San Francisco hospital, offers participants the option of removing gang-related tattoos. Participants must be between twelve and twenty-three years of age, live in San Francisco, provide ten hours of community service before joining the program, complete fifty hours of community service throughout the course of the program, and have the desire to change their gang life. The laser treatments to remove the tattoos occur over the course of up to a year and can be quite painful. Given that the response of the city to gangs is to try to eradicate them, encourage citizens to call the police, and put gang members in jail, the community values CASI's approach.

Unlike Pentecostal groups who work with gang members, CASI does not demand religious conversion, or indeed any spiritual practice of its clients. It is enough that the client wishes to change his or her lifestyle for whatever reason. Yet CASI's religious orientation is clear after a visit to its office, which is full of symbols signifying both religion and nation. Pictures of Monsignor Romero, seen as a martyr to El Salvador, are found in numerous rooms. The Celina Ramos Health Center takes its name from the housekeeper who was killed, along with her daughter and six Jesuits, at the Jesuit University of Central America in 1989. The claim by CASI is that Romero provided the inspiration for their founding and work. Romero and Celina Ramos signify both religion (Catholicism, especially liberation theology) and religious martyrdom coupled with justice. They are powerful religious symbols that also signify national identity—in this case that of El Salvador. In the service of religious and national symbols, other religious and national symbols are removed from the bodies of youths.

Most of the gang members we interviewed said that their religious tattoos didn't have explicit religious meanings for them. They didn't necessarily know what the symbols meant, just that a cross, for example, meant that they belonged to the Pachucos or that the Virgin of Guadalupe signified Mexico or Mexican Americans. Lupita sarcastically makes the sign of the cross, saying, "You know how they are . . . most cholos have a cross or a Virgin of Guadalupe." And Cesar adds, "I tease with the kids that are gang members, they have like Jesus, the Virgin or the cross, the Sacred Heart. Very religious man, but you continue killing your own people, yeah, very religious."

Yet, members use explicitly religious symbols to mark what is deepest for them. As Hugo notes, "We tattoo a cross with the name of some who died to remember them, to honor them." Guadalupe, while signifying Mexico or Mexican American, might also symbolize mother. Jorge claims that "Guadalupe protects us like our mothers do; we respect our mothers." The ex-gang member Franco wonders whether "the tattoo 'forgive me mother for my crazy life' is to the Virgin or to biological mothers. But to get this tattoo, gang members must have recognized that their mothers are suffering for what they are doing. The tattoos that mark their bodies asking for forgiveness communicate that they do not like the suffering of their mothers."

How do the clients of the tattoo removal program leave gangs? This occurs in several ways. Ex-gang members often report positively of the community service hours demanded of them by CASI. They are required to perform ten hours of community service before starting the tattoo removal process. Roughly fifty hours of service are required for each tattoo removed; the young person thus becomes involved in the community in a new way. Upon "graduating" from the program, some even become counselors for new youths about to have their tattoos removed. In addition, CASI offers help in finding jobs or pursuing an education.

The new friendships formed in the program, with both staff and other clients, also provide close relationships within a safe and stable environment. As Guillermo states, "It gives me the space I was looking for in my gang; I feel comfortable and welcome." And Jorge explains, "The religious people who came to me on the streets, they know way more about me than the police, or even my family." Juan said that he was hanging out on a street corner when someone from CASI approached him and told him about the program, and he adds that "they also took me to movies and I liked that." In the words of Vásquez and Marquardt, this "reterritorialization provides the ex-gang member with a 'new home' and 'new family' . . . the rearticulation of family and a place called home is accompanied by the emergence of a new, cleansed self (a self with gang tattoos removed)" (2003, 135). Previously the gang was the group that resocialized its members of the group to countercultural norms and behaviors; now CASI, a religious group, becomes the alternative organization.

The tattoo removal process takes time, thus allowing new activities, social groups, and identities to be internalized. It took Juan over a year to have his numerous homemade tattoos removed. The prolonged period of time as well as the pain involved demonstrates a commitment on the part of these ex-gang members. Juan claims that after finishing the program he wants to "help kids . . . I want to warn children about life on the streets."

Both CASI and the Pentecostal or charismatic groups share the belief that

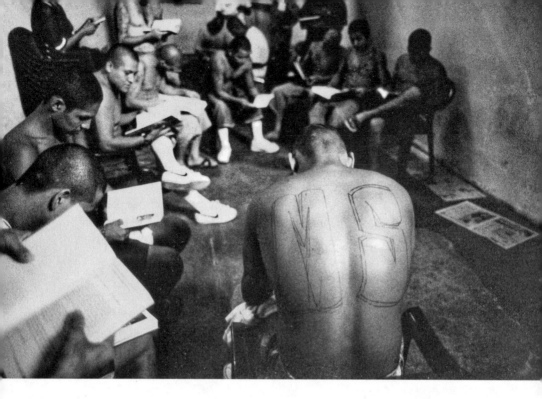

battles are, at least in part, "waged through control of the body" (León 2004, 212). Whereas "in charismatic worship, women and men give their bodies to God" (233), CASI reclaims bodies through tattoo removal. The body endures pain in the process as youths enter what might be viewed as a new rite of passage. Marcela yelled, "Just do it, just do it" before the nurse removed a scorpion tattoo from her stomach. At the end, the tears started coming, as she repeated over and over, "I can't believe I did this." Jackie, her nurse in the program, says, "She was so strong . . . it takes courage, strength, guts, I don't think a lot of people realize how much strength it takes for these kids to do this." New narratives replace the bodily text of the tattoo, as tattoo removal transforms the body. The changed body, as well as membership in a new collective body, opens public spaces previously closed to gang members.

Religious groups, whether CASI or Pentecostal churches, may allow gang members to "break with their communal hyper-individualism and to articulate a new relational self" (Vásquez and Marquardt 2003, 136). We don't claim that religious groups are the only alternative organizations that effect this break, however the methods they use are instructive in that they consciously reterritorialize and rearticulate values. Most participants in the program want to leave gangs for reasons like getting married and having children, getting a job, escaping the violence of gang life, or just "growing up," and CASI may provide a means to reach these goals. For gang members who "No tengo donde ir," a religious group provides a concrete place to go; the gang member's old life is literally replaced.

Religious groups such as CASI serve as buffers by mediating institutions between young people, the state that wishes to incarcerate or deport them, and the larger society that excludes and despises them. As admirable as projects initiated by religious groups such as CASI may be, they remain small, localized, and do little to address broader socioeconomic and political realities. Both civil society and the government have the responsibility to shape preventive projects rather than focusing on ineffective punitive measures that stigmatize all youth.

Transnational Salvadoran gangs grow as the opportunity for meaningful collective life shrinks. Young people respond to social and economic break- down and pervasive collective insecurity by creating alternative socialization processes. Solutions proposed to address youth gang membership and vio- lence by churches, nongovernmental organizations, police, and the state tend to target individuals rather than address structural conditions (Rocha 2000a). Global processes of social, economic, and state breakdown yield widespread displacement; in this context youth gang violence can be seen as "coherent modes of social structuration" (Rodgers 2006, 269). Religious groups may help ex-gang members reimagine their place in the city and forge new collective identities in conditions of displacement.

These strategies may help individual gang members, yet larger complex so- cial issues remain. Global inequalities, geographical and cultural displacement, weak and uncivil societies, cultures of violence, school desertion, family diffi- culties, and unemployment converge to push youths to reshape their identities as gang members—the "expelled" children, who may be as young as nine and ten years of age, desperately attempt to survive on the streets. Macrostruc- tural and macrohistorical forces weaken all major institutions—the state, the family, law enforcement, schools, economic structures—which then fail these "expelled" youths. The failure of these institutions locally combines with larger geopolitical realities. Economic policy, migration legislation, and national security concerns within the United States and El Salvador, as well as between the two countries, contribute to violence and poverty there, migration here, deportation there, and so forth in an ongoing cycle that increasingly alienates vulnerable youth. In our regional version of intensifying globalization, states fear that increased "disorganized" violence by nonstate actors (gangs) under- mines their monopoly on violence (Rodgers 2006, 268).[10] Increased repressive measures against marginalized youth emerge from this fear. Gangs directly express, in the raw, what happens in society. They are social mirrors.

We end where we started: namely, with Carlos, looking out the window and telling us, "Mira, todo lo que te puedo decir es que antes todo era obscuridad y ahora, luz" (Look, all I can tell you is that before, everything was dark and now it is light). To which we say, "Esperamos que sí" (we hope so).

NOTES

1. Unless otherwise noted, all quotations are from the interviews conducted by the authors during their fieldwork in San Salvador during summer 2003 and in San Francisco from 2001–2003.

2. We want to thank Liliana Harris who first introduced us to the tattoo removal program, drew our attention to gangs in San Francisco, and conducted the initial fieldwork. Thanks also to Daniela Bazan who conducted interviews in Los Angeles.

3. All names of individuals have been changed throughout this chapter. In addition the acronym CASI is a pseudonym for a San Francisco-based self-help organization.

4. A *maquila* or *maquiladora* is a factory that imports duty-free and tariff-free equipment and materials for manufacturing or assembly and then exports the products. The products are generally exported back to the country that sent the materials.

5. Alan Eisner, "Laura Bush Seeks Help for Young Gang Members," *Washington Times*, February 15, 2005.

6. "Trying To Get Home: Triste's Story," *Salvanet*, September–October, 4.

7. The former Immigration and Naturalization Service (INS) is now three agencies: Immigration and Customs Enforcement (ICE), Citizenship and Immigration Services (CIS), and Border Patrol (BP)—all of which are under the jurisdiction of the Department of Homeland Security.

8. Charlie LeDuff, 2005. "100 Members of Immigrant Gang are Held." *New York Times*. March 15, A19. A series of newspaper articles that appeared in the *New York Times*, the *Miami Herald*, the *Arizona Star*, and other papers in 2004 attempted to make links between Mara Salvatrucha and Al Qaeda because gang members were allegedly spotted in Honduras with an Al Qaeda member. Although the reports were discredited, they demonstrate the desire to make the link between gangs and terrorists.

9. Rocha notes that in Nicaragua, tattoos on middle-class individuals are generally placed in areas that can be covered by clothing. Tattoos on lower-class youths tend to be in more visible sites such as the hands or the face.

10. When we consider that one-third of the population in El Salvador is between the age of twelve and twenty-five years and that most of these individuals are impoverished, the fear of loss of control (from the state's perspective) makes sense.

Transnational *Hetzmek*

From Oxkutzcab to San Francisco

PATRICIA FORTUNY LORET DE MOLA

> Up to the age of three or four months, infants are borne in their
> mothers' arms. Thereafter . . . they are carried astride the left hip
> of their mother or older sister, supported by the woman's left arm.
> The first time the child is placed in this position it is called . . .
> "hetzmek." *By spreading his legs around the hip of the woman who*
> *carries him, he is made ready to walk long distances.*
> —R. Redfield and A. Villa Rojas, *Chan Kom: A Maya Village*
> (emphasis added)

In May 2002 I traveled to San Francisco, California, to interview Yucatecan immigrants from the town of Oxkutzcab (on Mexico's Yucatán Peninsula) who attend the Mission Presbyterian Church in the heart of that city's Mission District. My time in Oxkutzcab a few months earlier had allowed me to witness people's increasing mobility and the growing intensity of the bonds that unite these two places, and my brief stay in San Francisco would not only corroborate this finding but also open up a whole new panorama on the accelerating movement of migrants from Oxkutzcab in southern Yucatán to the beautiful California city of San Francisco. My work unveiled the fact that beginning in the 1970s a multiplicity of evolving social networks had been established between these two areas. As such this finding belies Yucatán's relatively modest place in Mexican migration to the United States, which represents just 0.51 percent of the total—a number that is tiny in comparison to the high-density states of Guanajuato, Jalisco, and Michoacán, which together account for a third of all Mexicans living in "the North." Indeed, Mexico's entire southeastern region sends only an average of 7 percent of migrants, while the "historical" migration-sending region in the west accounts for 50 percent. Even in the southeast, Yucatán takes second place to the state of Veracruz, which has 6 percent (Durand and Massey 2003). Migration to the United States has been dominated by western Mexico since the nineteenth century (Durand, Massey, and Zenteno 2001) and was described by Jorge Durand and Douglas Massey

(2003) as "historic," "massive," and "short-range." Because it has lasted more than one hundred years, it involves the majority of migrants (ten million) and takes place between neighbor nations.

In contrast to other sites of intensive migration, Mexican-U.S. transnationalism has deep historical roots that date back to the early twentieth century,[1] when Mexican railroads were connected to rail systems north of the border. As Mexico's northern states were scarcely populated at that time, workers were recruited from the more densely populated states farther south, such as Jalisco, Guanajuato, and Michoacán. From 1943 to 1946, U.S. railroads hired 130,000 Mexican workers (Durand 2001, 3), a trend that went unchanged until the 1980s.[2] The topic of Mexican immigration to the United States has been extensively researched over the past few decades,[3] in part because, as Douglas Massey points out, the specific case of Mexico-U.S. migration constitutes the "largest sustained flow of immigrants anywhere in the world." Massey also asserts that many theoretical ideas about migration have been based precisely on empirical studies of Mexican migration (1999, 47). Pioneering studies from the early twentieth century by Paul Taylor (1970 [1928]) and Manuel Gamio (1930) found transnational ties a long time ago that continue to be documented by contemporary studies (Durand 1996; Kearney 1986, 1991, 1995; Rouse 1991; Roberts, Reanne, and Fernando 1999). Similar to the rest of Mexico, Yucatán shows an important degree of transnationalism expressed through the many ties that have emerged between San Francisco and Oxkutzcab, including networks based on social or neighborhood ties and on kinship, friendship, and the church. Thus Yucatecan migrants are reproducing, re-creating and reinventing their hometowns in "the North" through the frequent, systematic movement of people and their social-cultural baggage, which has forged these two places into one transnational community.[4]

Despite the restrictions imposed in recent decades, Mexico-U.S. migration has not slowed but rather in fact has increased, and new types have emerged. In the 1980s, most migrants were unskilled laborers from rural areas, but in the 1990s more skilled, white-collar workers of urban origin began to join the migratory tide (Alarcón 1999)—though agricultural laborers still dominate, constituting some 86 percent of the agricultural workforce in the United States. Durand and Massey (2003) explain that today migrants to "the North" come from almost all areas of Mexico and have spread into new regions across almost the whole nation. Yucatecan migrants form part of these new waves from rural towns and large or medium cities who end up in different U.S. towns. Although they are small in number, the study of Yucatecan migrants is worthy because it provides new elements to compare with the traditional migration from the western and northern states of Mexico, and thus will bring new insight to better understand indigenous migration from other parts of the country.

According to data gathered by the Institute for the Development of Maya Culture in Yucatán (INDEMAYA, a state government agency),[5] around twenty-five thousand Yucatecans are currently living in just two California counties: San Francisco and Marin. Compared to the hundreds of thousands of immigrants from western and, more recently, central Mexico, this figure seems insignificant and may explain why Yucatán is often ignored in the growing literature on migration, both in Mexico and in the United States. Yucatecan Mayas are considered new migrants, not only because their migratory history is shorter — probably dating from the 1970s — but also because of the few empirical studies that exist. Rachel Adler (2004) conducted an ethnographic study of the so-called Kaal migratory route from Yucatán to Dallas, Texas, in which she reconstructs the history of the social networks that joined these localities through transnationalism and then develops the concept of "agenda" to explain that population's migratory plans and projects and their impact on social change.

The media in Mexico and the United States have not ignored the relatively recent arrival of Yucatecans in the San Francisco area. In April 2002 the reporter Garance Burke wrote an article for the *San Francisco Chronicle Magazine* that described how "Maya" migrants from Yucatán adapted to their new environment while preserving their "Maya-ness," thanks to an organization called Grupo Maya that unites them with "other Mayans from Guatemala and El Salvador." In Mexico, a short article was published in a Mexico City newspaper in November 2002 in which the author describes the emergence of what she calls "the Mayas of San Francisco."[6] This journalist described the economic forces that motivate Yucatecan men to leave their homes in Oxkutzcab, thereby underlining the rapid economic progress many migrants achieve that stands in stark contrast to the low incomes they earn at home. This research was facilitated by the Presbyterian Mission Church in San Francisco's Mission District, where many Yucatecan migrants live, and it includes general data on the amount of remittances sent home each month. The ethnicity issue is mentioned as a positive factor that can be awoken through migration.

Focused on a specific community in Yucatán — Oxkutzcab — the data I discuss here present a different image of the growing intensity and extent of Mexican migration to the United States by showing how this particular migratory flow is permeated by a Yucatecan flavor and shaped by individual social actors who play prominent roles in this human drama. I elucidate transnational migration through the migrants' own life histories as they have unfolded in two sites: Oxkutzcab and San Francisco. These cities are linked, for instance, by an

Internet site (Oxkutzcab.com) located in Oxkutzcab through which people can communicate the feelings of joy or sorrow caused by their separation. Presbyterian congregations in the two countries—the Monte de la Transfiguración Church in Oxkutzcab and the Mission Church in San Francisco—also figure importantly in this study; first, because most social actors are involved in religious activities in both cities; and, second, due to the creation of formal and informal ties among the members and leaders of these two churches.

This essay is divided into five sections. First, I describe the milieu of the "community of origin" in relation to the migratory process; second, I develop the *hetzmek* model, which I use as a metaphor to interpret the context of Yucatecan migration. In the Maya language, the term hetzmek refers to a particular way of carrying three- or four-month-old babies, in which they are "perched" on their mothers' (or some other woman's) hip, with their feet swinging freely on either side of the adult's body. Like babies carried hetzmek style, transnational migrants are also suspended between two places, separated by the U.S. border. In the third section, I present data gathered in the two localities, while the fourth section presents an analysis of the genealogy of one extended family that illustrates the social and cultural changes that its members experienced as a result of international migration. The final section describes and analyzes the links between two Presbyterian churches and the advantages they offer to believers separated by migration.

THE COMMUNITY OF ORIGIN

Oxkutzcab is a small town nestled among fertile hills in the Maya Puuc (hilly) region on the southern Yucatán Peninsula, the only mountainous area on a peninsula with an almost completely flat topography that lies only twenty to thirty meters above sea level. Oxkutzcab's neighbors are the municipalities of Maní (to the north), Akil (east), Ticul and Santa Elena (west), and Tekax and the state of Campeche (south). After Mexican independence in the early nineteenth century, Oxkutzcab became part of the *partido* of Tekax (a political division similar to a large county). In the 1840s, it achieved great development and became one of the most important towns in the state, but during the "Caste Wars" (1847–1901) it was almost destroyed and entered a period of severe impoverishment. Then, in 1879, a railway line from Mérida to Peto passed near the town, thereby providing a means to transport people and farm products (mainly citruses and other fruits from the Puuc region) to other areas of the state. The name Oxkutzcab comes from the Maya roots *ox*, *kutz*, and *cab*, meaning "three times fertile" or the land of *ramón* (a local tree), tobacco, and honey.

Both meanings refer to the area's bountiful soil. Today, Oxkutzcab is known for its production of citrus and other fruits (oranges, lemons, *mamey, chicozapote,* mangos, avocado, guava, papaya, etc.).

In this municipality, 70 to 79 percent of the people speak Maya, but the vast majority of them are bilingual in Spanish. The daily life of many is marked by the age-old traditions and beliefs of their ancestors. Despite this, I prefer not to use the term Maya to refer to Oxkutzcab's contemporary inhabitants because they do not use it in their daily lives but only when anthropologists or reporters ask them about their identity. The Maya identity, in fact, constitutes a category that was imposed from above by colonial or nation-state powers as well as by archeologists, historians, and anthropologists.[7] On the peninsula the question of ethnicity is clear-cut,[8] as Quetzil Castañeda plainly explains: "Unlike the Maya of Chiapas and Guatemala who had a grand-media provoking cultural revitalization and resurgence . . . The peoples of Yucatán . . . have a dramatically different history of conquest, colonization, independence and incorporation into a larger nation-state" (2004, 38). The words "Indian" and "Indigenous" are not used; instead, people speak of "mestizos," which refers locally to the particular kind of dress worn by adult women and some older men.[9] Adults call themselves *mayeros,* to emphasize that they speak Maya. For most Yucatecans who live outside the large cities, the term "Maya" refers only to the "ancient Mayas . . . the grand pyramid builders."

The Mexican national census for 2000 indicates a population of 25,483 inhabitants for Oxkutzcab. In April 2004 it was given the status of "city," with its economy based on citrus fruit production and marketing (sweet and sour oranges, grapefruit, tangerines, and Italian lemons, among others). Known as the "orchard of Yucatán," Oxkutzcab is one of the most important production centers on the peninsula. However, local markets are small and wages are low. The economic census shows that 40 percent of working people are in the agricultural sector. These figures demonstrate the enormous social inequality that prevails and also the scant job opportunities. In local markets, producers sell a variety of citrus fruits to local and regional buyers. Though citrus production is high and the quality is good, prices are low: for example, in October 2003 a twenty-kilogram box of oranges cost just US$0.70. With such low returns on the sales of their harvests, growers are often forced to travel long distances to sell produce, though commercialization has become more difficult even in distant places due to stiff competition. The few jobs available offer wages far below those paid in the peninsula's major cities and tourist resorts, such as Mérida, Campeche, or Chetumal (Quintana Roo).

In the 1970s and 1980s, Cancún attracted workers from all over the penin-

sula, first to construct highways and hotels, and then to work in the service sector. Since 1990, Playa del Carmen, and later the Riviera Maya, became magnets
for migrant workers from Yucatán, due to the intensive development. Thus,
migration is now a familiar phenomenon to many Yucatecans. The vast majority of international migrants first spend a few years in one or more tourist
resorts—which function as intermediate destinations—before venturing off to
the United States. In many cases, the jobs they take there help them develop the
abilities they need to accede to the next level of migration, though it must be
said that the opening of the Cancún resort in the 1970s absorbed many workers,
thus cushioning or even delaying the more systematic movement of Yucatecans
to the United States that began in the mid-1980s.

International migration began modestly in Yucatán with a few peasants who
were recruited in the final years of the Mexico-U.S. binational migratory agreement known as the Bracero Program (1942–1964).[10] In September 1965, seventeen farmers from Oxkutzcab registered as "aspiring braceros."[11] As occurred
in the rest of the country, some of those temporary migrants did not return
when their contracts expired but rather stayed as undocumented workers in
the United States. Though many did return eventually, the seeds of migration
had been sown. Those pioneer migrants established niches in labor markets
north of the border that continue to attract new undocumented migrants even
today. Studies in Oxkutzcab in the 1980s reveal the level of economic prosperity
that those braceros achieved: "55% of the prosperous peasants or their children
were braceros in the U.S., and with the money earned they purchased fields
or infrastructure needed for productive development" (Terán Contreras 1987,
186). Such data suggest that early international migrants discovered an alternative that offered an escape from poverty and that in subsequent years those
pioneers became models to be emulated.

Today's systematic flow of Yucatecans to "the North" is impelled not only
by personal ambition but also by the socioeconomic structure of their hometowns, which provide insufficient jobs and opportunities. Without wishing to
reduce this problem to economic causes, it must be said that Mexico's agricultural sector simply cannot generate enough employment or propitiate people's
economic advancement. Moreover, though early migratory flows in the 1970s
and 1980s were modest, they triggered a kind of social-cultural disposition
toward international migration in rural towns like Oxkutzcab and the southern Yucatán in general, where similar situations emerged in municipalities
like Peto,[12] Muna, Akil, Tekax, and others along the frontier between the corn-
producing zone and the ranching area, like Cenotillo,[13] where social networks
have multiplied. The result is that proven strategies are available to all potential

migrants, as are networks that help them cross the border, find lodgings and, often, obtain jobs at their destination. Clearly, migration from Oxkutzcab and nearby towns in Yucatán to San Francisco and other U.S. cities will tend to increase and become more complex in the years to come. Although it is true that overpopulation, poverty, and economic stagnation in the country of origin can "create pressures for migration . . . these conditions are not sufficient by themselves to produce large new migration flows" (Sassen 1998, 38). Major cities such as San Francisco pull large inflows among the new migrant groups because of "the rapid expansion of the supply of low-wage jobs in the United States and the casualization of the labor market associated with the new growth industries" (45).[14]

RE-CREATING HETZMEK

As Nancy Farris states, "Modern ethnographic literature contains descriptions of many domestic rituals, especially relating to childbirth, illness and death that seem to have been copied almost textually from colonial sources" (1984, 288). Older and more recent ethnographic studies indicate that the hetzmek ritual is common to Yucatecan Mayas throughout the peninsula and even among those who live in Belize.[15] In fact, with certain variations it continues to be celebrated today in modern urban settings such as Mérida (Bracamonte y Sosa 2004; Peón Arceo 2000; Fernández Repetto 1988; Negroe Sierra 1988; Farris 1984; Redfield 1941; Villa Rojas 1978). Given the impressive staying power of this ancestral custom, I felt it would be interesting to find out if it also persists among Presbyterian migrants from Oxkutzcab. Having withstood for centuries the influence and pressures of the colonial period, independence, the revolution, and the modern Mexican nation-state, has it been able to resist the processes of globalization and migration that now affect Yucatecans?

Regarding the first question, ever since the Presbyterian Church began evangelizing rural Yucatán in the late nineteenth century, it has had a syncretistic character that facilitates its expansion. As Robert Redfield, in his classic work from the late 1930s, *The Folk Culture of Yucatán*, points out: "It does not appear that the group of Evangelical Protestants [Presbyterians] constitutes an important center of skepticism with regards to pagan gods and ceremonies. As a whole, the Protestants pay relatively little attention to the *yuntzilob*, yet many of these men make offerings and some take part in group ceremonies with other agriculturalists" (1941, 235). Though Redfield does not specifically mention the hetzmek ritual in his book, it is likely that it was also practiced among those early Presbyterian converts, as it is a private rite performed in the domestic sphere rather than a public ceremony held in the cornfields, like the one mentioned in the above quotation. I found that modern Presbyterians do indeed continue to perform this ritual. While working on this case study, I was told that most believers perform the rite when babies are three or four months old, that it seems perfectly natural, and that it may be celebrated in Spanish or Maya. To give one example, Hebert Villafania's daughter Kelly performed hetzmek for her eldest son Emiliano by herself.[16] Instead of carrying out the rite with another adult who would have become the baby's godparent, she carried her son around the table and handed him the implements that are part of the normal ritual. This case is worth mentioning because in her effort Kelly re-created an old tradition through the incorporation of new, modern elements. While clearly valuing hetzmek, Kelly decided to ignore the rules that normally govern its performance. Another case occurred while Jorge Villafania was in San Francisco and thus was unable to attend his daughter's rite. He told his wife, Concepción (Conchy), to take the baby to a distant town on the road to Chetumal,[17] where his aunt would participate and become the godmother. It is hardly surprising to learn that people travel great distances to perform this ritual when we realize that such is its importance for migrants that they celebrate it thousands of miles away, north of the border. This was the case of Nalda, Tomás, and Cornelia Villafania's eldest daughter, whose two children, Ana and Peter, had hetzmek performed in San Francisco. On that occasion, the family went so far as to fly in an aunt from Oxkutzcab.

Hetzmek is a rite of passage or initiation that integrates infants into a community. Though its specific forms and meanings have changed through time and space, its central idea persists: to prepare children to become useful adults in the future. Its performance requires the presence of godparents, or at least a godfather or godmother, according to the sex of the child. This person takes the baby, straddles it over his or her left hip and begins to walk in circles around a table or a traditional thatched hut. The number of laps may vary, either nine or thirteen. Then the child is offered a series of objects that symbolize—according to its sex—the activities she or he will perform as an adult. Tradition holds that boys be given a hoe, a machete, and an axe, implements used to work the cornfields, as well as a shotgun, to make them good hunters, while girls receive thread, cloth, and needles to learn embroidery (Villa Rojas 1987, 412, 413). Today, however, children of both sexes also receive paper and pencils. Godparents give babies objects that the parents stipulate but are free to innovate. One godfather in Oxkutzcab confided that he had given his godson a cellular telephone so he can communicate with him when he is older. In some places, in addition to implements children receive foods such as boiled eggs, *pinole* (toasted, ground corn) *chaya*, and pumpkin seeds.[18] The baby, of course, may reject some of the objects and attempt to take others that are beyond her or his reach. What we see here is a dynamic established between the structure (rules) of the ceremony and the agency of godparents and godchildren. Like all rituals, hetzmek is flexible and permits a degree of innovation, reinvention, or improvisation, as long as the rules that constitute its ritual or repetitive aspects are respected.

When a Maya baby is placed in hetzmek, he or she is straddled across the godparent's hip with one leg hanging behind the adult's body and the other in front of it. This position can be seen as a metaphor of the movement or oscillation between two places. Thus, also metaphorically, the adult body represents two supporting and grounding organizations: the extended family and the Presbyterian churches on both sides of the border, as discussed below. And the migrant's world is divided into two parts, with one foot in San Francisco and the other in Oxkutzcab. Though migrants may feel at home in either place, they feel nostalgia and often evoke memories of the other place, as it is also their home, though they are not physically there. In this sense, they are "like liminal subjects who are in neither one place or another, the characteristics of the ritual subject (passenger) are ambiguous, they are in neither the first nor the second group or place, they cannot be situated, they are invisible . . . They have no status, property, distinctions [or] secular attire that indicates their rank or role, nor any position in the society or group" (Turner 1988, 101, 102).

In the context of hetzmek, the transnational life of Yucatecan migrants between Oxkutzcab and San Francisco involves a series of continuous oscillations: economic progress versus the need for affection; vulnerability versus safety; homeland (birthplace) versus a forbidding country; and better wages and a higher living standard versus political and social uncertainty, especially for the undocumented. During their time in "the North," migrants often feel homesick and yearn to return to the "other place" to be with their loved ones. However, upon returning to the closeness of family and friends, surrounded by affection, in a country where they can exercise their rights as citizens and their political risks are almost nil, they also recall the "other place," which represents a "horn of plenty" (jobs, high wages) that offers economic and social security. This oscillation between certainty and precariousness, abundance and poverty, and affection and loneliness captures the contradictions that plague transnational migrants: to reach their desired, but always far-off goals they must bear this arduous back-and-forth movement between two physical spaces that reminds us of the hetzmek position in which the baby's legs hang freely, separated but also supported by the adult body, or "the family and the church."

ENCOUNTERS WITH MIGRANTS

I visited Oxkutzcab for the first time in August 2001 to begin this study,[19] and I returned occasionally in 2003. Shortly after my arrival I met Don Crescencio in the local market, and while I was drinking a Coke at his stand he told me how he had been a bracero in the mid-1960s.[20] Though he worked for just one month because the program was drawing to a close, he saved $550. He then invested the money in a potable water tank and a business that delivered water in a town that had no potable water system. Some years later, his business became redundant when a water system was installed in Oxkutzcab. Today, he tills his cornfield (*milpa*) in the morning and attends his market stall in the afternoon. Don Crescencio's tale mirrors those of thousands of immigrants from Yucatán and other places around the world: he left his country as a legal migrant to work on American farms and today, forty years later, he is right back where he began—a self-employed man who complements his income with subsistence agriculture. We learn that people make decisions within the confines of the historical contexts that frame them, but that they can also act upon those limits when compelled by desires and goals. However, no matter how much effort such social actors invest in their personal projects, they are always subject to structural limitations.

The ethnographic fieldwork I undertook in Oxkutzcab was facilitated greatly by the Villafania clan and its relations. The fact that they are a well-known, respected family in the Puuc was a clear advantage for me. While making arrangements for my stay in August 2001, Jorge, the youngest of the Villafania children, generously offered me lodgings at his family's house. He and his brother Wilson were excellent hosts, and at the local Presbyterian Church, El Monte de la Transfiguración, they introduced me to a number of church members—many of whom I hoped to interview.[21] My friendship with this family also proved of great benefit when I went to San Francisco a few months later.

During my stay with this family, I was able to trace the saga of their migration by listening to the grandparents and three adult children who were in Oxkutzcab (Hebert, Wilson, and Jorge) as they recounted their own stories and those of their absent siblings (Abraham, Nalda, Luis Alfredo, and Carlos). I learned that, like the Villafanias, many other families in the town were separated by migration. During a religious service at my hosts' house, I met the parents of many young migrants who were anxious for news of their absent children. Whether they had migrated or not, parents always feel concern and anxiety for their offspring who travel to a foreign country as undocumented workers.

When they had free time from their various jobs, Jorge and Wilson took me to meet old folks and young men who also had tales to tell.[22] Every morning after breakfast, Doña Cornelia showed me photos from San Francisco (or San Pancho, as they call it) so that I could see the absent members and thus be able to identify her nephews, nieces, grandchildren, and great-grandchildren who lived far away up North. Hung on the walls of the sitting room were many family photos, both old and new. For example, there was a photo from Tomás and Cornelia's wedding that showed their great-grandparents in traditional Maya dress, alongside which were recent pictures of families that had been living in San Francisco since the late 1980s, unable to return home. Cornelia proudly showed me photos of four of her sons who once shared a nice modern apartment in San Francisco. Others showed her most successful son, Luis Alfredo, with his American wife and daughters. There were also prints of Cornelia and Tomás on trips to different places in the United States where they visited their children, met new grandchildren, or attended important celebrations such as a granddaughter's *quinceañera* (a girl's celebration of her fifteenth birthday) party. I began to understand a little more about the daily life of a family with a long migratory experience, one that has lived with the constant anxiety and sadness caused by the prolonged and indefinite absences of children, husbands, fathers, or brothers, and the joy that reigns during the moments when they return.

In addition, I had the opportunity to observe a family that enjoys the advantages of migrant remittances: extra income that allows them to resolve health problems and accidents, to afford small luxuries such as birthday parties for nieces and nephews, to buy a new plot of land or a new truck to transport fruit, to pay an extra fieldworker to give Tomás more time to devote to his church work, or to purchase a modern refrigerator or stove. Of course, the family had acquired various TV sets, VCRs, DVDs, and digital music players that are ubiquitous in migrant homes. Most importantly, however, all of the families (with one exception) had attained one of the most palpable material and social rewards of the successful migrant: a large, comfortable modern house. My first visit allowed me to observe the social processes of migration and appreciate their pros and cons from the perspective of the community of origin. Although I did not obtain a "representative sample" of informants, I was certainly able to gather the first of my notes for my migration project in Yucatán.

The Second Site

A few months after my stay in Oxkutzcab I flew to San Francisco to observe the other side of the migration process. Making my first contact there required only a phone call from my hotel room to an apartment shared by eight or ten young men from Oxkutzcab and a neighboring village called Maní. Tino, a young man from the latter village, answered the phone. After a quick explanation of my motives for the trip, he graciously invited me to their place on New Market Street, as it was his day off. I spent most of that sunny day in a Yucatecan hammock in his apartment listening to his story.

> I came to San Francisco three years ago with a group of fifteen [Yucatecans] and found work a month later through some friends I knew. I'm the only man in my family. I have two married sisters and some younger unmarried ones, so I'm also the first one from my family to come to San Francisco. Before coming I worked in construction in Cancún for a while and then in the Las Dunas Hotel. The first time I came was a short stay. The second time I stayed longer. I went back to Ox for four years with my wife Marta and my seven-year-old daughter. My dad gave me part of the family's land. The first time I came, I invested my savings in a small house on that plot in Maní as I go there a lot because my family is from there. The second time, with the money I earned I bought a ten by fifty [meter] urban lot in Oxkutzcab, and four fields of one hectare each. Now what I earn I send to Marta to finish building my second house in Oxkutzcab, where she's from. Sometimes I stay in Maní, sometimes in Oxkutzcab. I send almost all I earn to Marta, though occasionally I send [money] to my mother.[23]

Tino converted to Presbyterianism upon marrying Marta. He is an easygoing, spirited young man of thirty-two, whose mother tongue is Maya though he is bilingual in Spanish and understands basic English. Tino's trips to San Francisco took place in the 1990s but, like most Yucatecan migrants, he had an intermediate experience of migration in Cancún. His trajectory is that of the successful migrant who knows how to invest his dollars. In San Francisco he usually works double shifts in restaurants, though when I met him he had cut back to just one, which netted him approximately US$2,000 per month after taxes.[24] This young man organizes his expenses efficiently and sends home almost all of his earnings. At an agency in the Mission District that afternoon, I witnessed a transaction in which he sent US$700 to his wife. Tino is a transnational who has adapted well to his destination. As we strolled along the street he greeted numerous people, many of whom were also from the "land of the pheasant and deer" (i.e., Yucatán). In his free time, he enjoys taking day trips around the "Golden Gate City" and he knows the public transportation system like the back of his hand. At midday, loyal to the Yucatecan tradition of generosity, he invited me to lunch at a nearby fast-food Arab restaurant. We spent the rest of the afternoon walking down the main street of the Mission District until we reached the Presbyterian Church.

Tino's story is a personal reflection offered by a specific subject who responded in a particular context. Though I cite it at length I make no attempt to create an archetype of the Yucatecan migrant, because each individual's experience is distinct. During the interviews, many informants showed a tendency to emphasize the positive aspects of their migratory experiences and conceal the negative, as undoubtedly did Tino. Though during our long chat his words were well-intentioned, I sensed that my status as a researcher led him—consciously or not—to try to impress me.

While at the church chatting with its pastor, Mauricio Chacón, I received a phone call from Jorge Villafania, who had returned to San Francisco a few weeks before and had quickly learned of my arrival. Having served as my guide in his beloved hometown of Oxkutzcab in August 2001, he was anxious to lead me through the streets of his second city, San Francisco, and to assist me in my research. This unexpected encounter with the youngest son of the Villafania clan was clear evidence of the extensive mobility among yucatecos, of the tight bonds that link Yucatán and California, and of how migrants from Oxkutzcab (like babies in hetzmek) have one foot in each place. I could not have found a better guide to San Francisco. Jorge introduced me to his brothers Abraham and Carlos, to his sister Nalda, to his brother-in-law Daniel Espinosa, and to several nephews, nieces, and other relatives who were living in San Francisco at the time. The only brother I was unable to meet was Luis Alfredo, who had moved to Baltimore with his nuclear family several years before.

To better understand the complex motives and factors involved in international migration and relate them to the social, cultural, and economic consequences that this total process implies, the figures in this essay explain some important details of the extended family that functions as this study's unit of analysis. In the next section, I knit together data from both sites in an attempt to approach the more complete and complex reality of this emerging pattern of international migration among Yucatecans.

A "VERBAL PORTRAIT" OF ONE FAMILY OF YUCATECAN MIGRANTS

The extended Villafania family, including relatives by blood and marriage, consists of some fifty people. The founding couple is Tomás Villafania and Cornelia Bolio (figures 1 and 2), both of whom are from Oxkutzcab. The second generation includes their eight children (six sons, two daughters), all born in their

FIGURE 1. Place of birth

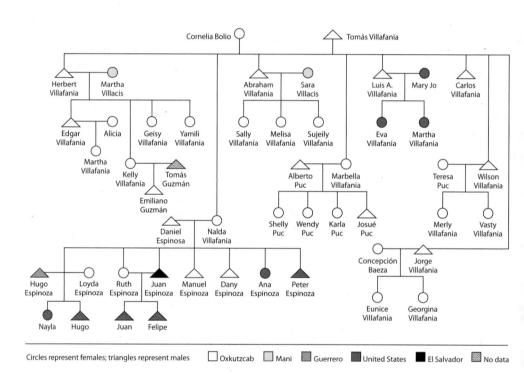

Circles represent females; triangles represent males   □ Oxkutzcab ▣ Mani ▨ Guerrero ■ United States ■ El Salvador ▨ No data

FIGURE 2. Biological generations

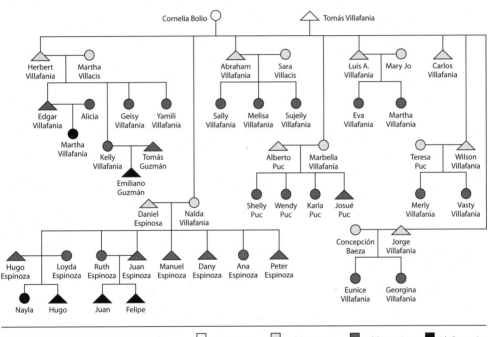

Circles represent females; triangles represent males   ☐ 1st Generation   ☐ 2nd Generation   ■ 3rd Generation   ■ 4th Generation

FIGURE 3. Languages

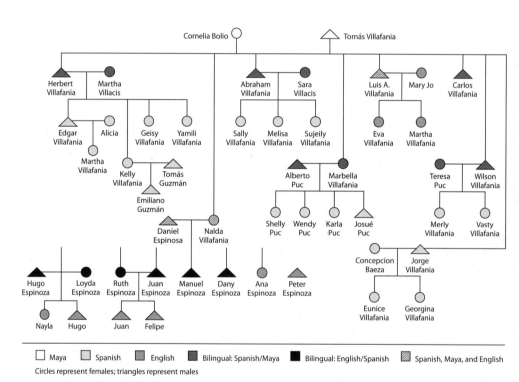

Maya ☐   Spanish ☐   English ☐   Bilingual: Spanish/Maya ☐   Bilingual: English/Spanish ☐   Spanish, Maya, and English ☐

Circles represent females; triangles represent males

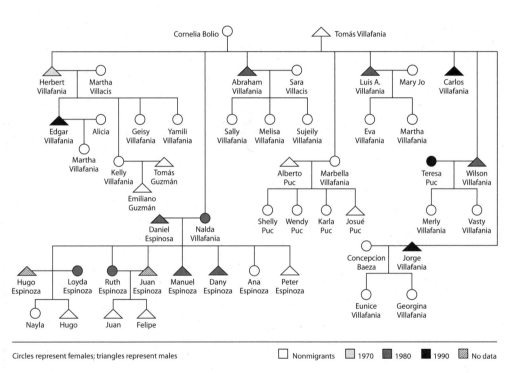

FIGURE 4. International migration

Circles represent females; triangles represent males

Nonmigrants   1970   1980   1990   No data

FIGURE 5. Place of residence and households

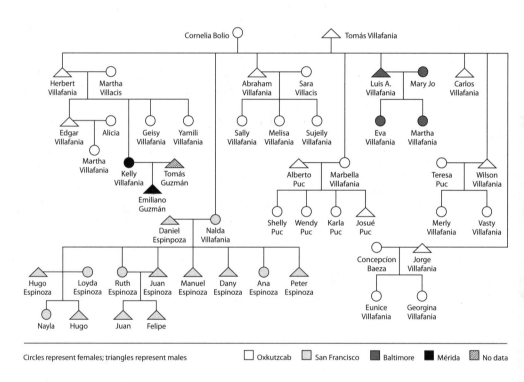

Circles represent females; triangles represent males   Oxkutzcab San Francisco Baltimore Mérida No data

FIGURE 6. Religious affiliation

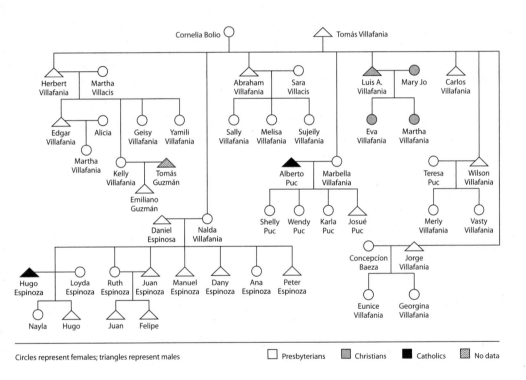

Circles represent females; triangles represent males

☐ Presbyterians ▨ Christians ■ Catholics ▨ No data

parents' hometown, and seven spouses (one son, Carlos, is single). Martha and Sara Villacis, Hebert's and Abraham's wives, respectively, are from Maní. Mary Jo, Luis Alfredo's spouse, is American; while Daniel Espinoza, Alberto and Teresa Puc, and Concepción Baeza were born in the city of Oxkutzcab. The third generation comprises twenty-three grandchildren and the spouses of the four eldest ones. Of the grandchildren, Ana and Peter Espinoza—Nalda's children—were born in San Francisco, while Luis Alfredo's two daughters, Eva and Martha, came into the world in Baltimore, Maryland. The other nineteen grandchildren were born in Yucatán. Hugo, Loyda's husband, is from the state of Guerrero, while Juan, Ruth's spouse, is from El Salvador. At the time of my research, the fourth generation consisted of six great-grandchildren, four of whom were born in the North and two in Oxkutzcab. The mother tongue of the founders, Tomás and Cornelia, is Maya, though they are also fluent in Spanish (figure 3). Members of the second generation are also bilingual but, in contrast to their parents, Spanish is their first language. Except for Marbella and Alberto, English is the migrants' third language, especially in everyday conversation. The third generation is the most complex: four of its members have English as their mother tongue, though they understand some Spanish, and six are totally bilingual and bicultural in Spanish and English. Several remember a little Maya that their grandparents spoke, and they continue to learn it thanks to the influx of new migrants. The other seventeen members of the third generation converse in Spanish and understand some Maya. Four people in the fourth generation have English as their first language and understand a little Spanish, while the other two communicate in Spanish but also understand Maya.

Tomás and Cornelia have never migrated to or worked in the United States, but they have legal papers and have visited their children several times, especially Luis Alfredo in Baltimore who, thanks to his legal status as a citizen gained when he married an American woman, was able to obtain visas for his parents so that they can travel legally. Their last trip was in April 2002, when they stayed in San Francisco for two weeks to attend their eldest daughter Nalda's twenty-fifth wedding anniversary before going to Baltimore. This clan's migratory history began in 1976, with Hebert, the eldest son (figure 4). He was followed by the third boy, Luis Alfredo, who would not be dissuaded from making the trip that would change his destiny at the tender age of sixteen, in 1981. On that occasion he was accompanied by his elder brother, Hebert, who already had experience. Luis Alfredo obtained his residence papers in 1986 and decided to stay in the United States. Two years after Luis Alfredo, it was the turn of the second son, Abraham, who crossed the border in 1983 and made four more trips to San Francisco. He lived in the United States for a total of fourteen years, with a longest stay of almost seven years.

Neither Marbella, the fourth child, nor her husband, Alberto, have migrated, but Wilson, sixth in line, went to San Francisco in 1986 when he was eighteen. He has been there three times. On his second trip, in late 1990, he was followed a month later by his wife, Tere, and their infant daughter. On that occasion both spouses worked in the same restaurant for a year and a half, while his sister, Nalda, looked after their baby. Nalda, the eldest daughter, left home in 1989 with her husband, Daniel, and their four children. They stayed in the United States for ten years before returning to attend their youngest brother's wedding in 1999. Carlos Efraín, the second-youngest of the eight children, first left Oxkutzcab in 1992 and has lived in San Francisco on three occasions, once for seven years and twice for brief stays. He has been back in Oxkutzcab since July 2003. Jorge, the youngest, followed his siblings' footsteps in 1993 when he was twenty. So far, he has made four trips to San Francisco, but he came back home in April 2003. Nalda's four children—the third biological generation—left Yucatán in 1989 when they were very small, so for them, especially Manuel and Daniel, the trip to San Francisco was really just an adventure. Edgar Villafania Villacis, Hebert's son, left Oxkutzcab in 1994 when he was sixteen.

Seven of the children (second generation) are either living or have lived at some time in San Francisco. Today, eighteen members of the extended family live in the United States: four are in Baltimore and the other fourteen are in San Francisco (figure 5).[25] The largest group is Nalda's nuclear family. Her husband, Daniel, is from an old migrant family in Oxkutzcab. He first went to San Francisco alone in the early 1980s, and it was not until 1989 that he took Nalda and their four children (Loyda, Ruth, Daniel, and Manuel) with him. Some years later they had two more children in San Francisco: Ana and Peter. Though the first four were born in Oxkutzcab, they were raised and educated in San Francisco. Now, they are young second-generation adults. Nalda and Daniel's two eldest daughters are married and have lived in San Francisco ever since they went back in 1989. Loyda's husband is from the state of Guerrero (Mexico), while the youngest daughter, Ruth, is from El Salvador. Each of these women had two children in San Francisco, who thus are members of the third migrant generation of Yucatecans there.

As the figures show, this thirty-year migratory tradition has generated a series of important cultural intersections that find expression in the use of three different languages—Maya, Spanish, English—and the combinations of them preferred by different individuals. The processes of transformation, inclusion, combination, and, possibly, the gradual disappearance of Maya in the younger generations are reflected in, and cut across, other variables such as place of birth, migratory generation, and biological generation.

With regard to religious affiliation, all of the consanguineal relatives in this group are Presbyterians who have been active in the congregation in Oxkutzcab or in the church in San Francisco, depending upon their residence (figure 6). The clan's evangelical roots date back at least half a century. Doña Cornelia converted when she was eleven, while Don Tomás did so as a lad of seventeen. Obviously, they were converts when they married and thus raised their children in the values and beliefs of their new faith. Luis Alfredo and his family in Baltimore belong to an evangelical denomination and he has studied to be a minister in the United States, though he attends the local Presbyterian Church (Monte de la Transfiguración) when staying with his family in Oxkutzcab. Marbella's husband, Alberto, is still nominally a Catholic, though she and the children participate in the local temple's religious activities. Loyda's husband, Hugo, from Guerrero, does not share his wife's evangelical faith but also has not interfered in her religious orientation. Kelly is formally a Presbyterian, but she attends church only sporadically as she lives in Mérida.

Migrant Histories

The overall view behind these life stories involves the modern globalized world in which goods, capital, information, images, and ideas flow rapidly and freely from one country to another with few border restrictions, little government control, and almost no obstacles. This brings to mind groups of "mobile people" who enjoy similar unrestricted conditions, like the tiny global elite who travel at ease and always carry the proper visas and passports—people whom Ulf Hannerz (1996) calls cosmopolitans. However, many other individuals, including Third World migrant workers, also move constantly on a global scale, though for very different reasons and under radically distinct circumstances from those enjoyed by cosmopolitans (for example, the notion of "global people" by Zygmunt Bauman [2000]). Unlike the "global people," the vast majority of migrants mobilize to search desperately for jobs and better wages in order to attain a higher living standard. These people pay taxes, usually lack legal immigration documents, risk their lives, and "travel light" with no luggage, as they may have to cross deserts, hide from border patrols, swim across rivers, or sail perilously on turbulent oceans. Often they find themselves in the unpleasant situation of abandoning their loved ones for long periods of time. Unlike twenty-first-century tourists, they do not travel for pleasure and curiosity, looking for new and exotic experiences in the third world. In fact, third world migrant workers may move around the planet even more than that small, privileged traveling minority. In addition to the disadvantages mentioned above, these "economic migrants" may have to pay three times as much for tickets than do tourists or cosmopolitans. To explore these contrasts between global people and migrant workers, I use the stories narrated by members of the extended Villafania family, based on their back-and-forth movement from Yucatán to San Francisco since the late 1970s.

Hebert

The first son, Hebert, began this family's migratory tradition in the 1970s as a young man in his early twenties. His mother, Doña Cornelia, recounted that as a child of five he often talked about going to the North, where he would be able to buy a real pickup truck and live in a comfortable house. He knew of Don Tomás Bermejo, perhaps the pioneer migrant from Oxkutzcab, who had traveled to San Francisco in the mid-1960s, attended the Presbyterian church in the Mission District, and in 1965 opened a restaurant (named Tommy's, on Geary Avenue) that served Yucatecan dishes. It seems that many people, both relatives and nonrelatives, had followed Don Tomás and worked in his restaurant or in other establishments. Hebert told me the following:

> Though my Dad didn't want me to go because he knew it was dangerous, I left for the first time in 1976. I had been married for a year [then]. My last job here in Oxkutzcab was in construction. The person who helped me now works in the [municipal government], he's the mayor's brother-in-law. Everything was arranged by a woman from Maní . . . a labor contractor from a Seventh-Day Adventist Church. She paid to get us across the U.S. border and set us up in different spots. I ended up in the fields in Fresno, California, picking grapes, tomatoes, and olives. They used to pay ten cents per box, and I had to fill 120 boxes a day because in the rainy season there was no work and you had to eat what you'd earned. I also picked oranges, but that wasn't hard for me [because] I'm skilled at it. In those years I sent money to my Dad and to my wife, so I couldn't save much. La Migra used to catch us and treat us like dogs . . . kicking us. I spent two years there [then] I went to Nogales, Tecate, La Paz, Cabo San Lucas, and Tijuana. We used to cross the famous road at the Mexico-U.S. border, running between cars and big trucks. Sometimes, after we'd run for a few kilometers, the border patrol would catch us and send us back. I swam across the river twice. The second time I went [1981], I stayed for five years without coming back. While Luis and I were there, we helped Abraham come [1983], so there were three of us,

not just two. Then we helped Wilson [1986], by paying his coyote [the person who led him across the border]. Luis and I always paid. [Upon returning to Oxkutzcab once and for all in late 1986], I bought my truck ... we're building a house. My younger brother Abraham worked for almost six years [then] got his house, a lot. While they were there [Carlos] went, then Jorge, and the rest. Luis didn't come back, he got married there and is an engineer.

Hebert worked in the fields around Fresno for two years before returning home. He got a job in construction in Cancún and helped his father-in-law clear his fields in Maní. Two-and-a-half years later, in 1981, he was back in the United States for his second trip. On that occasion he took with him his younger (and rather restless) brother, Luis Alfredo, though it was really Abraham's turn, because he is older. During his five years in San Francisco, Hebert saved enough capital to build a house and buy a truck with which he made his living back in Yucatán until he lost his sight because of diabetes in early 1990. At that time, his son, Edgar, took over the business and became the family breadwinner.

Edgar Villafania Villacís crossed the border on March 11, 1994, at the age of seventeen; much younger than his father had been when he first emigrated. His urgency to leave his hometown led him to abandon his studies when he had just begun the first year of high school (*preparatoria*). His father gave him part of the money he needed for the trip and to pay the coyote. Edgar told me that he crossed the border quite easily and arrived in San Francisco three days later to meet his uncles Abraham and Wilson. Shortly afterward he got a job as a dishwasher in a restaurant, but he only stayed there for six months because he considered his wages of $180 very low. Anxious to leave San Francisco and see other places, he was helped by a woman friend to make his way to Portland, Oregon, where he took a job in a cucumber-packing plant. Another friend gave him the false papers he needed to get the job. There, he shared a room with other young men from his home area and communicated frequently with his family in Yucatán. He earned $450 per week at the cucumber plant, but when the season ended he had to look for another job. A few days later he was hired to pick blackberries. Though his wages were similar to what he had earned at the plant he couldn't stretch them as far, so he only stayed in that job for six months. At that time a friend from his hometown (*paisano*) asked him for a loan of $2,000, but he never paid it back. Then, on top of that loss, he was unemployed for a few months and found it impossible to help his parents or save money. Eventually, he found work in the packing department of a record company, working twelve-hour shifts every day for eight dollars an hour. This job allowed him to pay off some debts and occasionally send a few dollars home.

But he was eager to drive so he invested his savings in a car, and thus was unable to help his parents for a time.

In late 1998, after a stay of four years and with a lot of experience under his belt, he decided to return to Oxkutzcab to attend his uncle Jorge Villafania's wedding. During that short visit he met Alicia who became his girlfriend (and later his wife). Despite being tied down by the obligations of courtship (or perhaps because of them) Edgar migrated for a second time in early 1999, though he kept up his relationship with Alicia by phone. Back in the United States, he returned to Oregon and was received again at the record company. Though he was doing well there, he lost the opportunity when two friends he had recommended turned out to be poor employees who shirked their tasks and were soon fired, together with Edgar. His next job was in construction, working for a firm that had contracts in several cities, so he was able to travel to Vancouver, Canada, and to Seattle and Tacoma in Washington State. Many of his fellow workers there were also Yucatecans, so he felt quite at home among them. While that job lasted, he earned $500 a week and was able to send a fixed amount home to his mother. With the remittances he saved during that time in addition to a bank loan, Edgar's father, Hebert, bought a large truck that cost 200,000 pesos. In 2000, Edgar returned home once and for all, as he had decided to get married. It was then that he began to manage his father's business in order to support his own incipient nuclear family, his parents, and his two unmarried sisters who were still in school; Hebert had begun to lose his sight and was forced to leave his son with this responsibility.

Today, this young exmigrant works as a fruit and vegetable merchant. Twice a week (Mondays and Thursdays) he fills his truck with produce in Oxkutzcab and drives to Valladolid, Cancún, and other municipalities in Yucatán to sell it. Since his uncle Abraham returned from San Francisco in July 2003, they have worked the business together: "It's hard work all right . . . you have to get up early, go to the market [and] look for the best prices . . . if you buy cheap, you sell cheap . . . if you buy expensive, you sell expensive. . . . You have to adjust to the other guys' prices."

The stories of migration presented above underline the differences in the historical circumstances in which they took place. Hebert's almost accidental arrival in Fresno's agricultural fields contrasts with Edgar's fairly smooth trip to San Francisco and then on to Portland. The constant flow of peasants from southern Yucatán in the 1970s and 1980s has led to the creation of new routes, itineraries, networks, and labor niches that today stretch across several states, in addition to California. Though the experiences of this father and son share certain elements, they also reveal the changes that have taken place in the towns of origin and destination. For example, Edgar had begun high school, while Hebert only finished primary school. Edgar's higher level of education gave him a certain plasticity or flexibility that allowed him to gain employment in several kinds of companies. Though Hebert, the first of the Villafania clan to migrate, was limited to working in agriculture, he was responsible for beginning to weave the networks that would facilitate the later arrival of his five brothers.

The distance of twenty years between the dates of Hebert and Edgar's first trips altered the nature of each man's migratory experience and reflects the development of a "migration culture" in this family. It is clear, for example, that even at a young age Edgar had access to social capital generated by two networks—one based on relatives, another on friends and neighbors—that gave him a wider margin of choice. When he decided to leave San Francisco, where he had stayed with his paternal uncles and other relatives, to try his luck independently, he knew that he could count on alternative social contacts beyond his relatives' network. While the dense social network (extended family) he enjoyed surely eased his process of adaptation, it may also have become a burden he felt he needed to get away from before it took control of his life. Thus, he went off in search of greener pastures (Portes 1998, 9).

Hebert and Edgar are both devout Presbyterians who belong to the congregation in their hometown, but neither one of them mentioned religion in their stories. In Hebert's case this can be explained by the fact that his narrative refers to a period in which he worked as an agricultural laborer and it was difficult for him to attend services in churches that are usually located in cities. Edgar didn't mention religion either, but that was because he spent most of his time in Oregon, where little is yet known about religious organizations whose services might represent a refuge for migrant workers.

THE PRESBYTERIAN FAITH AS A BRIDGE

To illustrate the relevance of Presbyterianism in the fieldwork site, I offer here a brief synopsis of the origin and development of this Christian denomination in Yucatán. This evangelical denomination first made contact with Yucatecans in the nineteenth century through Protestant missionary initiatives that began in 1877. Reverend Maxwell Philips was the first missionary of the Northern Presbyterian Church to live in Mérida. He initiated public services in 1882, but his work was interrupted when two of his daughters perished in an epidemic. New missionaries were sent that same year, though, and the first Presbyterian Church, El Divino Salvador was also founded. Shortly afterward, it baptized its first 49 believers. Despite a negative reaction by the Catholic clergy, the Presbyterian congregation had grown to 121 by 1893. Around that time, the Presbyterian Alfonso Herrera organized several mutual aid societies and began to preach the Gospel in jails and hospitals. From these beginnings, Presbyterian missions soon spread to the towns of Progreso, Ticul, and Muna, and into the neighboring state of Campeche. In 1914, a meeting of Protestant missionaries was held in Cincinnati, Ohio, in which Mexican territory was divided up among several denominations that were active there. The Yucatán Peninsula was assigned to the Northern Presbyterians, who had already undertaken their missionary work. This stimulated the growth of churches that continued to receive economic aid from affiliates in the United States. The Presbyterians concentrated their proselytizing efforts in Yucatán, and thus evangelism soon became consolidated throughout the state. In the ensuing years other sectors of the population were prepared to receive the Protestant gospel.

Proselytism and acceptance advanced slowly in the early twentieth century because almost the entire population—including that of Mérida, where efforts were focused—was made up of monolingual speakers of Maya. To resolve this issue, a mission called the Agencia Exploradora was created in the 1920s to organize missionary work directed at Maya speakers. However, this was a short-term solution to a language problem that required a long-term solution if the widely dispersed Maya-speaking population was to be reached. Hence, two missionaries, Elva and David Legters, arrived in Yucatán in 1936, settled in Xokenpich (near Chichén Itzá), and began the arduous task of translating the bible into Yucatecan Maya. They remained for thirty years working on this project, with aid from the Wycliffe Bible Translators—a U.S. organization founded by W. Cameron Townsend and L. L. Legters (Dame 1968, 162). Presbyterian missionaries called *obreros* were trained, paid wages, and supplied with literature, which they sold for personal gain. All obreros were from the peninsula, though some were trained at the Presbyterian seminary in Tlalpan, Mexico City.

The Presbyterian faith then began to spread out from Mérida toward the rural areas of Yucatán. Despite the revolutionary crisis of 1910 to 1925, new congregations were founded in Akil, Oxcutzcab, Teabo, Valladolid, Río Lagartos, and other sites. A second Presbyterian Church, Antioquía, was established in Mérida in 1921. A key area of Presbyterian mission work was education, which was encouraged by the founding of the Turner Hall American School and the Instituto Bíblico del Sureste in 1927, which trained leaders and pastors for churches throughout the peninsula. According to Asael Hansen and Juan Bastarrachea (1984, 254) by 1935 the American School had 250 students, of whom 20 percent were Presbyterians (at that time there were 308 Presbyterians, or 0.3 percent of Mérida's 100,000 inhabitants).

In order to determine the number and types of Protestant churches in Yucatán's municipalities,[26] I conducted a survey from 1980 to 1982—the results of which reflected the growth of Protestantism and its increasing diversity in the Yucatán (Fortuny 1982). Out of a total of 307 congregations registered, 38.1 percent belonged to the so-called "mainstream" churches, primarily Presbyterians and Baptists.[27]

In my more recent research in 2002 I found that some sixty believers from Yucatán, most of them Oxkutzcabeños but some from Mérida, attended Sunday service at the Mission Church in San Francisco. I also found out that in 1990 an Oxkutzcabeño named Mizraim discovered that this temple pertained to the same evangelical denomination that he had joined back home. He passed this news on to Jorge Villafania and both were soon attending services there. After a few months of regular attendance, Mizrain decided to elaborate a plan designed to bring the two congregations (one in Yucatán, the other in San Francisco) closer together. Upon hearing that two deacons from the church in California were going to Cancún, he asked them to include a side trip to Oxkutzcab in their itinerary so that they could meet the congregation and its pastor, Miguel Ángel Matei. The deacons arrived in January 2000 with photos of all the Oxkutzcabeños that attended the Mission Church, which they showed to their relatives back home. This emotional encounter led to a series of agreements for future pastoral visits.

Seven months later, in July 2000, the minister from the Mission Church, Mauricio Chacón, visited the congregation in Yucatán for the first time. He worked diligently for three days shoring up the incipient relationship between the two congregations, meeting with authorities from the local church, and preaching several times at the temple. He conducted interviews and dialogues with relatives of the migrants that attended his church in California, and in so doing he became a bridge between the migrant believers and their families. By becoming acquainted personally with the situation and needs of the wives, children, siblings, and parents of the "absent ones," Pastor Mauricio gained a better understanding of the forces and motivations that produced the "exodus" of the "brothers" that attended his church in the United States. This rapprochement between the religious leaders and their respective congregations also made it possible to elaborate more suitable strategies for supporting and orienting believers, not only in their spiritual life but also in moral, emotional, and even material concerns. This, in turn, led to other resolutions: for example, it became clear that the pastor at Monte de la Transfiguración in Oxkutzcab, Miguel Ángel

Matei, had to visit San Francisco. This plan, however, faced one large obstacle: a lack of funds. However, back in California Pastor Mauricio took up the task of obtaining the money needed to pay for the trip by his Yucatecan colleague and his wife. Finally, in May 2001 Pastor Matei and his spouse enjoyed a two-week stay in the Golden Gate City, where they saw firsthand the living conditions of the believers from Oxkutzcab who had chosen to migrate. During their visit, many activities were organized at the Mission Church to encourage dialogues and personal interviews between minister and migrants. The Oxkutzcabeños took maximum advantage of the visit to catch up on recent news about their loved ones. This opportunity to speak personally to the pastor with whom they had shared so many experiences had very positive effects, and the success of this first trip meant that future visits were planned for both ministers.

In addition to planting contentment and certainty among the faithful, creating mechanisms to support or protect church members, and establishing better communications between church leaders and their congregations, these recently forged links allowed both pastors to better regulate their parishioners. One mutual agreement stipulates that Pastor Mauricio will give believers who return to Yucatán a card certifying that they attended church regularly in California. I learned of at least one case of a believer who never went to church while in San Francisco and who, upon his return home, was expelled from the church for eight months. This may be an exception, though, as Pastor Matei understands that the living conditions and demands of work in the United States are radically different from those of Oxkutzcab. On various occasions he has explained to the faithful that while they are in California they are free to attend services at the church they find most convenient in practical terms of distance and time, though he emphasizes that they should make an effort to go to church regularly so as not to lose the habit of doing so.

These churches represent social spaces in which the devout migrants find a certain protection from the calamities and perils of the street. The Yucatecan pastor understands that life up North is difficult to bear due to the emotional instability often caused by the lack of affection and moral support that members' families would provide if circumstances were different. By the same token, work pressures and the social and psychological effects of life in a foreign country where one must adapt to unfamiliar cultural patterns also contribute to creating feelings of insecurity and apprehension. Another weighty factor that is beyond the control of religious authorities is the legal status of undocumented migrants. Some migrants learn to live outside the law without this affecting their daily lives, but others find that this condition brings anxiety and the fear that they might be caught and deported at any time.

Pastor Matei keeps a register of all of the members of the congregation who are away at any particular time, so that if problems arise he can contact them through his colleague in the United States. The wives of the migrants can also go to the church to receive news about their husbands or communicate with them (and vice versa), so the church as a bridge has come to mean a great deal to believers on both sides of the border; perhaps especially to the undocumented migrants who constitute the majority of the believers living in San Francisco. Finally, the church building itself plays an important role as a meeting place for migrants.

The variety of activities held at the church in California offers opportunities for Yucatecans to get together and to progress. In May 2002 I saw that the church offered courses in English, Spanish, and computers. Due to the continuous influx of new migrants into San Francisco, it also sponsors more informal social and cultural exchanges. For example, those who speak Maya may teach that language to the young people who arrived long ago. Pastor Mauricio is considered enormously charismatic, and his Latin origin (El Salvador) and the cultural affinities he shares with Yucatecans have facilitated their relationship and reinforced the faith among believers. Mauricio Chacón is an open-minded, liberal minister who inspires trust in his congregation. Perhaps it was due to the personal qualities of this pastor from El Salvador that, a few months after attending services there, Jorge Villafania organized a young people's group among Yucatecans that meets almost every afternoon to participate in a series of activities, both social and religious. Though this group had only a few members, some of whom were Catholics, the nature of its youth-oriented activities and the common origin of its members allowed it to operate for several months, until Jorge decided to return to Oxkutzcab. This social space was positive for young people, as it encouraged them to stay in school and participate in 'clean' recreational activities, thus protecting them from the trouble of daily life in San Francisco.

The objectives reached through this linkage included an agreement to send all alms paid by Yucatecan migrants to the congregation back home, whose local membership is made up mostly of low-income families. During Easter Week 2001 members in San Francisco sent money to their hometown, which was used to purchase food for a week for 260 believers attending classes at the Escuela Bíblica de Verano. Later, another series of projects was established to support the congregation in Oxkutzcab.

Through the activities they have carried out and others that are planned, these two Presbyterian congregations have achieved results that can be summarized as follows: first is the improved organization of the religious institution through letters, authorizations, and permissions, and the greater possibilities of keeping migrants in contact with their families; second is that the congregation, with its scant material resources (Oxkutzcab), can now organize more events thanks to the alms sent by their brothers in the faith up North.

CONCLUSIONS

The itineraries, routes, and maps that the Villafania travelers have drawn constitute a kind of social microscope that reflects the wider processes of international migration from this municipality in Yucatán, which has sent a significant number of migrant workers north. The extended family examined above has a series of structural conditions that facilitate the evolution of kinship-based social networks. Six young men from this family of eight created the initial conditions that made it possible to set up and then gain access to routes or trajectories, job markets, lodgings, and, in this case, even religious spaces that would then be used by others. At certain moments, each brother obtained and accumulated new information that added to the clan's fund of social capital and thus benefited later migrants. Back in the 1980s, Hebert, Abraham, and Luis Alfredo paved the way for their younger brothers Wilson, Carlos, and Jorge, as well as their nephew Edgar, all of whom migrated in the 1990s. In addition Nalda, by migrating with her entire nuclear family and settling in San Francisco, made an important contribution to the family's social capital. Throughout the 1990s she and her husband Daniel's home served as a temporary or semipermanent dwelling place for her migrant brothers. In the long run, the evolution of kinship-based social networks like the one developed by the Villafanias reduces the costs of migration, both monetary and in terms of risk.

Moreover, Nalda's children who grew up in the United States benefited from the constant influx of uncles, aunts, and other relatives from Yucatán. During Abraham's most recent stay in San Francisco, he devoted much time to activities at the Mission Church, which allowed him to spend time with his nephew, Manuel Espinosa Villafania (Nalda's son). Such exchanges and interrelations among the members of different biological generations propitiate a smoother adaptation to the destination for adult migrants, while also offering younger migrants the opportunity to relearn the customs of their homeland. During their interviews in May 2002, Loyda, Ruth, and Manuel mentioned the advantages of being able to turn to their aunts and uncles when they had problems with their parents, or in other situations. Manuel emphasized the satisfaction he felt upon learning a little Maya thanks to the afternoons he spent at the church with his uncle Abraham. Religious groups such as the one formed by

Jorge Villafania play a role as reference points that influence the formation of new identities among individuals who may have access to no other social networks in their destinations. The face-to-face interaction that such groups entail can replace family relations, while the moral and emotional support that communally organized civil or religious associations supply tends to keep young migrants from joining the gangs or street bands that so often engender violence and drug abuse.

The almost uninterrupted presence of one or more brothers in San Francisco, together with Nalda's family's permanent residence, provide spaces in which migrants can find affection, emotional support, protection, and useful information, in addition to offering a place where cultural customs can be relived or reactivated. All of the younger brothers mentioned in this case study returned to Oxkutzcab in the first half of 2003 to celebrate their parents' wedding anniversary in July. Since then, they have remained quietly in their hometown. Wilson and Jorge have at least two jobs and also participate in tilling the family's fields. Abraham works with his nephew Edgar in marketing fruits and vegetables, while Carlos has a full-time job at an agricultural supply company in the local market. Nalda and Luis Alfredo, with their respective families, are the only children who continue to live up North, as they have legal residence papers and citizenship. The political situation in the United States and the new national security measures instituted after 9/11 have serious repercussions for the dynamics of Mexican migration, as crossing the border illegally becomes more perilous every day. So, like the baby's legs that swing pendulum-style over its mother's hip, the lives of the Villafania clan oscillate between here and there, such that it is impossible to predict their future.

NOTES

I wish to thank Lois Lorentzen for kindly inviting me to collaborate in the transnational Religion and Immigration Project in Yucatan, a study made possible by the generosity of Lois, the University of San Francisco, and the Pew Charitable Trusts. I am indebted to Quetzil Castañeda for his valuable commentaries and suggestions for improving this essay, especially the idea of using hetzmek. Three aspiring Yucatecan anthropologists aided me in the project: Mirian Solís Lizama accompanied me during the final stage of research, when her experience as a student of migration in Yucatán and her gift for ethnographic fieldwork prove invaluable; Pedro Jesús Chalé helped in the search for socio-economic data on the municipality of Oxkutzcab; and Zoila Jiménez generated the genealogical charts on computer. I am deeply indebted to all three.

1. Transnationalism is defined as the reproduction of social and cultural relations in

territories outside the political jurisdiction or nation-state of the groups of national migrants. Transnationalism is forged by the continuous waves of migrants who travel back and forth between their communities of origin and their destinations, such that this ongoing exchange and lending of customs and traditions from one place to another transforms the two social spaces into one, metaphorically speaking.

2. After World War I, U.S. businessmen could not count on migrant labor from Southern and Eastern Europe because of restrictive immigration laws, so they turned to Mexican labor, which continued, according to one report, to "come from just three states: Guanajuato (10 percent), Jalisco (14 percent), and Michoacán (9 percent), which together accounted for roughly a third of all movement during the period" (Durand, Massey, and Zenteno 2001, 109). During the Bracero Program (1942–1964) the three most important sending states were also those in the west, a trend that continued unaltered from 1960 to 1980.

3. Massey, Durand, and Malone 2002 offers an excellent overview of this literature.

4. In this essay the concept of community is used in two different ways: the first is as the name of migrants' place of origin (as it is understood in literature on migration), and the second is the wider sense that refers to the shared cultural framework implicit in being born in a defined territory to which actors—in this case, migrants— feel a sense of cultural, social, and affective belonging.

5. The Spanish name of the agency is Instituto para el Desarrollo de la Cultura Maya. The data were published in a local paper, *Diario de Yucatán*, on February 2004. This government agency has opened a program called Ayuda al Migrante (Helping Migrants), which has been operating diligently since March 2003. Among its results is an attraction-expulsion diagnosis of migrants applied in the State of Yucatán, as well as a "Guide for the Yucatecan Migrant" that includes basic information designed to protect the migrant population.

6. G. Burke writes for the *Boston Globe*. On the cover of the *San Francisco Chronicle Magazine* the article is entitled "Mayan Migration. A Proud Culture Finds a Home in the Bay Area," while inside the title reads "From Oxkutzcab with Love." The article includes seven pages with photos of Yucatecans in different settings in San Francisco. For additional information, see Naomi Adelson, "La nueva migración indígena: Los Mayas de San Francisco," *Masiosare* (weekly supplement to *La Jornada*), November 10, 2002.

7. See the essays in the special issue of the *Journal of Latin American Anthropology* (vol. 9, no. 1, spring 2004), edited by Quetzil E. Castañeda and Ben Fallaw, on the Maya identity of Yucatán. These essays question the social classifications and the historical ethnogenesis of Maya ethnicity.

8. "Too often the public eyes of the international media and academic community assimilate all Maya to a homogenizing category of a uniform identity." That position erases the specificities of Mayan Zapatistas from Chiapas, Mexico, Pan-Mayanists of Guatemala, and Mayans of the Yucatán Peninsula (Castañeda 2004, 37).

9. Women wear the *huipil*, a white cotton dress embroidered in many colors. The em-

broidery, which may be done by machine or by hand, is placed across the chest area and also along the lower fringe, below the knees. Some elderly men who live in small, rural villages still wear short, white pants called *calzón* and sandals known locally as *alpargatas*.

10. During the operation of the Bracero Program five million Mexican laborers traveled to the United States, where they worked primarily in that nation's agricultural sector (Durand 2001).

11. This fact is proven by a document marked "no. 247," dated September 4, 1965, that bears the seal of the municipal presidency of Oxkutzcab and the signature of the municipal president, Mr. Carlos Granados A. In September 1965, a year after the Bracero Migratory Agreement ended, later recruits would have had to travel with H2A visas, which were special permits for agricultural laborers. For those dates, we found in the Archivo General del Estado copies of lists of men who aspired to become braceros; these lists included at least twenty municipalities and five hundred men from the city of Mérida "who were to present themselves in Empalme, Sonora, to be contracted in the United States of North America as migrant workers." The list for Mérida was signed by the Oficial Mayor de Gobierno, Lic. Nicolás López Rivas, and it was dated September 13, 1965.

12. See Ojeda 1998 for an informative, descriptive study of international migration in the municipality of Peto.

13. Mirian Solís Lizama conducted extensive fieldwork in 2002 and 2003 in Cenotillo, Yucatán, for her B.A. thesis. She found an intensive and extensive network of relations and mechanisms that facilitate migration and lower the costs involved. Migration there is a generalized phenomenon that has been practiced for two generations (Solís Lizama, personal communication with the author, March 12, 2004).

14. Saskia Sassen explains why any analysis of the new immigration would be "incomplete without an examination of the changes in labor demand in the United States . . . The continuation at high and ever-increasing levels [of the migration flows] is directly related to the economic restructuring in the United States. This restructuring also helps to explain the concentration of most of the new immigrants in large cities" (1998, 46).

15. The term Maya refers exclusively to the native people of the Yucatán Peninsula and the language they speak. In English, this word is both singular and plural. The term Maya refers to the people of Guatemala, Belize, and other parts of Mexico who speak a language that belongs to the Maya family. Their primary identity, however, is not Maya.

16. Kelly is married to a soldier. During my stay with the family in Oxkutzcab, she was in Mérida with her young son, attending classes at the Universidad Autónoma de Yucatán where she is studying to be a pharmacist.

17. More precisely, to Kilómetro 50, which today marks the limit of the municipality of José María Morelos in the state of Quintana Roo.

18. Villa Rojas explained the significance of the foods used in this rite. The egg (*hé*) means open, "to open or awaken [the child's] understanding"; *chaya* (*chay* or *xay*)

means "two parts," "to bifurcate thought such that [the child] will know how to differentiate between the 'good' and 'bad' of each thing"; *pinole* (*kah*) refers to remember, thus "giving [the child] a good memory"; while pumpkin seeds are thought to "make his intelligence flourish" (1978, 414).

19. Lois Lorentzen had given me the phone number of the Villafania brothers in Oxkutzcab because they attended the Mission Presbyterian Church in San Francisco and were well known to the pastor.

20. The binational migrant program known as Bracero lasted from 1942 to 1964. During that time five million Mexican workers traveled to the United States to work, primarily in the agricultural sector as farm labor (Durand 2001). When I told Don Cresencio's story to the anthropologist Jorge Durand, he said, "You see, everything started with the Braceros" (thereby referring to the massive Mexico-U.S. migration of today) (Durand, personal communication with the author, Guadalajara, Jalisco, November 2002).

21. The Villafanias offered me Luis Alfredo's second-floor apartment, which had two bedrooms, a bathroom, a modest kitchen, and a small living room that opened onto a large terrace, from which I could see Abraham's house. I ate with Conchy, Jorge, Doña Cornelia and Don Tomás. On my last day, Wilson and Tere prepared a special lunch of chicken and baked potatoes for my "send-off," to which they invited Pastor Matei and the other members of the Villafania clan who were in Oxkutzcab at the time.

22. Jorge was working at his father's plot of land (*parcela*) during the early mornings, and Wilson was busy with his new small business working with video and digital photos.

23. Unless otherwise noted, all quotes are from my fieldwork interviews in Oxkutzcab and San Francisco August 2001 and throughout 2002 and 2003.

24. A great majority of the Yucatecans working in San Francisco have found jobs in restaurants, or maybe in maintenance, but it is always in the service sector. Just as in other large cities, San Francisco has "gained jobs managing and servicing the global network of factories" (Sassen 1998, 46).

25. The Villafania lineage can be divided into eight households, based on procreation (children and grandchildren) and the establishment of different places of residence, though expected patterns of physical residence are not necessarily always fulfilled (figure 5). Household "A" includes the "founders" and their unmarried son, Carlos. This family built four houses on a lot located a few blocks from the center of town. The first house belongs to Hebert and the second to Carlos, while Tomás and Cornelia live in the third one with Jorge and his nuclear family living in the fourth. Luis Alfredo constructed a two-bedroom apartment on the second floor of his parents' house, which he uses when he is home on vacation. These dwellings are protected by an iron fence of elegant design that lends a touch of distinction to the complex. Hebert's house, where he lives with his wife and unmarried daughters, is shared with his married son Edgar and his family. Kelly, Hebert's second daughter, lives in Mérida with her son. Hebert and his offspring make up household "B." Abraham

built a modern residence on a lot on the other side of the street, near his parents' home, where he lives with his wife, Sara, and their three daughters and a newborn son, Luis Abraham, who is not included in the genealogy. This group constitutes household "C." The largest household ("D") is formed by the family that migrated to San Francisco in 1989. It includes Nalda, Daniel, and their descendants. In the argot of migration, this household pertains to the "one-and-a-half," or "second," generation, but the grandchildren belong to the "third generation" of migrants of Spanish-Yucatecan origin. Loyda, Ruth, and later on Manuel, left their parents' home when they married to live in separate houses with their respective nuclear families. Ruth's nuclear family was living in her mother-in-law's house. Loyda, her husband, and children lived in a rented apartment in the Mission District, very close to the Presbyterian Mission Church. Manuel and his wife had a child in 2004 and also live apart from Nalda and Daniel. Household "D" is the one that holds the migrant members together in their constant traveling, and therefore it represents—together with the church—the footing and rooting of the migrants. However, it also represents the other side of the process of migration; namely the dispersion of people into many very small households—a situation quite unlike that in their place of origin, where families try to keep as close as possible. Marbella is separated from her husband, Alberto, and lives with her three children in a precarious home perched on a lot next to her brother Wilson. She and her children make up household "F." Household "E" consists of Luis Alfredo, his American wife, Mary Jo, and their two daughters, Eva and Martha, who live in Baltimore, where Luis Alfredo owns a small construction company. Like his brother Abraham, Wilson used his remittances to build a modern residence on a lot that his wife inherited, just a few blocks from his paternal home. He lives there with his wife and two daughters, who make up household "G." Jorge, his wife Conchy, and their two small daughters comprise household "H," in a house they share with his parents.

26. Yucatán has 106 municipalities. The survey was conducted in all but the municipality of Mérida.

27. Pentecostal churches accounted for 34.8 percent, while 23.3 percent were marginal Protestant churches, such as the Seventh-Day Adventists, the Latter-Day Saints, and the Jehovah's Witnesses (Fortuny 1982, 7–8). These data give an idea of the prominence of the Presbyterian and Baptist churches.

The Latino "Springtime" of the Catholic Church

Lay Religious Networks and Transnationalism from Below

SARAH HORTON

It is an evening in June 2002 and members of one of El Salvador's popular lay Catholic organizations, the Catholic Ministry of Kerygma, have gathered in San Salvador for the annual anniversary celebration of the lay brotherhood. Nearly eight thousand members fill the coliseum, partitioned behind banners representing each of the group's twelve zones within El Salvador. These zones, roughly corresponding to the nation's fourteen *departamentos*, or districts, each contain the members of roughly forty lay communities who share their experiences of their "walk with the Lord." This is typical of the decentralized organization of the lay movements sparked by the Catholic Church's New Evangelization, of which Kerygma is one local example. Yet Kerygma clearly blends the local with the global. Underneath one banner stand the representatives from Zone 7 in California's San Francisco Bay Area. These San Franciscan Latinos—Salvadorans, Mexicans, and one Cuban American—have flown to San Salvador specifically to celebrate alongside their Salvadoran "brothers" in the movement.

This essay examines the lay Catholic movements sparked by the New Evangelization as comprised of networks that, like Kerygma, unite Latino Catholics across borders. Scholars have argued that the Catholic Church's bureaucratic structure may make it less suited to respond to the challenges of a global religious market, as it may be less capable of adapting its message to local circumstances and of responding flexibly to rapid change (Berryman 1999; Menjívar 1999, 594; Smith and Prokopy 1999). However, following on the reforms of Vatican II, the New Evangelization has increasingly promoted lay initiative by allowing popular religiosity to enliven and in effect "pluralize" the traditional Catholic Church. Indeed, I argue that it is the very networklike structure of lay movements like Kerygma and the Catholic Charismatic Renewal that enables the Church to adapt to globalization. Such decentralized movements allow the Church to capitalize upon transnational networks of Latino immigrants, thereby revitalizing it through "transnationalism from below" (Smith and Guarnizo 1998).

Yet while such lay movements maintain transnational connections to their counterparts in El Salvador, the institutional Church in the United States has been less fully able to tap their potential. By focusing on two lay Catholic movements—the Catholic Ministry of Kerygma and the Catholic Charismatic Renewal—in one particular Catholic parish in the Archdiocese of San Francisco, I wish to draw attention to the paradox inherent in the "highly dynamic, open" structure (Castells 2000, 501) of such transnational lay networks. I show that lay movements revitalize the official Catholic Church through transnational connections while eluding archdiocesan control, with their decentralized organization both enlivening the Church while posing a challenge to its hierarchical organization.

EXAMINING RELIGIOUS ORGANIZATIONS AS NETWORKS

A number of scholars have suggested that religion should be "deterritorialized" by viewing both religious organizations and congregations as a series of interconnected networks (Berryman 1999; Vásquez and Marquardt 2003). As Manuel Vásquez and Marie Marquardt persuasively argue, "because networks transgress borders and often link multiple spatio-temporal arrangements, a focus on them allows us to embed the personal and local in larger processes" (2003, 228). Thus the focus on religious organizations not as homogeneous entities but rather as bundles of intersecting institutional and lay networks offers new analytical purchase on the study of religion and globalization. By focusing on the congregation not as a unit bounded in space and time but rather as a site in which transnational religious currents cross, this analysis helps illustrate the dynamism inherent even in locally emplaced institutions. Moreover, a focus on the congregation as a node in connected networks that both segment and rearticulate analytically captures the "disjunctures" in the landscape of religion in a global economy (Appadurai 1996).

Analyzing religious organizations as networks builds upon the work of Manuel Castells's *The Rise of the Network Society* (2000). Castells uses the rise of the new information technology as "an entry point" (4) to examine the global restructuring of capitalism. Castells argues that under an "informational" society—one in which industry is based upon the accumulation of information—organizations that have a networklike structure are best equipped to adapt to the new environment of fast-paced technological change. Whereas Castells takes the flexible corporations of the new informational society as the paradigmatic form of such networklike organizations, we may extend his analogy to religious organizations as well. Thus Phillip Berryman (1999) has shown that it is the networklike organization of the Pentecostal movement—its decentralization, horizontal integration, and flexibility—that has allowed it to successfully adapt to myriad local environments and thus spread throughout Latin America.[1]

To highlight the advantages of networklike organizations in the new informational society, Castells contrasts them with the large, leaden bureaucracies that dominated Fordist mass production. Whereas the former are characterized by a relatively flat authority structure and "horizontal integration," the traditional corporate model of the latter is defined by a pronounced hierarchy and "vertical integration" (2000, 168–77). The sharp hierarchical distinction between workers and managers in such traditional corporations impedes their ability to flexibly adapt to everyday changes in local demand (166–67). In contrast, the "flexible production" of networklike organizations facilitates their response to changes in local conditions by fostering a greater degree of "teamwork, decentralized initiative, [and] greater autonomy of decision on the shop-floor" (170).

Castells's description of the type of corporation that once flourished under Fordist production—of vertical bureaucracies characterized by "standardized mass production and oligopolistic markets" (179)—may well describe the organization of the traditional Catholic Church. Yet the reforms of Vatican II decentralized the Church in order to build alliances with the masses—namely by encouraging local initiatives, reducing hierarchical control over the priesthood, and increasing lay participation (Smith and Prokopy 1999, 12–13). The New Evangelization program initiated by Pope John Paul II has only intensified the Church's emphasis on lay participation, while simultaneously attempting to reassert the authority of the diocesan structure (Gill 1999). The official concluding document of the 1992 conference of Latin American bishops, for example, recognizes "prayer groups, apostolic movements, new forms of life and of contemplative spirituality, as well as various expressions of popular religiosity" as among the tools for the church's renewal (cited in Gill, 1999, 30). Thus the Vatican may be seen as attempting an organizational "restructuring" akin to the corporate restructurings of the global informational economy by encouraging "teamwork, decentralized initiative, [and] greater autonomy of decision on the shopfloor" (Castells 2000, 170).

As I describe below, the lay Catholic movements that have flourished at

St. Anne's—such as Kerygma and the Catholic Charismatic Renewal—have indeed adopted a "networklike" form of organization. Similar to Berryman's description of Pentecostalism (1999), such organizations are characterized by horizontal integration, flexibility, and decentralized decisionmaking. Yet before I describe the organization and activities of these two organizations at St. Anne's parish, I will discuss the history behind the Church's embrace of lay movements, specifically the history of its promotion of the Catholic Charismatic Renewal because this particular lay movement has been the centerpiece of the Vatican's New Evangelization.

THE CATHOLIC CHARISMATIC RENEWAL

The Catholic Charismatic Renewal began in 1967 when a group of students and faculty at Duquesne University in Pittsburgh experienced a "spiritual awakening of Baptism in the Holy Spirit" (Csordas 1997, 4). Marked by Pentecostal-like features such as speaking in tongues, "resting" or fainting in the Spirit, and healing through the laying on of hands, the Renewal emphasizes the direct connection of lay members to the Lord through the Holy Spirit. As one leader in the Charismatic Renewal within the archdiocese explained, "It's like having a DSL line to the Lord." While the early movement owed much to the influence of Protestant Pentecostals, the Renewal has since been fully integrated into the mainstream Catholic Church as not only a movement but also a distinctive "style that penetrates a wide spectrum of ritual and pastoral models" (Peterson and Vásquez 2001, 190).

While the early movement began at a grassroots level, officials in the Catholic Church took note of it as early as the 1970s; Pope Paul VI addressed its annual conference in 1975. By the 1980s, the movement had gained status as a distinctive form of Catholicism and had received approval within the international Catholic Church hierarchy. Pope John Paul II was an especially vocal advocate for the movement. During the 1980s and 1990s, the Renewal increasingly became a mainstay of the Vatican's program of internal "restructuring" (Gill 1999, 17), notably by forming the cornerstone of its attempts to reevangelize nominal Catholics and stem the tide of evangelical defection. For example, the 1992 Santo Domingo meeting of Latin American bishops took up the theme of "the New Evangelization," and centered largely on the Renewal.

Like the other forms of lay religious expression that have followed it, the Renewal shares more with Pentecostalism than its emphasis on "a born-again spirituality of a 'personal relationship' to Jesus" (Peterson and Vásquez 2001,

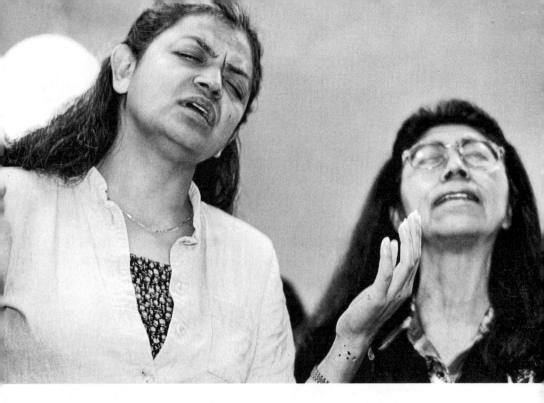

190). Like Pentecostalism, the Renewal relies strongly on lay initiative, moderated by the careful influence of pastoral guidance. Lay leaders may lead prayer groups, run healing masses (though not heal), and form Bible study groups, all of which provide intense interaction in a more personal manner than does the traditional parish structure (Peterson and Vásquez, 2001, 189). While the Vatican intends the Renewal to remain under pastoral direction, its fostering of lay initiative in effect "pluralizes" the offerings of the traditional church. Many Charismatics refer to the Renewal's fostering of lay participation as the "springtime of the Catholic Church," invoking the image of the Renewal's generation of a diverse array of lay Catholic "flowerings."

For example, the Renewal's integration into the Archdiocese of San Francisco largely reflects this more decentralized, networklike organization. The Renewal is officially directed by an advisory board of twenty priests and members of the laity who supervise its activities throughout the archdiocese. The archbishop's liaison to the Charismatic Renewal presides over this board, reporting directly to the archbishop. Members of the Advisory Board meet regularly with the various components of the Renewal in the archdiocese, including the leaders of its Filipino, Anglo, and Latino prayer groups. Thus the structure of the Renewal, compared to that of the official church, is relatively flat, with the Renewal board serving as an intermediary between the official Church and lay leaders. Yet the greatest action of the Renewal—that which defines and constitutes the Church's "springtime"—still occurs at the grassroots, where lay leaders have initiated over one hundred prayer groups since the Renewal officially began.

SUPERCEDING SPACE AND ANNIHILATING TIME: TRANSNATIONAL LAY NETWORKS AND THE "SPRINGTIME OF THE CATHOLIC CHURCH"

As noted above, the Catholic Charismatic Renewal can be seen as a network-like organization characterized by a horizontal "open structure" that allows the flourishing of local prayer groups amid its decentralized control (Castells 2000, 177). As Anna Peterson and Manuel Vásquez have suggested (2001, 189), the Renewal's very decentralization allows for myriad local interpretations of its message, thus enabling it to better adapt to local circumstances than is the case in the mainstream Church. In addition, I suggest that the very network-like organization of the Renewal and other lay Catholic movements sparked by the New Evangelization allows them to tap into grassroots transnational networks. Whereas the Catholic Church's bureaucracy and vertical organization may prevent it from mobilizing transnational grassroots ties, the horizontal organization of lay religious movements allows them to take advantage of contacts that span borders. Thus within the Archdiocese of San Francisco it is such movements' grassroots transnational connections with Latin America that are fueling the mainstream church's renewal. These connections have led to the flowering of Spanish-speaking prayer groups that outnumber the English-speaking prayer groups in the archdiocese, thereby contributing a distinctly Latin American flavor to the Church's "springtime."

To illustrate this, I will describe below the transnational actions of two lay organizations at St. Anne's parish in San Francisco. Both groups adopt a decentralized model in which lay leaders organize and guide parishioners' devotions with minimal pastoral oversight. Organized and directed by Salvadoran lay members, both groups capitalize upon grassroots transnational connections with similar movements in El Salvador. While Kerygma is a "franchise" organization, or offshoot, of a Salvadoran ministry that sprang up independently in San Francisco, the Charismatic Renewal has drawn lay leaders in the movement largely trained in Central America. Yet before I examine the activities of these largely Salvadoran organizations at St. Anne's, I will describe the history of the migration of Salvadorans to the parish.

Salvadoran Migration to San Francisco and St. Anne's Parish

St. Anne's parish, founded in 1893, sits at the outskirts of San Francisco's vibrant Mission District. Until the Second World War the parish was largely comprised of Irish and German immigrants, but currently 70 percent of its parishioners are immigrants from Latin America. The largest group of parishioners hails from Central America, primarily from El Salvador and Nicaragua. Since the 1980s the Mission District has become a bustling "little Central America." Restaurants serve Salvadoran *pupusas* alongside Nicaraguan *quesillos*, and sidewalk grocers tout to passersby their wide array of mangos, *jocotes*, yucca, and plantains. Reflecting the dominance of Salvadorans in the parish, the archdiocese assigned the first Spanish-speaking priest—who himself is from El Salvador—to St. Anne's in 2001.

While San Francisco's population of Salvadorans may be smaller than that of Los Angeles or of Washington, D.C., it has a longer history of Salvadoran migration than any other American city (Menjívar 2000, 9–11). Since the early twentieth century when San Francisco became the chief processing center for coffee from Central America, Central American coffee-producing elites came into contact with San Francisco businesspeople. The construction of the Panama Canal and its route through San Francisco later brought many working-class Central Americans to San Francisco to work for the shipping lines. Yet it was not until the Second World War that Salvadoran migration to the region was institutionalized, as the shipyards and maritime industries in San Francisco began assiduously recruiting Central Americans to fuel wartime production. During this period, Central Americans outnumbered the Mexican-born migrants (Godfrey 1988). By the late 1940s, Central Americans had begun increasingly to move into the Mission District, as the wartime boom allowed the area's Irish and German immigrants to find more luxurious accommodations. By the 1970s, Latinos had become a majority in the Mission District, thus making it the vibrant Latino enclave it is known as today.

While Salvadoran immigrants have had a visible presence in the Mission District since the 1940s, Salvadoran migration peaked during the 1980s with the onslaught of El Salvador's civil war. Between 1980 and 1991, more than a century of civil unrest and sharp social stratification erupted in a fierce conflict between the country's military and rebel forces, in which more than eighty thousand people were killed. This conflict displaced more than a fifth of the country's population from their homes (Peterson, Vásquez, and Williams 2001, 13). As Cecilia Menjívar (2000, 11) shows, 45 percent of the Salvadoran-born population in San Francisco in 1990 had arrived during the peak war years between 1980 and 1990.

The heavy migration from El Salvador during the civil war established the foundation for further migration, and Salvadorans continued to migrate to the United States even after the peace accords were signed, as poverty, high unemployment, and a series of natural disasters have contributed to the status of Salvadorans as one of the fastest-growing Latino immigrant groups in the United States. The parish reflects this long history of Salvadoran migration, as each wave of Salvadorans has brought its own devotional practices. For example, the parish boasts both the traditional Salvador del Mundo, the devotional group that celebrates the nation's annual saint's day festival, as well as the Ministerio Católico de Kerigma, a more recent, Charismatic-like group born of the New Evangelization.

Kerygma: A "Franchise" Springing from the Grassroots

In the parish hall behind St. Anne's church, La Fiesta del Señor—or the general assembly of Zone 7 of the Catholic Ministry of Kerygma—is underway. The coordinator of the group is playing pulsing notes on his synthesizer, while the preacher amps his electric guitar and two women meld their voices into a chorus. The preacher opens the assembly by reminding the crowd of the ministry's upbeat message: "This is a very happy moment for us; we are here to forget all our worries because we are in the presence of the Holy Spirit. We have come here full of troubles and worries, but the Lord will make them disappear."[2] Members dance and clap their hands as they begin singing, "Tú eres mi escudo, tú mi fortaleza; tú eres la gloria que levanta mi cabeza!" (You are my shield, you are my strength; you are the glory that raises up my head.) This is but the first rock-inspired Charismatic song of the assembly that has drawn members from the zone's five communities in the Bay Area—including newly evangelized immigrants from El Salvador, Mexico, Puerto Rico and Cuba.

Kerygma, the Greek term for the "proclamation of the good news," is a ministry founded in San Salvador in 1992. The ministry is not part of the official Charismatic Renewal but rather is one of three vibrant lay movements in El Salvador that respond to the New Evangelization by combining Charismatic features with fervent rock-inspired worship. Kerygma is one of the most popular of such lay movements in El Salvador; it is recognized by the Catholic Church and has more than six thousand members. Kerygma depends upon the organization of members in each of its twelve zones into lay communities of ten to fifteen people. Much like the "covenant communities" common in the early stages of the Charismatic Renewal, these small groups share their religious experiences and apply biblical readings to their lives (Peterson and Vásquez 2001, 189). Thus Kerygma, like the Charismatic Renewal, is a decentralized movement that fosters lay involvement in order to "re-evangelize" the nominally Catholic and recruit new members.

Kerygma's founding in the San Francisco Bay Area in 2001 illustrates the prominent role that transnational networks of immigrants from Latin America have played in sparking an "outpouring of Spirit" (Boucher and Boucher 1994, 4) in the archdiocese. The New Evangelization's decentralization of control and fostering lay initiative has allowed immigrants to found such movements in the archdiocese. Meanwhile, the lay movements' network-like structure mimics that of transnational immigrant networks, thus allowing them to benefit from New Evangelization activities in Latin America while continuing to evangelize in the United States.

The San Francisco chapter of Kerygma may be viewed as a "franchise" (Berryman 1999, 27) of the Salvadoran ministry—an offshoot that attempts to offer the same "product" as its mother group. As one of the founders, who had had ten years of experience with the ministry in El Salvador, stated: "We wanted to re-create Kerygma exactly the way it is in El Salvador." Yet it is striking that while "franchise" religious groups typically begin with a directive and support from central headquarters, Kerygma was in fact initiated by lay members rather than by organizational leaders. Rather than stemming from a pastoral initiative, or even an initiative of the ministry in El Salvador, the San Francisco chapter of Kerygma began with the decisions of two local Salvadoran immigrants. After founding the first community, these two layleaders then contacted the parent ministry's leader, Walter Cáceres, for support.

While Salvadoran immigrant networks brought Kerygma to the San Francisco Bay Area, networks of recently arrived immigrants in the United States allow the group to evangelize. Like other movements stemming from the New Evangelization, Kerygma takes its inspiration from "covenant communities." As Peterson and Vásquez describe, such "covenant communities . . . provide intense interactions in small groups, in contrast to the relatively impersonal character of the traditional Roman Catholic parish structure" (2001, 189–90). The pastor at St. Anne's pointed out the suitability of this organizational form for recent immigrants: "They come to each other and they visit each other. That creates a kind of link among them that we cannot do in the Big Church . . . Maybe they are in need of that, in need of somebody greeting them and caring. In the Big Church everybody just wants to come and fulfill their sacrament, it is more anonymous." Partly due to the success of this model, Kerygma's Zone 7 has grown to contain five communities: three in San Francisco and one each in Concord and San Rafael.

This lay community model clearly is networklike in structure, thereby fostering what Castells might call "teamwork," "decentralized initiative" (2000, 170), and "horizontal integration" (176). Importantly, for the group's evangelization and growth it also helps forge support groups of recently arrived immigrants. These small communities become "safe havens" for largely immigrant group members to share life problems, thus attracting a substantial number of new converts to the Catholic flock. One such convert is Mariana, an immigrant from Puerto Rico who grew up a "Sunday Catholic." Having left her family in Puerto Rico twenty years ago, Mariana said she found herself at midlife feeling "lost" and without support. She felt she had fallen in a "deep rut"; she was drinking and smoking "like a chimney" and life seemed worthless. Mariana recalled that she turned to a coworker, a fellow immigrant, for help. The coworker, a member of the San Francisco Kerygma community, brought Mariana to a retreat and served as her "steward." "I remember that during the retreat she was watching me all the time, making sure that I wouldn't go outside and smoke," Mariana said. She recalled that this demonstration of concern deeply impressed her, and it gave her the sense of community she felt she lacked. Thus Kerygma's immigrant networks allow it to evangelize, while its lay community model responds well to the alienation that some immigrants find in their lives in the United States.

While the San Francisco chapter of Kerygma assiduously evangelizes among networks of U.S. Latinos, it has also maintained strong ties to its mother ministry in El Salvador. Every four months the group holds retreats to recruit new members, which are attended by the ministry's leader in San Salvador, Walter Cáceres. The leader of the San Francisco chapter also remains in close communication with Cáceres; the two speak weekly about the ministry's activities and plans for growth in the United States. In 2002, to cement these ties, the ministry's leader officially recognized the San Francisco chapter as Zone 7 of the ministry's twelve zones. Thus Zone 7 continues to form part of an "imagined" Kerygma community within El Salvador (Anderson 1991), as lay leaders within the zone also travel to El Salvador to take part in the annual anniversary celebration of the ministry's founding.[3]

The ease of contact between the leaders of Kerygma in San Francisco and its leaders in San Salvador recalls Castells's observation about the facility of global communication in networklike organizations. Castells argues that a network is a dynamic, "open structure" (2000, 502) that may consist of an infinite number of components or "nodes." Within a given network, the distance (or "intensity and frequency of interaction") between each node is equivalent, thus rendering the social structure horizontal and flat. Linked through virtual connections and telecommunications, the social distance between cross-border nodes in lay networks is no greater than that between nodes in the archdicoese itself. Ironically, it is the Renewal's lay networks that allow the mainstream Church to "supercede space and annihilate time" (502) — the desired characteristics of any organization wishing to succeed in the new global economy.

Thus the founding of Kerygma in San Francisco illustrates the fostering by laity of "transnationalism from below" (Smith and Guarnizo 1998) — the transnational ties forged and maintained via networks of ordinary Salvadorans rather than via corporations or elites. Rather than being a transplant founded by the ministry from El Salvador, Kerygma's Zone 7 is a "franchise" organization that sprouted from the grassroots up. Because of the New Evangelization's decentralization of control, then, Salvadoran immigrants are able to import new lay movements, thereby maintaining their ties with these movements' parent organizations. As I note below for the case of the Charismatic Renewal, the vitality of such immigrant networks has been a major source of organizational flexibility for the Catholic Church. Such transnational networks have revitalized lay Catholic movements in the United States, perhaps contributing to the desired goal of the late Pope John Paul II for the "resacralization" of the United States (see Vásquez and Marquardt 2003, 187–88).

The Charismatic Renewal at St. Anne's: "Hacer Vivir" a la Iglesia Católica

On a Friday evening in the Chapel of the Immaculate Conception in St. Anne's Church a group of Latino immigrants are praying during the weekly Charismatic healing mass. In a gesture of continuity with the traditional Marian emphasis in Latin American Catholicism, the mass begins with a fervent rosary. Then, unlike most mainstream Catholic masses, however, the traditional Charismatic devotional songs begin. With the low-tech accompaniment of guitar, maracas, and tambourines, congregants begin singing, "Alza las manos y alaba al Señor" (Raise your hands and praise the Lord), and, at the invitation of the leader, they reach out their hands as if to "touch the Holy Spirit." The leader of the group then breaks into a brief sermon to remind each member of their vital role in the Renewal: "As the Apostle Paul said in the Bible, God has given each of us a different spiritual gift. The day of the Pentecost, they showed their gifts well. And we too have our own gifts — whether it's to sing well or to have faith — and each gift exists to edify the Church. For Christ didn't die on the

cross—he continued to *live*—and we too have to make the Church come alive (hacer vivir a la iglesia)."

This statement—that the Charismatic Renewal's mission is to make the mainstream Church "come alive"—well illustrates the role of the Spanish-speaking Renewal within the Archdiocese of San Francisco. While there are over one hundred Charismatic prayer groups officially connected to the archdiocese, officials acknowledge that the Spanish-speaking prayer groups are significantly larger than the English-speaking prayer groups. Over the past decade, with continuing immigration from Latin America, the Renewal's Spanish-speaking prayer groups have overtaken the size of both its English-speaking Anglo and Filipino prayer groups combined. As a token of recognition of this growth, the archbishop in 2004 specifically appointed a second liaison to the Charismatic Renewal to work with the Spanish-speaking prayer groups. The liaison for the Spanish-speaking Renewal himself recognized the prominent role of transnational Latin American connections in creating the vitality of the Renewal in the archdiocese: "A lot of the movement's strength here comes from Latin America. It is through immigration that the Renewal is making our Church come alive, bringing the strength of their devotion to our prayer groups here."

This strength—and the fact that it has derived from the Renewal's ability to tap the vitality of transnational networks that link Charismatics in San Francisco to those in Latin America—is reflected in the prayer group at St. Anne's.

Indeed, the couple who founded the Charismatic group at St. Anne's twenty years ago came from El Salvador, where the Charismatic movement was just beginning (Peterson and Vásquez 2001). The pair was trained as lay leaders in El Salvador, completing the six, six-month required courses. Moreover, many of the group's members themselves became Charismatics in their countries of origin, thus illustrating the strength of the movement there. Cecilia, a Salvadoran woman in her sixties, recalls that she at first rejected the Charismatic congregation in her hometown of Santa Tecla because their songs "sounded like Protestant songs." Yet a friend eventually persuaded her that Charismatics were Catholics and then convinced her to attend a Bible study group. "And I liked the involvement—the way they had vigils, retreats, and healing masses. I joined because they say that through the Charismatics you can deepen your relationship to God," Cecilia said. Thus the Spanish-speaking Renewal in the archdiocese has clearly benefited from the strength of the Renewal in Latin America, and in El Salvador specifically.

Yet the Renewal in San Francisco has also benefited from transnational networks of lay members that span borders, as those in the movement have invited preachers and groups with whom they were familiar "back home." The annual Spanish-speaking Charismatic conference, for years in the hands of lay members, brought respected preachers from various Latin American countries, attracting upward of five thousand people. The prayer group at St. Anne's hosted a local priest from El Salvador for a special healing mass. Finally, the pastor at St. Anne's, himself a Charismatic, invited from El Salvador a Charismatic-inspired music ministry with whom he had personally been involved, "Jesús es Señor." This invitation did not come through the archdiocese's Office of the Charismatic Renewal, but rather was born of this pastor's personal connections. Thus, like Kerygma, the Renewal helps tap grassroots transnational networks to help revitalize the institutional church in San Francisco.

While Kerygma's success derives largely from its horizontal integration, the success of the Charismatic movement in the archdiocese may be due in part to its fostering of decentralized initiative and lay autonomy. Interviews with members of the St. Anne's prayer group suggest the appeal of the Renewal's emphasis on their contribution to the church through their possession of spiritual "gifts," or *charisms*, gained through the Holy Spirit. As the leader of the prayer group told his congregants, "It's no more than what St. Paul said in the Bible— he said that we all have spiritual gifts. Whether your gift is to speak in tongues or to sing well, they all exist to edify (*edificar*) the Church." This statement that each person's possession of distinct spiritual gifts helps "edify" the church is yet another example of the teamwork inherent in "flexible production," thus converting the individuals in the prayer group into specialized members of a spiritual team.

Cecilia's daughter, for example, said she was only a "Sunday Catholic"—that is, she went to church but for mass only. "We call them a *ratera*—it's somebody who steals. And I say I was a ratera—because I went for just a rato, or a short time," she said. Yet when her mother persuaded her to attend the Charismatic prayer group, she slowly became more interested in deepening her faith. While attending healing masses and prayer groups, she felt that she was graced with spiritual gifts granted by the Holy Spirit—the gifts of discernment, prophecy, tongues—even the ability to sing. "I had never been able to sing before. And all of a sudden, I tried, and I could strike even the hardest notes . . . So God did that. He knew I was having troubles (in my faith), so He was giving me all these gifts," she said. Thus the Renewal not only fosters the autonomy of lay leaders—their "greater autonomy on the [church] floor" (Castells 2000, 170)—but that of ordinary lay members as well. For Cecilia, her possession of spiritual gifts derived through the prayer group convinced her that her involvement in Church was important; that she had particular gifts only she could use to help contribute to the Church's renewal.

THE LIMITS OF NETWORKS: BARRIERS TO CONSISTENCY AND COMMUNICATION

While both Kerygma and the Charismatic Renewal revitalize the traditional Church through their ability to tap into transnational networks of lay members, their fostering of lay involvement exists in dynamic tension with the Church's attempt to assert control. Both movements are only loosely integrated into the traditional archdiocesan structure. As one Charismatic priest in the archdiocese described it, "In my experience, the English Charismatic groups are more attached to the churches than the Spanish ones. Because the English-speaking Charismatics perhaps can play a more visible role in the church hierarchy, perhaps they feel closer to the church as an institution. The Spanish movement is even more a lay movement." While Latino Charismatics are loyal to Catholicism and interpret their Charismatic involvement as a continuation—rather than radical break—with their Catholic faith (Peterson and Vásquez 2001, 193–94), their lack of integration into the church structure may diminish their loyalty to the American church hierarchy. Thus while such movements illustrate the dynamism of a networklike organization, they also demonstrate the fragility of the alliances between decentralized networks and the Church.

While others have noted the parallel between new forms of religious organization and Castells's description of "network enterprises" (Berryman 1999, 31), few have paid attention to the tension inherent in this organizational form. Here again Castells provides an entry point for analysis. For Castells, networks are composed of segments that are "both autonomous and dependent *vis-à-vis* the network, and may be a part of other networks" (187). Because of the autonomy and dependence of the various components of the network, the viability of the unit as a whole depends on the components sharing common goals as well as their effective communication. In short, decentralization alone is not sufficient for success in the informational economy, as organizations of networks must demonstrate what Castells calls "consistency" (of goals) and "connectedness" (or the ability to communicate) in order to successfully bridge their component parts (187).

This helps illuminate the contradictions inherent in the networklike form of lay movements such as the Charismatic Renewal. As we have seen, such movements follow a network logic that emphasizes decentralized control, flat hierarchy, "teamwork," and greater autonomy among its members. Yet this decentralization not only allows lay movements the flexibility to adapt a universal Catholic message to respond to local conditions but also creates the possibility of its autonomous parts' segmenting and recombining with other religious networks. As Castells argues, the very dynamism of networks stems from their ability to "innovate and adapt relentlessly" (177), to form "strategic alliances," and to segment and recombine as market conditions demand. Thus the decentralization of religious networks is both a source of revitalization and a threat to the institutional church, as the latter must continually strive to ensure "consistency" and "connectedness" among its component parts.

The advisory board to the Renewal, for example, has long had difficulty ensuring both connectedness and consistency among the Latino prayer groups of the archdiocese. The board, in fact, was first created after two major "defections" by large Charismatic prayer groups: the first was the archdiocese's first Charismatic community, which left the archdiocese in 1977 to join a Charismatic community in South Bend, Indiana; and the second was a large Latino prayer group that left its parish in 1982 to merge with the Pentecostal group the Assemblies of God. Moreover, when the Renewal's advisory board was created, only half of the Spanish-speaking prayer groups agreed to a more formal relationship with the institutional church while the other half remained outside the church or joined with Pentecostal churches. In explaining the history that his position was created to correct, the current liaison to the Charismatic

Renewal emphasized the need for supervision of the Renewal's lay activities: "There is some concern that the Renewal could serve as a trampoline to the other churches."

The Charismatic priest at St. Anne's, in fact, said that he felt a calling to become a priest in order to provide "guidance" to the Charismatic movement. This priest had given the Charismatic group a set of guidelines stating that "they are called to be faithful to the hierarchy in the Catholic Church." He then added that "the problem is that the leaders of the Charismatic movement believe that they are a side church, a parallel church . . . They believe that they don't need guidance from the clergy and feel that they're enlightened by God— which is wrong according to our Catholic traditions and church teachings. And then their members will not participate in parish activities without their explicit approval." Indeed, the Renewal's networklike structure has facilitated communication and organization among Spanish-speaking networks outside the parish structure of the archdiocese. While prayer groups are supposed to be supervised by the priest of the parish in which they reside, these prayer groups often meet in private homes without direct priest supervision.

Like the Renewal, the San Francisco chapter of Kerygma is also only loosely tied to the archdiocese. The group had originally begun at a different Catholic parish in the city, but the pastor there had asked them to move because he did not like the group's worship style. The leader then moved the group to St. Anne's, where the Charismatic priest there gave it safe haven. While the leader of the group does attend parish meetings at St. Anne's, the group receives neither formal recognition nor supervision from archdiocesan officials. This may be due to both language barriers and its small size. In El Salvador, in contrast, the ministry forms part of the Colegio Arquidiocesano de Laíco, or Lay People Movements; the leaders of the ministry communicate regularly with an assigned priest and meet monthly with the archbishop.

While networks are always dynamic and flexible structures, one particular source of instability in the connection between such lay Catholic movements and the archdiocese is the lack of a Spanish-speaking infrastructure to integrate them. Castells writes that networks are "open structures, able to expand without limits, integrating new nodes as long as they are able to communicate within the network" (2000, 502). Thus, the Spanish-speaking Renewal's organization as a "parallel church" is not due only to its decentralization and emphasis on local initiative but also to the archdiocese's lack of infrastructure to integrate Spanish-speakers within its hierarchy (see Sullivan 2000).

The Renewal's drawing of strength from Latin America, for example, is due in part to the lack of Spanish-language catechesis and training for lay leaders in the archdiocese. The six, six-month seminars that the Salvadoran leaders of the St. Anne's group took in El Salvador are not offered in Spanish in the United States. Thus the archdiocese lacks the infrastructure to direct and guide the "flowering of faith" exhibited by the Spanish-language Renewal. In short, language barriers make the social distance between the Spanish-speaking Renewal and the archdiocese greater than that between nodes within the Renewal's transnational networks from Latin America, thus increasing the tension between the Renewal's decentralization and archdiocesan control.

CONCLUSION

What has this study taught us about the relationship between transnational Salvadoran networks, the Church hierarchy, and the flowering of lay religious expression in Catholic parishes across the United States? First, we have seen how the networklike structure of these two lay Catholic movements allows them to tap into the vitality of such movements in Latin America. The New Evangelization's decentralization of control and fostering of lay initiative has allowed lay leaders to form new organizations—such as Kerygma and the Charismatic prayer group—at St. Anne's. Within lay networks, modern travel and communication systems have made the social distance between nodes across borders equivalent to that between nodes within lay networks in San Francisco itself. Thus lay leaders in these two organizations facilitate the flow of pastors and groups from Latin America, and in so doing contribute to a form of "transnationalism from below" (Smith and Guarnizo 1998). These cross-border religious ties are not institutionalized but rather are fostered by vibrant "grassroots transnational networks composed of laypersons" (Sandoval 2002).

Anthony Gill (1999, 35) argues that one source of institutional flexibility for the Catholic Church in Latin America has been its pluralization of faith—its offering a "diverse array of 'Catholicisms' under one institutional umbrella." The New Evangelization's decentralization of control perhaps unintentionally contributed to the multiple distinct "flowerings" of lay Catholic expression in a transnational context. In emphasizing "autonomy" and "local initiative" (Castells 2000, 170), lay Catholic movements allow lay members to creatively adapt Catholic teachings to local circumstances. Thus in a context of recently arrived immigrants, the "lay community" model utilized by Kerygma becomes a valuable support group for immigrants adjusting to an alienating new life. Meanwhile, immigrant parishioners seeking greater church involvement interpret the Charismatic emphasis on the various charisms, or gifts gained through the Holy Spirit, as evidence of their important role in the church's revitalization. This local reinterpretation thus hybridizes a universal Catholic message while refashioning it to meet local needs, and as such it contributes to the strength of the movement at the lay level (see Peterson and Vásquez 2001, 188–209).

While the networklike organization of such groups enables religious importation, the homology—and overlap—in structure between lay movements and immigrant networks themselves facilitate such movements' evangelization and growth. Both Kerygma and the Renewal have spread in the United States by utilizing immigrant networks. Because such networks are often excluded from the official Catholic hierarchy, however, their communication occurs largely outside official parish and archdiocesan channels. Communication barriers have impeded the snug integration of the Spanish-speaking lay movements into the institutional church, making the social distance between nodes within the archdiocese at times greater than that across borders. The lack of Spanish-speaking infrastructure impedes the Renewal's full integration into the archdiocese, in turn contributing to the Renewal's appearance as a "parallel church." The peripheral status of both of these lay movements in the archdiocese's parish structure further illustrates the need to examine immigrant devotion not merely within the confines of the parish but rather in the vital—and often informal—lay networks that nourish the institutional church.

NOTES

1. While the analogy between religious "restructuring" and the restructuring of the global economy may be analytically helpful, scholars have rightfully cautioned us that reducing religious pluralism to the existence of increasingly competitive "religious markets" can only take us so far (Berryman 1999, 25; Vásquez and Marquardt 2003). As Vásquez and Marquardt argue, "Rather than a single predictable market characterized by scarcity, there are multiple overlapping religious 'markets' defined by the abundance and cross-fertilization of options" (2003, 23). Moreover, while their distinctive organizational form may help particular new religious forms flourish, attention must also be paid to the content of such religions' message.

2. Unless otherwise indicated, all quotes by church leaders and members are taken from my fieldwork research and interviews conducted in San Salvador and San Francisco in 2003.

3. Thus the Catholic Ministry of Kerygma attempts to harness the power of its transnational chapter in San Francisco to solidify the power of the nation, redefining its expatriate community as part of a Catholic Salvadoran nation through their designation as "Zone 7." This may be seen as a form of what has been called "deterritori-

alized" nation-state formation, a practice common in countries like El Salvador that are dependent upon their transmigrants' remittances (Basch, Schiller, and Szanton-Blanc, 1995; see also Mahler 1998). Yet at the same time, the designation of the San Francisco chapter as "Zone 7" decenters the Salvadoranness of the nation, as Puerto Rican, Mexican, and Cuban Kerygma members represent Zone 7 at the ministry's annual anniversary assembly.

PART 4

Civic and Political

Engagement

We Do Not Bowl Alone

Cultural and Social Capital from Filipino Faiths

JOAQUIN JAY GONZALEZ III, ANDREA MAISON,
AND DENNIS MARZAN

Memorial Day is a cherished American holiday, one that is made even more significant by the tragic events of 9/11 and the war on terrorism. It is a special day for remembering war heroes and veterans, but it is perhaps even more popular as a day for travel and recreation with family and friends. On one recent Memorial Day, we visited Classic Bowl in Daly City, one of the largest bowling centers in the San Francisco Bay Area. On this day, all sixty lanes were occupied by just one group—the bowlers and audience were ministers and brethren from Global Church of Christ (GCC),[1] one of the largest Filipino independent Christian churches. Many members of the church's Daly City locale bowl together every week, and sometimes even twice a week. Brethren from throughout the northern California district have been gathering to bowl at annual tournaments like this one since the 1970s. The event is a mix of serious athletic competition and lighthearted partying. Members of the bowling teams wear matching shirts embroidered with the names of their church locales. Behind them, the room teemed with crowds of nonbowlers—spouses, children, and friends—who used the tournament as an opportunity to visit with GCC members from other locales. Gathered around tables or sitting on the floor, they shared homemade feasts and traded the latest *balita* (news), *kwento* (stories), and *chismis* (gossip). Evidently, bowling is one of the ways that the widespread membership of the GCC in northern California forms social and cultural bonds in American society.

At this Memorial Day tournament, the enormous bowling center was packed with thousands of GCC members as far as the eye could see. The sea of Filipino faces and strains of various Filipino languages that filled the huge room spoke about Daly City's status as the largest Filipino "barrio" in the San Francisco Bay Area. As the largest city in San Mateo County in terms of population, Daly City has the largest Filipino population outside of the Philippines. More than 40 percent of its 103,000 residents are of Filipino descent. For Filipino immigrants this place also evokes one of the popular bowling centers in downtown Manila, where it is normal to see so many Filipinos engaged in this popular pastime.

This gathering is more than an impressive display of Filipino culture, however, because it illustrates a compelling exception to the claims made by the Harvard political science professor Robert Putnam in his acclaimed book *Bowling Alone: America's Declining Social Capital* (2000). Putnam's central thesis is that civic engagement and social connectedness have declined in the United States over the past several decades—a theme he expands globally in *Democracies in Flux: The Evolution of Social Capital in Contemporary Society* (2004). In this text, he and a number of colleagues argue that this dire situation is also endemic in a number of Western countries. Consequently, the sustained success of democratic societies has been compromised. However, segments of the American population—in this case, Filipino migrants to the United States—are increasing their participation in organized group activities, particularly through their churches. Indeed, their heavy involvement in these social and cultural functions facilitates their own success within American civil society as well as their positive contributions to business and politics.

In this essay we examine how Filipinos are bringing back social capital to the fabric of American society through the churches they have taken over from declining congregations or have established on their own. We also show how they blend Filipino cultural practices and religious festivals to create new and stronger social and cultural capital. Finally, we analyze the unique nature of the transnational sociocultural capital continuously being spread by the Filipino diaspora.

ON SOCIAL AND CULTURAL CAPITAL IN AMERICA

Although Putnam is not the first to "capitalize" on human networks, connections, norms, and religion, his neo-Tocquevillian discussions of social capital and its significant decline in America have certainly become a centerpiece of recent discussions (Putnam 1993, 1995, 1996, 2000, 2004). Putnam's work has generated literature across scholarly disciplines and global geographies (e.g., Halpern 1998; Kolenkiewicz 1996; Norton, Latham, and Sturgess 1997; Schuller 1997; Whiteley 1999). Special issues of leading publications, including the *Journal of International Development, American Behavioral Scientist,* and *The American Prospect* have scrutinized Putnam's argument, operational definition, and empirical evidence. Two edited volumes—one originating from top academics in the United States (Edwards, Foley, and Diani 2001) and one from the

United Kingdom (Baron, Field, and Schuller 2000) — illustrate the range of the discussions. Just as loyal followers of Putnam's thesis have multiplied, so have skeptics (e.g., Edwards and Foley 1997, 1998; Foley and Edwards 1999; Portes 1995, 1998; Portes and Landolt 1996; Putzell 1997), and some criticize his heavy reliance on "quantifying associational memberships." Undeterred, in *Democracies in Flux* Putnam (2004) and a group of leading scholars have examined the state of social capital in eight advanced democracies around the world and came up with more evidence supporting his thesis.

Putnam says that an intensification of social networks, which comes through the growth of churches, increases the norms of reciprocity and trustworthiness that glue a society together. "Civic virtue," Putnam adds, "is most powerful when embedded in a dense network of reciprocal social relations. A society of many virtuous but isolated individuals is not necessarily rich in social capital" (2000, 19). Churches and other religious organizations have played a unique role as incubators of civic virtue in the United States (65–79). However, social capital also comes in two forms, both of which are necessary for a healthy society. On the one hand, there is "*bonding* social capital" which is the inward-focused connections of a social group. They create strong in-group loyalty that needs to be balanced by "*bridging* social capital" — the outward-looking social ties that "encompass people across diverse social cleavages" (22–23). Stephen Warner (2000) says that religious groups create their identities by segregating themselves from other groups, but that these groups also are key sites of bridging activity. Religious groups produce matching rhetorics, what Paul Bramadat (2000, 59–68) has called "fortress" and "bridging" rhetorics.

Some analysts say that Putnam overemphasizes his measurements of the social connections and disconnections of a society and does not account for the independent, causal role of culture. For instance, in *Forms of Capital* Pierre Bourdieu (1986) distinguished three forms of cultural capital: "embodied capital," which represents what an individual knows and can do; "objectified capital," which is found in material objects; and "institutionalized capital," which is found in schools.

It is no secret that a primary source of America's social and cultural capital is its more than a hundred thousand churches, mosques, temples, synagogues, and other places of worship. Savvy politicians demonstrate the power of this capital by tapping churches and other religious organizations during elections. For those seeking office, having a charismatic preacher as a close friend can be as good as having solid party support. In doing so, they are actually participating in an old American tradition. Since the early days of nationhood, America's religious organizations have been the breeding grounds of volunteerism, philanthropy, and civic behavior (Greeley 1997). They are not only places of worship but also spaces for cultivating civic engagement and sites for political recruitment, incorporation, co-optation, and empowerment (Verba, Schlozman, and Brady 1997). But even this enduring institution, according to Putnam, has not been spared serious decline in terms of membership and related activities. He claims that the technological developments of communication and recreation and the changing attitudes toward politics and the role of women are partly to blame for this trend. Although many thought that the spiritual and patriotic fervor following 9/11 would start a sustainable renaissance of faith- and church-based volunteerism, recent controversies, such as the many allegations of sexual abuse by Catholic priests, have virtually wiped out any gains (see Boston Globe 2003; Gibson 2003). The aftershocks of these morbid revelations will probably be felt for a long time and thus further erode memberships, contributions, patronage, and networking within religious organizations.

In *Bowling Alone* Putnam notes that, while the number of bowlers has increased 10 percent over the past thirty years, league bowling is down 40 percent. Given this decline in organized recreational activity, it is not surprising that far fewer Americans are affiliated with political, civic, and religious organizations. This is particularly the case among American-born descendants of European immigrants through the twentieth century. Even black churches, once a source of African American empowerment, have witnessed a noticeable thinning of their congregations. As a result, many faith-based spaces and networks of churches, schools, and social services have been abandoned. Memberships have also been consolidated for the sake of maintaining administrative and operational overheads.

This essay joins a number of sociological studies of American churches that argue that not all secular and spiritual gathering places in American communities are declining (see Lincoln and Mamiya 2003; Roozen and Nieman 2005). On the contrary, a number of them have been revitalized, are full (or even expanding), and contribute to efforts in community organizing and American democratization (Jacobsen 2001; Warren 2001). However, a number of churches may no longer be filled with the European American (white or Caucasian) or African American faces that have historically comprised their memberships. Instead, immigrants from places considered "new," including East and Southeast Asia, Latin America, the Caribbean, and the Middle East, have replenished these faith-based institutions and their production of social and cultural capital, particularly in America's "gateway cities" (Carnes and Yang 2004; Jeung 2004; Min and Kim 2002; Warner 2000; Warner and Wittner 1998; Yoo 1999). Many churches in San Francisco have become sites for Filipinos to bond with

each other while simultaneously bridging with the non-Filipino, non-Asian world. Further, the church is a site for the renewal, preservation, and transmission of cultural capital in the forms of community activities, traditions, rituals, family values, and work ethics.

THE GROWTH OF FILIPINO COMMUNITY AND THE RISE OF THEIR CHURCHES IN SAN FRANCISCO

San Francisco's cultural, racial, and ethnic diversity today is the logical result of its history as a Spanish missionary site in the 1700s, a center for the events of the gold rush, and a staging location for America's forays to the Eastern Hemisphere. The heavy commercialization of San Francisco brought in many waves of immigrant groups starting in the early 1800s. By the middle of the century, the city had already become a mixed bag of Irish, English, German, Italian, Mexican, and Chinese cultures. But the Irish presence, at 33 percent of the city's population, was particularly felt in politics, business, and religion. Eventually Angel Island emerged as one of the premier immigration stations in the west—a place where new immigrants were "screened and processed." In the early 1900s Portuguese, Japanese, and Filipinos came to the area, and around the same time the African American community arrived in significant numbers.

The twentieth century brought in peoples from all geographic regions of the world, from Latin America to South Asia. The U.S. Immigration and Naturalization Service (INS) became one of the most visible public agencies in the San Francisco Bay Area, and the terms "INS" and "green card" were mainstreamed into the local discourse of San Franciscans.

The results of the 2000 census show a significant demographic shift in the San Francisco Bay Area.[2] The American-born white population of San Francisco is now less than half of the total number. African Americans represent less then 8 percent of the total population. The numbers of both racial groups show a rapid decline from the 1990 census. Meanwhile, Asians, Pacific Islanders, and Hispanics now make up close to 50 percent of San Francisco residents. Since the 1965 Immigration Act increased the influx of "new" immigrants, these newcomers have not only replaced declining economic capital but also brought with them social capital in the form of organizational affiliations and social practices; indeed, they brought not only churches but the quintessentially American practice of league bowling.

The Filipino community in the San Francisco Bay Area, estimated at more than 320,000 according to the 2000 census, is a major part of the larger diasporic migration to the United States, which now numbers two million. Migratory waves from the Philippines, after its 1898 annexation by the United States, led to the steady growth of attendance by Filipino migrant workers at local Catholic and Protestant churches. The growing number of Filipino immigrants also increased church attendance rates at that time. Between 1920 and 1929, 31,092 Filipinos entered California, and more than 80 percent of them went through the Port of San Francisco (California Department of Industrial Relations 1930). The end of the Second World War and the 1972 declaration of martial law in the Philippines and the passage of the 1965 U.S. Immigration Act further intensified the conditions that drew Filipinos to the United States.

Up to the 1930s most Filipinos were hired in the farm areas to work as agricultural workers, but many also stayed in the cities to work as domestic helpers and manual laborers in the hotel industry. American Protestant and Catholic missionaries came to the villages and told Filipinos about America and the many jobs and opportunities in the agricultural and service industries. In addition, there was also a large group of *pensionados* or U.S. government scholars who came to study at American universities.

Through several decades San Francisco was the most popular gateway city for Filipino immigrants. By 1960 there were 12,327 Filipinos in the city of San Francisco. The arrival of Filipinos in large numbers after 1965 came as religious institutions in San Francisco were declining. By the late 1960s, many older

TABLE 1. Filipino population in the San Francisco Bay Area in 2000

County	Number of individuals	County	Number of individuals
Santa Clara	76,060	Contra Costa	34,595
Alameda	69,127	Sonoma	2,697
San Mateo	59,847	Napa	1,759
San Francisco	40,083	Marin	1,389
Solano	36,576	TOTAL	322,133

Source: U.S. Census Bureau. Available at http://www.census.gov/main/www/cen2000.html.

San Francisco Catholic and Protestant churches had serious declines in active memberships and financial contributions. Downtown churches started to close at an alarming rate, and because of a lack of money for maintenance many churches closed permanently. Commercialization, fires, and earthquakes drove people out of the area; Sunday mornings were especially quiet, with a notable absence of strollers and churchgoers. Then, with the arrival of large numbers of Filipinos and other Asian immigrants, the declining churches started to revive. Itinerant congregations competed to see who could lease space in previously empty churches. By 1990 the number of Filipinos in San Francisco had more than tripled since 1960, and by 2000 over 320,000 Filipinos resided in the Bay Area (see table 1). As indicated in the essay by Joaquin Gonzalez in this volume, the Filipino immigrant revitalization of local religion is strikingly evident in the Roman Catholic churches. The Filipinos have driven up attendance and finances while also changing the culture of the Catholic churches in the area. In the vast Archdiocese of San Francisco, which encompasses the counties of San Francisco, San Mateo, and Marin, one out of every four Catholics is of Filipino descent. According to official estimates from 2000, there are now more than 90,000 registered Catholic parishioners in the archdiocese out of an estimated population of more than 150,000 Filipinos.[3]

FILIPINIZATION AS SOCIAL AND CULTURAL CAPITAL FORMATION

Filipinization occurs when segments of a society or spaces in it experience varying degrees of Filipino cultural, political, and financial influence, support, ownership, or control. Churches are "abandoned" because of funding issues due to a lack of participation. One instance is the outright takeover by the independent Philippine-based Global Church of Christ of what was previously an influential Christ the Scientist church in the heart of San Francisco. Filipinization is a form of active adaptation and acculturation given the changing dynamics of American social and political events, especially in gateway regions like the San Francisco Bay Area. Thus, the Filipino community is constantly responding to changing scenarios, opportunities, and challenges in their new home—in the process forming both bonds and bridges for social and cultural capital, which they weave into the quilt of American society. Through the churches they joined or established, Filipino immigrants have contributed tremendously to building San Francisco civil society and its social and cultural capital. Through commitment to their churches, Filipinos bring with them their social relations, kinship ties, networks, emotional commitment, traditions, beliefs, customs, and practices that promote community self-help, the spirit of trust, and self-reliant attitudes and behavior. These are manifested in the well-recognized Filipino values of *bayanihan* (community self-help attitude), *bisita* (kin visits), *panata* (vow), *pagkamagalang* (respectfulness), *bahala na* (leave it to God), *utang na loob* (debt of gratitude), and *pakikisama* (getting along with others). These traits and practices allow Filipino migrants to connect to mainstream U.S. society in both "bridging Filipinization" or "bonding Filipinization" ways. The church is not just a site that they Filipinize in bonding terms but a space they use to bridge themselves to Filipinize U.S. society.

For instance, to foster a strong sense of community and pride many San Francisco churches have made accommodations to popular Philippine languages and dialects such as Tagalog, Ilocano, Cebuano, Kapampangan, Bicolano, and Ilonggo. Some Tagalog hymns have even found their way into the English services. Reverend Jeremiah Resus says that the blending of spirituality and the immigrant experience at his Saint James Presbyterian Church has aided the creation of a perspective that frames new identities orientated toward feeling accepted, assimilation, and enduring hardships. The church, he says, "is a place that changes perceptions of reality and supplies perspective to face challenges in life. As a community, St. James provides a sense of identity for immigrants . . . Membership in the church allows the process of assimilation, movement into American life, a sense of belonging."[4] The pastor also says that the church provides a sense of belonging through encouraging marriages and job seeking.

Filipino immigrants also use their churches for community gatherings, group meetings, dances, fiestas, graduations, parades, processions, bingo nights, birthday parties, anniversaries, cultural presentations, and so forth. Many senior citizens and retirees gain companionship and camaraderie from their churches. For instance, members of the San Francisco Filipino American

Seventh-Day Adventist Church regularly visit elderly and sick fellow members who are in the hospitals, care facilities, or living alone at home. The need for senior citizen care has grown over the years with the influx of Filipino war veterans, many of whom are in their seventies and eighties and have no family support system in the United States. Filipino American churches also reach out to the San Francisco Bay Area community at large, and they contribute thousands of dollars in public services to Bay Area cities. Some common civic activities are blood drives, tree plantings, public-area cleanups, and food distribution to homeless and other needy people. Some churches also provide space for community. Local politicians have officially hailed many of these contributions, which further integrate Filipino churches and their memberships into larger San Francisco society. Local social service organizations regularly visit Filipino American churches to spread information and educate members on welfare, health, and other programs.

Filipino congregations also contribute to San Francisco society by helping new Filipino immigrants in their adjustment to America. As Reverend Capuli of Grace United Methodist Church claims, "The grace of God makes people productive members of society (for instance, taxpayers, professionals with valuable services to offer) and individuals with strong moral character and which value family." At some churches, members provide assistance to newcomers by volunteering to pick them up when they arrive at the airport. Basements and other areas in private homes often become temporary housing until fellow members find their own places to stay. New members are often carpooled to church services while they are still familiarizing themselves with roads and public transportation routes. At these churches the bulletins boards are typically filled with important leads from job opportunities to baby-sitting offers. Church members have been known to hire fellow members to work for their companies. Training sessions to upgrade skills are even offered through some churches for free. Some interest-free loans are exchanged between trusting members, especially those who are related or who come from the same province or town. Used cars and trucks are lent out, donated, or sold at a substantial discount.

Filipino churches such as the Saint Francis and Grace United Methodist Church and the Saint James Presbyterian Church rent out space for preschool education. They also allow local nonprofit organizations such as Alcoholics Anonymous, or candidates for local office, to use their space free of charge. Saint Francis and Grace United Methodist Church provided valuable meeting space for San Francisco Mayor Willie Brown during his first campaign for public office. The church effectively became a key point of contact with the neighborhood and the larger network of Bay Area Filipinos. The congregation also allows community groups in the Sunset District to use their space, including other churches that do not have buildings.

With the support of their San Francisco congregations, the mission work of Filipino American churches has been able to expand in the United States, the Philippines, and many other countries. Many Filipino American churches finance American Christian missionaries in the Philippines. They also give much-needed financial and spiritual support to projects and programs of their "home" churches in the Philippines. Pastors in the Philippines attest to the valuable contributions of Filipinos in America to the restoration and beautification of old historic churches as well as the building of new chapels. After all, their home churches are probably the places where Filipinos who have migrated to America prayed for God to facilitate their departure from the Philippines. When natural calamities strike, such as earthquakes, fires, and typhoons in the United States, the Philippines, or elsewhere around the globe, Filipino American churches have provided relief goods and members to help in disaster management. For instance, Saint Francis and Grace United Methodist Church sent to the Philippines scholarships for seminary and college students, money to clinics in Palawan, and aid to the victims of the Mount Pinatubo disaster. These acts of giving are part of their *utang na loob* (debt of gratitude) to their homeland, and some new immigrants may feel that it is part of their *panata* (vow) not to forsake the place where they were born, which serves as a distant source of social energy.

FILIPINO RELIGIOUS FESTIVALS

Festivals and food represent another way that social and cultural capital is transfused into San Francisco life. Nearly every day of the year there is some sort of religious festival being celebrated in a village, town, city, or province in the Philippines. During the Spanish rule, Catholic festivals and fiestas were encouraged for religious purposes. In modern times, the traditional Catholic festivals blended with the local native beliefs and practices, and celebrations come with a distinctly Philippine flavor. Philippine fiestas are a kaleidoscope of colors, fireworks, games, eating, drinking, dancing, gambling, and beauty contests. Hence, given the more than 300,000 Filipinos in the San Francisco Bay Area it is not surprising that there would be a celebration somewhere.

Filipinos in the Bay Area have celebrated the Feast of the Black Nazarene by honoring the hundred-year-old statue of the miraculous "dark-colored Christ." Immigrants from Aklan, true to their regional loyalties, focus on the Ati-Atihan festival, which is a carnival-like celebration in honor of the infant Jesus, the town's patron saint. Filipino Americans from Marinduque host the Moriones festival during the Lenten weeks, while those who came from Sariaya, Tayabas, and Lucban in Quezon Province celebrate the Pahiyas festival in honor of San Isidro, the patron saint of farmers. Commemoration of these religious events does not necessarily have to be held in religious spaces like the church but can take places in the streets of San Francisco, like the annual Christmas lantern parade, as well as parks and spaces such as local hotel ballrooms, convention centers, restaurants, and bars. There are annual Filipino fiestas (*pistahan*) held in Yerba Buena Gardens, as well as a fiesta at the Civic Center in front of City Hall that begins with a grand parade on Market Street. Some events have been hosted in public schools, like Bessie Carmichael Elementary School's Santacruzan, while others have been done in Catholic schools. Bicolanos from San Francisco have rented boats for the Peñafrancia festival, a devotion to the miraculous image of the Nuestra Señora de Peñafrancia. Not to be outdone the Cebuanos of the Bay Area host the Sinulog—a dance ritual in honor of the miraculous image of the Santo Niño, which is reputed to be the oldest festival in the Philippines.

TWO CASE STUDIES IN TRANSNATIONAL SOCIOCULTURAL CAPITAL FORMATION

The following two case studies provide microviews of the process of transnational sociocultural capital formation in two of the most influential Filipino Christian congregations in the San Francisco Bay Area: the Global Church of Christ in Daly City, California, which is a local branch of an independent Philippines-based Christian church; and San Patricio's Catholic Church,[5] which is located in downtown San Francisco.

The Global Church of Christ, Daly City

Members of the Global Church of Christ (GCC) say that helping each other is the "Global Church of Christ state of mind." They call each other *kapatid* (the brethren). The worldwide network of GCC churches is like an extended family. When a member is planning a move from Daly City, California, to New York City, a brethren will first check to see if there is a GCC church in the area. In acts such as this the church provides central support for its members who are new immigrants. At the same time, however, it tends to be so supportive as to be insular—the church is a bank of social capital for its members but is a bit of a monastery too.

On every first Saturday of the month, members of the Daly City branch of the GCC bring friends and neighbors to church. These services, called Grand Evangelical Missions (or GEMs, for short), are rare opportunities for outsiders to learn about the insular fundamentalist church. After hymns and prayer, Resident Minister Brother Lorenzo takes his stance before an open Bible at the pulpit. Gripping the podium with both hands, he looks intently at the audience. He asks, "What does God command us to do, brothers and sisters?" Then he pauses and looks at the congregation. He picks up the Bible and points at a passage: "In 1 Corinthians 12:25, God commands his chosen people to 'be united in the same mind and the same judgment.' God has so adjusted the body that there may be no discord . . . but that the members may have the same care for one another." "Brothers and sisters," he declares, "God commands us, his chosen people, to think and act together. We must be unified." For the fundamentalist Global Church of Christ, members attend to the biblical imperatives quoted by Brother Lorenzo as behavioral guides designed to strengthen the social cohesiveness of the congregation. Their leaders teach that helping one another succeed as individuals benefits the church as a whole. A central part of the church's spiritual mission is what some might call building social capital.

The church encourages its constituents to have a sense of personal connectedness to one another that transcends distance. Church members believe that they will always find unqualified acceptance and support from the brethren anywhere. Brethren easily can detail the practical and emotional support that the church provides them when they are away from home or settling someplace new. For instance, Marie, a young woman from the Daly City locale, was planning to move to Connecticut to attend medical school.[6] Before she left, she talked about her anxiety about the transition. "The biggest reassurance I have," she said, "is the knowledge that there is a Global Church of Christ congregation in my new neighborhood. It will serve as my 'home away from home.'"

Official church structures also help the transition of migrant brethren to new locations. First, members are strongly encouraged to move to a place where there is another Global Church of Christ locale. So when Marie considered Connecticut College she checked to see if there were a GCC congregation nearby. The English-language *God's Message* and the Tagalog-language *Pasugo*, weekly magazines published by the church, list contact information for every Global Church of Christ congregation throughout the world, so that members like Marie can locate GCC congregations in unfamiliar places. In Connecticut the brethren will give Marie rides to and from church, enroll her in the Kadiwa singles group, and introduce her to new friends.

Mr. and Mrs. Santos are also migrant church members who moved from

Manila, Philippines, to Daly City to live with their daughter. Before they moved, they informed the resident minister of their church in Manila, who forwarded their files to the resident minister in Daly City. The new congregation prepared to welcome them. In Daly City the Santos were made part of a group of three families whose spiritual, emotional, and physical well-being is overseen by a church officer. In addition to leading prayers in the Santos's home, the officer might also ensure their practical needs. He might inquire if they were success-ful in locating the local Social Security office; if they needed help securing a driver's license; or if they knew about Pacific Super, the nearby supermarket stocked with Filipino goods. In addition the Daly City GCC has classes such as English as a second language and driver education that are geared toward new immigrants like the Santos. The specialized assistance and social structures that the church provides are relatively consistent from place to place.

In the Philippines the GCC has a long-standing tradition of partnering with social service agencies to provide for needy members and nonmembers. There are many examples of these services such as free medical and dental care, housing for people dislocated by natural disaster, and literacy programs. In addition to these long-term programs, the church also organizes its members for one-time activities like blood drives and planting trees in sites damaged by erosion. These practices are carried over to the United States also.

Bay Area GCC churches regularly join in civic activities of the Red Cross and local governments. Over the course of a year GCC Bay Area churches have done blood and food drives, free cholesterol screenings, and neighborhood cleanups and tree plantings. Local government officials have taken notice of these ac-tivities. For instance, on June 28, 2001, Mayor Carol L. Klatt declared "Global Church of Christ Week" in Daly City. The Daly City Council has also awarded the Global Church of Christ with a number of community citations including the award for Most Outstanding Volunteer Group. As Mayor Klatt stated: "The congregation's civic activities and volunteer effort occur year-round, time and again, they have come through, regardless of the odds and obstacles."[7]

Local officials also recognize the potential political power of the church. Indeed, Daly City has an official partnership across the Pacific with Quezon City in the Philippines—the location of the headquarters of the Global Church of Christ as well as several important educational, medical, and religious in-stitutions. Consequently, Michael Guingona, a former mayor of Daly City and a Filipino American official who sat on the Sister City Commission, was care-ful to make a courtesy call on the Global Church of Christ's leadership in the Philippines.[8] The GCC sees the church also as giving back to the community in unseen but more fundamental ways. First, they believe that the church's moral

278 GONZALEZ, MAISON, AND MARZAN

code encourages its members to be law abiding, hardworking, and oriented toward community service. In other words, it encourages people in the Protestant ethic and in good citizenship. Second, the church says its missionary work, which spreads these values to others, is thus also a public service.

At the GEM service we attended, all of the visitors were invited to a casual buffet lunch after the conclusion of the formal services. Churchgoers streamed out of the worship area and made their way to the social hall, where a veritable feast had been laid out. Once in the hall, the quiet crowd turned animated and noisy. Loud talk and laughter filled the room, where several rectangular folding tables placed end to end formed a vast buffet of restaurant-purchased and homemade Filipino and American food. Large aluminum trays piled high with *pancit, pritong manok* (fried chicken), and Filipino-style spaghetti from local restaurants crowded alongside homemade dishes in smaller, individualized containers. *Pinakbet, mechado, kare-kare* and other regional favorites spoke both of the congregation's geographic diversity and love of food.

As we entered the social hall, our GCC hosts sprung into action like a well-rehearsed team, staking out a table and enough folding chairs for each member of our group. One woman sat at the table and reserved seats with our purses and jackets, while the rest of us joined the crowds at the well-stocked buffet. We made our way to the food tables and scooped a little bit of rice, *pinakbet*, and *pancit* onto our plates. One of our companions urged us to try some of the other, home-cooked dishes. "This is *bopis*—it's my favorite! You've got to taste it!" she insisted, passing a serving spoon. She also directed our attention to a paper plate laden with bits of sweetened yam. We noticed that her plate was heaped in layers, with several fried sardines perched atop a generous pile of rice, noodles, and vegetables. Back at our table we ate and, speaking in Tagalog, talked about food: not only about recipes, condiments, and the best local sources for Filipino ingredients but also the memories that Filipino food conjured about "home." As this example shows, by stimulating people to speak Tagalog and conjuring reminiscences of the Philippines, food not only helps "bond" members together but also is used to "bridge" members from church to community, society, and their two homelands—the United States and the Philippines.

San Patricio's Catholic Church, San Francisco

San Patricio's Church builds on the sense of continuity between life in the Philippines, where the majority are Catholic, and life in the United States. Filipino ushers greet new immigrants and seat them among the congregants, who are mostly Filipino also. More often than not the celebrant is a Filipino priest.

In spite of the church's Gothic Revival architecture, the new Filipino immigrant usually feels that he or she might still be in Manila, especially during the monthly Tagalog mass.

Icons refer to popular devotions in the Philippines, like those of the Mother of Perpetual Help and the Divine Mercy that flank the high altar. The Holy Infant Jesus (Santo Niño) is enshrined close to the center of the sanctuary, reflecting the affection that Filipino Catholics feel for the baby. San Lorenzo Ruiz, the first Filipino saint, also has his own shrine. Even the Black Nazareno, an icon of Christ revered by many male Filipinos at the Quiapo Church in Manila, has a place.

Many Filipino Catholics are not content to pay their respect to their saints simply through prayer. Indeed, through their touches, caresses, and bestowal of affection as if the saint were a living person they have worn off the paint on San Lorenzo Ruiz's feet and on the Nazareno's right hand. For the Filipino parishioners, San Patricio's Church is one of the few places where they can engage in this active form of devotion without being self-conscious. They can also pray and confess in their native languages by interacting with bicultural priests. Dual citizenship—that is, allegiance to both the Philippines and the United States—is an accepted mental state here in this church. Filipinos claim that this definitely eases in their acculturation.

The present population of Filipino immigrants tends to obscure the fact that, as San Patricio's, the church was one of the citadels of Irish Catholicism in

the Bay Area. Indeed, after most of the Irish left the neighborhood, the church was a forlorn space empty of all but priests. Filipinos have filled the church with life and also have the run of the parish, from the rectory to the lay organizations. All resident priests and deacons are Filipinos who were born and trained in the Philippines, and the parish frequently hosts visiting Philippine priests. Even the nuns come from a Filipino religious order, the Religious of the Virgin Mary, founded in Manila during the seventeenth century.

The Filipino presence has led to the formation of new parish organizations and the revitalization of existing ones. For example, the San Patricio's chapter of the Holy Name Society, an international Catholic confraternity, has its roots in the chapter established at the parish of Guadalupe in Makati, a city in metropolitan Manila. In fact, the Filipino immigrant population has become the main influence on the social life of the parish. Every December for the last two decades there has been a celebration of Misa de Gallo (also known as Simbang Gabi), the nine early-morning masses before Christmas, which is a ritual particular to the Philippines. The parish also recently reinstituted Filipino-style breakfasts after mass, and there are plans for a Filipiniana night for the feast of San Lorenzo Ruiz. The highlight of many parish organization meetings is the food and refreshments.

Many new Filipino immigrants, especially those from small towns, operate within the mental construct of a Philippine *poblacion* (or town plaza), wherein the church is at the center of the plaza with the various governmental institutions and social gathering places around it. Because San Patricio's helps Filipino immigrants adjust to American life by reinforcing Filipino cultural values and behaviors, it continues its loyalty toward the parish. In San Francisco's South of Market area, San Patricio's is the center of gravity that draws Filipinos back even when they have moved to the suburbs.

For example, the parish's lay organizations provide the newly arrived with an instant network of individuals that share common interests and adjustments to a new country. Personal connections are made and a common religious devotion is experienced. Indeed, personal connections play a major role at San Patricio's. Parishioners frequently consult the priests for advice and assistance about problems. Further, although San Patricio's does not have many formal social programs, the church draws upon the Catholic Archdiocese of San Francisco's extensive social outreach resources.

San Patricio's also has informal partnerships with neighborhood-based organizations like West Bay Filipino Multi-service Center, South of Market Teen Center, the South of Market Health Center, the South of Market Job Training Center, Arkipelago Bookstore, Filipinas Restaurant, the Veteran's Equity

Center, and the Bessie Carmichael Elementary School. Further, these local groups and the church often play the role of advocate for Filipinos. They have successfully lobbied the U.S. Congress to provide recognition to Filipino veterans of the Second World War by granting to them American citizenship and health benefits. These organizations have also leveraged funds from the City and County of San Francisco for Filipino youths and their families. Church leaders and parishioners have testified in City Hall hearings and meetings on issues that affect at-risk youths and veterans and the South of Market Project Area Committee. There is a symbiotic relationship between the church and these community-based organizations: the parish helps new arrivals maintain a connection to the Philippines while the neighborhood organizations help them make a successful start in their new home in the United States.

San Patricio's is one of the few places where Filipino Catholics can consistently attend devotions particular to the Philippines, such as the Simbang Gabi, the early-morning masses celebrated during Christmas season. It is usually after such devotions when food is served to the congregation, whether it is breakfast after Simbang Gabi or an early evening snack after a novena to the Santo Niño de Cebu. In most instances, as with the Simbang Gabi and the novena, the religious ceremony is a prelude to the hospitality of serving meals that, regardless of devotion or occasion, reflect a mixture of Filipino traditions and the current social realities of many Filipino immigrants in the South of Market area. Like town fiestas in the Philippines, certain individuals or parish groups sponsor the meals—that is, the donors serve as the *hermano mayor* (grand sponsor) of the event. However, given the relatively low income of most of the parishioners, the meals are usually modest; familiar dishes such as *pancit* or *lumpia* are served that feed a crowd but do not strain the budget. In the case of the Simbang Gabi breakfasts in December, the sponsors always make sure that the food provides both physical and spiritual warmth—for example, *champorado* (chocolate rice porridge), *arroz caldo* (chicken and rice stew), and *sotanghon* (chicken soup), usually accompanied by bread or hot *pan de sal* (rolls).

Regardless of the fare, people are always served graciously; and the parish volunteers who help serve always have a kind word to give. For those who come alone and leave alone, this meal is a source of comfort that goes beyond physical satisfaction. The community opens its arms in welcome, and again, like the hermanos mayor, the volunteers make sure everyone is able to partake of the meal, and the generosity of the donors makes sure there is more than enough to go around. The parish takes the time to acknowledge the sponsors and the donors, and the meals are greatly appreciated by those in attendance.

The aim of the Simbang Gabi to foster a sense of community is quite apparent, given the communal setting and the socialization that goes on during the meal. However, it can also be read as a means of remembering not only one's identity as a Catholic but also one's identity as a Filipino. In much the same way that the Eucharist is considered the most sacred characteristic of Catholic worship—the act that affirms unity with the mystical body of Christ—the meals taken after mass affirm unity with the local community of Filipinos, and thereby serve as a secular version of communion within the context of tradition. To partake in the meal indicates an acceptance of tradition and a willingness to see it continue for years to come—to remember and to act accordingly.

The significance of the church's traditions reaches beyond its walls. The parishioners of San Patricio's are not conscious of this, but to celebrate Filipino traditions and to share them with the outside community goes beyond the mere notion of national pride. As noted above, hospitality happens at home, and to celebrate Simbang Gabi—one of the most-loved religious traditions among Filipino Catholics—outside of the Philippines indicates a desire by Filipinos to make their present surroundings home. The Filipinos of San Patricio's don't just want to celebrate Christmas—they want to celebrate as they did back in their old home and share it with their new neighbors in their new home. By appropriating what was formerly borrowed space and making it a place where transplanted *kababayan* can experience a sense of continuity with what they left behind, the Filipinos of San Patricio's have created a sort of haven with church walls and made the parish an informal center of cultural promotion and preservation. From the hermano mayor to the festivities and the food, San Patricio's has come full circle from one group of immigrants to another. The Irish national church of the West Coast has become the newest addition to the poblacion for the Filipinos of San Francisco.

CONCLUSION

Filipino immigration to the San Francisco Bay Area has provided a critical mass of loyal churchgoers that are Filipinizing social and cultural capital, in both bonding and bridging ways, in the San Francisco area. In particular, religious and ethnic organizations almost collapsed in some areas. This situation meant that there were too many atomized individuals per block for a healthy community to be built on mutual recognition, trust, and ownership of the public life. Some areas had become socially blighted and anomic.

Originating from a country with a long history of Christianity and faith-based organizing, Filipino immigrants have transformed vacated church spaces and places into sanctuaries for incorporation and acculturation rooted in Filipinized cultural traits, norms, beliefs, exchanges, interactions, and iconography. With the "blessings" of their churches, they have formed Filipino associations and built networks that simultaneously maintain transnational linkages and local social power centers. They have also transfused their feasts, festivals, rituals, and food not just in their religious sites but also to American business and society. Mainstream supermarkets such as Safeway and Albertson's carry Filipino ingredients like *pansit canton* (egg noodles) and *patis* (fish sauce).

Even in an era of church and state separation, there is much room for convergence through social and cultural capital development to meet the needs of rapidly changing communities. Many San Francisco Bay Area governments have discovered this and are trying to create an atmosphere that stimulates sociocultural capital formation among its diverse populations. The Global Church of Christ's civic involvement in Daly City has been praised many times by mayors, city councils, and other government offices, and many citations and awards are displayed on the walls of the GCC's northern California district office. A single phone call to the GCC by Mayor Cathy Brown of the City of Livermore is all it took to bring in brethren volunteers who cleaned streets, landscaped public areas, and painted over graffiti. In remarking on these efforts she stated: "If you have two thousand volunteers, it does not even compare to the number of city staff we have, so you have probably done a year's work." The volunteers did civic work that would have cost the city hundreds of personnel hours and ten of thousands of dollars. In 2002, Oakland Mayor Jerry Brown made the same phone call to the GCC in Oakland and got the same results.

With the strong support of Filipino religious leaders, the City and County of San Francisco has established a fifteen-member Commission on Immigrant Rights to protect the civil rights of new immigrants and dismantle barriers to their full civic engagement. San Francisco is one of the few cities in the United States to have such a commission. Not surprisingly, a number of active parishioners of San Patricio's Church have been appointed by the mayor to be commissioners. In another unprecedented move, the commission now requires all city and county agencies to provide better language access. More than forty thousand Filipino residents of the city benefited from this move. With gentle lobbying from Filipino Christian residents, the San Francisco Board of Supervisors has also promoted pro-immigrant policies like declaring San Francisco a "Sanctuary City" for all immigrants, legal or illegal.

We have seen San Patricio's parishioners and Global Church of Christ members organizing and attending the Pistahan Celebration at the Yerba Buena Gardens and the Fiesta Filipina Exposition at the Civic Center in front of City Hall—both of which are large-scale San Francisco festivities cosponsored by the City and County of San Francisco and major corporations such as AT&T, Wells Fargo Bank, PG&E, and Western Union. Moreover, San Francisco hosts cultural days for most of its major ethnicities—including Philippine Independence Day on June 12—at which religious organizations display their civic commitments.

Bowling together is a cherished feature of Filipino faith, fellowship, and feasting. Bowling and church are both integral parts of the Filipino culture. Indeed, the Filipino love for bowling has produced many bowling greats, including *Guinness Book of World Records* holder Rafael "Paeng" Nepomuceno, a six-time world champion. He is one of the inspirations of the Philippines' global diaspora of church-going immigrants. Filipinos are bringing back "bowling together" to a "bowling-alone" America. Besides filling up bowling lanes on Memorial Day, Filipino culture has melded into more American civic spaces and community activities—from Simbang Gabi in Catholic churches to San Francisco's famous gay pride parade. As a process the Filipinization of America forms both bonding and bridging social and cultural capital. Bonding capital is manifested as *kasamahan* (feelings of togetherness and companionship) while bridging capital is practiced through *bayanihan* (spirit of communal unity and cooperation)—both of which are clearly demonstrated at the San Patricio's Church and at Global Church of Christ.

NOTES

Portions of this chapter were first published as "We Do Not Bowl Alone: Cultural and Social Capitals from Filipinos and Their Churches," in T. Carnes and F. Yang, eds., *Asian American Religions: The Making and Remaking of Borders and Boundaries* (New York: New York University Press, 2004).

1. "Global Church of Christ" is a pseudonym used to preserve anonymity.
2. Accessible on the website of the U.S. Census Bureau, http://www.census.gov/main/www/cen2000.html.
3. The figures here are based on information from interviews with Noemi Castillo, director of the Office of Ethnic Ministries, Archdiocese of San Francisco, May-June, 2001.
4. Unless otherwise noted, all quotations are from the interviews conducted by the authors during their fieldwork in the San Francisco Bay Area, 2001–2003.
5. Pseudonym used to preserve anonymity.
6. To preserve privacy, all personal names given in this essay are pseudonyms.
7. Mayor's Message, June 28, 2002.
8. Similarly, San Francisco is the sister city of Manila, with a joint commission that has representation from active Filipino Christians.

Counterhegemony Finds Place in a Hegemon

Activism through Filipino American Churches

JOAQUIN JAY GONZALEZ III AND
CLAUDINE DEL ROSARIO

The evening of Friday, May 18, 2001, was glorious, with crystal-clear skies and a smooth gentle breeze. In a small neighborhood elementary school just outside of San Francisco, California, Catholic priests, brothers, and sisters were gathering. As they trickled into the brightly lit lunch hall, the atmosphere felt increasingly like a barrio fiesta rather than an encounter of respected spiritual leaders. With their laughter and banter in Taglish (mixed Tagalog and English), Tagalog, Ilocano, Bicolano, Cebuano, Kapampangan, Waray, Boholano, and other dialects it was clear that they could not be described as ordinary "American" clergy. All sixty-three members in attendance that night were Filipino religious migrants, and as such they formed an unprecedented assembly. They all knew that their mission in the United States was not simply to quench the spiritual thirst of hundreds of thousands of Catholics of Filipino ethnicity who have resettled in the country but also to minister to the larger, diverse multicultural Catholic communities in Marin, San Francisco, and San Mateo counties. Between alternating mouthfuls of crunchy *lechon de leche* (roasted suckling pig), tasty *adobong manok* (chicken soy stew), and succulent *lumpiang sariwa* (fresh vegetable eggrolls), the men and women of the cloth exchanged animated stories of ministering to an "overseas Fililpino flock." They commented on the multitude of American and Filipino issues they encounter that their Philippine seminary or convent education never prepared them for. From a corner of the room an elder pastor, jokingly nicknamed Bishop, quipped loudly that one approach he definitely imported from home was how to raise consciousness and rally in the streets, when needed, on social problems—whether American or Filipino. Silence then filled the room, until a young nun in the back piped up in Taglish: "Bishop, parang Pilipino people power sa America!" (Bishop, it's like using Filipino-style people power in America!).[1] In response everyone laughed—apparently in agreement.

Immigrant religious leaders and their followers have become a major source of spiritual, cultural, social, and political capital formation in many gateway cities in the United States. Hence, their "organized action" in society versus dysfunctional policies could definitely be seen as counterhegemonic. The San Francisco Bay Area, home to thousands of Filipino immigrants and their hundreds of spiritual congregations, is no exception. After all, the acceptable political and spiritual socialization that Filipino migrants subscribe to deviates from what the larger American society prefers and is exposed to—a dichotomized path for spiritual and political life. Church and state should be separated by clear mental and institutional boundaries, particularly in government spaces. City hall is the appropriate venue for politics, policy, and advocacy, while the cathedral, mosque, and synagogue are the proper spaces for prayer, rites, and worship. Public policies should reflect this dichotomy in terms of process and product. But not to the Filipino migrant psyche it seems.

Our initial participant observations (which are also shared in this volume in the essays by Joaquin Gonzalez, Andrea Maison, and Dennis Marzan) led us to explore further the dynamics of this sociopolitical phenomenon, as guided by the thoughts expressed as follows: Given the large influx of Filipino pastors, Filipino religious workers, and Filipino members of various Christian faiths into the United States and the many acculturation and immigration issues that emerge, what kinds of unique civic engagement and incorporation exchanges between congregants, state, and society have resulted? From a more radical standpoint, have Filipinos been effective at using their immigrant spiritual politicization as a Trojan horse that would allow them to get into the core of American society and make positive inroads into its hegemonic structures? And, most important, what are the conditions that have allowed a fused transnational spiritual and political capital formation to develop?

We began with the assumption that the evolutionary process of intertwined transnational spiritual and political capital formation among Filipino immigrants in the San Francisco Bay Area illustrates a form of counterhegemony as grounded in the early critical points raised by Karl Marx, Max Weber, Paulo Freire, Antonio Gramsci, and the eminent Filipino historian Reynaldo Ileto on social revolution and the church. After discussing the conceptual underpinnings of this perceived counterhegemony, we gathered historical evidence of both state-church hegemony and the resulting civil society counterhegemony in the more than three hundred years of colonization and Hispanization under Spain and the more than hundred-year-old relationship of colonization and neocolonization and a continuing process of Americanization.

Following the Filipino diaspora across the Pacific, we compiled more materials on the movement of this counterhegemonic socialization and behavior to the United States through the Filipino diaspora of pastors, religious workers, and parishioners—many of whom came early on as agricultural workers and later on as professionals. Crossing to the United States also meant that we needed to extend our initial speculation. Essentially, this mass movement of people and culture from the Philippines constitutes a form of reverse coloni-zation, where American political, social, and economic institutions and spaces experience varying degrees of Filipinization. In this essay the scope of this counterhegemonic impetus is evaluated in more depth through a case study on the growth and development of fused transnational spiritual and political capital formation. The case illustrates how Filipino Catholic Churches use this to constructively engage local and national public policies that have negative effects to their community. We conclude the essay with some lessons from the case and challenges to the sustainability of this unique process.

REVISITING HEGEMONY AND THE CHURCH

There is a growing body of research about religion- and congregation-based political organizing in the United States (among others, see Dillon 2003; Harris 1998; Jacobsen 2001; Ramsay 1998; Wood 2002). The nature of the relationship between church and activism has always been controversial—philosophers have written about it for centuries, and policymakers continuously try to avoid stepping on matters of religion and faith. Nevertheless, the literature on lib-eration theology and faith-based organizing abounds in such discussion, espe-cially in the Latin American political context (see Cleary and Steigenga 2004; Martin 1990; Smith 1991; Swatos 1995; Torres 1992). The civil rights movement and the rise of African American churches also illustrated the power of con-gregation organizing versus both the hegemony of American society and the hegemony of the Christian Church (see Lincoln and Mamiya 2003; Sales 1994; Warren 2001). Although liberation theology and religious activism are popu-lar areas of social science research, especially among Filipino and Philippine studies scholars (among others, see Apilado 1999; Harris 2004; Kwantes 1998; Nadeau 2002; Wiegele 2005), there are only a few works that look at the dynam-ics and praxis within emerging Filipino diasporic communities (e.g., Aguilar-San Juan 1994; Võ 2004), particularly in their American religious experience (e.g., Filipinas Book Team 2003; San Buenaventura 1999). As noted above, our thoughts in this essay are grounded on the classic works of counterhegemonic theorists such as Marx, Weber, Freire, Gramsci, and Ileto.

Our research seeks to provide contemporary empirical evidence from the

Filipino diaspora on Karl Marx's famous controversial statement that religion is the opium of the people: "The foundation of irreligious criticism is: Man makes religion, religion does not make man . . . Religious suffering is, at one and the same time, the expression of real suffering and a protest against real suffering. Religion is the sigh of the oppressed creature, the heart of a heartless world, and the soul of soulless conditions. It is the opium of the people" (1844, 145). Eventually Marx influenced many critical thinkers, political activists, and oppressed workers, including Freire who in *Pedagogy of the Oppressed* strongly agreed with him that churches and their teachings definitely fostered a lack of critical consciousness to marginalized groups in civil society: "Preaching sin and hell, churches appeal to the fatalistic and frightened consciousness of the oppressed. The promise of heaven becomes a relief for their existential fatigue. The more the masses are frowned on in a culture of silence, the more they take refuge in churches that offer pie in the sky by and by. They see church as a womb where they can hide from an oppressive society . . . This directs their anger against the world instead of the social system that runs the world . . . leaving untouched their real source of oppression" (1970, 131–32). Marx, Friere, and the structuralist-Marxist school of thought argued that religion advanced a false consciousness in which people, particularly oppressed people, find solace and relief from their existential fatigue through praying to be saved in another world, the afterlife. They are comforted by this idea, which distracts them from confronting and addressing the material reality and injustices of the present world. In essence, they sought to destroy the hegemonic superstructure made of rich elites, including churches, who only enriched themselves using corrupted feudalistic and capitalistic substructures, by creating a new economic foundation grounded on the tenets of socialism. A counterhegemonic or proletariat revolution led by peasants, factory workers, and other oppressed groups was therefore necessary.

From another perspective, Max Weber in his famous work *The Protestant Ethic and the Spirit of Capitalism* provided a counterargument to the Marxists' views on the primacy of the economic base in relation to institutions, especially churches and their religious teachings. If the Catholic Church is corrupt and inadequate, then one should seek an alternative institution within civil society that would be compatible with a capitalist substructure—for example, Protestantism. Protestant teachings could offer the much needed counterhegemonic deliverance for the oppressed and downtrodden. There is no need to change the economic base to socialism. After all, within the Protestant ethos, "Man is dominated by the making of money, by acquisition as the ultimate purpose in his life. Economic acquisition is no longer subordinated to man as the means for the satisfaction of his material needs." (Weber 1958, 53).

Gramsci in *Selections from the Prison Notebooks* (1971) elaborated further on the importance of superstructures or civil society entities. As alluded to in Michael Omi and Howard Winant's book *Racial Formation in the United States* (1994), Gramsci is known to have popularized in-depth thinking on the notion of hegemony in civil society. Hegemony is defined as the conditions necessary in a given society for the achievement and consolidation of rule by a dominant group (Omi and Winant 1994, 67). In other words, it is the conditions that allow for oppression. Society as a whole is persuaded to agree upon an ideology that is favorable to the dominant class. This ideological dominance is achieved by the ruling class through a combination of consent and coercion. The relationship between the two is dialectical, and hegemony cannot exist without both aspects. At times, consent is the primary force at work, but at other times, when consent is not easily won, coercion or force becomes the primary means of maintaining hegemony. The dominant class must make compromises and forge alliances with its fundamentally opposing classes in order to gain and maintain political and ideological leadership. In turn, the subordinate classes are persuaded to hold values and beliefs that are consistent with the economic dominance of the ruling class. Although rule can be obtained by force, it cannot be secured and maintained, especially in modern society, without the element of consent. Gramsci conceived of consent as far more than merely the legitimization of authority. In his view, consent extended to the incorporation by the ruling group of many of the key interests of subordinated groups, often to the explicit disadvantage of the rulers themselves (Omi and Winant 1994, 63).

This is in keeping with Marx's hypothesis that the superstructures perpetuate and maintain the base. Gramsci built upon Marxist ideas by focusing in on civil society and demonstrating that it is the terrain upon which the proletariat must engage in counterhegemonic activities. He describes the "war of position," which is a very gradual process through which the people must undergo moral and ideological reform to eliminate the class bias of the existing hegemony. Ideology is the key to transforming society—it is what gives a common denominator to all members of a historical bloc. This is where civil society comes in—at the point where a "war of position" is a necessary first step in revolution to win the consent of the people. Without consent, power may be seized from the ruling class, but force would eventually be needed to maintain it.

But is it possible for a group in civil society to win a "war of position"? Could counterhegemony emerge from a hegemonic superstructure, like the church? According to the historical evidence presented by Ileto in *Pasyon and Revolution* (1979) this emergence does seem possible. Ileto's work is significant because it illustrates how Philippine civil society is able to position itself for counterhegemonic projects within the hegemonic superstructures of both Spanish and American church and state. Ileto's work echoes the counterhegemonic battles described in the vast literature on liberation theology. Ileto makes connections between a popular Filipino religious text *Casaysayan nang pasiong mahal ni Jesucristong panginoong natin* (Account of the Sacred Passion of our Lord Jesus Christ), or the *Pasyon*, and Filipino revolutionary movements against Spanish and American colonizers between 1840 and 1910. Although Spain imposed Catholicism upon the Philippines, Ileto argues that the Filipino people were able to create their own brand of Christianity from which a language of anticolonialism evolved in the late nineteenth century.

A common stereotype of Filipinos that Ileto references is that of a passive, deferential, and hospitable family-bound individual. Ileto warns against this stereotype by taking into consideration the many instances throughout history when popular movements threatened to overturn the ruling structures—counterhegemony at its best. His study examines the possibility that folk religious traditions, which usually promote passivity, actually "have latent meanings that can be revolutionary" (10). Ileto claims that the Filipino masses' familiarity with the *Pasyon's* revolutionary images allowed them a cultural preparedness to live out similar scenarios in response to adverse conditions under Spanish and American hegemony. He analyzes the text of the *Pasyon* and emphasizes its importance as a "mirror of the collective consciousness." Its narration of Christ's suffering, death, and resurrection conveys a transition from darkness to light, despair to hope, misery to salvation, and the like.

Analogously, in times of political and economic despair the masses were able to take action under the leadership of individuals who promised "deliverance from oppression." The themes of the *Pasyon* were parallel to the nation's transition from the dark age of Spanish exploitation and dominance to the bright age of freedom. Ileto illuminates themes within the *Pasyon* that do not encourage passivity and acceptance of the status quo under Spanish or American hegemony. One example is that although Filipinos regard family as the basic unit, the *Pasyon* teaches that a time comes when one must heed a higher calling, which may require separation from family. This is exemplified through the emphasis on the relationship of Jesus with his grieving mother and his explanation that he must leave her because he had a greater mission to fulfill—saving humankind. Further, the masses could identify with Christ in the

Pasyon—he is described there as a poor, seemingly harmless man of humble origins, and he and his followers exhibit timid, modest, and sad behavior. To the colonizers, this was an ideal image for keeping natives in a subservient state. Despite this lowly behavior on the surface, however, the "real" story brewing in the minds of the Filipinos was one of defiance to authority and commitment to an ideal.

In sum, Marx, Friere, Weber, and Gramsci establish through their philosophical rationalities, and Ileto via his Philippine empirical research, that it is quite possible for counterhegemony or social revolution to emerge from within hegemonic institutions such as the church and the state.

HEGEMONY AND COUNTERHEGEMONY FROM THE UNITED STATES TO THE PHILIPPINES AND BACK

Ileto's work is significant to our study of church, civil society, and counterhegemony because it shows how religious ideals have shaped the Filipino sociopolitical consciousness over centuries of colonization. Ileto's thoughts in *Pasyon and Revolution* go beyond the points raised by Marx, Friere, Weber, and Gramsci by asserting that the indigenous Filipino thinking shaped religion and the practice of religion, eventually inspiring counterhegemonic behavior against two powerful hegemonic colonizers. In this section, we move further up the dialectical chain by examining how Spain and the United States began a legacy of church hegemony that carried over to Filipino immigrants. But, later on, these same U.S.-based church institutions experience varying degrees of Filipinization, which new migrant faithful used successfully to "colonize" their former American colonizer. Filipinization within the hegemony of American church institutions has similar consequences to the decolonization" process within the hegemony of the American society described by Leny Strobel (2001), who highlights the importance of naming and telling Filipino stories; of opening the doors to Filipino memory and imagination; of using Filipino languages to express one's deepest values; of replacing colonial knowledge with Filipino cultural and historical knowledge; of building Filipino community institutions; and of integrating Filipino indigenous spirituality in one's lives.

State and Church Hegemony under Spain and the United States

Hegemony has shaped the consciousness of Filipinos since the time of Spanish colonization. The Catholic Church and its missionaries were used as tools for establishing and perpetuating Spain's hegemony over the Philippines. Although

Magellan is known as the first Spanish explorer to reach the Philippines, it was not until the Legazpi expedition reached the islands in 1565 that the Spanish were able to establish colonial rule. What made this expedition more success-ful than the first was that Spain used the combination of the sword (the army) and the cross (the Catholic Church) to subjugate the native people. The work of the Filipino historian Renato Constantino documents how Legazpi arrived armed with Augustinian missionaries, who were soon followed by Franciscans, Jesuits, and Dominicans. These missionaries became the pretext for Spanish colonialism in which the colonizers aimed to "bring the light of Christianity to the natives" (1998, 67). The Spanish Empire was deemed to be in the service of "both majesties": God and the King. This was the basis for the union of church and state, which became an important aspect of Spanish rule in the Philippines. The colonial power used the church to pacify the people and to manufacture the consent that was needed to establish hegemony over the islands. Through the research of Steffi San Buenaventura, we have an example of Gramsci's "consent and coercion." Buenaventura cites John Leddy Phelan's work in determining that while Mexico and Peru were colonized through the "violent conquest by sword . . . , the Spanish colonization of the Philippine archipelago was primarily a conquest-by-the-cross, whereby Spanish missionaries envisioned their work as a spiritual conquest of the minds and hearts of the natives, a supplement to, and the ultimate justification for, the military conquest" (2002, 36).

Over the course of three centuries, Catholic friars were sent from Spain to eradicate the natives' religious beliefs in "false" idolatry. Ultimately, the friars in the Philippines had more power than the king's administrators because they were larger in number and had more permanent positions. They were entrusted with so many civil duties that over time they were involved in every aspect of community life. The friars were in charge of schools, taxation, military enlist-ment, municipal budgets, health, police, and even the local dramas that were staged at the fiestas. Over time, they seized much of the ancestral lands from indigenous peoples.

> Taxes, tributes, exorbitant rents and arbitrary increases of the same, forced labor and personal services—all these intensified the hardships of natives who now had to give a good part of their products to their landlords. In addition, some administrators practiced other petty cruelties which caused much suffering among the people. In 1745, in the Jesuit ranches of Lian and Nasugbu, Batangas, for example, the people accused the religious not only of usurping the cultivated lands and the hills that belonged to them, but also of refusing to allow the tenants to get wood, rattan, and bamboo for their

personal use unless they paid the sums charged by the friars. (Constantino 1998, 72)

Though the most brutal forms of hegemonic activity linked to the church occurred during Spanish colonization, the activity is certainly not limited to that time. Dawn Mabalon documents how supportive Protestant leaders were of American imperialism. She quotes Reverend Wallace Radcliffe who stated, "I believe in imperialism because I believe in foreign missions . . . The peal of the trumpet rings out over the Pacific. The Church must go where America goes" (2003, 116). The United States won the Spanish American War in 1898 and bought the Philippines from Spain. But they also used their army to suppress any resistance to this purchase, and in so doing killed over 1.5 million people during the Philippine-American War. Mabalon writes that "missionaries even defended the atrocities committed by soldiers in the Philippines, calling Filipinas/os 'treacherous and barbaric' and 'defective in reasoning'" (117). During the period of American occupation, religion, particularly Protestantism, served as an important justification for acquisition and domination. President McKinley's theological justification for continuing occupation is well known. He claimed that the United States had the responsibility to "uplift and civilize and Christianize" Filipinos (24).

San Buenaventura asserts that "the coming of Protestantism ended the Roman Catholic monopoly on Christianity in the Philippines" (2002, 37). While the majority of Filipinos remained loyal to the Catholic Church, many chose to join the American religion, which San Buenaventura links to its representation of freedom and liberty. But despite what it was supposed to represent, Protestantism failed to give Filipinos the sense of self-determination that they desired because it denied them participation at higher levels of leadership within the church. Although there was a high level of enthusiasm from Filipinos, those who sought involvement were relegated to lower positions of leadership as "Filipino helpers."

While the Spanish relied heavily on the church to maintain power and dominance over the people, the Americans were able to utilize other forms of civil society, particularly education. A new band of hegemonic missionaries were deployed to the Philippines. The Thomasites, as they were called, arrived in the Philippines in 1902 and established an American educational system and English as the primary teaching language. Today, English is still taught alongside Tagalog and is the main language used for teaching in the Philippines. The educational system continues to manufacture consent, while U.S. military presence on the islands provides a formidable tool of coercion when needed.

Church Hegemony Follows Filipino Immigrants Stateside

American hegemony constitutes both the "push" and the "pull" factor for Filipino immigration to the United States. The influence of the American educational system, the presence of the U.S. military, and the domination of American corporations are major factors in the shaping of Filipino "common sense" in Philippine cities. American brandnames are far more desirable and well-known than are local ones. All of the famous Filipino actors and actresses seen on TV everyday are the ones who look the most "white," which demonstrates how the hundreds of years of both American and Spanish colonialism have affected Filipinos' perception of themselves. Strobel writes about how colonial civil society has shaped Filipino psychology: "The experience of colonization has prevented Filipinos from becoming too critical of American hegemony. Colonial mentality has made whiteness a reference point. Consequently, Filipinos are also often judged by outsiders and by each other on the basis of Western cultural standards, e.g. lazy, undisciplined, passive, obsequious, never on time. Even Senator Shahani endorsed a 1988 study of the Philippine character which blamed Philippine culture, rather than imperialism and colonialism, for the weaknesses of Philippine society" (2001, 38). It makes sense, then, that many Filipinos truly believe that life in the United States is superior to life in the Philippines. Strobel points out the historical determinants of Filipino immigration to the United States, such as the colonial relationship between the United States and the Philippines and the "global capitalist system that influences the movement of peoples from poor to the affluent countries" (36). The remnants of the colonial days along with "globalization" are some of the factors that keep the Philippines so poor, which then "pushes" Filipinos out. In turn, the glamorization of American whiteness and wealth "pull" into the United States those who are able to go there.

When the United States opened its doors in 1965, many Filipinos saw the event as their golden opportunity to chase the "American dream." Many Filipinos who were just graduating from college or their professional schools were trained in the American-style schools where they learned that the United States is the land of freedom and opportunity. The common perception is that by living in the United States they would be able to provide their family with the more-superior education offered in there and thus have more opportunities to succeed and to prosper. As Strobel writes: "From 1965 to 1976, more than 250,000 Filipinos entered the United States. This group was composed predominantly of Filipinos from the urban middle class; most were college graduates, professionals, and highly skilled workers. Identified as the 'brain drain' generation, they are products of an American-patterned education in the Philippines. Their world view, beliefs, and values have been shaped by this educational system and the hegemony of American culture in the Philippines. This has resulted in reverse ethnocentricism—the preference for things foreign or American, or in Filipino slang, 'stateside'" (2001, 37). The U.S. census for 2000 states that there are more than 320,000 Filipinos in the San Francisco Bay Area alone. But the reality of "freedom" and "opportunity" is less than perfect, as can be seen throughout the history of Filipino presence in the United States. During early immigration when Filipino men were hired as agricultural workers, they faced many forms of discrimination. There were antimiscegenation laws and the infamous sign on the door of many shops and restaurants that read, "No Filipinos allowed."

In the first part of the twentieth century, Stockton, California, with its extensive agricultural industry, had the highest number of Filipino residents outside of the Philippines. Mabalon explores the ways in which churches in Stockton remained conservative in the earlier part of the century by siding with the more dominant forces of society rather than with the disenfranchised Filipino community of the time. Until 1962, Stockton was part of the massive Catholic Archdiocese of San Francisco. Mabalon's work is very revealing in terms of how Filipinos were perceived by the Catholic Church. Her primary sources show that anti-Filipino racism was one of the factors that pushed Filipinos away from the Church. In fact, she gives undeniable evidence that the Catholic Church supported the 1935 Filipino Repatriation Act in order to address what was called the "Filipino problem." Mabalon cites documents from San Francisco Archbishop John J. Mitty who stated, "I wish to emphasize my conviction, based upon Filipino sentiment that repatriation will go far in solving the difficult Filipino problem." Although this conviction was supposedly based upon Filipino sentiment, "only 2082 Filipinas/os out of a population of more than 100,000 in Hawaii and the US mainland volunteered to be repatriated." In later letters in which he was pushed to address the "Filipino problem," Mitty drafted statements that blamed the Filipinos who "want white collar jobs and flashy clothes." He believed that their difficulty stemmed from the "instability of character of the Filipinos" (2003, 63). He ultimately removed those statements from his final letters to the papal representative in the United States, but the drafts that Mabalon was able to obtain reveal Archbishop Mitty's negative attitude toward Filipinos.

Mabalon's work shows the unwillingness of the Catholic Church in Stockton to address problems facing the Filipino community, despite the large population of Catholic Filipinos. As Father McGough of Saint Mary's Church in Stockton stated: "I regret I have nothing to offer in the way of a solution for these people." Another priest at Saint Mary's stated that Filipinos are already "lost to the church." Mabalon's argument takes off from where Fred Cordova left off in his *Filipinos: Forgotten Asian Americans* (1983), in which he devotes a chapter to discussing the Church and religion in the Filipino American community. He points out that although 90 percent of Filipino Americans were thought to be Catholic, the Catholic Church did not make much of an effort to respond to the needs of their community. Coming from a Philippine society rooted in Catholicism for more than three hundred and fifty years, Filipino Americans often were denied access to sacramental marriages involving Catholic Filipino men and Catholic Caucasian women; to Christian burials involving indigents; to Sunday masses involving individual Filipinos in all-white parishes; to Catholic education involving poor brown children; and to confession involving those not able to speak English.

San Buenaventura has studied the religious experiences of Filipino American communities in Hawaii and in Southern California, and her extensive research uncovers the role that non-Catholic religion played in perpetuating hegemony. In her words, migrant workers arrived in "a plantation system that encouraged the Christianization of its labor force. Because of the Protestant origins of the sugar industry . . . , the creation of ethnic missions within the Congregational and Methodist Churches was a natural step in inculcating Christian teachings and virtues to the 'Asiatic' plantation workers and in instructing them in American democratic principles through the process of Americanization. To them, it was also necessary to nurture Christian religion among the converted workers so as to ensure the continued civilizing effect of Christianity on their outlook and conduct . . . to prevent having a 'Filipino social problem' . . . Protestant missionaries worked on the assumption that the Filipinos needed special Christian moral guidance" (2003, 158).

Whether it was an unwillingness to accept Filipino immigrants or a desire to control their behavior, religious institutions in the United States have a long history of continuing the legacy of oppression within the church, as is documented by Filipino American scholars such as Strobel, Mabalon, Cordova, and San Buenaventura. They confirm the preconditions for counterhegemony laid out by Marx, Friere, Weber, Gramsci, and Ileto. However, the Filipino American researchers allude to a unique transnational counterhegemony, which we examine below.

COUNTERHEGEMONY COMES TO AMERICA: A CASE STUDY
FROM THE FILIPINO DIASPORA

The counterhegemonic consciousness arising from the subtexts of Spain and America's Christian teachings led to the emergence of spin-off groups from Catholic and Protestant churches. Beyond what Ileto described as Pasyon prayer sessions inspiring Filipinos to move from mass apathy to militant activism versus Spain in 1840 and against the United States in 1910 were the similar hegemonic actions by Filipino Catholic priests. The Filipino priests Mariano Gomez, Jose Burgos, and Jacinto Zamora were martyred in public on the recommendation of their Spanish church superiors for sharing their "progressive views" with their parishioners, particularly the native Filipino population. This only fueled the anger of Filipino nationalists like Jose Rizal, who penned two novels exposing blatant church-state corruption and abuses. Disgruntled, Rizal eventually left the Catholic Church and became a Mason. One Filipino Catholic Church pastor, Gregorio Aglipayan, established a breakaway group called the Philippine Independent Church (or Aglipayans), which was refused recognition by the Vatican. In another case a lay member disillusioned by both Catholic and Protestant churches founded his own progressive church called the Global Church of Christ during the American occupation of the Philippines.[2]

In the decades after the annexation of the Philippines by the United States, Filipino migrant Catholics, Aglipayans, Iglesias, El Shaddais, Baptists, Methodists, Seventh-Day Adventists, Episcopalians, Congregationalists, Presbyterians, Lutherans, Mormons, and Jehovah's Witnesses came en masse to California not only to continue to spread the faith and Filipinize American spiritual spaces but also to mainstream into state-society relations various forms and degrees of Filipino-inspired counterhegemonic engagement. There was some evidence of counterhegemonic activities among the early immigrants despite the strong American church-state hegemony discussed earlier. In both the small towns and large cities in California, the many Masonic lodges (e.g., Caballeros de Dimasalang) venerating the legacies of Filipino heroes like Jose Rizal, Andres Bonifacio, and Emilio Aguinaldo were clear evidence of counterhegemonic thinking and action among early immigrants. Around the same time that liberation theology began to flourish—during the 1950s and 1960s—Stockton's church people changed their attitude toward Filipinos. Mabalon cites instances of counterhegemony through her work, in which she finds that the Franciscan priests (a religious order that is dedicated to serving the poor) focused their resources on the Filipino and Mexican migrant workers in the area. In fact, Father Alan McCoy, a liberal Franciscan priest, along with Larry Itliong and

Dolores Huerta worked to form the Agricultural Workers Organizing Committee (AWOC). The AWOC was responsible for the historic Delano Grape Strike, and it would later unite with Cesar Chavez to create the United Farm Workers Union, but few writers mention that it has roots in the church.

The contemporary case study below demonstrates in depth these varying forms and degrees. We organized the case study to delve into the following key factors and conditions that allowed for counterhegemony to grow and prosper: compelling political issues, leadership structure, socioeconomics of the congregation, and parish interest groups.

San Patricio's Catholic Church

Less than a week after the September 11, 2001, attack on the United States, Filipino community activists along with the leaders of San Patricio's Church in San Francisco, California, organized a prayer vigil.[3] It was the first ethnic community in the Bay Area to take a collective stand on progressive issues after the tragedy and it was hosted by San Patricio's and strongly endorsed by its Filipino pastor, Monsignor Ferdinand Santos.[4] The call was for the maintenance of peace, a stop to the anti-Arab and Muslim American violence, and for the United States to take a step back and examine its foreign policy as the possible motivation for the attacks. Many speakers also named U.S. imperialism as the reason why other nations would want to attack the country.

Within this Filipino "plaza," with San Patricio at the center, is the Filipino Educational Center, where Filipino youths attend after-school programs held in Tagalog. The Mint Mall, which is two blocks away from San Patricio's, houses a Filipino bookstore, restaurant, Filipino businesses, and nonprofit organizations. Also only two blocks away is Bindlestiff Studios, the epicenter of radical Filipino performing arts in San Francisco, which gives local actors, actresses, poets, spoken word artists, and musicians a place to develop and showcase their craft. Filipino student organizations and Filipino American studies in the universities and in one high school in the Bay Area help students in the process that Strobel has labeled cultural identity formation. The Church, although it is often overlooked, is a site where some of the most powerful cultural rearticulation and counterhegemonic struggles take place.

In the Bay Area the Catholic Church is the only place where Filipino migrants can gather and feel immediately at home. In a world of unfamiliarity, the Church is familiar, comfortable, and empowering. Furthermore, it provides services to new immigrants that help them to acculturate. In some Bay Area churches, masses are offered in Tagalog and confessions are heard in several Filipino languages. One of the female congregation members of San Patricio's commented on how the church gives her a sense of belonging: "Every time I attend mass I can see that all the altar servers, the priests, the lay ministers, the lectors . . . and also the music ministry, they are all Filipinos and that makes me proud because the other people who attend the mass who are not Filipinos will see how close we are, how big the community is." Many of the Filipino traditions of celebrating holidays are practiced in Bay Area churches. For example, as mentioned in earlier chapters, San Patricio's celebrates a nine-day early-morning novena mass called Simbang Gabi (or Misa de Gallo), which is a treasured form of celebrating Christmas for Filipinos. The children of parishioners often sing church songs in Tagalog and go to catechism classes where their parents feel that they learn Filipino values such as galang (respect for elders). Filipino congregants feel that the Church is a way to feel like part of the Filipino community.

The redevelopment of San Francisco into a cosmopolitan city has caused serious displacement to its Filipino residents and workers who take refuge in pockets of the city with low-income housing units. The tearing down of the International Hotel in what was then a ten-block Manilatown symbolized a victory for commercial developers but it also galvanized Filipinos and their community allies into political action. Affordable housing became an issue for those who came to the central valley of California in the early 1900s as rural agricultural workers and wanted to retire and be with fellow Filipinos in San Francisco. The demolition of the International Hotel was followed by a suspicious fire that gutted the Delta Hotel, another popular low-income residence for Filipinos.

The City of San Francisco's redevelopment of the South of Market area affected not only residential areas but also a number of old commercial buildings on Sixth Street, which included the home of Bindlestiff Studios. Artists and musicians lobbied long and hard at city hall but eventually they had to move to a new location. Hitting close to the heart of Filipino spirituality was the decision by the Archdiocese of San Francisco to close Saint Joseph's Church and the adjoining Catholic school, which predominantly served Filipino parishioners and students. The Filipino pastor Monsignor Ferdinand Santos was transferred to San Patricio's Church, however, and the loyal Filipino congregation followed.

The neighborhoods where most of San Patricio's parishioners live are some of the poorest and depressed areas of San Francisco. The South of Market and Tenderloin are areas where petty crime, drug sales and drug use, homelessness, youth gang violence, and vandalism are all part of daily life. Nevertheless, new immigrants, especially Filipinos, continue to move to these areas because of the accessibility to downtown jobs (and eliminating the cost of commuting), the availability of low-rent apartments, and the close proximity to Filipino shops

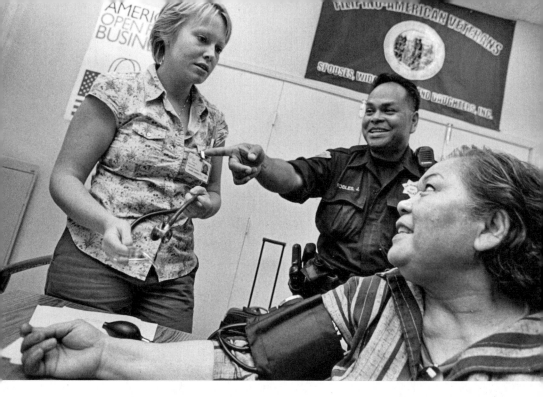

and services—including grocery stores, barber shops, tailors, restaurants, and, in the case of South of Market, religious life. It is easier to earn and save money in these neighborhoods. However, the social trade-offs to many Filipino families for these economic benefits are increased drug use among teens, school drop-out rates, teen pregnancies, cases of depression in youth and seniors, and incidences of HIV infection. Additionally, the test scores at the local elementary school are some of the lowest in the county.

In the early 1990s the long-awaited naturalization of Filipino veterans of the Second World War brought another wave of new migrants to San Patricio's. Because of the long Congressional delay in acting on this matter, most of the veterans who arrived were already in their sixties and seventies and had no medical benefits. Their main source of support was Social Security income, which they had supplemented with odd jobs as busboys, doormen, security guards, garbage collectors, school janitors, newspaper deliverymen, and handymen at the hotels, businesses, schools, and restaurants in the area.

Just like all Catholic churches, the leadership structure at San Patricio's is hierarchical, with the top position of pastor followed by the associate pastors, the deacon, and the parish staff. Two Filipino nuns from the Religious of the Virgin Mary, an order established in the Philippines, are staff members in charge of the parish's finances and their religious educational program. In spite of the standard hierarchy, however, the behavior and actions of leaders and followers exhibit an organizational culture that is Filipino in its nature. Monsignor Ferdinand Santos, the charismatic pastor, is the ultimate authority within the parish. However, over the years, as demands for his guidance and counsel have increased, he has learned to delegate much of the work to his trusted and loyal associates and the staff, and there is much leeway in how they handle affairs. Owing to the demands placed on the pastor (who is probably the most popular person not just in the parish but in the entire Filipino American community), he cannot help but have the other Filipino priests shoulder some of the work, especially in dealings with the parish's many organizations.

Lay parish activities are coordinated by the parish council, which meets weekly on Tuesday evenings. The twenty-one different parish organizations send representatives to the council, with the exception of the four youth groups, which have their separate council. The parish council acts as both a consultative and deliberative body in that it coordinates the parish's social life. Decisions on activities and related issues are then relayed back to the organizations, which usually have the responsibility of implementing them. As for the youth, the youth council serves as an umbrella entity encompassing the youth choir, the altar servers, and the youth chapter of the Legion of Mary. As a result, the youth organizations frequently share the same members.

In the minds of many of his parishioners, Monsignor Santos represents a form of political, economic, and social patron (in the patron-client arrangement). In the Philippines, patrons are usually prominent citizens (e.g., the mayor or the local lawyer). Where such a structure is missing, as in the United States, the locus of power is the parish, and thus it is the monsignor who is able to influence decisions, bestow favors, and "bless" community events and most importantly actions. The monsignor's leadership in the parish and in the larger community is seen through the respect that is given for his blessings. His blessings can be explicit or implicit, social or political, formal or informal, direct or indirect. For instance, the monsignor gave his explicit blessings to the September 11, 2001, activities and sits on the board of directors of the Veterans Equity Center. He has also given more implicit blessings to mass actions for the International Hotel and Bindlestiff Studios, to more social services for families, and to the fight for low-income housing. He tries his best to be at all social and political events, or at least to send some of his loyal associate pastors or lay assistants. Even when he is absent, as long as people know that the monsignor is their supporter or that he has an awareness of the issue, then they feel blessed. Thus, although he is never in front of counterhegemonic exercises like marching to city hall and rallying on Market Street this does not mean that he is not supporting the events or that he has not informed his parishioners of them.

Community leaders know that they have the monsignor's blessings when they engage in mass actions to address burning issues.

Most of the time parishioners seek the monsignor's help with spiritual matters, but there are times when an individual asks for his assistance in regard to everyday matters — such as housing problems or immigration status. The monsignor intimated to us in an interview that he is not very comfortable with this kind of solicitation, but he is obliged to help however he can. This is how clergy are trained in the Philippines, and this is what is expected of them by parishioners. Most of the time, the monsignor refers such requests to government and nongovernmental agencies who are better equipped to help — notably, Catholic Charities, Westbay, the South of Market Area Teen Center, the Mayor's Office of Neighborhood Services, and the Board of Supervisor's Office. People view the monsignor as a benefactor, and they are willing to follow him as long as he is able to dispense favors. The individuals he helps are also able to use him as a reference and obtain better access to services, especially from Filipino agencies. In a way, as a patron in the United States, Monsignor Santos is able to create a more subtle but effective form of counterhegemony. Hence, this new and more activist role is quite different from the traditional notion of a "patron." It is more similar to the role of the legendary Zorro — who held the roles of haciendero and masked revolutionary leader.

The primary ethnicity in San Patricio's is Filipino. It was predominantly Irish until about the 1970s, but with the demographic shift in the surrounding neighborhoods came the change in the congregation's makeup, along with the parish's merger with Saint Joseph's. Because Filipino parishioners are notorious for not formally registering at the church, accurate population figures are lacking. As such, the term "parishioners" is used loosely here; "parish regulars" would probably be a more accurate description. In terms of age, the congregation is fairly old. A good number of the individuals who take part in daily parish activities are in the fifty-to-seventy age bracket. There is a significant youth movement within the parish (consisting mainly of families), but the older members form the bulk of the population of the parish. Further, women seem to dominate the congregation; in many of the parish events observed, women frequently outnumber men three to one.

The South of Market and Tenderloin areas are dominated by apartment buildings and single resident occupancy hotels, and single-family homes are rare. The congregation reflects the neighborhoods' socioeconomic status, with many of the older congregants living in low-cost housing provided by the parish and the community, such as the Alexis House and the San Lorenzo Ruiz Center. There are exceptions, though, as many parishioners come from communities outside San Francisco. The type of employment by parish members is varied and tends to follow age patterns; the older parishioners are either retired or unemployed, while the younger parishioners have steady employment, either part time or full time. There are parishioners with professional jobs, though not in management—many work close by as office workers in the Financial District or in retail establishments close to the church in the Union Square area. Many of the older parishioners, especially males, immigrated to the United States to press for veterans benefits that were denied to them by the United States government despite their service during the Second World War.

Generally speaking, the younger members of the parish seem to be more affluent than the older parishioners. Given the different waves of Filipino migration, the younger parishioners are usually from the "brain drain" generation and their children. As for the veterans and their spouses, they could be classified as an extension of the original itinerant Filipino field workers of the 1910s to the 1940s, though the veterans came much later. In terms of their present socioeconomic situation and their location, the veterans have much more in common with the field workers than with their "brain drain" contemporaries. Encounters between the older and younger generations of parishioners resemble those in the Philippines. The older generation has the run of the parish while the younger members have mostly a secondary role. While youth members participate in liturgy (e.g., as the altar servers or in the young adult choir), adult members regularly perform the duties of ushers, lectors, and Eucharistic ministers. The average household income, however, is still much lower than other Catholic parishes.

The parish organizations are a good indication of the relative status of older and younger parishioners. Of the twenty-five different parish organizations, only four are geared toward the younger parishioners. However, the presence of independent youth organizations is significant in that it addresses the question of legacy. Given the advanced age of many of the parishioners, the youth represent the future lay leaders of the parish, and their involvement in parish activities seems like a preparation for this future assumption of leadership roles. There are connections between the older groups and the younger groups—the younger members of the adult organizations serve as informal mentors to the youth parishioners, often identifying each other as fictive kin: the mentors act more as older siblings to the youth instead of having a more formal relationship.

Generational dynamics also exist among adult parishioners, with younger adults showing deference to older adults. Though most call each other either "brother" or "sister," there are times when individuals are addressed as either

"*kuya*" (older brother) or "*ate*" (older sister), usually in more informal settings. This is another example of the prevalence of fictive kin relationships that are brought over from the Philippines, much like the relationship between the youth parishioners and their mentors. The regionalism that usually characterizes Filipino settings seems much more muted in the parish environment. It can be attributed to the homogenizing effects of religious faith—that is, having something as significant as faith diminishes the effects of other differentiating factors, such as regional origins. In addition, the need for ethnic solidarity in a foreign country can also be a determining factor. As such, San Patricio's is a center for the creation of a new Filipino identity rooted in the American experience, and the old regionalisms of the past are now used mostly as material for jokes.

Politically speaking, San Patricio's parishioners live in two worlds. Not only are domestic politics and issues important, but what goes on in the Philippines is also followed with interest. The easy availability of both Filipino-language and Filipino-oriented media as well as the frequent visits of priests from the Philippines help keep the parish informed of social and political developments in the home country.

Parishioners are informed about political issues inside the church through sermons by the priests. In addition, Filipino establishments in the South of Market area town plaza frequently feature racks holding free Filipino newspapers, and Filipino-operated newsstands—especially around downtown and in the South of Market area—sell Filipino newspapers and magazines. The Filipino Channel (TFC) is a cable channel operated by the Philippines-based media company ABS-CBN, and it is readily available on cable networks in Daly City and in other areas with a significant Filipino population. For people without access to cable television, two local channels (KTSF and KMTP) have Filipino-language programming.

In terms of activism and engaging in counterhegemonic activities, some choose to be more involved than others in terms of joining their fellow parishioners on the street protests. Many choose to sympathize through prayers and financial contributions. Their strong Catholic faith helps determine their stance on morality, but they are conscious of where they stand in the United States. Parishioners seem to reflect the view of the majority of Filipino immigrant families—namely, a mix of social conservatism (usually around the areas of personal and sexual issues) and political progressiveness. Many of the parishioners are conscious of the Filipino veterans' struggle for equity, especially in light of those in poverty, and they are also conscious of Filipino Americans' low position on the political ladder. Like many other Filipino Americans, parishioners in San Patricio's Church view the American dream as not only personal prosperity but also political and social validation—which is why the election of a Filipino as mayor of Daly City in November 2001 was of major importance among the local Filipino American community.

Church leaders believe that their primary concern is the spiritual welfare of their parishioners. Hence, their counterhegemonic engagement is in the form of partnerships between the parish and community-based organizations. Apart from daily masses, other religious rituals, and other devotional activities, the parish sponsors religious education programs for children as well as the program Rite of Christian Initiation for Adults for new converts to Catholicism or adult candidates for confirmation. In relation to the parish's liturgical functions, the church also has three different choirs (adult, youth, and the Latin choir that sings at the weekly Latin mass), an organization for the lay ministers (ushers, lectors, and Eucharistic ministers), and another organization for the youth altar servers.

And of course there are the parish organizations. As mentioned above, coordinating the social activities between these organizations (of which there are twenty-five) is the Parish Council. Apart from the eight chapters of the Legion of Mary, the organizations deal with liturgical functions (as described above) and are related to a particular order or devotion (Charismatic Prayer Group, Divine Mercy, Holy Name Society, Lay Carmelite, Sacred Heart Devotion, Saint

Vincent de Paul Society), or a particular saint (Confraternity of Saint Joseph, Mother Ignacia del Espiritu Santo, Sodality of the Blessed Virgin Mary), or to young people (as in the youth parish council).

Historically, many of the social activities for these organizations—such as parties and meetings—have been held in the main parish hall. However, with the recent renovation of the church, social activities have been scaled back and the larger events have either been cancelled or held outside the church. Although some activities—such as the block rosaries popular among the Marian organizations, a devotion where an image of the Virgin is passed among the members' homes for a certain period and rosaries are said during the intervals—traditionally occur outside the church, for organizations that were more dependent on the parish's facilities, the displacement has been problematic. It is only within the past two years that the social life that revolved around San Patricio's precincts began to revive. Before and after the formal meetings and prayer sessions, and during informal parties and functions, are times to discuss community issues.

To address the issues, many of San Patricio's church leaders (including Monsignor Santos) and parishioners are actively involved in neighborhood-based organizations through their Social Justice Committee and its linkages with the West Bay Filipino Multi-service Center, the South of Market Teen Center, the South of Market Health Center, the South of Market Job Training Center, Arkipelago Bookstore, Filipinas Restaurant, and the Filipino Veteran's Equity Center. Many parishioners are board members of neighborhood organizations, or are organizers, staff members, volunteers, financial contributors, and proprietors. As a Filipino institution San Patricio's has close linkages with these civil society groups. Further, these community-based organizations and San Patricio's often play the role of mutual advocate for Filipinos. They have successfully lobbied the U.S. Congress to provide recognition to Filipino veterans of the Second World War by grants of American citizenship. These organizations have also leveraged funds from the City and County of San Francisco for Filipino youths and their families. They have lobbied for resolutions to be passed by the San Francisco Immigrant Rights Commission and the San Francisco Board of Supervisors. They have also lobbied for the successful appointment of qualified Filipinos (some who are San Patricio's parishioners) to city, county, and state-level commissions, boards, and other government posts. San Patricio's leaders and members have also supported letters and petitions brought to them by these community-based groups addressed to San Francisco mayors, California governors, California congressional delegations, and even U.S. presidents. Counterhegemony at San Patricio's is reflected in the symbiotic relationship between the church and these civil society organizations: the church helps new arrivals maintain an important socio-spiritual connection to the Philippines while the neighborhood organizations help them make a successful start in their new home in the United States.

CONCLUSIONS

Based on our extensive archival and ethnographic research, we have attempted to provide conceptual, historical, and empirical evidence to the emergence of counterhegemonic activities within the Filipino American religious experience in San Francisco.

Conceptually and historically, Marx, Weber, Friere, and Gramsci provided us with a philosophical framework to examine counterhegemony through the church. However, Ileto introduced us to a more culturally adapted analytical lens by pointing out that Filipino counterhegemony against Spanish and American colonizers was inspired by the subtexts of religious teachings used for hegemonic means. We extended further Ileto's Philippine assertion and Strobel, Mabalon, San Buenaventura, and Cordova's Filipino American documentations by arguing that given the proper conditions (i.e., compelling issues, leadership structure, socioeconomics of the congregation, and parish interest groups) Philippine church-inspired counterhegemony could be transferred and utilized effectively by Filipino immigrants to challenge hegemonic structures in American society. Ironically, Filipino immigrant counterhegemonic activities versus the American church and state were inspired by the same Spanish and American Catholic and Protestant teachings. Starting with indigenous Masonic lodges, then Catholic and Protestant churches, the diaspora in the sixties and seventies also brought many pastors and congregations into independent Filipino churches like the Global Church of Christ and the Aglipayan Church. Many American spaces and congregations were Filipinized with the decline in traditional church memberships. For instance, the all-American Lutheran Church in Pacifica, California, was taken over by the predominantly Filipino Seventh-Day Adventist congregation in the early 1970s.

Our participant observation at Catholic churches in the San Francisco Bay Area allowed us to study this sociopolitical phenomenon in more depth, and we found the following conditions to be critical to counterhegemony. First, counterhegemony begins with compelling national and local political issues. These problems are close to the hearts and minds of the immigrant congregation and also to their larger ethnic community. Some of their members might be directly affected, but many issues are those of the larger Filipino community in California. San Patricio's congregation had a plethora of concerns, many of which drew them outside the confines of their churches. Additionally, the political environment of tolerance, radicalism, and acceptance in progressive San Francisco is more conducive and open to counterhegemony than in most cities in the United States.

Second, charismatic religious and lay leadership are critical to identifying and acting on the compelling issues. Leaders must be comfortable using the many years of political organizing experience developed in the Philippines. The form of leadership can be an explicit, hands-on style as is the case at San Patricio's Church. Church leaders can be in front of a march protesting injustices to members of the community or they can simply send "signals of consent" from behind the altar during the homily in a mass.

Third, the socioeconomic background of the congregation is a critical element to effective counterhegemony. However, parish members' current class standing (whether middle or lower class) and their region of origin in the Philippines are less important to counterhegemonic activities than are their Filipino political socializations and willingness to combine spiritual energy and mass action to address congregational and community issues.

Finally, parish interest groups are key determinants of successful mass action and linking with community groups. The San Patricio's case illustrated the significance of engaged parish interest groups like the Rite of Christian Initiation of Adults and the Social Justice Committee. Parish interest groups are important for winning small battles in city hall and commission hearings as well as big battles such as that with the U.S. Congress for veterans' benefits. The groups are also the key to continuing struggles against chronic health problems and social issues like HIV infection, drug addiction, homelessness, and health insurance.

Now that we have learned about some of the conditions that contribute to counterhegemonic activity in two Filipino American churches, we would like to draw out the possible implications and lessons for the Filipino American community as well as for the Church. There are a number of strengths and challenges that we would like to elaborate upon in the hopes that they will inspire future research as well as collaboration between the Church and the community.

First, there has been an abundant supply of compelling issues—notably, internal or external threats—especially among immigrant communities. Our case study provides good reason for the community to look increasingly to the church for support on issues that affect them. The case study shows that there is a large base of "people power" to draw upon when the community is faced with threats. And since religion has such a central role among Filipino migrants' lives, it may make sense for other churches that are heavily populated by Filipinos to take up issues of social justice that affect the Filipino American community. The challenge to this issue-driven activism is in building a lasting counterhegemonic movement that sees beyond the issues to more permanent social change. While there are always issues that call for social action, they may not always be as universally compelling as we have seen in our two case studies. Ultimately, this should not result in a lull in the church's activity around social justice and counterhegemony. The movement should be maintained even when there are no immediate issues, and education in social justice should continue so that this movement can be more strategic than "fighting fires" or responding to issues as they arise.

Second, leaders come and go. The challenge for the Filipino American leaders that have been so pivotal in the activism of these churches is to foster enough leadership in the parishes to continue to build upon what they have started. Leaders like Monsignor Santos have been critical in the Filipino community's success in addressing social justice, but what happens when they are appointed to different churches or retire? It is absolutely essential that while these progressive leaders are in place they are able to build a movement that is strong enough to survive even when another leader comes in. San Patricio's is on the right track by fostering leadership through the parish interest groups that have many active members to ensure some continuity after these charismatic priests and nuns move on to new places.

Third, we learned that it is not just the less-affluent working class that has the motivation to stand up against hegemonic forces. In fact, it is sometimes the more stable middle class that has the time and energy to do the work. The community needs to start paying more attention to this group rather than indulging in the tendency to overlook them as too conservative to fight for change.

Finally, what if parish organizations choose to focus only on traditional Filipino devotions, venerations, and prayer groups? What if community groups refuse to partner with the parish church? What if the archdiocese decides to regulate all counterhegemonic activities, just as it discouraged some Filipino socioreligious practices such as holding masses outside of the church? Overcoming these barriers is the key not just to sustaining the gains from counterhegemony but also replicating and spreading the positive lessons across Filipino churches and for the empowerment of other immigrant communities.

Coming full circle, although Marx said that religion is the "opium of the masses," he also said that it is the "sigh of the oppressed creature, the heart of a heartless world and the soul of soulless conditions." Religion inspires followers to have faith that they can do something to fight for their collective heart and soul as the world becomes more heartless and soulless in this era of globalization, racism, and oppression. Applying dialectics to the church as a hegemon allows for a new, more involved Filipino American church with endless potential for counterhegemonic projects and fighting for more lasting equitable conditions in this society. In the end "man makes religion," so it will be women and men who make religion into what it needs to be to address oppression and heartlessness.

NOTES

1. Unless otherwise noted, all such quotations are from the interviews conducted by the authors during their fieldwork in the San Francisco Bay Area, 2001–2003.
2. "Global Church of Christ" is a pseudonym used to protect anonymity.
3. San Patricio's Church is a pseudonym used to protect anonymity.
4. Ferdinand Santos is a pseudonym used to protect anonymity.

Appendix A

Research Questions

The incorporation of new immigrants into U.S. society forces us to ponder what it means to be a member of this society. To address this question, non-immigrant America must enter a dialogue with those who have more recently arrived and who are making decisions as to the level, type, and intensity of civic and social incorporation into U.S. society they wish to pursue. If voting, for example, is a mark of civic and political incorporation, are the large majority of Euro-Americans who don't vote somehow not fully incorporated? According to Robert Bellah, dramatic declines in American associational life over the past several decades have led to a "crisis of civic membership" (1999, 20). In what ways do the religious institutions of new immigrant communities illuminate the possible meanings of civic incorporation? How do religious groups foster civic and political incorporation for new immigrants as well as maintain culture identity and ties to countries of origin? The overarching theme of religion, immigration, and incorporation into civil society can be illuminated by exploring the following questions:

1. How do immigrant religious groups encourage and support or reject participation in the political, civic, and associational life of San Francisco and of the larger U.S. political and civic scene?

   — Do religious communities and organizations encourage naturalization, voting, and participation in local and national political forums?
   — Are ethnic religious groups, or those serving ethnic and minority communities, active in political movements and issues? Do these groups educate their congregants on issues relevant for their immigrant group and for society at large? Are immigrants who are religiously affiliated more or less politically involved than secular immigrants?

— Are voluntary associations common in U.S. society perceived to be relevant to recent immigrants? Do religious groups encourage the participation of new immigrants in voluntary associations? What sorts of voluntary associations and informal networks do religious groups encourage immigrants to form and join?

2. In what ways do religious congregations foster the transnational character of new immigration? Does dual citizenship impede incorporation into San Francisco and the United States?

— What expectations do new immigrants have concerning participation in civil society prior to coming to the United States? What is religion's role in changing or supporting these expectations?

— Are any of the religious groups truly transnational? Do religious leaders consider themselves to have congregants in both San Francisco and the country of origin? Is dual citizenship (when possible) promoted? How involved are immigrants in politics in their countries of origin? How informed do immigrants keep of social and political events in their country of origin and in the United States? Are immigrant religious leaders and congregants affected by, and active in, political issues and movements in their countries of origin?

— Do religious groups send financial assistance to congregations, associations, or individuals in their countries of origin? What other sorts of ties or linkages to sending countries are encouraged by religious groups? For example, do religious groups disseminate information about sending countries?

— Are immigrants who are religiously affiliated more or less likely to maintain ties to their countries of origin compared to secular immigrants?

— Do civic and societal values and attitudes change differentially in the process of acculturation as a function of religiosity and of personal involvement in religious communities?

3. What social services do religious congregations provide for new immigrants?

— Are religious organizations direct providers of basic needs such as housing, jobs, food, clothing, legal services, and medical and mental health assistance? Do religious organizations and communities pro-

vide emotional and psychological support to new immigrants, and is this an important factor in conversions?
— Do religious leaders and congregations actively pressure public agencies to provide needed services to new immigrants? Do religious groups provide assistance in negotiating public social services for new immigrants?
— Are religious groups more likely to promote informal networks of assistance and self-help groups or to encourage members' use of public assistance?
— Are certain styles of participation in economic life favored or promoted by immigrant congregations? Are occupational choices and work attitudes shaped by religious practice and belief?
— Are active members of religious organizations more likely to receive assistance in meeting social and personal needs than are secular immigrants?

4. Do religious congregations actively attempt to preserve the culture of new immigrants?

— How important is native language use for the religious congregation? In what language are worship services conducted? How important is it for children to be fluent in their parents' native language? Does the religious congregation offer classes in language and culture?
— Are religious festivals and holy days honored the same as those celebrated in the country of origin?
— What cultural values are especially important for this immigrant group? Do religious groups promote the cultural values of immigrants' country of origin or affirm U.S. cultural values?
— Are religiously affiliated recent immigrants more likely to preserve language and culture than are secular immigrants?

5. What is the relationship between immigrant family relations, religion, and incorporation?

— Do gender and family roles change as immigrants become incorporated? Do religious groups try to influence gender relations? Child-rearing practices?
— How are intergenerational conflicts and differences in intergenerational relations mediated by religiosity and religious communities?

— Do religious values ever exacerbate intergenerational conflicts? How does the role of the religious congregation differ depending on one's generational location?

— Do religiously affiliated immigrants experience more or less intergenerational conflict than secular immigrants?

In addressing these research questions, we understand that incorporation is not a unidimensional process. Many recent immigrants operate on multiple fields or dimensions of incorporation—to San Francisco, to the United States, to an altered status in their countries of origin, as well as to a new immigrant community. And, as Ana Maria Diaz-Stevens and Anthony Stevens-Arroyo (1998, 40) note, the receiving community is not a static force. In cities with large ethnic populations, such as San Francisco, a process of "transculturation" or biculturalism takes place in which there is a mutual assimilation between immigrant group and host city. In recognizing that behavioral acculturation is a complex process, we utilize a number of indicators as evidence of behavioral incorporation and personal biculturalism. Borrowing from Milton Gordon's assimilation variables as well as from more recent literature on acculturation, we use current instruments that are psychometrically strong (e.g., Marin and Gamba's Biculturalism Scale; Liu's Acculturation index; Alba and Nee's new assimilation theories) and develop new culturally appropriate and psychometrically strong indices to measure social and political incorporation (Gordon 1964; Marin and Gamba 1996; Alba and Nee 1999). Among the indices used are proficiency in English; level and fluency of original language maintenance; ethnic and national self identification, including citizenship status; participation in U.S.-based political activities, including voting, running for office, and membership in political groups and movements; access to and preference for foreign, U.S. mainstream, and ethnic media; participation in voluntary associations, including large-scale entrance into clubs and institutions of the host society; intermarriage; ethnic group preferences for peers and friends; preferences for change of cultural patterns to those of host society, including celebration of host society holidays; and economic participation, including access to a range of occupational categories and upward mobility in employment. In addition, we analyze the level of adherence and personal significance given to basic cultural values as individuals undergo the process of acculturation and the role played by religiosity and religious affiliation and involvement in changing or supporting those values. Again our assumption, reflecting current research in the field of acculturation, is that this process is bidimensional in nature (with one dimension being "U.S. mainstream" and the other reflecting the culture of origin). Throughout, our assumption is that religion, both in terms of personal adherence as well as community involvement, serves as a moderating variable in all of the aspects of incorporation noted above. What this study allows us to further analyze is not only the extent of that mediation but also how the effects may vary by generation, gender, length of residence in the United States, religiosity, and other relevant variables.

Appendix B

Family Member Questionnaire of
the USF Religion and Immigration Project

FAMILY QUESTIONNAIRE (ADULT)

Thank you for agreeing to meet with me. I am going to ask you a lot of questions. I will tape record you because it makes it easier for me to remember what you have said. Please feel free to tell me anything that comes to your mind. I won't put your name on this and no one will know who made these comments except you and me.

So now, tell me:

BACKGROUND INFORMATION

Where were you born?
How long have you lived in the United States?
Did other family members come to the United States with you?
Do you have other family members still living in [country of origin]?
How long have you lived in San Francisco?
Where else have you lived?
You are now a member of [their religious group]. How long have you been a
    member or attended [their religious group]?
    PROBE [To probe is to ask additional questions related to the central
    question, i.e., Why did you join?]

I. POLITICAL AND CIVIC INCORPORATION

A. Now, please tell me, during the time that you have lived in the United
   States, has anyone told you that you should become a United States
   citizen?

PROBE [Who? What did they say? What reasons did they give you?]

B. If you are a U.S. citizen, has anyone suggested that you vote in elections held in the United States?
PROBE [Who? What did they say? What reasons did they give you?]

C. Does your country allow you to remain a citizen and also to become a U.S. citizen?

D. Are you a citizen in the United States and in [country of origin]?

E. How about voting in elections in [country of origin]? Has anyone told you that you should vote in those elections?
PROBE [Who? What did they say? What reasons did they give? Were there specific things they wanted you to vote about? Please describe.]

Now, let's talk about YOUR CHURCH/TEMPLE in the United States:

F. In the last 12 months, has anyone in your church/temple suggested that you should vote *in* U.S. elections?
PROBE [Who? What did they say?]

G. In the last 12 months, has anyone in your church/temple suggested that you vote in elections in [country of origin]?
PROBE [Who? What did they say?]

H. In the last 12 months, has anyone in your church/temple talked to you or said something in church about the political situation in the United States?
PROBE [Who? What did they say? What political situation concerned them?]

I. In the last 12 months, has anyone in your church/temple talked to you or said anything in church or at meetings regarding the social problems of the United States?
PROBE [Who? What did they say? What social problems concerned them?]

J. In the last 12 months, has anyone in your church/temple asked you to attend a political demonstration or a protest?
PROBE [Who? What was it about?]

K. In the last 12 months, have you participated in demonstrations or protests with members of your church/temple?

PROBE [Which ones? Who organized the activity? What motivated you to participate?]

L. How do you think your pastor/priest feels about you becoming a U.S. citizen?

M. Has anyone talked about a club or organization in your church/temple?
PROBE [Who? Which church/temple club or organization? What did they say about this club/organization? Did they ask you to join this club/organization?]

N. Do you belong to any club or association that is related to your church/temple?
PROBE [Which one? What do they do?]

O. Has your pastor/priest suggested or recommended that you join a club or association?
PROBE [What did he/she say? What reasons did he/she give?]

II. TRANSNATIONAL MIGRATION AND RELIGION

A. What is the nationality of most members of your church/temple?

B. What is the nationality of the leader of your church/temple?

C. Do you have family members still living in [country of origin]?
PROBE [Who?]

D. Do you return to [country of origin] to visit family and/or friends?
PROBE [How often? In the last 12 months how many times have you visited (country of origin)?]

E. Does your church/temple encourage you to visit, call, or write to family and friends in [country of origin]?
PROBE [What do they say? What reasons do they give?]

F. Did you belong to a [church or temple] in your home country?
PROBE [What was the name of the church/temple? Where was it located?]
[If "YES"—proceed to question G below.]
[If "NO"—proceed to question H]

G. Before coming to the United States, did your church/temple in [country of origin] ask you to participate in political activities? Social activities?
PROBE [What activities? What did they say? What reasons did they give?]

H. Before to coming to the United States, did you expect to become part of political or social activities in the United States?
PROBE [What activities?]

I. Does your church/temple in the United States ask you or encourage you to participate in political or social activities?
PROBE [Which activities? What is said? What reasons are given?]

J. Do you keep informed about political and social issues in [country of origin]?
PROBE [Which political and social issues? How do you keep informed?]

K. In the last 12 months, has anyone in your church/temple talked to you or said something in church about the political situation in [country of origin]?
PROBE [Who? What did they say?]

L. Are you involved in politics in [country of origin]?
PROBE [Please describe your involvement.]

M. Is the leader of your church/temple involved in the politics and/or social issues in [his/her country of origin]?
PROBE [How is your leader involved?]

N. In the last 12 months, has anyone in your church/temple suggested ways of being involved in the politics of [country of origin]?
PROBE [What did they say?]

O. Does your church/temple have a sister or partner church in [country of origin]?
PROBE   [If "NO"—proceed to question Q]
          [If "YES"—   (1) What is the name of the church/temple?
                       (2) Where is it located?
                       [***proceed to question P below***]

P. Do members of your church/temple in the United States visit this sister or partner church/temple?
PROBE [Who visits? How often and for what types of events?]

Q. Do members of the church/temple in [country of origin] visit your church/temple here in the United States?
PROBE [Who visits? How often and for what events? Have they visited in the last 12 months?]

R. Does your church/temple here in the United States send money to churches/temples, groups, or individuals in your home country?
PROBE   [If "YES": (1) To whom? For what?
(2) Have they sent money in the last 12 months?
- To whom? For what?]

III. SOCIAL SERVICES FOR NEW IMMIGRANTS

First I want you to think of PEOPLE WHO JUST ARRIVED *in the United States.*

A. Does your church/temple provide help with finding housing for people who have just arrived in the United States?
PROBE [What type of help do they offer? How do they offer this help?]

B. Does your church/temple help with finding jobs for new arrivals?
PROBE [What type of help do they offer? How do they offer this help?]

C. Does your church/temple provide food to new arrivals?
PROBE [To whom? How do they offer this help?]

D. Does your church/temple provide legal services for new arrivals?
PROBE [To whom? What kind of legal help?]

E. Does your church/temple provide medical help for people who have just arrived in the United States?
PROBE [To whom? What kinds of medical help?]

F. Does your church/temple provide counseling services for new migrants?
PROBE [To whom? What kind of services?]

G. Are there other important services that your church/temple offers to people who have just arrived in the United States?
PROBE [Can you please describe these services? How are they provided?]

Now I would like you to think of PEOPLE WHO HAVE LIVED IN THE UNITED STATES FOR MORE THAN ONE YEAR.

H. Does your church/temple provide help with finding housing?
PROBE [What type of help do they offer? How do they offer this help?]

I.   Does your church/temple help with finding a job?
     PROBE [What type of help do they offer? How do they offer this help?]

J.   Does your church/temple provide food?
     PROBE [To whom? How do they offer this help?]

K.   Does your church/temple provide legal services?
     PROBE [To whom? What kind of legal help?]

L.   Does your church/temple provide medical help for people?
     PROBE [To whom? What kinds of medical help?]

M.   Does your church/temple provide counseling services?
     PROBE [To whom? What kind of services?]

N.   Are there other important services that your church/temple provides to
     people who have just arrived in the United States?
     PROBE [Can you please describe these services? How are they provided?]

O.   In the last twelve months, has anyone at your church/temple given you
     information about social services in San Francisco/San Jose?
     PROBE [What information did they give you? What reasons did they
     give?]

P.   Does your church/temple work with the government or other groups in
     San Francisco/San Jose to get housing, jobs, medical help, or other ser-
     vices?
     PROBE [Which groups? What do they do together?]

Q.   Do members of your church/temple help each other with housing, jobs,
     or other needs?
     PROBE [Can you describe these needs? How do they help each other?]

R.   Can you please describe the types of services that you have received from
     your church/temple?
     PROBE [How long have you been using these services? How have they
     helped you and your family?]

IV. CULTURAL PRESERVATION

A.   Have you experienced any language difficulties in the United States?
     PROBE [Can you describe two different situations in which you experi-

enced language difficulties? Where were you and what happened? What were you feeling? How did you deal with these situations?]

B. What do you think are the hardest things about not speaking English and living in the United States?

C. Has [church/temple] helped you overcome some of these difficulties?

D. What language is used during services at your church or temple?

E. Is the language used at services in your church or temple important to you?
   PROBE [Please explain why.]

F. Do your children speak [Spanish, Tagolog, Vietnamese, Mandarin, Cantonese]?

G. How important is it to you that your children speak your language?

H. Does your church/temple offer educational programs or classes in your language?
   PROBE [Please describe these classes.]

I. Does your church/temple offer classes in the traditions and culture of [country of origin]?
   PROBE [Please describe these classes.]

J. Does your church/temple celebrate the same religious festivals/holy days that you had celebrated in [country of origin]?
   PROBE [Which religious festivals / holy days?]

K. What values from [country of origin] are most important to you?
   PROBE [Why are these values important to you? How are they expressed?]

L. Does your church/temple promote the values from [country of origin]?
   PROBE [Which values? How do they promote these values?]

M. What do you think are the most important American values in the United States?
   PROBE [Why are they important?]

N. Does your church/temple promote U.S. values?
   PROBE [Which values? How do they promote these values?]

V. FAMILY AND GENDER RELATIONS

A. Think about how men and women in your generation treat each other. Do you think it's different from how men and women from your parents' generation treated each other?
PROBE [How is it different? Why do you think this is?]

B. Have you noticed any differences in how men and women from [country of origin] treat each other now that they live in the United States?
PROBE [What are these differences? In your opinion, why do they treat each other differently now that they are in the United States?]

C. Have you noticed any differences in how children who move here from [country of origin] treat their parents now that they live in the United States?
PROBE [How do they treat their parents differently? In your opinion, why do they treat their parents differently now that they are in the United States?

D. Do children who are raised in the United States behave differently than children who are raised in [country of origin]?
PROBE [How do they behave differently? In your opinion, why do they behave differently?].

E. Does your church/temple tell children how to behave towards their parents?
PROBE [What does your church /temple tell them? How does your church / temple tell them?]

F. Does your church/temple tell you how to raise your children?
PROBE [What does your church / temple tell you? How does it tell you?]

G. Does your church/temple talk about how husbands and wives should treat each other?
PROBE [What is said? How is this taught?]

H. Does your church/temple tell men how they should treat women?
PROBE [What do they say? What reasons are given?]

I. What tasks or activities did men and women perform in your church/ temple in [country of origin]?

J. What tasks or activities do men and women perform in your church/ temple in the United States?

References

Adler, R. H. 2004. *Yucatecans in Dallas, Texas: Breaching the border, bridging the distance*. Boston: Pearson.

Agamben, G. 1998. *Homo Sacer: Sovereign power and bare life*. Trans. Daniel Heller-Roazen. Stanford, Calif.: Stanford University Press.

Agoncillo, T. 1990. *History of the Filipino people*. Quezon City, Philippines: Garotech.

Aguilar-San Juan, K., ed. 1994. *The state of Asian America: Activism and resistance in the 1990s*. Boston: South End Press.

Alarcón, R. 1999. La integración de los ingenieros y científicos mexicanos en Sillicon Valley. In G. Mummerd, ed., *Fronteras fragmentadas*. Zamora, Mexico: El Colegio de Michoacán.

Almaguer, T. 1993. Chicano men: A cartography of homosexual identity and behavior. In H. Abelove, M. A. Barale, and D. M. Halperin, eds., *The lesbian and gay studies reader*. New York: Routledge.

Almaria, C. R., ed. 1993. *Evangelization in Asia: Proceedings of the Asian Congress on Evangelization*. Quezon City, Philippines: Claretian Publications.

Alonso, A. M. 1995. *Thread of blood: Colonialism, revolution, and gender on Mexico's northern frontier*. Tucson: University of Arizona Press.

Altman, D. 1993 [1973]. *Homosexual: Oppression and liberation*. New York: New York University Press.

——. 1982. *The homosexualization of America, the Americanization of the homosexual*. New York: St. Martin's Press.

——. 2001. *Global sex*. Chicago: University of Chicago Press.

Alvarez, R. 1987. *Familia: Migration and adaptation in Baja and Alta California, 1800–1975*. Berkeley: University of California Press.

——. 1995. The Mexican-U.S. border: The making of an anthropology of borderlands. *Annual Review of Anthropology* 24: 447–70.

Anderson, B. 1991. *The imagined community: Reflections on the origins and spread of nationalism*. New York: Verso.

————. 2002. *Imagined communities: Reflections on the origin and spread of nationalism*. Rev. ed. London: Verso.

Anzaldúa, G. 1987. *Borderlands: La frontera*. Berkeley, Calif.: Aunt Lute.

————. 1990. *Making face, making soul / Haciendo caras: Creative and critical perspectives by women of color*. Berkeley, Calif: Aunt Lute.

Apilado, M. C. 1999. *Revolutionary spirituality: A study of the Protestant role in the American colonial rule of the Philippines, 1898–1928*. Quezon City, Philippines: New Day Publishers.

Appadurai, A. 1990. Disjuncture and difference in the global cultural economy. In R. Featherstone, ed., *Global culture: Nationalism, globalization and modernity*. Newbury Park, Calif.: Sage.

————. 1996. *Modernity at large: Cultural dimensions of globalization*. Minneapolis: University of Minnesota Press.

Araujo, S., A. Peña, M. R. Barbosa, S. Falcón, S. Galván, A. García, and C. O. Uribe. 2002. El culto a la Santa Muerte: Un estudio descriptivo. University of London, http://udelondres.com.

Arendt, H. 1958. *The origins of totalitarianism*. Cleveland, Ohio: Meridian Books.

Argüelles, L., and B. R. Rich. 1985. Homosexuality, homophobia, and revolution: Notes toward an understanding of the lesbian and gay male experience, part 2. *Signs* 11.1: 120–36.

Aridjis, H. 2003. *Santa muerte: Sexteto del amor, las mujeres, los perros y la muerte*. Mexico City: Alfaguara.

Asad, T. n.d. What do human rights do? An anthropological enquiry. *Theory and Event*, http://muse.jhu.edu.

Atkinson, P., and M. Hammersley. 1994. Ethnography and participant observation. In N. K. Denzin and Y. S. Lincoln, eds., *Handbook of qualitative research*. Thousand Oaks, Calif.: Sage Publications.

Balfour, I., and E. Cadava. 2004. The claims of human rights: An introduction. *South Atlantic Quarterly* 103.2/3: 278–96.

Balls Organista, P., K. C. Organista, and K. Kurasaki. 2003. The relationship between acculturation and ethnic minority mental health. In K. M. Chun, P. Balls Organista, and G. Marin, eds., *Acculturation: Advances in theory, measurement, and applied research*. Washington, D.C.: American Psychological Association.

Bandura, A. 1977. *Social learning theory*. Englewood Cliffs, N.J.: Prentice-Hall.

Banlaoi, R. 2002. The role of Philippine-American relations in the global campaign against terrorism: Implications for regional security. *Contemporary Southeast Asia* 24: 24–36.

Baron, S., J. Field, and T. Schuller, eds. 2000. *Social capital: Critical perspectives*. Oxford: Oxford University Press.

Barta, P. 1998. Lambskin borders: An argument for the abolition of the United States' exclusion of HIV-positive immigrants. *Georgetown Immigration Law Review* 12 (winter): 323–59.

Basch, L., N. Schiller, and C. Szanton-Blanc. 1995. *Nations unbound: Transnational projects, postcolonial predicaments, and deterritorialized nation-states*. Amsterdam: Gordon and Breach.

Bauman, Z. 2000. *Globalization: The human consequences*. Cambridge: Polity Press.

Baviera, A., and L. Yu-Jose. 1998. *Philippine external relations: A centennial vista*. Manila: Foreign Service Institute.

Beckford, J. 1998. Religious movements and globalization. In R. Cohen and S. M. Rai, eds., *Global social movements*. London: Athlone Press.

Bello, W. 1983. Springboards for intervention, instruments for nuclear war. *Southeast Asia Chronicle* 89: 45–71.

Berlant, L. 1997. *The queen of America goes to Washington City*. Durham, N.C.: Duke University Press.

Berry, J. W. 1980. Acculturation as varieties of adaptation. In A. Padilla, ed., *Acculturation: Theory, models, and findings*. Boulder, Colo.: Westview.

———. 2003. Conceptual approaches to acculturation. In K. M. Chun, P. Balls Organista, and G. Marin, eds., *Acculturation: Advances in theory, measurement, and applied research*. Washington, D.C.: American Psychological Association.

———. 2006. Acculturation: A conceptual overview. In M. H. Bornstein and L. R. Cote, eds., *Acculturation and parent-child relationships: Measurement and development*. Mahwah, N.J.: Lawrence Erlbaum Associates.

Berryman, P. 1999. Churches as winners and losers in the network society. *Journal of Interamerican Studies and World Affairs* 41.4: 21–34.

Bérube, A. 1990. *Coming out under fire: The history of gay men and women in World War II*. New York: Free Press.

Blackwood, E., and S. E. Wieringa, eds. 1999. *Female desires: Transgender practices across cultures*. New York: Columbia University Press.

Blumhofer, E. L., R. P. Spitler, and G. Wacker, eds. 1999. *Pentecostal currents in American Protestantism*. Urbana: University of Illinois Press.

Bockting, W. O., B. E. Robinson, and B. R. S. Rosser. 1998. Transgender HIV prevention: A qualitative needs assessment. *AIDS Care* 10.4: 505–26.

Boellstorff, T., and W. L. Leap, eds. 2004. *Speaking in queer tongues: Globalization and gay language*. Urbana: University of Illinois Press.

Bokenkamp, S. R. 1997. *Early Daoist scriptures*. Berkeley: University of California Press.

Bonus, R. 2000. *Locating Filipino Americans: Ethnicity and the cultural politics of space*. Philadelphia: Temple University Press.

Bornstein, M. H., and L. R. Cote, eds. 2006. *Acculturation and parent-child relationships: Measurement and development*. Mahwah, N.J.: Lawrence Erlbaum Associates.

Bosco, J., and P. Ho. 1999. *Temples of the Empress of Heaven*. Hong Kong: Oxford University Press.

Boston Globe. 2003. *Betrayal: The crisis in the Catholic Church.* New York: Little, Brown.

Boucher, J., and T. Boucher. 1994. *An introduction to the Catholic charismatic renewal.* Ann Arbor, Mich.: Servant Publications.

Boudewijnse, B., A. Droogers, and F. Kamsteeg, eds. 1998. *More than opium: An anthropological approach to Latin American and Caribbean Pentecostal praxis.* Lanham, Md.: Scarecrow Press.

Bourdieu, P. 1986. The forms of capital. In J. Richardson, ed., *Handbook of theory and research for the sociology of education.* New York: Greenwood Press.

Boyd, N. A. 2003. *Wide open town: A history of queer San Francisco to 1965.* Berkeley: University of California Press.

Bracamonte y Sosa, P. 2004. *Encuesta sobre marginalidad, pobreza e identidad del pueblomaya.* Mérida, Mexico: Empimaya.

Bramadat, P. 2000. *The church on the world's turf: An evangelical Christian group at a secular university.* Oxford: Oxford University Press.

Brands, H. W. 1992. *Bound to empire: The United States and the Philippines.* New York: Oxford University Press.

Brennan, D. 2004. What's love got to do with it? Transnational desires and sex tourism in the Dominican Republic. Durham, N.C.: Duke University Press.

Breyer, C. A. 1993. Religious liberty in law and practice: Vietnamese home temples in California and the First Amendment. *Journal of Church and State* 35 (spring): 367–401.

Brislin, R. 2000. *Understanding culture's influence on behavior.* 2nd ed. Fort Worth, Tex.: Harcourt, Brace, Jovanovich.

Brook, J., C. Carlsson, and N. J. Peters, eds. 1998. *Reclaiming San Francisco: History, politics, and culture.* San Francisco: City Lights Books.

Brown, S. 1999. Democracy and sexual difference: The lesbian and gay movement in Argentina. In B. D. Adam, J. W. Duyvendak, and A. Krouwel, eds. *Global emergence of gay and lesbian politics: National imprints of a worldwide movement.* Philadelphia: Temple University Press.

Brown, W. 2004. The most we can hope for: Human rights and the politics of fatalism. *South Atlantic Quarterly* 103.2/3: 451–63.

Bruner, E. M. 1986. Experience and its expressions. In V. W. Turner and E. M. Bruner, eds., *The anthropology of experience.* Urbana: University of Illinois Press.

Brusco, E. 1995. *The reformation of machismo: Evangelical conversion and gender in Colombia.* Austin: University of Texas Press.

Buddhist Text Translation Society. 1995a. *In memory of the Venerable Master Hsu Yun,* vol. 1. Burlingame, Calif.: Buddhist Text Translation Society.

———. 1995b. *In memory of the Venerable Master Hsu Yun,* vol. 2. Burlingame, Calif.: Buddhist Text Translation Society.

Buraway, M., A. Burton, A. Ferguson, K. J. Fox, J. Gamson, N. Gartrell, L. Hurst,

C. Kurzman, L. Salzinger, J. Schiffman, and S. Ui. 1991. *Ethnography unbound: Power and resistance in the modern metropolis*. Berkeley: University of California Press.

Burdick, J. 1993. *Looking for God in Brazil: The progressive Catholic Church in urban Brazil's religious arena*. Berkeley: University of California Press.

———. 1998. *Blessed Anastacia: Women, race and popular Christianity in Brazil*. New York: Routledge.

Burns, J. M. 2000. *San Francisco: A history of the Archdiocese of San Francisco*, vols. 1–3. Paris: Girold Gresswiller.

Burns, J. M., E. Skerrett, and J. M. White, eds. 2000. *Keeping faith: European and Asian Catholic immigrants*. Maryknoll, N.Y.: Orbis.

Bustamonte, J. A. 1983. Maquiladora: A new face of international capitalism on Mexico's northern frontier. In J. Nash and P. Fernandez-Kelly, eds., *Women, men and the international division of labor*. Albany: State University Press of New York.

Butler, J. 1990. *Gender trouble: Feminism and the subversion of identity*. New York: Routledge.

———. 1993. *Bodies that matter: On the discursive limits of "sex."* New York: Routledge.

———. 2004. *Undoing gender*. New York: Routledge.

Cabezas, A. L. 1999. Women's work is never done: Sex tourism in Sosua, the Dominican Republic. In K. Kempadoo, ed., *Sun, sex and gold: Tourism and sex work in the Caribbean*. Lanham, Md.: Rowman and Littlefield.

Calderón, H., and J. D. Saldivar. 1991. *Criticism in the borderlands: Studies in Chicano literature, culture, and ideology*. Durham, N.C.: Duke University Press.

California Department of Industrial Relations. 1930. *Facts about Filipino immigration into California*. San Francisco: Department of Industrial Relations.

Canaday, M. 2003. Who is a homosexual? The consolidation of sexual identities in mid-twentieth-century American immigration law. *Law and Social Inquiry* (spring): 351–85.

Canclini, N. G. 1995. *Hybrid cultures: Strategies for entering and leaving modernity*. Minneapolis: University of Minnesota Press.

Canlas, M. C. 2002. *SOMA Pilipinas studies 2000*. San Francisco: Arkipelago.

Cantú, L. 1999. Border crossings: Mexican men and the sexuality of migration. Ph.D. dissertation, University of California, Irvine.

———. 2002. De ambiente: Queer tourism and the shifting boundaries of Mexican male sexualities. *GLQ: A Journal of Lesbian and Gay Studies* 8:139–66.

Carnes, T., and F. Yang, eds. 2004. *Asian American religions: The making and remaking of borders and boundaries*. New York: New York University Press.

Carrier, J. 1992. Cultural factors affecting urban Mexican male homosexual behavior. In W. Dynes and S. Donaldson, eds., *Ethnographic studies of homosexuality*. New York: Garland.

Carrillo, H. 2002. *The night is young: Sexuality in Mexico in the time of AIDS*. Chicago: University of Chicago Press.

———. 2004. Sexual migration, cross-cultural sexual encounters, and sexual health. *Sexuality Research and Social Policy: Journal of NSRC* 1.3: 58–70.

Castañeda, Q. 2004. We are not indigenous: An introduction to the Maya identity of Yucatán. *Journal of Latin American Anthropology* 9.1: 36–63.

Castellanos, L. La Santa de los desperados. *La Jornada*, May 9, 2004, http://www .jornada.unam.mx.

Castells, M. 2000. *The rise of the network society*. Malden, U.K.: Blackwell Publishing.

Castillo, N. M. 2001. *Ethnic diversity in parishes: Archdiocese of San Francisco*. San Francisco: Archdiocese of San Francisco.

Cesar, W. 2001. From Babel to Pentecost: A social-historical-theological study of the growth of Pentecostalism. In A. Corten and R. Marshall-Feratani, eds., *Between Babel and Pentecost: Transnational Pentecostalism in Africa and Latin America*. Bloomington: Indiana University Press.

Chace, P. G. 1992. Returning thanks: Chinese rites in an American community. Ph.D. dissertation, University of California, Riverside.

Chant, S. ed. 1992. *Gender and migration in developing countries*. London: Belhaven Press.

Chao, R. K. 1994. Beyond parental control and authoritarian parenting style: Understanding Chinese parenting through the cultural notion of training. *Child Development* 65: 1111–119.

Chauncey, G. 1995. *Gay New York: Gender, urban culture, and the making of the gay male world, 1890–1940*. New York: Basic Books.

Chavez, L. R. 1985. Households, migration and labor market participation: The adaptation of Mexicans to life in the United Status. *Urban Anthropology* 14: 301–46.

———. 1986. Immigration and health care: A political economy perspective. *Human Organization* 45: 344–52.

———. 1989. Migrants and settlers: A comparison of undocumented Mexicans and Central Americans in the United States. *Frontera Norte* 1: 49–75.

———. 1994. The power of the imagined community: The settlement of undocumented Mexicans and Central Americans in the United States. *American Anthropologist* 96.1: 52–73.

Chavez, L. R., E. Flores, and M. Lopez-Garza. 1990. Here today, gone tomorrow? Undocumented settlers and immigration reform. *Human Organization* 45: 193–205.

Chávez, Monsignor G. R. 2002. Church speaks out on immigrant rights. *Salvanet* (September/October): 3.

Chen, Y. 2000. *Chinese San Francisco, 1850–1943: A transpacific community*. Stanford, Calif.: Stanford University Press.

Chesla, C. 1995. Hermeneutic phenomenology: An approach to understanding families. *Journal of Family Nursing* 1.1: 68–78.

Chow, R. 1993. I's you, and no me: Domination and "Othering" in theorizing the "Third World." In L. S. Kauffman, ed., *American feminist thought at century's end: A reader*. Oxford: Blackwell Publishing.

Choy, C. 2003. *Empire of care: Nursing and migration in Filipino American history*. Durham, N.C.: Duke University Press.

Choy, P. 1984. San Francisco Chinatown historic development. In G. Lin, ed., *The Chinese American experience: Papers from the Second National Conference on Chinese American Studies*. San Francisco: Chinese Historical Society of America; Chinese Culture Foundation of San Francisco.

Chun, K. M. 2006. Conceptual and measurement issues in family acculturation research. In M. H. Bornstein and L. R. Cote, eds., *Acculturation and parent-child relationships: Measurement and development*. Mahwah, N.J.: Lawrence Erlbaum Associates.

Chun, K. M. and P. D. Akutsu. 2003. Acculturation in ethnic minority families. In K. M. Chun, P. Balls Organista, and G. Marin, eds., *Acculturation: Advances in theory, measurement, and applied research*. Washington, D.C.: American Psychological Association.

Chun, K. M., P. Balls Organista, and G. Marin. 2003. *Acculturation: Advances in theory, measurement, and applied research*. Washington, D.C.: American Psychological Association.

Chun, K. M., K. L. Eastman, G. C. S. Wang, and S. Sue. 1998. Psychopathology. In L. C. Lee and N. W. S. Zane, eds., *Handbook of Asian American psychology*. Thousand Oaks, Calif.: Sage Publications.

Cleary, E., and T. Steigenga. 2004. *Resurgent voices in Latin America: Indigenous peoples, political mobilization, and religious change*. New Brunswick, N.J.: Rutgers University Press.

Clements-Nolle, K., R. Marx, R. Guzman, and M. Katz. 2001. HIV prevalence, risk behaviors, health care use, and mental health status of transgender persons: Implications of public health intervention. *American Journal of Public Health* 91.6: 915–21.

Cockburn, C. 1998. The Women's movement: Boundary-crossing on terrains of conflict. In R. Cohen and S. M. Rai, eds., *Global social movements*. London: Athlone Press.

Coleman, J. 1988. Social capital in the creation of human capital. *American Journal of Sociology* 94: 85–120.

———. 1990. *Foundations of social theory*. Cambridge, Mass.: Harvard University Press.

Collinson, H. 1990. *Women and revolution in Nicaragua*. London: Zed Books.

Constantino, R. 1989. *Recalling the Philippine-American war*. Quezon City, Philippines: Education Forum.

————. 1998. *The Philippines: A past revisited.* Manila: Renato Constantino.

Cordova, F. 1983. *Filipinos: Forgotten Asian Americans.* Dubuque, Iowa: Kendall/ Hunt.

Corten, A. 1997. The growth of the literature on Afro-American, Latin American and African Pentecostalism. *Journal of Contemporary Religion* 12.3: 311–34.

————. 1999. *Pentecostalism in Brazil: Emotion of the poor and theological romanticism.* New York: St. Martin's Press.

Corten, A., and R. Marshall-Feratani, eds. 2001. *Between Babel and Pentecost: Transnational Pentecostalism in Africa and Latin America.* Bloomington: Indiana University Press.

Cox, H. 1995. *Fire from Heaven: The rise of Pentecostal spirituality and the reshaping of religion in the twenty-first century.* Reading, Mass.; Addison Wesley.

Cruz, J. M. 1998. Los factores posibiladores de la violencia en El Salvador. In R. Papadoulus, ed., *Violencia en una sociedad en transición.* San Salvador, El Salvador: Programa de las Naciones Unidas para el Desarrollo.

Csordas, T. 1997. *Language, charisma, and community: The ritual life of a religious movement.* Berkeley: University of California Press.

Dame, L. 1968. *Maya mission.* Garden City, N.Y.: Doubleday.

Dank, B. M. 1973. *The development of a homosexual identity: Antecedents and consequences.* Ph.D. dissertation, University of Wisconsin.

Das Dores Campos Machado, M. 1998. Family, sexuality and family planning: A comparative study of Pentecostals and Charismatic Catholics in Rio de Janeiro. In B. Boudewijnse, A. Droogers, and F. Kamsteeg, eds., *More than opium: An anthropological approach to Latin American and Caribbean Pentecostal praxis.* Lanham, Md.: Scarecrow Press.

Dasgupta, P., and I. Serageldin, eds. 2000. *Social capital: A multifaceted perspective.* Washington, D.C.: World Bank.

Davis, M. 2001. *Magical urbanisms: Latinos reinvent the U.S. big city.* London: Verso.

De Genova, N., and A. Y. Ramos-Zavas. 2003. *Latino crossings: Mexicans, Puerto Ricans and the politics of race and citizenship.* New York: Routledge.

Delmendo, S. 1998. The star entangled banner: Commemorating one hundred years of Philippine independence and Philippine-American relations. *Journal of Asian American Studies* 13: 67–79.

D'Emilio, J. 1983. Capitalism and gay identity. In H. Abelove, M. A. Barale, and D. M. Halperin, eds., *The lesbian and gay studies reader.* New York Routledge.

Dillon, M., ed. 2003. *Handbook of the sociology of religion.* Cambridge: Cambridge University Press.

Do, H. D. 1999. *The Vietnamese Americans.* Westport, Conn.: Greenwood Press.

Donayre, M. 2002. Bi-national couples: Alliance of fear. *Gay and Lesbian Review Worldwide* 9.2: 25.

Donham, D. 1998. Freeing South Africa: The "modernization" of male-male sexuality in Soweto. *Cultural Anthropology* 13.1: 3–21.

Doran, C. F. 1971. *The politics of assimilation: Hegemony and its aftermath*. Baltimore: Johns Hopkins Press.

Drogus, C. 1997. Private power or public power: Pentecostalism, base communities and gender. In E. I. Cleary and H. W. Stewart-Gambino, eds., *Power, politics and Pentecostals in Latin America*. Boulder, Colo.: Westview.

Droogers, A. 1994. The normalization of religious experience: Healing, prophecy, dreams, and visions. In K. Poewe, ed., *Charismatic Christianity as a global culture*. Columbia: University of South Carolina Press.

————. 1998. Paradoxical views on a paradoxical religion: Models for the explanation of Pentecostal expansion in Brazil and Chile. In B. Boudewijnse, A. Droogers, and F. Kamsteeg, eds., *More than opium: An anthropological approach to Latin American and Caribbean Pentecostal praxis*. Lanham, Md.: Scarecrow Press.

————. 2001. Globalization and Pentecostal success. In A. Corten and R. Marshall Feratani, eds., *Between Babel and Pentecost: Transnational Pentecostalism in Africa and Latin America*. Bloomington: Indiana University Press.

Durand, J. 1996. *El norte es como el mar: Entrevistas a trabajadores migrantes en Estados Unidos*. Guadalajara: Universidad de Guadalajara.

————. 2001. El programa bracero. En la forma, un convenio bilateral: En el fondo un convenio obrero-patronal. Paper presented at Mesa Redonda Binacional: Programas de Trabajadores Temporales Mexico-Estados Unidos, Guadalajara.

Durand, J., and D. Massey. 2003. *Clandestinos: Migración México-Estados Unidos en los albores del siglo XXI*. Zacatecas, Mexico: Universidad Autónoma de Zacatecas and Miguel Ángel Porrúa.

Durand, J., D. Massey, and R. M. Zenteno. 2001. Mexican immigration to the United States: Continuities and change. *Latin American Research Review* 36: 107–27.

Eastman, A. C. 2001. Pandillas juveniles en América Latina: Una alerta social no escuchada? In M. L. Santacruz Giralt and A. Concha-Eastman, *Barrio adentro: La solidaridad violenta de las pandillas en El Salvador*. San Salvador, El Salvador: Universidad Centroamericana José Simeón Cañas.

————. 2001. Prologo. In M. L. Santacruz Giralt and A. Concha-Eastman, *Barrio adentro: La solidaridad violenta de las pandillas en El Salvador*. San Salvador, El Salvador: Universidad Centroamericana José Simeón Cañas.

Ebaugh, H. R., and J. S. Chafetz, eds. 2000. *Religion and the new immigrants: Continuities and adaptation*. Walnut Creek, Calif.: AltaMira Press.

————. 2002. *Religion across borders: Transnational immigrant networks*. Walnut Creek, Calif.: AltaMira Press.

Eck, D. 2001. *A new religious America: How a "Christian Country" has now become the world's most religiously diverse nation*. San Francisco: Harper.

Edwards, B., and M. Foley. 1997. Social capital and the political economy of our discontent. *American Behavioral Scientist* 40: 669–78.

————. 1998. Civil society and social capital beyond Putnam. *American Behavioral Scientist* 42: 124–39.

Edwards, B., M. Foley, and M. Diani, eds. 2001. *Beyond Tocqueville: Civil society and the social capital debate in comparative perspective*. Hanover, N.H.: University Press of New England.

Espenshade, T., and V. King. 1994. State and local fiscal impacts of U.S. immigrants: Evidence from New Jersey. *Population Research and Policy Review* 13: 225–56.

Espín, O. 1999. *Women crossing boundaries: A psychology of immigration and transformations of sexuality*. New York: Routledge.

Espinosa, G., V. Elizondo, and J. Miranda. 2003. *Hispanic churches in American life: Summary of findings*. Notre Dame, Ind.: Institute for Latino Studies at the University of Notre Dame.

Espiritu, Y. L. 1992. *Asian American panethnicity: Bridging institutions and identities*. Philadelphia: Temple University Press.

————. 2003. *Home bound: Filipino American lives across cultures*. Berkeley: University of California Press.

Ewick, P., and S. S. Silbey. 1998. *The Common Place of Law: Stories from Everyday Life*. Chicago: University of Chicago Press.

Farris, N. M. 1984. *Maya society under colonial rule*. Princeton, N.J.: Princeton University Press.

Fast, J., and J. Richardson. 1982. *Roots of dependency: Political and economic revolution in nineteenth-century Philippines*. Quezon City, Philippines: Foundation for Nationalistic Studies.

Feher, M. 2000. *Powerless by design: The age of the international community*. Durham, N.C.: Duke University Press.

Femia, J. V. 1981. *Gramsci's political thought: Hegemony, consciousness, and the revolutionary process*. Oxford: Clarendon Press.

Fernandez-Kelley, P. M. 1983. *For we are sold, I and my people: Women and industry in Mexico's frontier*. Albany: State University of New York.

Fernández Repetto, F. J. 1988. Resistencia cultural y religiosidad popular: Los gremios de Chuburná de Hidalgo, Mérida, Yucatán. Master's thesis, Universidad de Oaxaca, Mexico.

Feuchtwang, S. 2001. *Popular religion in China: The imperial metaphor*. London: Routledge.

Filipinas Book Team. 2003. *Filipinos in America: A journey of faith*. South San Francisco: Filipinas Publishing.

Finch, B. K., B. Kolody, and W. A. Vega. 2000. Perceived discrimination and depression among Mexican-origin adults in California. *Journal of Health and Social Behavior* 41.3: 295–313.

Foley, M., and B. Edwards. 1999. Is it time to disinvest in social capital? *Journal of Public Policy* 19: 669–78.

Foley, M. and D. R. Hoge, eds. 2007. *Religion and new immigrants: How faith communities form our new citizens.* New York: Oxford University Press.

Fortuny Loret de Mola, P. 1982. Inserción y difusión del sectarismo religiouso en el campo yucateco. *Yucatán: Historia y economia,* September/October 1982, 3–23.

———. 1998. Women's empowerment through religion: Stories of female converts in two Mexican cities. Paper presented at Trinity University, San Antonio, Texas.

Foucault, M. 1980. *The history of sexuality. Volume 1: An introduction.* New York: Vintage Books.

Fox, R. 1991. *Recapturing anthropology.* Santa Fe, N.M.: School of American Research.

Freese, K. 2005. *The death cult of the drug lords: Mexico's patron saint of crime, criminals, and the dispossessed.* Fort Leavenworth, Kans.: Foreign Military Studies Office.

Freire, P. 1970. *Pedagogy of the oppressed.* New York: Seabury Press.

Fremon, C. 2004. *G-Dog and the homeboys: Father Greg Boyle and the gangs of East Los Angeles.* Albuquerque: University of New Mexico Press.

Friedman, J. 2003a. Globalisation, dis-integration, re-organization: The transformations of violence. In J. Friedman, ed., *Globalization, the state and violence.* Walnut Creek, Calif.: AltaMira Press.

———. 2003b. *Globalization, the state and violence.* Walnut Creek, Calif.: AltaMira Press.

Gamio, M. 1930. *Mexican migration to the United States.* Chicago: University of Chicago Press.

Garber, M. 1992. *Vested interests: Cross-dressing and cultural anxiety.* New York: Routledge.

Garrard-Burnett, V. and D. Stoll, eds. 1993. *Rethinking Protestantism in Latin America.* Philadelphia: Temple University Press.

Gartner, J. 1996. Religious commitment, mental health, and prosocial behavior: A review of the empirical literature. In E. P. Shafranske, ed., *Religion and the clinical practice of psychology.* Washington, D.C.: American Psychological Association.

Geertz, C. 1973. *The interpretation of cultures: Selected essays.* New York: Basic Books.

George, R. M. 1992. Traveling light: Of immigration, invisible suitcases, and gunny sacks. *Differences* 4.2: 72–99.

Gevisser, M. and E. Cameron, eds. 1995. *Defiant desire: Gay and lesbian lives in South Africa.* London: Routledge.

Gibson, D. 2003. *The coming Catholic Church: How the faithful are shaping a new American Catholicism.* San Francisco: HarperCollins.

Gill, A. 1999. The struggle to be soul provider: Catholic responses to Protestant growth in Latin America. In C. Smith and J. Prokopy, eds., *Latin American Religion in Motion.* New York: Routledge.

Glick Schiller, N. 1999. Transmigrants and nation-states: Something old and something new. In C. Hirschman, P. Kasinitz, and J. DeWind, eds., *Handbook of international migration*. Durham, N.C.: Duke University Press.

Godfrey, B. 1988. *Neighborhoods in transition: The making of San Francisco's ethnic and nonconformist communities*. Berkeley: University of California Press.

Golay, F. H. 1998. *Face of empire: U.S.-Philippine relations, 1898–1946*. Madison: University of Wisconsin Press.

Gomez Peña, G, D. Keiller, and R. Barta. 1993. *Warrior for gringostroika: Essays, performance texts, and poetry*. St. Paul, Minn.: Graywolf Press.

González-López, G. 2003. *De madres a hijas*: Gendered lessons on virginity across generations of Mexican immigrant women. In P. Hondagneu-Sotelo, ed., *Gender and U.S. migration: Contemporary trends*. Berkeley: University of California Press.

———. 2005. *Erotic journeys: Mexican immigrants and their sex lives*. Berkeley: University of California Press.

Gramsci, A. 1971. *Selections from the prison notebooks*. New York: International Publishers.

Grasmuck, S., and P. R. Pessar. 1991. *Between two islands: Dominican international migration*. Berkeley: University of California Press.

Greeley, A. 1997. The other civic America: Religion and social capital. *American Prospect* 32: 68–73.

Green, J. N., and F. E. Babb. 2002. Introduction: Gender, sexuality, and same-sex desire in Latin America. *Latin American Perspectives* 29.2: 3–23.

Guarnizo, L., and M. P. Smith. 1998. The locations of transnationalism. In M. P. Smith and L. Guarnizo, eds., *Transnationalism from below*. New Brunswick, N.J.: Transaction.

Guerra Vásquez, G. A. 2004. Homies unidos: International barrio warriors waging peace on two fronts. In S. Maira and E. Soep, eds., *Youthscapes: The popular, the national, the global*. Philadelphia: University of Pennsylvania Press.

Gupta, A., and J. Ferguson. 1992. Beyond "culture": Space, identity, and the politics of difference. *Cultural Anthropology* 7.1: 6–23.

Gupta, A., and J. Ferguson, eds. 1997. Culture, power, place: Ethnography at the end of an era. In A. Gupta and J. Ferguson, eds., *Culture, power, place: Explorations in critical anthropology*. Durham, N.C.: Duke University Press.

Guttman, M. 2003. Introduction: Discarding manly dichotomies in Latin America. In M. Guttman, ed., *Changing men and masculinities in Latin America*. Durham, N.C.: Duke University Press.

Haddad, Y., J. I. Smith, and J. L. Esposito, eds. 2003. *Religion and immigration: Christian, Jewish, and Muslim experiences in the United States*. Walnut Creek, Calif.: AltaMira Press.

Halberstam, J. 1998. *Female masculinity*. Durham, N.C.: Duke University Press.

Halley, J., and W. Brown, eds. 1999. *Left legalism/left critique*. Durham, N.C.: Duke University Press.

Halpern, D. S. 1998. *Social capital, exclusion and the quality of life*. London: Institute for Public Policy Research.

Hannerz, U. 1989. Notes on the global ecumene. *Public Culture* 1.2: 66–75.

———. 1996. *Transnational connections: Culture, people, places*. London: Routledge.

Hansen, A. and J. Bastarrachea. 1984. *Mérida: Su transformación de capital colonial a naciente metropoli en 1935*. Mexico City: Instituto Nacional de Antropología.

Harding, S. 1993. Reinventing ourselves as other: More new agents of history and knowledge. In L. S. Kauffman, ed., *American Feminist Thought at Century's End: A Reader*. Oxford: Blackwell Publishing.

Harrell, S., and C. Huang, eds. 1994. *Cultural change in postwar Taiwan*. Boulder, Colo.: Westview.

Harris, A. 2004. *Dare to struggle, be not afraid: The "theology of struggle" in the Philippines*. Quezon City, Philippines: Claretian Communications.

Harris, M. 1998. *Organizing God's work: Challenges for churches and synagogues*. London: Macmillan.

Hartmann, H. 1994. The family as the locus of gender, class, and political struggle: The example of housework. In A. C. Herrmann and A. J. Stewart, eds., *Theorizing feminism: Parallel trends in the humanities and social sciences*. Boulder, Colo.: Westview.

Hawley, C. 2004. Catholic Church upset by Mexico's St. Death. Worldwide Religious News, http://wwrn.org.

Henwood, K. L., and N. F. Pidgeon. 1992. Qualitative research and psychological theorizing. *British Journal of Psychology* 83: 97–111.

Herdt, G. 1996. *Third sex, third gender: Beyond sexual dimorphism in culture and history*. New York: Zone Books.

Hermann, A. C., and A. J. Stewart, eds. 1994. *Theorizing feminism: Parallel trends in the humanities and social sciences*. Boulder, Colo.: Westview.

Herrera-Sobek, M. 1984. Mexican immigration and petroleum: A folklorist's perspective. *New Scholarship* 91: 99–110.

Heyman, J. M. 1990. The emergence of the waged life course on the United States–Mexico border. *American Ethnologist* 172: 348–59.

———. 1991. *Life and labor on the border: Working people of northern Sonora Mexico, 1886–1986*. Tucson: University of Arizona Press.

———. 1995. Putting power in the anthropology of bureaucracy: The immigration and naturalization service at the Mexico–United States border. *Current Anthropology* 362: 261–87.

Higgins, M., and T. Coen. 2000. *Streets, bedrooms, and patios: The ordinariness of diversity in urban Oaxaca*. Austin: University of Texas Press.

Hing, B. 1993. *Making and remaking Asian America through immigration policy, 1850–1990*. Stanford, Calif.: Stanford University Press.

Hirsch, J. S. 2003. *A courtship after marriage: Sexuality and love in Mexican transnational families*. Berkeley: University of California Press.

Hondagneu-Sotelo, P. 1994. *Gendered transitions: Mexican experiences of immigration*. Berkeley: University of California Press.

———, ed. 2007. *Religions and social justice for immigrants*. New Brunswick, N.J.: Rutgers University Press.

Hooley, J. 1997. Transgender politics, medicine and representation: Off our backs, off our bodies. *Social Alternatives* 16.1: 31–36.

Howe, C. 2002. Undressing the universal queer subject: Nicaraguan activism and transnational identity. *City and Society* 14.2: 237–79.

———. In press. *Eroticscapes: Sex, social justice and Nicaragua's new media era*. Durham, N.C.: Duke University Press.

Hull, K. E. 2003. The cultural power of law and the cultural enactment of legality: The case of same-sex marriage. *Law and Social Inquiry* 28.3: 629–57.

Huntington, S. P. 1996. *The clash of civilizations and the remaking of world order*. New York: Simon and Schuster.

Hutchinson, E. P. 1981. *Legislative history of American immigration policy, 1789–1965*. Philadelphia: University of Pennsylvania Press.

Iglesia Ni Cristo. 2000. *An introduction to the Iglesia Ni Cristo: The history and Christian fellowship*. Daly City: Northern California (video).

Ignacio, E. N. 2005. *Building diaspora: Filipino cultural community formation on the Internet*. New Brunswick, N.J.: Rutgers University Press.

Ignatieff, M. 2001. *Human rights as politics and idolatry*. Princeton, N.J.: Princeton University Press.

Ileto, R. 1979. *Pasyon and revolution: Popular movements in the Philippines, 1840–1910*. Manila: Ateneo de Manila University Press.

Indra, D. M., ed. 1999. *Engendering forced migration: Theory and practice*. New York: Berghahn Books.

Isasi-Diaz, A. M., and Segovia, F. 1996. *Hispanic/Latino theology: Challenge and promise*. Minneapolis: Fortress Press.

Jacobsen, D. A. 2001. *Doing justice: Congregations and community organizing*. Minneapolis: Fortress Press.

Jeung, R. 2004. *Faithful generations: Race and new Asian American churches*. New Brunswick, N.J.: Rutgers University Press.

Johnson, M. H. 2006. *National policies and the rise of transnational gangs*. Washington, D.C.: Migration Policy Institute.

Kaplan, C. 1996. *Questions of travel: Postmodern discourses of displacement*. Durham, N.C.: Duke University Press.

Kauffman, L. S., ed. 1993. *American feminist thought at century's end: A reader*. Oxford: Blackwell Publishing

Kearney, M. 1986. From the invisible hand to visible feet: Anthropological studies of migration and development. *Annual Review of Anthropology* 15:331–61.

———. 1991. Borders and boundaries of the state and self at the end of empire. *Journal of Historical Sociology* 4.1: 52–74.

———. 1994. Desde el indigenismo a los derechos humanos: Etnicidad y política más allá de la Mixteca. *Nueva Antropología* 14: 49–67.

———. 1995. The local and the global: The anthropology of globalization and transnationalism. *Annual Review of Anthropology* 24: 547–65.

———. 1996. *Reconceptualizing the peasantry: Anthropology in global perspective.* Boulder, Colo.: Westview.

———. 2004. The classifying and value-filtering missions of borders. *Anthropological Theory* 42: 131–56.

Kearney, M., and Nagengast, C. 1989. Anthropological perspectives on transnational communities in rural California. Working Group on Farm Labor and Rural Poverty, California Institute for Rural Studies, Davis.

Kelly, G. P. 1977. *From Vietnam to America: A chronicle of Vietnamese immigration to the United States.* Boulder, Colo.: Westview.

Kennedy, E. L., and M. D. Davis. 1994. *Boots of leather, slippers of gold: The history of a lesbian community.* New York: Penguin.

Kinsey, A. C., W. B. Pomeroy, and C. E. Martin. 1948. *Sexual behavior in the human male.* New York: W. B. Saunders.

Kinsey, A. C., W. B. Pomeroy, C. E. Martin, and P. H. Gebhard. 1953. *Sexual behavior in the human female.* New York: W. B. Saunders.

Kniss, F., and P. D. Numrich, eds. 2007. *Sacred assemblies and civic engagement: How religion matters for America's newest immigrants.* New Brunswick, N.J.: Rutgers University Press.

Kolankiewicz, E. 1996. Social capital and social change. *British Journal of Sociology* 473: 427–41.

Kulick, D. 1998. *Travesti: Sex, gender and culture among Brazilian transgendered prostitutes.* Chicago: University of Chicago Press.

Kuo, W. H. 1984. Prevalence of depression among Asian-Americans. *Journal of Nervous and Mental Disease* 172: 449–57.

Kwantes, A. C., ed. 1998. *A century of Bible Christians in the Philippines.* Manila: OMF Literature.

Laclau, E., and C. Mouffe. 1992. *Hegemony and socialist strategy: Towards a radical democratic politics.* London: Verso.

Lalive d'Epinay, C. 1970. *El refugio de las masas.* Santiago de Chile: Ed. Pacifico.

———. 1983. Political regimes and millenarism in a dependent society: Reflections on Pentecostalism in Chile. *Concilium* 161: 42–54.

Lancaster, R. 1992. *Life is hard: Machismo, danger, and the intimacy of power in Nicaragua.* Berkeley: University of California Press.

Lavie, S., and T. Swedenburg, eds. 1996. *Displacement, diaspora, and geographies of identity*. Durham, N.C.: Duke University Press.

LeCompte, M. D., and J. J. Schensul. 1999. *Designing and conducting ethnographic research*. Walnut Creek, Calif.: AltaMira Press.

Lee, E. 2003. *At America's gates: Chinese immigration during the exclusion era, 1882–1943*. Chapel Hill: University of North Carolina Press.

Lee, J. H. X. 2002. Journey to the West: Tianhou in San Francisco. Master's thesis, Graduate Theological Union, Berkeley.

———. 2006. Contemporary Chinese American religious Life. In J. Miller, ed., *Chinese religions in contemporary societies*. Santa Barbara, Calif.: ABC-CLIO.

———. Forthcoming. Taiwanese Americans and religion. In H. Lingh and A. W. Austin, eds., *Asian American history and culture: An encyclopedia*. Armonk, N.Y.: M. E. Sharpe, East River Books.

Lee, R. G. 1999. *Orientals: Asian Americans in popular culture*. Philadelphia: Temple University Press.

Leidner, R. 2001. On whose behalf? Feminist ideology and dilemmas of constituency. In B. Ryan, ed., *Identity politics in the women's movement*. New York: New York University Press.

León, L. 2004. *La Llorona's children: Religion, life, and death in the U.S.-Mexican borderlands*. Berkeley: University of California Press.

Leonard, K., A. Stepick, M. Vásquez, and J. Holdaway. 2005. *Immigrant faiths: Transforming religious life in America*. Walnut Creek, Calif.: AltaMira Press.

Levitt, P. 2001. *The transnational villagers*. Berkeley: University of California Press.

———. 2007. *God needs no passport: Immigrants and the changing American religious landscape*. New York: New Press.

Lewin, E. 1998. *Recognizing ourselves: Ceremonies of lesbian and gay commitment*. New York: Columbia University Press.

Lin, I. 1996. Journey to the Far West: Chinese Buddhism in America. *Amerasia Journal* 22.1: 107–32.

Lin, M. 1996. AAS Abstracts. China session 25: Popular religion and the problem of Taiwanese identity. Taiwan Studies Group, http://www.aasianst.org.

Lincoln, C., and L. Mamiya. 2003. *The black church in the African American experience*. Durham, N.C.: Duke University Press.

Liu, W. T., M. Lamanna, and A. Murata, eds. 1979. *Transition to nowhere: Vietnamese refugees in America*. Nashville, Tenn.: Charter House Publishers.

Loewenstein, L. K. 1984. *Streets of San Francisco: The origins of street and place names*. San Francisco: Lexikos.

Lomas, J. 1998. Social capital and health: Implications for public health and epidemiology. *Social Science and Medicine* 47.9: 1181–88.

Lombardi, E. 2001. Enhancing transgender health care. *American Journal of Public Health* 91.6: 869–72.

Loreta Mariz, C. and M. Das dores Campos Machado. 1997. Pentecostalism and women in Brazil. In E. I. Cleary and H. W. Stewart-Gambino, eds., *Power, politics and Pentecostals in Latin America*. Boulder, Colo.: Westview.

Loue, S. 1990. Homosexuality and immigration law: A re-examination. *Journal of Psychiatry and Law* 18 (spring/summer): 109–35.

Luibhéid, E., and L. Cantú Jr., eds. 2005. *Queer migrations: Sexuality, U.S. citizenship and border crossings*. Minneapolis: University of Minnesota Press.

Lumsden, I. 1996. *Machos, maricones, and gays: Cuba and homosexuality*. Philadelphia: University of Pennsylvania Press.

Lyon, J., and K. Wilson. 1987. *Marcos and beyond*. Roseville, Australia: Kangaroo Press.

Mabalon, D. 2003. Life in Little Manila: Filipinas/os in Stockton, 1917–1972. Ph.D. dissertation, Stanford University.

Maggay, M. 1989. *Communicating cross-culturally: Towards a new context for missions in the Philippines*. Quezon City, Philippines: New Day.

Mahler, S. J. 1998. Theoretical and empirical contributions toward a research agenda for transnationalism. In M. P. Smith and L. E. Guarnizo, eds., *Transnationalism from below*. New Brunswick, N.J: Transaction Publishers.

———. 1995. *American dreaming*. Princeton, N.J.: Princeton University Press.

Mahler, S. J. and D. Ugrina. 2006. Central America: Crossroads of the Americas. Washington, D.C.: Migration Policy Institute, http://www.migrationinformation.org

Manalansan, M. F., IV. 1997. In the shadows of Stonewall: Examining gay transnational politics and the diasporic dilemma. In L. Lowe and D. Lloyd, eds., *The Politics of culture in the shadow of capital*. Durham, N.C.: Duke University Press.

———. 2003. *Global divas: Filipino gay men in the diaspora*. Durham, N.C.: Duke University Press.

Marcuse, H. 1966. *Eros and civilization: A philosophical inquiry into Freud*. Boston: Beacon.

Marin, G., P. Balls Organista, and K. M. Chun. 2003. Current issues and findings in acculturation research. In G. Bernal, J. E. Trimble, F. T. L. Leong, and A. K. Burlew, eds., *Handbook of ethnic minority psychology*. Thousand Oaks, Calif.: Sage Publications.

Mariz, C. L., and M. das Dores Campos Machado. 1997. Pentecostalism and women. In E. I. Cleary and H. W. Stewart-Gambino, eds., *Power, politics and Pentecostals in Latin America*. Boulder, Colo.: Westview.

Markus, H. R., and S. Kitayama. 1991. Culture and the self: Implications for cognition, emotion, and motivation. *Psychological Review* 982: 224–53.

Marshall-Feratani, R. 2001. Mediating the global and local in Nigerian Pentecostalism. In A. Corten and R. Marshall-Feratani, eds., *Between Babel and Pentecost: Transnational Pentecostalism in Africa and Latin America*. Bloomington: Indiana University Press.

Martin, D. 1990. *Tongues of fire: The explosion of Protestantism in Latin America*. Oxford: Basil Blackwell.

Marx, K. 1844. An Introduction to a Contribution to the Critique of Hegel's Philosophy of Right. *Deutsch-Französische Jahrbücher*, February, 1–3.

Massey, D. 1999. Why does immigration occur? A theoretical synthesis. In C. Hirschman, P. Kasinitz, and J. DeWind, eds., *The handbook of international migration: The American experience*. New York: Russell Sage Foundation.

Matsuoka, F. 1995. *Out of silence: Emerging themes in Asian American churches*. Cleveland, Ohio: United Church Press

Maupin, A. 1976. *Tales of the city*. New York: HarperCollins.

McClure, H., L. Soloway, and C. Nugent. 1997. *Preparing sexual orientation-based asylum claims: The handbook*. Chicago: Heartland Alliance for Human Needs and Human Rights.

McDonnel, K. 1980. *Presence, power, praise: Documents on charismatic renewal*. Collegeville, Minn.: Liturgical Press.

McKay, S. 2006. *Satanic mills or silicon islands: The politics of high-tech production in the Philippines*. Ithaca, N.Y.: Cornell University Press.

Menjívar, C. 1999. Religious institutions and transnationalism: A case study of Catholic and evangelical Salvadoran immigrants. *International Journal of Politics, Culture, and Society* 12.4: 589–612.

———. 2000. *Fragmented ties: Salvadoran immigrant networks in America*. Berkeley: University of California Press.

Mercado, L. N. 1982. *Christ in the Philippines*. Manila: Divine Word University.

Merry, S. E. 1990. *Getting justice and getting even: Legal consciousness among working-class Americans*. Chicago: University of Chicago Press.

Miller J., C. L. Maxson, and M. W. Klein. 2001. *The modern gang reader*. Los Angeles: Roxbury Publishing Company.

Miller, S. 1982. *Benevolent assimilation: The American conquest of the Philippines, 1899–1903*. New Haven, Conn.: Yale University Press.

———. 1998. Gender and victimization risk among young women in gangs. *Journal of Research in Crime and Delinquence* 35: 429–53.

Min, P. Y., and J. H. Kim, eds. 2002. *Religions in Asian America: Building faith communities*. Walnut Creek, Calif.: AltaMira Press.

Montero, D. 1979. *Vietnamese Americans: Patterns of resettlement and socioeconomic adaptation in the United States*. Boulder, Colo.: Westview.

Moore, J. 2002. Foreword. In J. D. Vigil, *A rainbow of gangs: Street cultures in the mega-city*. Austin: University of Texas Press.

Murray, S. O. 1992. The "underdevelopment" of modern gay homosexuality in Mesoamerica. In K. Plummer, ed., *Modern homosexualities: Fragments of lesbian and gay experiences*. London: Routledge.

———. 1996. *American gay*. Chicago: University of Chicago Press.

Myers, H. F., and N. Rodriguez. 2003. Acculturation and physical health in racial and ethnic minorities. In K. M. Chun, P. Balls Organista, and G. Marin, eds., *Acculturation: Advances in theory, measurement, and applied research.* Washington, D.C.: American Psychological Association.

Nadeau, K. 2002. *Liberation theology in the Philippines: Faith in a revolution.* Westport, Conn.: Praeger Publishers.

Naficy, H. 1991. The poetics and practice of Iranian nostalgia in exile. *Diaspora* 1.3: 285–302.

Nagengast, C., and T. Turner. 1997. Introduction: Universal human rights versus cultural relativity. *Journal of Anthropological Research* 53.3: 269–72.

Nalven, J. 1982. Health research on undocumented Mexicans. *Social Science Journal* 192: 73–88.

———. 1984. A cooperation paradox and an 'airy tale along the border. *New Scholarship* 91–92: 171–200.

Negroe Sierra, G. M. 1988. La Identidad Social y sus transformaciones en Chuburná de Hidalgo, Mérida, Yucatán. Master's thesis, Universidad de Oaxaca, Mexico.

Nemoto, T., D. Luke, L. Mamo, A. Ching, and J. Patria. 1999. HIV risk behaviors among male-to-female transgenders in comparison with homosexual or bisexual males and heterosexual females. *AIDS Care* 11: 297–312.

Nguyen, C. T., and A. W. Barber. 1998. Vietnamese Buddhism in North America. In C. S. Prebish and K. Tanaka, eds., *The faces of Buddhism in America.* Berkeley: University of California Press.

Norris, P. 1996. Does television erode social capital? A reply to Putnam. *PS: Political Science and Politics* (September): 1–7.

Norton, A., M. Latham, and G. Sturgess, eds. 1997. *Social capital: The individual, civil society and the state.* Sydney: Centre for Independent Studies.

Nyitray, V. L. 2000. Becoming the empress of Heaven: The life and bureaucratic career of Tianhou/Mazu. In E. Bernard and B. Moon, eds., *Goddesses who rule.* New York: Oxford University Press, 2000.

———. 2006. Questions of gender in Tianhou/Mazu scholarship. In H. Chang and C. R. Yeh, eds., *Contemporary religions in Taiwan: Unities and diversities.* Taipei: SMC.

———. n.d. Do my eyes clearly see? Unpublished manuscript.

Ojeda, C. R. 1998. *Migración internacional y cambio social: El caso de Peto, Yucatán.* Bachelor's thesis, Universidad Autónoma de Yucatán, Mexico.

Omi, M., and H. Winant. 1994. *Racial formation in the United States: From the 1960s to the 1980s.* New York: Routledge.

Ong, A. 1999. *Flexible citizenship: The cultural logics of transnationality.* Durham, N.C.: Duke University Press.

———. 2003. *Buddha is hiding: Refugees, citizenship, the New America.* Berkeley: University of California Press.

Palloni, A., D. Massey, M. Ceballos, K. Espinosa, and M. Spittel. 2001. Social capital and international migration: A test using information on family networks. *American Journal of Sociology* 106.5: 1262–98.

Palmberg, M. 1999. Emerging visibility of gays and lesbians in Southern Africa: Contrasting contexts. In B. D. Adam, J. W. Duyvenaak, and A. Krouwel, eds., *The global emergence of gay and lesbian politics*. Philadelphia: Temple University Press.

Pan, E. Y. Z. 1995. *The impact of the 1906 earthquake on San Francisco's Chinatown*. San Francisco: Peter Lang.

Papachristos, A. V. 2005. Gang world. *Foreign Policy* 140: 49–55.

Park, R. E. 1950. *Race and culture*. Glencoe, Ill.: Free Press, 1950.

Parker, R. 1997. Migration, sexual subcultures, and HIV/AIDS in Brazil. In G. Herdt, ed., *Sexual cultures and migration in the era of AIDS*. Oxford: Clarendon Press.

———. 1998. *Beneath the Equator: Cultures of desire, male homosexuality, and emerging gay communities in Brazil*. New York: Routledge.

Parreñas, R. 2001. *Servants of globalization: Women, migration, and domestic work*. Stanford, Calif.: Stanford University Press.

———. 2005. *Children of global migration: Transnational families and gendered woes*. Stanford, Calif.: Stanford University Press.

Patton, C., and B. Sanchez-Eppler, eds. 2000. *Queer diasporas*. Durham, N.C.: Duke University Press.

Paxton, P. 1999. Is social capital declining in the United States? A multiple indicator assessment. *American Journal of Sociology* 105.1: 88–127.

Pedraza-Bailey, S. 1985. *Political economic migrants in America: Cubans and Mexicans*. Austin: University of Texas Press.

———. 1991. Women and migration: The social consequences of gender. *Annual Review of Sociology* 17: 303–25.

Peón Arceo, A. 2000. Rituales del ciclo de vida en Tuzik, Quintana Roo. *Temas Antropológicos: Revista Científica de Investigaciones Regionales* 22.1: 54–77.

Perez, G. M. 2004. *The near northwest side story: Migration, displacement and Puerto Rican Families*. Berkeley: University of California Press.

Perry, Reverend T. D. 1972. *The Lord is my shepherd and he knows I'm gay: The autobiography of the Reverend Troy D. Perry*, as told to Charles L. Lucas. Los Angeles: Nash Publishing.

Perry, Reverend T. D., and Swicegood, T. L. P. 1990. *Don't be afraid anymore: The story of Troy Perry and the Metropolitan Community Churches*. New York: St. Martin's Press.

Pessar, P., ed. 1997. *Caribbean circuits: New directions in the study of Caribbean migration*. New York: Center for Migration Studies.

Peterson, A. L. 2001. The only way I can walk: Women, Christianity, and everyday life in El Salvador. In A. L. Peterson, M. A. Vásquez, and P. Williams, eds., *Chris-

tianity, social change, and globalization in the Americas. New Brunswick, N.J.: Rutgers University Press.

Peterson, A. L., and M. A. Vásquez. 2001. 'Upwards, never down': The Catholic Charismatic Renewal in transnational perspective. In A. L. Peterson, M. A. Vásquez, and P. J. Williams, eds., *Christianity, social change, and globalization in the Americas*. New Brunswick, N.J.: Rutgers University Press.

Peterson, A. L., M. A. Vásquez, and P. J. Williams, eds. 2001. *Christianity, social change, and globalization in the Americas*. New Brunswick, N.J.: Rutgers University Press.

Phelan, S. 1993. (Be)coming out: Lesbian identity and politics. *Signs* 18.4: 765–790.

———. 1997. *Playing with fire: Queer politics, queer theories*. New York: Routledge.

———. 2001. *Sexual strangers: Gays, lesbians, and dilemmas of citizenship*. Philadelphia: University of Pennsylvania Press.

Phinney, J. 1990. Ethnic identity in adolescents and adults: Review of research. *Psychological Bulletin* 108: 499–514.

———. 2003. Ethnic identity and acculturation. In K. M. Chun, P. Balls Organista, and G. Marin, eds., *Acculturation: Advances in theory, measurement, and applied research*. Washington, D.C.: American Psychological Association.

———. 2006. Acculturation is not an independent variable: Approaches to studying acculturation as a complex process. In M. H. Bornstein and L. R. Cote, eds., *Acculturation and parent-child relationships: Measurement and development*. Mahwah, N.J.: Lawrence Erlbaum Associates.

Pido, A. J. 1986. *The Filipinos in America: Macro/micro dimensions of immigration and integration*. New York: Center for Migration Studies.

Poewe, K. ed. 1994. *Charismatic Christianity as a global culture*. Columbia: University of South Carolina Press.

Pomeroy, W. J. 1970. *American neo-colonialism: Its emergence in the Philippines and Asia*. New York: International Publishers.

Poore, G. 1996. Three movements in a minor: Lesbians and immigration. *Off Our Backs* (August–September): 12–13, 22.

Portes, A. 1995. *The economic sociology of immigration: Essays on networks, ethnicity and entrepreneurship*. New York: Russell Sage.

———. 1998. Social capital: Its origins and applications in modern sociology. *Annual Review of Sociology* 24: 1–24.

Portes, A., and P. Landolt. 1996. The downside of social capital. *American Prospect* 7.26: 18–21.

Portes, A., and R. G. Rumbaut. 1996. *Immigrant America: A portrait*. Berkeley: University of California Press.

Posadas, B. M. 1999. *The Filipino Americans*. Westport, Conn.: Greenwood Press.

Prebish, C. S., and K. K. Tanaka, eds. 1998. *The faces of Buddhism in America*. Berkeley, Calif.: University of California Press.

Prieur, A. 1998. *Mema's house, Mexico City: On transvestites, queens, and machos.* Chicago: University of Chicago Press.

Putnam, R. 1993. *Making democracy work: Civic traditions in modern Italy.* Princeton, N.J.: Princeton University Press.

———. 1995. Bowling alone: America's declining social capital. *Journal of Democracy* 6: 65–78.

———. 1996. The strange disappearance of civic America. *American Prospect* 24: 34–48.

———. 2000. *Bowling alone: The collapse and revival of American community.* New York: Simon and Schuster.

———, ed. 2004. *Democracies in flux: The evolution of social capital in contemporary society.* New York: Oxford University Press.

Putzell, J. 1997. Accounting for the dark side of social capital: Reading Robert Putnam on democracy. *Journal of International Development* 9.7: 939–49.

Quijano, E. E. 2003. *Santa Muerte: El libro total.* Mexico City: Editorial La Luna Negra.

Ramírez, R. L. 1999. *What it means to be a man: Reflections on Puerto Rican masculinity.* New Brunswick, N.J.: Rutgers University Press.

Ramsay, M. 1998. Redeeming the city: Exploring the relationship between church and metropolis. *Urban Affairs Review* 33.5: 595–616.

Ranck, L. 2002. Gays and lesbians in the U.S. immigration process. *Peace Review: Journal of Social Justice* 14.4: 373–77.

Ratti, R., ed. 1993. *A lotus of another color: An unfolding of the South Asian gay and lesbian experience.* Boston: Alyson Press.

Redfield, R. 1941. *The folk culture of Yucatan.* Chicago: University of Chicago Press.

Redfield, R., and A. Villa Rojas. 1990 [1934]. *Chan Kom: A Maya village.* Prospect Heights, Ill.: Waveland Press.

Reed, R. 1990. Migration as mission: The expansion of the Iglesia ni Cristo outside the Philippines. In R. Reed, ed., *Patterns of migration in Southeast Asia.* Berkeley: Center for South and Southeast Asian Studies/International and Area Studies, University of California.

Reimers, D. 1992. *Still the golden door: The third world comes to America.* New York: Columbia University Press.

Roberts, B. R., F. Reanne, and L. A. Fernando. 1999. Transnational migrant communities and Mexican migration to the U.S. *Ethnic and Racial Studies* 22.2: 238–66.

Rocha, J. L. 2000a. Pandillero: La mano que empuña el mortero. *Revista Envio* 216, http://www.envio.org.

———. 2000b. Pandillas: Una cárcel cultural. *Revista Envio* 219, http://www.envio.org.

———. 2003. Tatuajes de pandilleros: Estigma, identidad y arte. *Revista Envio* 258, http://www.envio.org.

———. 2005. The *Traido*: A key to youth gang continuity. *Revista Envio* 288, http://www.envio.org.

Rodgers, D. 2006. Living in the shadow of death: Gangs, violence, and social order in urban Nicaragua. *Journal of Latin American Studies* 38.2: 267–92.

Rodríguez, A. P. 2005. Cultural narratives of Salvadoran transnational migration. *Latino Studies* 3: 319–41.

Rodríguez, J. M. 2003. *Queer Latinidad: Identity practices, discursive spaces.* New York: New York University Press.

Rofel, L. 1999. Qualities of desire: Imagining gay identity in China. *Gay Lesbian Quarterly* 5.4: 451–74.

Román, D. 2000. Visa denied. In J. Boone et al. eds., *Queer frontiers.* Madison: University of Wisconsin Press.

Romano, V. 1965. Charismatic medicine, folk-healing and folk-sainthood. *American Anthropologist* 67.5: 1151–73.

Rosaldo, R. 1989. *Culture and truth: The remaking of social analysis.* Boston: Beacon.

———. 1994. Social justice and the crisis of national communities. In F. Barker, P. Hume, and P. Iverson, eds., *Colonial discourse/postcolonial theory.* Manchester: Manchester University Press.

Roozen, D., and J. Nieman, eds. 2005. *Church, identity, and change: Theology and denominational structures in unsettled times.* Grand Rapids, Mich.: Wm. B. Eerdmans Publishing.

Roscoe, W. 1991. *The Zuñi man-woman.* Albuquerque: University of New Mexico Press.

Rouse, R. 1991. Mexican migration and the social space of postmodernism. *Diaspora* 1: 8–23.

———. 1992. Making sense of settlement: Class transformation, cultural struggle and transnationalism among Mexican migrants in the United States. In L. Basch, C. Blanc-Szanton, and N. Glick Schiller, eds., *Towards a transnational perspective in migration: Race, class, ethnicity, and nationalism reconsidered.* New York: New York Academy of Science.

Rubel, A. J. 1969. Concepts of disease in Mexican American culture. *American Anthropologist* 62.5: 3–13.

Rumbaut, R. 1985. Mental health and the refugee experience: A comparative study of Southeast Asian refugees. In T. C. Owan, ed., *Southeast Asian mental health: Treatment, prevention, services, training, and research.* Rockville, Md.: National Institute of Mental Health.

Said, E. 1979. Zionism from the standpoint of its victims. *Social Text* 1: 7–58.

Saldívar, J. 1991. *Criticism in the borderlands: Studies in Chicano literature, culture, and ideology.* Durham, N.C.: Duke University Press.

Sales, W. 1994. *From civil rights to black liberation: Malcom X and the Organization of Afro-American Unity.* Cambridge, Mass.: South End Press.

Salzinger, L. 2003. *Genders in production: Making workers in Mexico's global factories.* Berkeley: University of California Press.

San Buenaventura, S. 1999. Filipino folk spirituality and immigration: From mutual aid to religion. In D. K. Yoo, ed., *New spiritual homes.* Honolulu: University of Hawaii Press.

———. 2002. Filipino religion at home and abroad: Historical roots and immigrant transformations. In P. G. Minand and J. H. Kim, eds., *Religions in Asian America.* Walnut Creek, Calif.: AltaMira Press.

Sandoval, E. 2002. Catholicism and transnational networks: Three cases from the Monterrey-Houston connection. In H. R. Ebaugh and J. Saltzman Chafetz, eds., *Religion across borders: Transnational immigrant networks.* Walnut Creek, Calif.: AltaMira Press.

Sangren, S. P. 1983. Female gender in Chinese religious symbols: Kuan Yin, Ma Tsu, and the 'Eternal Mother.' *Signs: Journal of Women in Culture and Society* 9.1: 4–25.

San Juan, E. 1998. *From exile to diaspora: Versions of the Filipino experience in the United States.* Boulder, Colo.: Westview.

Santacruz Giralt, M. L., and A. Concha-Eastman. 2001. *Barrio adentro: La solidaridad violenta de las pandillas.* San Salvador, El Salvador: Universidad Centroamericana Jose Simeon Canas.

Santacruz Giralt, M. L., and J. M. Cruz. 2001. Las maras en El Salvador. In *Maras y pandillas en Centroamérica.* San Salvador, El Salvador: UCA Publicaciones.

Sassen, S. 1996. *Losing control? Sovereignty in an age of globalization.* New York: Columbia University Press.

———. 1998. *Globalization and its discontents: Essays on the new mobility of peoples.* New York: New Press.

———. 2006. *Territory, authority, rights: From medieval to global assemblages.* Princeton, N.J.: Princeton University Press.

Savidge, Joyce. 1977. *This Is Hong Kong: Temples.* Hong Kong: Government Publications.

Schirmer, D. B., and S. R. Shalom, eds. 1987. *The Philippines reader.* Boston: South End Press.

Schuller, T. 1997. Building social capital: Steps towards a learning society. *Scottish Affairs* 19: 77–91.

Seaman, G. 1987. *Journey to the North: An ethnohistorical analysis and annotated translation of the Chinese folk novel "Pei-yu-chi."* Berkeley: University of California Press.

Sedgwick, E. K. 1990. *Epistemology of the closet.* Berkeley: University of California Press.

Segovia, F. 1996. In the world but not of it: Exile as locus for a theology of the diaspora. In A. M. Isazi-Diaz and F. Segovia, eds., *Hispanic/Latino theology: Challenge and promise.* Minneapolis: Fortress Press.

Seidman, S. 1996. *Queer theory/sociology*. London: Blackwell.

Shalom, S. R. 1981. *The United States and the Philippines: A study of neocolonialism*. Philadelphia: Institute for the Study of Human Issues.

Shaw, A. V., and L. H. Francia. 2003. *Vestiges of war: The Philippine-American war and the aftermath of an imperial dream, 1899-1999*. New York: New York University Press.

Shon, S., and D. Ja. 1982. Asian families. In M. McGoldrick, J. K. Pearce, and J. Giordano, eds., *Ethnicity and family therapy*. New York: Guilford Press.

Sinnott, M. 2004. *Toms and Dees: Transgender identity and female same-sex relationships in Thailand*. Honolulu: University of Hawaii Press.

Slootweg, H. 1998. Pentecostal women in Chile. In B. Boudewijnse, A. Droogers, and F. Kamsteeg, eds., *More than opium: An anthropological approach to Latin American and Caribbean Pentecostal praxis*. Lanham, Md.: Scarecrow Press.

Smilde, D. A. 1997. The fundamental unity of the conservative and revolutionary tendencies in Venezuelan evangelicalism: The case of conjugal relations. *Religion* 27: 343–59.

———. 2004. Contradiction without paradox: Evangelical political culture in the 1998 Venezuelan elections. *Latin American Politics and Society* 46.1: 75–102.

Smith, C. 1991. *The emergence of liberation theology: Radical religion and social movement theory*. Chicago: University of Chicago Press.

Smith, C., and J. Prokopy. 1999. Introduction. In C. Smith and J. Prokopy, eds., *Latin American religion in motion*. New York: Routledge.

Smith, H. 1991. *The world's religions: Our great wisdom traditions*. New York: HarperCollins.

Smith, J. Z. 1987. *To take place: Toward theory in ritual*. Chicago: University of Chicago Press.

Smith, M. P., and L. E. Guarnizo, eds. 1998. *Transnationalism from below*. New Brunswick, N.J.: Transaction Publishers.

Smutt, M. 1998. El fénomeno de las pandillas en El Salvador. In R. Papadopoulos, ed., *Violencia en una sociedad en transición*. San Salvador: Programa de las Naciones Unidas para el Desarrollo.

Smutt, M., and J. Miranda. 1998. *El Salvador: Socialización y violencia civil*. San Salvador, El Salvador: Imprenta Criterio.

Solis, M. M. 2000. *A brief history of St. Philip's Church, Salinas, California*. Salinas: St. Philip's Church and Sarimanok.

Solivan, S. 1996. Sources of a Hispanic/Latino American theology: A Pentecostal perspective. In A. M. Isasi-Diaz and F. Segovia, eds., *Hispanic/Latino theology: Challenge and promise*. Minneapolis: Fortress Press.

Spielberg, J., and A. Zavaleta. 1997. Historic folk sainthood along the Texas-Mexico border. In M. Kearney, A. Knopp, and A. Zavaleta, eds., *Studies in Matamoros and Cameron county history*. Brownsville: University of Texas.

Stevens, K. G. 2001. *Chinese mythological gods*. London: Oxford University Press.

Strobel, L. M. 1994. Cultural identity of third wave Filipino Americans. *Journal of the American Association for Philippine Psychology* 1 (summer): 37–54.

———. 1996. Born-again Filipino: Filipino American identity and Asian panethnicity. *Amerasia Journal* 22.2: 31–53.

———. 2001. *Coming full circle: The process of decolonization among post-1965 Filipino Americans.* Quezon City, Philippines: Giraffe Books.

Stychin, C. E. 1994. *A nation by rights: National cultures, sexual identity politics and the discourse of rights.* Philadelphia: Temple University Press.

Sue, S. 2003. Foreword. In K. M. Chun, P. Balls Organista, and G. Marin, eds., *Acculturation: Advances in theory, measurement, and applied research.* Washington, D.C.: American Psychological Association.

Sullivan, K. 2000. St. Catherine's Catholic Church: One church, parallel congregations. In H. R. Ebaugh and J. Saltzman Chafetz, eds., *Religion and the new Immigrants: Continuities and adaptations in immigrant congregations.* Walnut Creek, Calif.: AltaMira Press.

Swatos, W. 1995. *Religion and democracy in Latin America.* New Brunswick, N.J.: Transaction Publishers.

Sweetman, C. 1998. *Gender and migration.* London: Oxfam.

Takaki, R. 1987. *Strangers from a different shore: A history of Asian Americans.* New York: Penguin Books.

Taylor, P. S. 1970 [1928]. *Mexican labor in the United States,* vols. 1 and 2. New York: Arno Press.

Teachman, J., K. Paasch, and K. Carver. 1997. Social capital and the generation of human capital. *Social Forces* 75.4: 1343–59.

Teiser, S. F. 1995. Popular Religion. *Journal of Asian Studies* 54.2: 378–86.

Terán Contreras, S. 1987. La estratificación social y el mercado en Oxkutzcab Yucatán. Master's thesis, Escuela Nacional de Antropología e Historia.

Thich, M. D. 2000. Dam Luu: An eminent Vietnamese nun. In *Ky yen su ba Dam Luu.* San Jose: Van Boi Publishing House.

Torres, C. A. 1992. *The Church, society, and hegemony: A critical sociology of religion in Latin America.* London: Praeger.

Triste. 2002. Trying to get home: Triste's story. *Salvanet* (September/October): 4–5.

Trotter, R. T., and J. A. Chavira. 1981. *Curanderismo: Mexican American folk healing.* Athens: University of Georgia Press.

Trubeck, D. M. 1984. Where the action is: Critical legal studies and empiricism. *Stanford Law Review* 36: 575–622.

Tucker, R. C., ed. 1978. *The Marx-Engels reader.* New York: Norton.

Tuggy, A. L. 1978. Iglesia Ni Cristo: An angel and his church. In D. J. Hesselgrave, ed., *Dynamic religious movements.* Michigan: Baker Book House.

Turner, T. 1997. Human rights, human difference: Anthropology's contribution to an emancipatory cultural politics. *Journal of Anthropological Research* 53.3: 273–91.

Turner, V. 1988. *El proceso ritual: Estructura y antiestructura.* Madrid: Taurus.

Uba, L. 1994. *Asian Americans: Personality patterns, identity, and mental health.* New York: Guilford Press.

Ungar, M. 2001. Lesbian, gay, bisexual, and transgendered international alliances: The perils of success. In J. M. Bystydzienski and S. P. Schacht, eds., *Forging radical alliances across difference: Coalition politics for the new millennium.* London: Rowman and Littlefield.

Uslaner, E. 1999. Morality plays: Social capital and moral behaviour in Anglo-American democracies. In J. Van Deth et al., eds., *Social capital and European democracy.* London: Routledge.

Vallangca, R. V. 1977. *Pinoy: The first wave, 1898–1941.* San Francisco: Strawberry Hill Press.

Vanguardia. 2004. Una santa muy conocida: No está reconocida por el Vaticano. Vanguardia, http://Noticias.vanguardia.com.

Vásquez, G. A. G. 2005. Homies unidos: International barrio warriors waging peace on two fronts. In S. Maira and E. Soep, eds., *Youthscapes: The popular, the national, the global.* Philadelphia: University of Pennsylvania Press.

Vásquez, M., and L. Gómez. 2001. Youth gangs and religion among Salvadorans in Washington and El Salvador. In A. L. Peterson., M. A. Vásquez, and P. J. Williams, eds., *Christianity, social change, and globalization in the Americas.* New Brunswick, N.J.: Rutgers University Press.

Vásquez, M., and M. F. Marquardt. 2003. *Globalizing the sacred: Religion across the Americas.* New Brunswick, N.J.: Rutgers University Press.

Verba, S., K. L. Schlozman, and H. E. Brady. 1997. The big tilt: Participatory inequality in America. *American Prospect* 32: 74–80.

Vigil, J. D. 1998. *Barrio gangs: Street life and identity in Southern California.* Austin: University of Texas Press.

———. 2002. *A rainbow of gangs: Street cultures in the mega-city.* Austin: University of Texas Press.

Vila, P. 2000. *Crossing borders, reinforcing borders: Social categories, metaphors and narrative identities on the U.S.-Mexico frontier.* Austin: University of Texas Press.

Villa Rojas, A. 1978. *Los elegidos de Dios: Etnografía de los mayas de Quintana Roo.* Mexico City: Instituto Nacional Indigenista.

Villar, M. L. 1990. Rethinking settlement processes: The experience of Mexican undocumented migrants in Chicago. *Urban Anthropology* 19.1–2: 63–79.

———. 1992. Changes in employment networks among undocumented Mexican migrants in Chicago. *Urban Anthropology* 21.4: 385–97.

Võ, L. T. 2004. *Mobilizing an Asian American community.* Philadelphia: Temple University Press.

Wallovits, S. E. 1966. *The Filipinos in California.* Masters thesis, University of Southern California.

Warner, M. 1993. *Fear of a queer planet: Queer politics and social theory*. Minneapolis: University of Minnesota Press.

———. 1999. *The trouble with normal: Sex, politics, and the ethics of queer life*. New York: Free Press.

Warner, R. S. 1995. The metropolitan community churches and the gay agenda: The power of Pentecostalism and Essentialism. *Religion and the Social Order* 5: 81–108.

———. 2000. Religion and new post-1965 immigrants: Some principles drawn from field research. *American Studies* 41.2/3: 267–86.

———. 2005. *A church of our own: Disestablishment and diversity in American religion*. New Brunswick, N.J.: Rutgers University Press.

Warner, S., and J. Wittner, eds. 1998. *Gatherings in diaspora: Religious communities and the new immigration*. Philadelphia: Temple University Press.

Warren, M. 2001. *Dry bones rattling: Community building to revitalize American democracy*. Princeton, N.J.: Princeton University Press.

Watson, J. L. 1985. Standardizing the Gods: The promotion of T'ien Hou "Empress of Heaven" along the South China coast. In D. Johnson, A. J. Nathan, and E. S. Rawski, eds., *Popular culture in late imperial China*. Berkeley: University of California Press.

Weaver, T. 1988. The human rights of undocumented workers in the United States-Mexico border regions. In T. E. Downing and G. Kushner, eds., *Human Rights and Anthropology*. Cambridge, Mass.: Cultural Survival.

Weber, M. 1958. *The Protestant ethic and the spirit of capitalism*. New York: Charles Scribner's Sons.

Wells, M. K. 1962. Chinese temples in California. Master's thesis, University of California, Berkeley.

Weston, K. 1991. *Families we choose: Lesbians, gays, kinship*. New York: Columbia University Press.

———. 1998. *Long slow burn: Sexuality and social science*. New York: Routledge.

Whiteley, P. 1999. *Social capital and European democracy*. London: Routledge.

Wiegele, K. 2005. *Investing in miracles: El Shaddai and the transformation of popular Catholicism in the Philippines*. Honolulu: University of Hawaii Press.

Wieviorka, M. 2003. The new paradigm of violence. In J. Friedman, ed., *Globalization, the state and violence*. Walnut Creek, Calif.: AltaMira Press.

Wilcox, M. 2003. *Coming out in Christianity: Religion, identity and community*. Bloomington: University of Indiana Press.

Willems, E. 1967. *Followers of the new faith: Culture change and rise of Protestantism in Brazil and Chile*. Nashville, Tenn.: Vanderbilt University Press.

Williams, C. 1981. *Tongues of the spirit: A Study of Pentecostal glossolalia and related phenomena*. Cardiff: University of Wales Press.

Williams, D. R. 1926. *The United States and the Philippines*. New York: Doubleday, Page and Company.

Williams, P. 1997. The sound of tambourines: The politics of Pentecostal growth in El Salvador. In E. I. Cleary and H. W. Stewart-Gambino, eds., *Power, politics and Pentecostals in Latin America*. Boulder, Colo.: Westview.

Wilson, C. G. 1974. *Chinatown quest: One hundred years of Donaldina Cameron House, 1874-1974*. Rev. ed. San Francisco: California Historical Society; Donaldina Cameron House.

Wilson, N. 1995. *Our tribe: Queer folks, God, Jesus, and the Bible*. San Francisco: HarperCollins.

Wood, R. L. 2002. *Faith in Action: Religion, Race, and Democratic Organizing in America*. Chicago: University of Chicago Press.

Woolcock, M. 1998. Social capital and economic development: Toward a theoretical synthesis and policy framework. *Theory and Society* 27: 151–208.

Wuthnow, R. 2005. *America and the challenges of religious diversity*. Princeton, N.J.: Princeton University Press.

Yang. F. 1999. *Chinese Christians in America: Conversion, assimilation, and adhesive identities*. University Park: Pennsylvania State University Press.

———. 2000. The growing literature of Asian American religions: A review of the field, with special attention to three new books. *Journal of Asian American Studies* 3.2: 251–56.

Yang, M. M. 2000. Mass media and transnational subjectivity in Shanghai: Notes on recosmopolitanism in a Chinese metropolis. In J. X. Inda and R. Rosaldo, eds., *The anthropology of globalization: A reader*. London: Blackwell Publishers.

Yee, B. W. K., L. N. Huang, and A. Lew. 1998. Families: Life-span socialization in a cultural context. In L. C. Lee and N. W. S. Zane, eds., *Handbook of Asian American psychology*. Thousand Oaks, Calif.: Sage.

Yoo, D., ed. 1999. *New spiritual homes*. Honolulu: University of Hawaii Press.

Yu, H. 2001. *Thinking Orientals: Migration, contact, and exoticism in modern America*. New York: Oxford University Press.

Zhao, X. 2002. *Remaking Chinese America: Immigration, family, and community, 1940-1965*. New Brunswick, N.J.: Rutgers University Press.

Zhou, M. and C. L. Bankston. 1998. *Growing up American: How Vietnamese children adapt to life in the United States*. New York: Russell Sage Foundation.

Zilberg, E. 2004. Fools banished from the kingdom: Remapping geographies of gang violence between the Americas (Los Angeles and San Salvador). *American Quarterly* 56.3: 759–79.

Žižek, S. 2005. Against human rights. *New Left Review* 34: 115–31.

Contributors

LUIS ENRIQUE BAZAN works for Right Reality, a company that helps organizations improve their community service. He also edits *WAG Latino*, a weekly Spanish-language publication; coordinates social justice programs for the University of San Francisco; and is executive director of the Children's Aid Fund, an organization that creates projects for vulnerable children in developing countries.

JERRY BERNDT is an internationally renowned photographer whose prints are in the collections of the Museum of Modern Art in New York; Bibliotheque Nationale in Paris; and the Boston Museum of Fine Arts. His photos include works taken in Haiti, El Salvador, Guatemala, Rwanda, Poland, Portugal, Armenia, and throughout the United States.

KEVIN M. CHUN is a professor of psychology and the director of the Asian American Studies Program at the University of San Francisco. He completed his bachelor's degree in psychology at Santa Clara University, his doctorate in clinical psychology at the University of California, Los Angeles, and his psychology internship at the Palo Alto Health Care System of the Department of Veterans Affairs. His research focuses on family acculturation processes and their relation to health and psychosocial adjustment for Asian American immigrants and refugees. His publications include, with coauthors Pamela Balls Organista and Gerardo Marín, *Acculturation: Advances in Theory, Measurement, and Applied Research* and *Psychology of Ethnic Groups in the U.S.* (forthcoming).

CLAUDINE DEL ROSARIO is a first-generation Pinay, born and raised in New Jersey. Her undergraduate work was done at the University of California, Berkeley, and her master's degree in Asian American studies is from San Francisco State University. She worked as a research associate with the Religion and Immigration Project and teaches at the University of San Francisco's Yuchengco Philippine Studies Program. Claudine is a senior project manager at the San Francisco Mayor's Office of Community Investment. She has done consulting for grassroots community-based organizations, research on Filipino American churches, teaching and consulting for Filipino-focused educational programs at San Francisco high schools, and has taught Asian American history at the community college level.

HIEN DUC DO is a professor of social sciences and Asian American studies at San Jose State University and is past president of the Association of Asian American Studies. He is the author of *The Vietnamese Americans*, and he served as associate producer *of Viet Nam: At the Crossroads*, a documentary film that aired nationally on PBS and won the 1994 CINE Golden Eagle Award.

PATRICIA FORTUNY LORET DE MOLA received a doctorate from University College in London. She is a researcher at the Center of Research and Advanced Studies in Social Anthropology (CIESAS/Peninsular) in Mérida in Yucatán, Mexico. She is the editor of *Los otros creyentes* and of *Creyentes y creencias en Guadalajara*. In 1997 and 1998 she was a Fulbright scholar at St. Mary's University in San Antonio, Texas; in 2001, she was a Rockefeller fellow at the University of Florida in Gainesville; and in 2004 she was a resident scholar at the Rockefeller Center in Bellagio, Italy.

JOAQUIN JAY GONZALEZ III is an associate professor of politics and the director of the Maria Elena Yuchengco Philippine Studies Program at the University of San Francisco. He has authored and co-authored several books, including *Filipino American Faith in Action* and *Philippine Labour Migration*. He was a co-investigator of The Religion and Immigration Project (TRIP). After 9/11 he was appointed to the San Francisco Immigrant Rights Commission, and in 2005 he received special congressional recognition from the House leader Nancy Pelosi, and the George Christopher Chair in Public Administration from Golden Gate University. Jay has worked for the World Bank, the Institute on Governance of Canada, the Inter-American Development Bank, and the Philippine government. He has taught at De La Salle University in Manila and at the National University of Singapore. Jay is a veteran of the Philippine People Power revolution of 1986.

SARAH HORTON is on the research faculty in the Department of Anthropology, History, and Social Medicine at the University of California, San Francisco. Her areas of specialization include religious expression among Latino immigrants, the articulation of changing conceptions of immigrants' citizenship with neoliberal U.S. health care policies, and disparities in health care for Latino immigrants. She received a doctorate degree with distinction from the Department of Anthropology at the University of New Mexico in 2003. She was a postdoctoral fellow in the Department of Social Medicine at Harvard University from 2003 to 2005, where she studied new Salvadoran immigrant family formations under globalization. While at the University of California, San Francisco, she has undertaken new research on the role of heightened border enforcement policies on the health and family structures of Salvadoran and Mexican immigrants in California's segregated Central Valley.

CYMENE HOWE is an assistant professor in the Anthropology Department at Rice University, where her research centers on sexuality, gender, media, and human rights in Latin America and the United States. Her forthcoming book, from Duke University Press, is entitled *Erotiscapes: Sex, Social Justice, and Nicaragua's New Media Era.*

MIMI KHÚC is a Ph.D. candidate in religious studies at the University of California, Santa Barbara. Her work examines Vietnamese American strategies of meaning and memory, with a particular focus on second-generation immigrants. Other interests include Asian American studies more generally, Buddhism in the United States, New Age spirituality, and women-of-color feminism.

JONATHAN H. X. LEE is an assistant professor of Chinese and Chinese American studies in the Asian American Studies Department at San Francisco State University. Lee's research interests are in contemporary Chinese popular religion with a specific focus on Buddho-Daoism, in addition to studies of material religions, secularization, and the state in modernity, especially as it collides with traditional order under colonial and postcolonial conditions.

LOIS ANN LORENTZEN is a professor of social ethics, co-director of the Center for Latino Studies in the Americas, and was principal investigator for the Religion and Immigration Project (funded by the Pew Charitable Trusts) at the University of San Francisco. She is the author of *Etica ambiental*, coauthor of *Raising the Bar*, and co-editor *of Ecofeminism and Globalization: Exploring Culture, Context, and Religion; Religion/Globalization: Theories and Cases; The Women and War Reader; Liberation Theologies, Postmodernity and the Americas*; and *The Gendered New World Order: Militarism, the Environment and Development.* She is a member of the Jesuit Migrant Services: North and Central America research network. She has worked in refugee resettlement with Catholic Charities and the state of Minnesota, and she has a long interest in the plight of the world's displaced peoples.

ANDREA MAISON received a bachelor's degree in fine arts from Dickinson College, and a master's degree in art history from the University of California, Santa Barbara. Andrea has extensive experience working in the arts field as well as with Filipino American cultural projects and communities. She worked for the Smithsonian Institution in Washington conducting outreach to Filipino American and other Asian American audiences. She later joined the Religion and Immigration Project's Filipino research team in San Francisco. Andrea now lives in Florida, where her professional life includes teaching art history classes online, appraising art, and writing and editing articles about her research with the Religion and Immigration Project.

DENNIS MARZAN holds a bachelor's degree in history from the University of San Francisco and a master's degree in political sociology from the London School of Economics. Dennis is presently a program associate with the David and Lucile Packard Foundation in Los Altos, California. He was formerly a research associate with the Religion and Immigration Project.

ROSALINA MIRA was born in El Salvador and grew up in East Los Angeles, California. As an immigrant herself, she understands firsthand the importance of research projects that highlight the unique cultural contributions that immigrants make to the social landscape. Through her work at the Religion and Immigration Project at the University of San Francisco, she documented how newly arrived immigrants thrive amid severe adversity through religion- and faith-based communities and yet they are still a vulnerable population. She joins countless of others in campaigns that advocate immigrant rights, family rights, and educational opportunity. She is a current fellow at the Children's Defense Fund, Emerging Leaders Program and director of the Upward Bound Program at Cañada Community College in Redwood City, California.

SUSANNA ZARAYSKY was born in Leningrad, in the former Soviet Union. She emigrated with her family in 1980 and grew up in Silicon Valley, California. After graduating with honors from the University of California, Berkeley, with a degree in international political economy, she worked in international business and economic development. In Buenos Aires, Argentina, she worked as an editor and journalist for the *Buenos Aires Herald*. Having left the Soviet Union because of religious persecution, she felt a strong link to the Bosnian War, and in 2000 and 2001, she designed economic development projects in war-torn villages in Bosnia. Her research for this book is an extension of her profound interest in the role of religion, faith, and community for immigrants. She has written a book on easy foreign-language education, *Language is Music*; a budget travel guide, *Travel Happy, Budget Low*; and a memoir, *One-Eyed Princess in Babel*, about her immigration and identity search. More information on her work can be found at http://www.susansword.com and http://www.kaleidomundi.com.

Index

LOIS ANN LORENTZEN is a professor of social ethics at the University of San Francisco. She is a co-author of *Raising the Bar* and a co-editor of *Ecofeminism and Globalization*; *Religion/Globalization*; *The Women and War Reader*; *Liberation Theologies, Postmodernity and the Americas*; and *The Gendered New World Order*.

JOAQUIN JAY GONZALEZ III is an associate professor of politics and the director of the Maria Elena Yuchengco Philippine Studies Program at the University of San Francisco. He has authored and co-authored several books, including *Filipino American Faith in Action* and *Philippine Labour Migration*. He was a co-investigator of The Religion and Immigration Project (TRIP).

KEVIN M. CHUN is a professor of psychology and the director of the Asian American Studies Program at the University of San Francisco. He is a co-author (with Pamela Balls Organista and Gerardo Marin) of *Acculturation: Advances in Theory, Measurement, and Applied Research* and *Readings in Ethnic Psychology*.

HIEN DUC DO is a professor of social sciences and Asian American studies at San Jose State University. He is the author of *The Vietnamese Americans*.

All photographs in this book are by JERRY BERNDT and appear by permission of the artist.